Biopolitics

A Feminist and Ecological Reader on Biotechnology

EDITED BY

VANDANA SHIVA & INGUNN MOSER

D0224779

Zed Books Ltd
London & New Jersey

Third World Network
Penang, Malaysia

Biopolitics was first published by
Zed Books Ltd, 7 Cynthia Street, London N1 9JF, UK, and
165 First Avenue, Atlantic Highlands, New Jersey 07716, USA, and by
Third World Network, 228 Macalister Road, 10400 Penang, Malaysia,
in 1995.

Cover design by Andrew Corbett.
Laserset by Long House, Cumbria, UK.
Printed and bound in the United Kingdom
by Biddles Ltd, Guildford and King's Lynn

A catalogue record for this book
is available from the British Library.

US CIP data is available from
the Library of Congress.

ISBN 1 85649 335 0 Cased
ISBN 1 85649 336 9 Limp

Acknowledgement
Zed Books is grateful for permission to reprint Chapters 2 and 3 from Ruth
Hubbard, *The Politics of Women's Biology* (Rutgers University Press, 1990);
Chapter 4 from Evelyn Fox Keller, *Secrets of Life, Secrets of Death. Essays on
Language, Gender and Science* (Routledge, 1992); Chapter 5 from *Science as Culture*,
Vol. 3, Part 1, No. 14 (1992); Chapter 6 from *Issues in Reproductive and Genetic
Engineering*, Vol. 3, No. 2 (1990); Chapter 7 from D. Leskien and J. Spangenberg
(eds), *European Workshop on Law and Genetic Engineering – Proceedings* (BBU-
Verlag, 1990); Chapter 8 from *Science and Public Policy*, Vol. 18, No. 5 (1991);
Chapter 9 from E. Gulbrandsen and N. Witoszek (eds), *Culture and Environment:
Interdisciplinary Approaches* (SUM/TMV, University of Oslo, 1994); Chapter 10
from R. Diprose and R. Ferrell (eds), *Cartographies, Poststructuralism and the
Mapping of Bodies and Spaces* (Allen & Unwin, 1991); Chapter 12 from *Economic
and Political Weekly,* Vol. 26, No. 48 (Bombay, 1991); Chapter 13 from O. T.
Sandlund, K. Hindar and A. H. D. Brown (eds), *Conservation of Biodiversity for
Sustainable Development* (Scandinavian University Press, 1992); and Chapter 15
from *The Second Asian Development Forum* (CADI).

Contents

Foreword

This anthology is the result of a collaborative project between three inter-disciplinary centres at the University of Oslo: the Centre for Technology and Culture, the Centre for Women's Research and the Centre for Development and the Environment. The background to the project was an initiative by Vandana Shiva, guest researcher at the University of Oslo, to define a field of interest and a research agenda for critical studies in and of biotechnology in Norway. The anthology constitutes a step on the way and is included in this enterprise. Vandana Shiva and Ingunn Moser have been responsible for the work, together with a reference group consisting of researchers attached to the three centres. The centres would like to thank the Norwegian Department of the Environment, the Norwegian Ministry of Foreign Affairs and the Norwegian Agency for Development Cooperation to the Ministries for financial support to the project.

Centre for Technology and Culture
Centre for Women's Research
Centre for Development and the Environment

Preface

The aim of this anthology is to bring together, expose and offer a multitude of approaches, perspectives, tools and concepts with which to problematize the conditions, consequences, possibilities and limitations of biotechnology. We wish to present frameworks and contexts in which to locate and assess debates on biotechnological developments, and the tremendous hopes and fears attached to them. The field we clear must be large enough to enable us to get a firm grasp of ways of understanding nature, biology, knowledge and science in biotechnology, as well as the social structures, cultural contexts and ecological relations in which biotechnological developments are integrated. We hope to create a good and rich ecology in this field for cultivating critical discussion and movements for change.

However, one still has to make some limitations and demarcations. We are focusing in terms of area on the conditions for and the consequences of biotechnological development with regard to 'green' nature: food, agri-culture and biodiversity rather than people, medical gene therapy and

v

reproduction technologies. In saying this, however, we would hasten to add that our concern is not directed towards bread, beer, cheese, yoghurt or wine. The discourses on biotechnology came about because of and were motivated by developments within genetics and genetic engineering: the possibility of studying and manipulating the genetic hereditary material of living organisms in a systematic way, and transferring hereditary matter from one type of organism to another. The anthology focuses on this new group of technologies and the challenges separating modern gene/biotech-nology from traditional biotechnology. Modern biotechnology not only breaks down species barriers and time horizons in evolutionary processes, but also causes boundaries between science, technology, research and industry to collapse. This challenges fundamental suppositions and premises in the current discussions on science, science ethics and science politics.

Among the pressing challenges posed by modern biotechnological developments, the anthology discusses the relationship between bio-technology and biodiversity; the politics of biotechnology in North–South relations; the patenting of plant genetic material; values, conceptions of nature and understandings of knowledge within biotechnological research and development; the importance of ethics in a time when technological possibilities seem to have put traditions and ethical systems out of the running; and the issues of risk. We bring into focus the need for a critique of the politics of knowledge: to confront biotechnology with a critique of science and technology as politics and culture; and, vice versa, to confront this critique with the need to relate to nature and biology.

Accordingly, the question of modern science and technology, and their critiques, will be central. Most controversies over biotechnology are based on premises which are seldom made explicit or opened up to debate. Many conflicting points of view which reoccur in debates on biotechnology rest on differing understandings of nature, scientific knowledge and the relation-ship between our knowledge and nature. This is as applicable to discussions of biology as to discussions of risk, ethics and politics. Our contribution is to draw in these frameworks and strategies of knowledge and make them a part of the debate on biotechnology.

The structure and contents of the book are organized around this challenge and, using this as a criterion, we have selected contributions and explained exclusions. The anthology's principal challenge is to create acknowledgement and recognition of the problematic status of biotech-nology in discussions of global ecology and sustainable development, and to mobilize discourses and communities to act on this recognition. The intention is to strike a note for talks and exchanges, to build bridges and alliances. Up until now the concerns and challenges raised by women's and environmental movements, alternative directions within biology, medicine or agriculture, and critiques of science and technology have been sporadic and marginalized in controversies over biotechnology. The questions of science and technology, gender and ecology have been treated as separate axes, each of them only remotely verging on biotechnology. This collection of articles brings together these interests and questions in order to mobilize the awareness that they do meet in biotechnology, and must be both addressed and answered together. The challenge is to pose what Sandra Harding – for feminism – called 'the science question in feminism' to all participants in the discourses on global ecology and sustainable development. What is the biotechnology question in the debates on global ecology and sustainable development?

This challenge is pursued in four thematic sections, Parts 1–4. The general introduction puts the biotechnology question into contexts which are about previous experiences and current debates and challenges, and presents themes and challenges in each of the four sections. It provides an insight into and introduces central arguments in the material, and identifies new challenges which are generated at the intersection points between gender, ecology and biotechnology.

We would especially like to thank Elisabeth Gulbrandsen, Brita Gulli, Torben Hviid Nielsen and Per Sandberg for their continual commitment and investment in the development of this work. We also thank the students who participated in the interdisciplinary seminar on critical challenges in biotechnology during the spring of 1994. Their endeavours to communicate and learn across the disciplinary boundaries within the group was a great inspiration. Finally, we would like to thank the three cooperative centres who embarked on this multidisciplinary project: the Centre for Technology and Culture, the Centre for Women's Research and the Centre for Environment and Development.

Vandana Shiva and *Ingunn Moser*

Contributors

Rosalyn Diprose has degrees in biomedical science and philosophy, and is a lecturer in Philosophy at the University of New South Wales, Australia. Her publications include *The Bodies of Women: Ethics, Embodiment and Sexual Difference* (Routledge) and *Cartographies. Poststructuralism and the Mapping of Bodies and Spaces*, co-edited with Robyn Ferrell (Allen & Unwin).

Cary Fowler currently heads the International Conference and Programme for Plant Genetic Resources at the Food and Agriculture Organization of the UN. He holds a PhD from Uppsala University of Sweden. Dr Fowler completed his article while Associate Professor at the Norwegian Centre for International Agricultural Development (NORAGRIC), Agricultural University of Norway.

Donna Haraway's teaching and writing in feminist theory and science studies are addressed to the politics, histories and cultures of modern science and technology. Teaching in Women's Studies and the History of Consciousness Board at the University of California at Santa Cruz, her publications include *Primate Visions: Gender, Race, and Nature in the World of Moden Science* (Routledge) and *Simians, Cyborgs, and Women: The Reinvention of Nature* (Free Association Books).

Jesper Hoffmeyer is Professor at the Institute of Molecular Biology, University of Copenhagen, Denmark. His scientific work has been concerned with theoretical biology, theory of science and technology, and the nature–culture relation in its historical development. He has published several books, most recently *En snegl på vejen (in Danish)*. His publications in English include: 'Some Semiotic Aspects of the Psycho-Physical Relation: The Endo-Exosemiotic Boundary' in Thomas A. Sebeok and Jean Umiker-Sebeok (eds) (1991) *The Semiotic Web: Biosemiotics* (Mouton de Gruyter). Hoffmeyer was the editor of the magazines *Naturkampen* and *OMverden*, both of which were concerned with the nature–culture relation.

Henk Hobbelink, a Dutch agronomist, is the founder and coordinator of Genetic Resources Action International (GRAIN) – an international NGO based in Barcelona, Spain, which seeks to to raise public awareness about the dangers of genetic erosion, and to stimulate the development of a more equitable and sustainable global conservation system. Hobbelink is co-editor of *Seedling*, the newsletter of GRAIN, and his publications include *Biotechnology and the Future of World Agriculture* (Zed Books).

Ruth Hubbard, a Professor of Biology Emerita at Harvard University, has worked and written on the politics of women's biology and of health care since the 1970s and serves on the boards of directors of the Council for Responsible Genetics and the Massachusetts chapter of the American Civil Liberties Union. Among her many publications are *The Politics of Women's Biology* (Rutgers) and (with Elijah Wald) *Exploding the Gene Myth* (Beacon).

Evelyn Fox Keller received her PhD in theoretical physics at Harvard University, worked for a number of years at the interface of physics and biology, and is now Professor of History and Philosophy of Science in the Program in Science, Technology and Society at Massachusetts Institute of Technology, USA. She is perhaps best known as the author of *A Feeling for the Organism. The Life and Work of Barbara McClintock* (W. H. Freeman and Company), *Reflections on Gender and Science* (Yale University Press) and, most recently, *Secrets of Life, Secrets of Death. Essays on Language, Gender and Science* (Routledge). Her current research is on the history of developmental biology.

Regine Kollek is a biologist and member of the Board of Directors of the German Institute for Applied Ecology (Öko-institut). She has researched extensively in developmental biology, virology and genetics, and was a member of the scientific staff of the German Bundestag's Commission of Inquiry on the Potential and Risks of Genetic Engineering. Dr Kollek is currently working at the Hamburg Institute for Social Research on inter-disciplinary approaches to technology assessment.

Les Levidow is a Research Fellow at the Open University, England, where he has been studying the safety regulation of agricultural biotechnology. He has been Managing Editor of *Science as Culture* since its inception in 1987, and of its predecessor, the *Radical Science Journal*. He also worked at Free Association Books, where he co-edited several collections, including *Science, Technology and the Labour Process*; *Anti-Racist Science Teaching*; and *Cyborg Worlds: The Military Information Society*.

Ingunn Moser is a Research Fellow at the Centre for Technology and Culture, University of Oslo, Norway. Her work has been in feminist theory and science and technology studies, and is concerned with putting the challenges arising from the crises in environment and development on the agenda for the established research complexes.

Nicanor Perlas is President of the Center for Alternative Development Initiatives, Quezon City, Philippines. He was the recipient of the 1994 UNEP Global 500 Award for his work on sustainable agriculture and for galvanizing action against hazardous pesticides. Besides acting as a consultant to the UN, government and NGOs on sustainable agriculture and development, Perlas also provides technical assistance to NGOs and farmers' organizations practising large-scale sustainable agriculture in the Philippines.

Vandana Shiva – physicist, philosopher and feminist – is Director of the Research Foundation for Science, Technology and Natural Resource Policy, Dehra Dun, India. She has been active in citizens' action against environmental destruction, including the Chipko movement, and is highly critical of current agricultural and reproductive technologies. Her many publications include *The Violence of the Green Revolution: Third World Agriculture, Ecology and Politics* (Zed Books and Third World Network), *Monocultures of the Mind* (Zed Books and Third World Network) and, most recently, (with Maria Mies) *Ecofeminism* (Zed Books, London, Fernwood Publishing, Halifax, Kali for Women, New Delhi and Spinifex, Melbourne).

Joyce Tait is employed as Deputy Director, Research and Advisory Services for Scottish Natural Heritage. Her research has focused on technological development, environmental protection and the interactions between the two. She recently coordinated work on three major research projects dealing with agriculture-related biotechnological developments. Among her publications are *Biotechnology: Cognitive Structures of Public Groups* and *Release of Genetically Modified Organisms: Public Attitudes and Understanding* (both reports published by Centre for Technology Strategy, Open University).

Christine von Weizsäcker, trained as an evolutionary biologist, presides over a large family and lives in Bonn, Germany. As a freelance author, she has become an original voice in the public debate on the less reputable implications of technology and economics. She is particularly concerned about the marginalization of the domestic sphere in industrial society and argues for a modern reinvention of the 'commons'. In a similar vein, she has criticized genetic engineering as an invasion of the common heritage of life, calling for respect in the face of the intricate richness of evolution. She holds a doctorate in biology and has developed the concept of 'error-friendliness' as an evolutionary principle. Von Weizsäcker is active in the Warentest Foundation and is on the Executive Committee of the Heinrich Böll Foundation.

CHAPTER I

Introduction
Mobilizing Critical Communities and Discourses on Modern Biotechnology

INGUNN MOSER

Modern biotechnology is often promoted as an ecologically sound technology necessary for the realization of sustainable development and a common future. Discussions of the ethics and politics of this technological development are framed by the same interpretations and strategies; biotechnology is represented as being a morally necessary solution to the environmental and developmental crises – to hunger, poverty and pollution problems, the conservation of biodiversity and climatic change.

Increasingly the world is described as, and is becoming based on and dependent on modern science and technology. Yet this is nothing fundamentally new; science and technology are central elements in modern Western culture's self-understanding and self interpretation processes. Science and technology have played an active part in forming industrial society's relationship with nature, other people and cultures. What is the position with regard to the growing acknowledgement of the close connection between global environmental and developmental crises, and modern Western life forms? What roles do modern science and technology play in the developments which have become critical – in social, cultural and natural environments?

Modern science and technology are becoming increasingly more involved and integrated within political structures and financial institutions, as well as in our everyday lives and activities, in a culture threatening life on earth. This poses a challenge to science and technology to be more than suppliers of solutions, and to participants in research complexes to be more than 'helpers' and experts. In 1991 the Oslo conference on 'Humanistic perspectives on technology, environment and development' drew researchers from many countries to look at the social and cultural bearings of the global environmental and developmental crises, focusing particularly on the roles of science and technology in these processes. The conference report found that

> One of the conclusions to be drawn from the discussions at the conference was that we as participants in the research complex and the technological

communities of the North, must seek alternatives and create projects for change in our part of the world – and recognize ourselves also as part of the problem and not only as producers and suppliers of solutions.[1]

In a time of challenge to the authority and legitimacy of science and technology as sources of safe knowledge and solutions for the distress and sufferings of the world, it is of the utmost importance to understand the role of biotechnology, which gives rise to such immense hopes and fears, in cultural and political projects. This is the challenge we would like to add to the agenda with this book. The ambition is to create recognition and understanding of the need to problematize the involvement of biotechnology in the increasingly critical developments we experience today. We offer frameworks of understanding and contexts in which to locate and evaluate debates on biotechnological developments, and controversies on the possibilities and limitations of biotechnology. The aim is to mobilize critical communities and discourses on modern biotechnology as the market's last wonder cure for the environmental and developmental crises.

Technology in a Common Future

The World Commission on Environment and Development, and its report *Our Common Future* (1987), opened up space, fora and discourses which have brought together the world's political authorities, international bodies, grassroots movements, research and industry in concern over nature's survival and the aims of development. The Earth Summit in Rio de Janeiro in 1992 was a manifestation of the mobilization of a colourful community, marked by political conflicts, cultural opposites and differences in power and opportunities for being heard. Nevertheless, the meeting places and discourses represent possibilities of participation in the struggle to define problems and formulate challenges. Many have later asked *whose* world and common future all this talk is about: is this not simply a new push from the side of the rich and powerful to shift the focus from modern Western development crises to questions of global ecology and common interests? Is it more than a construction which secures the interests of the rich and powerful by asserting the need to manage this common future by the new, supposedly non-political expertise wielded by ecocrats with a background in modern Western science and technology?[2] The battle is not decided once and for all, however, and the controversies bobbing in the wake of the World Commission's work have a hand in changing the agenda and including new perspectives and challenges. A theme which has been forced into the open in this way is the question of the roles and conditions of science and technology in a sustainable common future.

Until recently this question has not been raised in the fora and discourses with most power to influence global development directions. Modern science and technology have been regarded as unambiguously progressive, necessary and neutral means for realizing undisputed political objectives such as growth, progress and development. Science and technology have been treated as suppliers of solutions, their managers and operatives as 'helpers' and experts. The relationship between modern science and technology and questionable developments in the social, cultural and natural environments in which we live has not been problematized – in spite of the recognition that modern science and technology are undeniably involved in both acute catastrophes and chronic environmental and developmental crises. The burdens imposed by technological development on social, political and natural environments have been known right from the early phases of industrialization, but were assessed as secondary effects or passing phenomena which future technological and scientific development was supposed to overcome. In the modern Western culture we have pinned our hopes on and invested our trust in science and technology, despite the uncertainty of their working to our advantage and delivering solutions to our problems.

This is still true of the World Commission's work on development and the environment, in the way it has been charted in *Our Common Future* and followed up in international negotiations, discussions and documents.[3] These documents request that science and technology should be brought to an even greater extent into the making of political decisions and policies on sustainable development. It is taken for granted that sustainable development will be increasingly dependent on modern scientific and technological expertise, which is supposed to be independent, objective and non-political. Science and technology are assumed to be given practices; they are identified with modern Western institutions of production of knowledge and are not problematized. Sure enough, scientific knowledge is associated with insecurity, and risks inevitably follow technological encroachments and systems, but science and the management regime of sustainable development must accept responsibility for these inherent uncertainties. The impression which remains is of a fundamental technical optimism, where risk can be overcome with the help of more science and technology, and where more science and technology can watch over, extend and move boundaries for the production and consumption patterns which we know to be critical for sustainable development.[4]

It is true that *Our Common Future* also intimates unease at the ambivalence of technological development, and expresses a need for a movement for change in research.[5] The political reorientation in science and technology politics in connection with policies for sustainable development will depend, however, on a more complex and integrated understanding of research processes and the historic, cultural and social relations to which they are bound, and which they bind. We need to work with science and technology as integrated in and integrating cultural and political projects, and to problematize our own development model, and the roles played in this by modern science and technology, in a historical and reflective way. But in order to be able to work with science and technology as problematic political and cultural projects, we need frameworks of understanding and discourses for our own ambivalence and unease. These are lacking today, not only in political and public debate, but also within research itself. Accordingly, the easiest thing is to go in for the supposedly safe and familiar 'free research' on the old terms, with confidence that the insecurity surrounding future developments within science and technology will turn out to our advantage. There are so many problems to solve, and time is so short – the doubt never gets a chance to be put to rest, the unease is never reflected.

Lessons of the Past

Promoting technology as the solution to political and ecological crises has a long history and tradition in the development of industrial societies and the modern world order. Dreams, suppositions, conditions and courses of action we know so well are repeated. Modern Western science and technology have been and are seen as the driving forces behind development, and as sources for solutions which offer security and abundance where there is insecurity and shortage. These cultural images and dreams have such a strong effect that costly experiences with technology are never reflected and worked through. They are rewritten and sink into a kind of collective oblivion. The other hidden and hushed-up stories in the narrative about science and technology in the Great Development are never brought out and used as a basis for a reconstruction of this narrative, a retelling of what we have become and what we can become.

But which stories are continuously rewritten? What can we learn from the protest movements and critical traditions which have been mobilized? What lessons and theoretical and political resources do we have at our disposal to grasp biotechnology as a part of the problem, and not only a part of the solution?

Modern science and technology have, in the authorized accounts, their own internal dynamics and logic, and their own internal control systems, which carry research 'forwards'. Academic liberty, logic, the experimental method, rational argumentation and a research community committed to achieving consensus on controversial findings are supposed to ensure that the best argument wins and humanity's universal interests guide research. It is independent of and transcends social and cultural contexts. Religion and tradition are forms of knowledge bound to social interests and closed cultural worlds. Science, on the other hand, is supposed to be objective and universal, superior to all other forms of knowledge. In this scenario, technology is the implementation of scientific knowledge in order to satisfy human needs.

Accusations of involvement in war, in social and race-related conflicts, and in ecological destruction have been raised against such an *internalist* understanding of science and technology. Social – or *externalist* – critiques of science and technology were mobilized by the wide protest movements against militarism, racism and sexism in the 1960s and 1970s.[6] The enlistment of science and technology in genocide during the Vietnam War, with the development of napalm bombs at the prestigious Harvard University, came as a shock both to researchers and students. Likewise, Rachel Carson's *Silent Spring* (1962), a study of the harmful effects of using the pesticide DDT, had the force of a surprise attack on the chemical industry which stood accused of waging a war on nature. These revelations discredited the pretensions of science and technology to distance and independence in relation to social structures and power relations, and thus their claims to objectivity and the achievement of progress. According to externalist understandings of science and technology, the social practices and processes which constitute research cannot be understood independently of the society from which they derive. Modern science and technology are therefore political. Researchers and students were radicalized and challenged to take responsibility for their participation in social conflicts.[7]

It follows from such a practically orientated understanding of science and technology that the demarcation between these forms of knowledge is blurred; modern science and technology are looked upon as fundamentally tangled and mutually dependent forms of knowledge. Developments within technology enable developments within science, and vice versa. With information technology and genetic engineering the distinction becomes more or less meaningless. What in this process is instrumental and applied knowledge, and what is basic research, explanation, interpretation or reflection, is no longer separable. Research is reality producing practices through interpretation, production of meaning and intervention. None of these elements in the research process occur in ideal space, where the social and political gravities are removed.

According to Hilary Rose, the externalist critics took up a tradition from Marxist natural scientists and scientific historians like Boris Hessen, John D. Bernal and Joseph Needham.[8] They had focused on economic production relations as determining power structures, both in society and in research.

In capitalist societies, technology and science would necessarily be the means of creating and preserving capitalist power relations in production. The possibilities for a new and better science and technology had to lie in the transition to another – socialist – society. However, the new social critiques steered clear of the economic reductionism and determinism of the early externalism. With the waves of theories on biological determinism and socio-biology in the 1970s, race and sex were also thrown into the discussions on the conditions of science. Natural scientists, science critics and activists in the protest movements were mobilized, formed alliances and confronted biological theories which purported to prove the genetic basis for intellectual inferiority in ethnic and social groups, as well as for male dominance and patriarchal social structures.[9]

Turning to critiques of biological determinism, the exploration of the other side of science in society – society in science – became just as urgent. Science and technology do not exist in society simply in the manner of sometimes serving illegitimate interests and producing ideology. Society is in science, and not just by coincidence. Not even researchers – with scientific tools and resources – can position themselves outside their cultural and social contexts. This is a much more alarming admission, which in its turn radicalized the social critiques. Science and technology are social and cultural projects, formed in power structures and coloured by dominating values in the societies and the cultures in which they occur. As such they are constituted on as well as constitutive of cultural and social conditions. Science and technology are reality-producing and -reproducing practices.

In the women's movement, a critique of science and technology was developed within a general critique of patriarchy as the determining power structure in society. Patriarchy was understood as a power system which functions through relations in reproduction, through the division of work between women and men. Patriarchy was seen as constitutive also of other power relations and hierarchies; the suppression of women, classes, ethnic groups, deviating sexualities and nature are all linked. Consciousness of the close connections between the suppression of women and of nature, of the meanings associated with women as nature – or more natural or closer to nature (versus men as culture and rationality) – and of the role of the sciences with regard to confirming and accentuating these power relations led feminists to challenge patriarchal power relations which also permeated science and technology. Here they were able to draw on the externalist critiques which looked upon science and technology as tools in the hands of the powerful, bringing in new or strengthening old power relations. In a feminist version, the critique of science and technology shed light on science and technology as an expression of patriarchal power and a means of controlling women and nature.[10]

In *The Death of Nature: Women, Ecology and the Scientific Revolution* (1980) Carolyn Merchant examined texts from the ancestors of science and technology with regard to their modern, Western and patriarchal values. Here she found the rationale for a violent science and technology aimed at mastering and controlling an unpredictable (feminine) nature: nature's secrets had to be wrestled from her, and she had to be pierced and dominated by force. The biologist Ruth Hubbard and the physicist Evelyn Fox Keller have studied how the understanding of genetics, evolutionary processes and human nature within biological sciences are based on, confirm and reproduce patriarchal views on reality, values and relations.[11] For example, it is often assumed that aggression, violence, egoism and rivalry are founded in our (male) genes, and that the struggle for existence and egoism makes us reproduce ourselves and produce as many offspring as our competitive fitness allows.

Studies of how power and politics work in our productions of knowledge have shown nature to be an arena for battles defining who we are and what we can become. Modern science and technology are powerful social constructions, the result of negotiations and struggles for defining realities and possibilities where power is distributed unequally.[12] For example, in modern Western culture, nature has been constructed as characterized by necessity, scarcity and the fight for survival. Darwinist theories on where we come from and which laws prevail can be said to reflect and project a raw and brutal social order on nature. In Darwin's time industrialization and urbanization made their breakthrough, and abandoned a multitude of people who had previously belonged to traditional farming communities in a new social reality which really had become a fight for survival. These biological theories were then used to legitimize the same individualistic competitive society. The breakthrough of the images and models of explanation of genetics and genetic engineering in popular culture during the last few years seems to have revitalized the most vulgar versions of these simple world images and the politics they reinforce.[13]

A feminist theory of science deconstructs – investigates, exposes and criticizes – these suppositions. It studies how they work and are played out both in the world of research and in the society in which the knowledge is used. A feminist science aims at developing alternatives which are based on other, more benevolent relations and conditions. The work and contributions of Ruth Hubbard, Evelyn Fox Keller and Donna Haraway represent these positive attempts to move on from critiques of scientific representations and practices as cultural and political productions, and to arrive at new representations, relations and practices.[14]

In a parallel critique from an ecological standpoint, Vandana Shiva sheds light on dominant science and technology as a modern, patriarchal and colonial project aimed at control of people and natural resources.[15] Central to this project are the ideas of development and progress conceived as freedom from and control over nature, and as moved forward by modern science and technology. The focus of this critique is on the destructive developments in the wake of transferrals of Western science and technology to other cultures and ecologies. It is no longer controversial to maintain that the Green Revolution – the transferral of Western industrialized models of agriculture to the so-called Third World – has been a failure.[16] It not only failed in its intention of solving the famine problem, but showed itself to be deeply involved in social and political processes which concentrated wealth and power in the hands of a few. From an ecological point of view, foreign and vulnerable monocultures were introduced at the cost of local diversity, together with an industrial agriculture, intensive in resources. As a result, poverty and environmental crises have become more extreme. Local communities have been robbed of their means of livelihood. Violent conflicts on the control of natural resources spiral.

We notice the resonance between three types of critique here: the critique of science and technology as cultural and social forms, the critique of science and technology as gendered constructions and the critique of science and technology as involved in ecological collapse and destruction. The point is to show that science and technology are never separable from social and political structures, cultural projects and ecological relations. In the 1960s and 1970s a truism was established that science and technology have their *political economies*, their political households. In this way the cultural project of modern science and technology was associated with economic, social and political relations.[17] Vandana Shiva goes further, and radicalizes the basis of this economy; she draws nature into the same political field. Accordingly, science and technology do not just have a political – capitalist, patriarchal and colonial – economy, but also a *political ecology*. Nature functions as a political category, nature is a term we fight about the meaning of in order to decide who we are and what we can become. Nature is a cultural and social construction through which we define and legitimize the differences between ourselves and others. In modern times science and technology have played a central role in these cultural processes of interpretation, construction and legitimization. By defining and characterizing something as nature and something else as culture, modern science and technology have contributed to creating and legitimizing differences, building and maintaining hierarchies and power relations, and attaching unequal values to different people, natures and cultures. Until recently, however, modern science and technology have been capable of denying their relation to nature as *a relation,* socially and culturally constituted, as more and other than naturalized necessity, and the only one and best form of knowledge.

Thus some of us have avoided confrontation with the political ecology of modern science and technology – its household with regard to ecological and social sustainability, use and administration of natural resources, and treatment of the living nature of which we ourselves are a part.

In the approaches presented above, modern biotechnology takes its place in an old narrative about science and technology involved in local and global politics, and enlisted in conflicts about the control of nature and people. These experiences and stories are about people being controlled or removed, natures and ecologies exploited, and cultures degraded and reduced to nature. As mentioned, these stories seldom enter the narrative of the heroic roles of science and technology in the Great Development. When modern biotechnology is now launched within a narrative such as this, which prefers to acknowledge only the great 'landmarks' which science and technology achieve in the service of mankind, it is urgent to (re)mobilize the critical traditions. In this anthology on biotechnology we draw on traditions which have their bases in forgotten lessons and stories. We will confront biotechnology with critiques of science and technology as integrated in and integrating for political and cultural projects, but, vice versa, we will also confront the critiques with the need to relate to nature and biology. Modern biotechnology also challenges the critical traditions and discourses on science and technology as politics and culture in their fundamental suppositions and prerequisites, interests and politics.

Problematic Integrations of Science, Society and Culture

In his introduction to the anthology *Global Ecology. A New Arena for Political Conflict* (1993), Wolfgang Sachs likens dependence on research and technology in the management of the world after the Rio Earth Summit in 1992 to driving a car (development) at high speed along the edge of the abyss, equipped with radar, monitors and highly educated expert personnel continuously monitoring, testing and manoeuvring the biophysical tolerances. For more than twenty years we have heard warnings of our coming closer to the drop, that we are driving right at it, but can still turn back in time. Have we then found a handy solution which lets us off stopping? As far as it goes, it represents little new: a political strategy for development carried on, and now even risk-controlled and managed, by modern science and technology.

The knowledge-producing institutions in modern societies can no longer be looked upon naïvely as enclaves or cocoons for detached and disengaged reflection on a world 'out there'. Modern research does not take place in elevated and isolated ivory towers, where researchers with a comfortable distance from everyday problems and conflicts of interest peer out over reality and deliver their 'objective' judgements. This should not be a controversial standpoint today. Most researchers would also agree on the point of the social and cultural dependence of modern science and technology: science and technology in society, society in science and technology. Even so, scientists, technologists, politicians and bureaucrats seem to carry on thinking of the knowledge-producing institutions as 'outside', or at least marginal, in relation to the 'real' conflicts, sufferings and institutional conditions under which we live. The research complex is also considered as less important within critical environmental and women's movements, even when science and technology are acknowledged to be enmeshed in gendered, racial, ethnocentric, colonial and capitalist projects and practices. We seem not to be able to stop thinking in terms of 'out there' and 'in here', and seeing the modern research complexes as marginal and less important with regard to where problems and changes are generated.

So much of our cultural trust is invested in scientific and technological solutions that each time it gets too problematic and disquieting we seem to slide back into simple models and solutions. When science and technology appear to be involved in the crises they were supposed to solve, the cry goes up for more freedom and independence for research rather than taking the bull by the horns – accepting responsibility for, and puzzling out, the social, cultural and ecological relations our knowledge (re)produces. It has been difficult, although science and technology obviously have a political life, to see how these politics operate in the practices and products of research. When we are confronted with these problematic relations, we often select defensive strategies. We do not seem to know how to approach and work to change the world-producing apparatuses which modern science and technology actually are. We lack a grasp of science and technology as culture, and as integrated in and integrating for the modern world order.[18]

One of the problems along the way is that the projects for change, for sustainable development and for a common future, suffer from constant pressures of time and the need to employ modern science and technology as the means to create a better world. There is never time for working for change in science and technology; the need for expertise and counter-expertise – better knowledge with more authority and legitimacy – seems to stand in the way. Judging by the accusations directed at post-modern critiques – when they query the legitimacy of modern science as the authoritative discourse of truth – we need, for moral and political reasons, a science so powerful and commanding that we cannot afford to question the other consequences of this power. Both women's and environmental movements have based their politics and policies on science being conquered as a tool for other interests. Science should be used in all its authority to point out risks, sutferings and injustices, to speak on behalf of those who do not have a voice to be heard, those with less power, those who are less privileged. The question of the extent to which science will let itself be used as a tool in this way – on the same terms – or whether one is trapped by a politics of knowledge which is part of the problem rather than the solution, becomes politically impossible.

It is a question, however, whether we can afford *not* to take the question seriously, and demand time to suspend the authority and puzzle out conditions for and effects of our knowledge-producing practices – as well as to work out new strategies. Each day we live and experience the consequences of a form of knowledge which has become so abstracted from the realities, relations and opinions it is knowledge of, that it undermines its own basis in life.

Against such accusations a traditional internalist statement would still look upon science and technology as independent undertakings, but insist that their borders must be continuously maintained and defended against intruders and exploiters with illegitimate motives and ambitions. Consequently, the question of science and technology in society would be a question of use or misuse, and the question of culture and society in science and technology a question of excluding (subjective and special-interest) values, of keeping science and technology straight. One 'rescues' science and technology by holding neither of them 'in themselves' liable for the problems, and blaming 'external' political circumstances.

But if we follow the argumentation in the critical traditions that I have presented, the question can no longer be about misuse or 'biased' research – because science and technology *are* social relations, *are* culture. Not even science has direct and unmediated access to the world and reality as it 'really' is. *None of us* are so privileged as to have a position outside worlds in crisis, which guarantees critical distance and innocent – objective – knowledge. This does *not* mean that all is relative and just as good and true, that it is all about untranslatable language games and a play with representations. It means, on the contrary, that focus is shifted away from questions about the truth and validity of particular theories, and towards questions of ethical and political implications and responsibility.[19] As researchers, we do not simply consider, analyse, understand and solve problems 'out there'; our knowledge production is a (re)productive force. Science does not simply reveal truth and unmask reality; it invents – or constructs – it too. I have tried to show and argue, by presenting experiences and lessons of the past which we seem to forget, that knowledge is veritably constructive, creative and productive, and it produces and distributes chances of life and death. As Evelyn Fox Keller says, this is 'nowhere so dramatically in evidence than in the successes of nuclear physics and molecular biology, that is, in the production of technologies of life and death'.[20] Once we acknowledge this as a fundamental condition for all forms of knowledge production, the challenge is to develop ways of holding researchers responsible for their production of knowledge.

The question has to be about how we can be made responsible for the knowledge we (re)produce. The answer has to begin with critical reflection on social and cultural conditions, on how these operate in and through scientific and technological production of knowledge. Some have more power to see and construct worlds than others, and modern biotechnology is a very powerful discourse in that respect. The credibility in the arguments about biotechnology serving humankind's interests depends, for example, on where and how one is localized in the world. How do we force localization on to the participants in these discourses? The answer must further be about making oneself accountable, and about developing new strategies and ways of working in science and technology which are more viable and life-sharing.

So, to speak of science and technology 'in themselves' or 'as such' is an abstraction, a construction or fiction. This can be seen each time new and promising developments appear to be leading to exploitation and maldevelopment; when the exertions of sincere, well-meaning researchers and politicians result in people losing their means of livelihood rather than in a better world. Science and technology are always realized in concrete social, cultural, historical and ecological contexts. Both the meanings and uses of knowledge are always contextual, they are never found outside time and space, social relations and structures, cultural hopes and fears. They *are* social and cultural constructions, and cannot be separated and isolated from the contexts within which they operate.

Likewise with the developments within modern gene technology and biotechnology: they cannot be discussed and evaluated outside the social, cultural and ecological relations in which they are integrated and integrate. One cannot, for example, promote biotechnology as a morally necessary solution for global poverty and environmental crises without causing several short circuits. The argument presupposes that more food means fewer poor, and that biotechnological research and development are directed towards the production of food for the poor. This is a prime example of our cultural faith in technological solutions. Technology, however, is unable to solve problems whose 'nature' is political and ecological: food is a distribution problem, a question of power and politics. In the market economy system, purchasing power is not distributed according to need. Neither, in this system, is biotechnological development directed towards the production of food for the poor. Biotechnological research and development occurs on the whole privately, conducted by large industrial enterprises and multinational corporations. The proportion of biotechnological research and development which is directed towards increasing the nutritional value in grain, rice or corn is negligibly small. Instead, what is pushed is the development of resistance to pesticides in industrially produced seed stock – enabling industry to sell their seed stocks, fertilizer and pesticides as integrated package solutions to the farmers. Another large industry is called 'industrial foods', industrially produced replacements of agricultural crops which were previously imported from countries in the South to countries in the North. Through the help of advanced biotechnology and the free flow of gene resources from South to North, farmers and nations in the South become economically more dependent on the North, and ecologically more vulnerable, while countries in the North become economically independent and at the same time enriched in relation to countries in the South.[21]

Thus, biotechnology cannot be discussed without addressing the urgent questions of the relation between biotechnology and biodiversity, the political role of biotechnology within North–South relations, biotechnology's role in a capitalist world economy, biotechnology's relation to cultural values such as nature's intrinsic value and respect for the integrity of all things living, or biotechnology's conceptions of knowledge and nature. Biotechnological developments produce and reproduce concrete circum-stances: contexts of meanings, relations and institutions. But this does not mean that other more benevolent and sustainable scientific and tech-nological developments are impossible. On the contrary, science and technology are determined neither by their internal dynamics and logic, nor by social and cultural power structures. They are social and cultural constructions, and can always be (re)constructed in new ways in new relations. Neither science and technology nor social, cultural and ecological relations are given once and for all. There are always other possible ways, more responsible, reflective and humble. We are not condemned to eternal reproduction, but must find out how we are to take responsibility for the co-production of science, technology and the contexts they are to enter into.[22]

Critical Challenges in Biotechnology

The main aim of this anthology is to create recognition and acknowledge-ment of the problematic status of biotechnology in discourses on global ecology and sustainable development, and to mobilize critical discourses and communities to act on the background of this admission. The intention is to strike a note for conversations and exchanges, to build bridges and form alliances. Until now the concerns and challenges raised by women's and environmental groups, alternative directions within biology, medicine and agriculture, and critiques of science and technology have been diffused and marginalized in controversies over biotechnology. The questions about science and technology, gender and ecology have been treated as separate axes, each of them only remotely verging on biotechnology. This collection of articles brings together these interests and questions in order to mobilize the awareness that they do meet in biotechnology, and thus must be addressed and answered together.

The need to regard the new biotechnological developments as problematic is urgent. This demands attention from natural scientists, students of the natural sciences, science critics, activists in women's and environmental movements, politicians, bureaucrats and committed people everywhere. Until recently, however, scientific inquiry has been understood to demand freedom and the absence of control. Science is supposed to bless us most when we leave it alone. The same liberty is demanded by industry and markets for their technological development. But biotechnology is not, and cannot be, just some scientists' business – nor even the business of some professional in the field of ethics. By no means should decisions on biotechnology research and development be left to markets, profit factors and industry. Through these institutions, biotechnology is woven into the developments we experience today as critical. As our world and everyday life become more and more affected by and dependent on biotechnology, and the problematic consequences are felt and experienced by more people, both local and global politics must address science and technology as involved and integrated in the problematic developments behind environmental and poverty crises.

Significantly, the new developments in biotechnology – with regard to food, agriculture and biodiversity – are seldom scrutinized and discussed from the perspectives of the critical movements and traditions which were mobilized in the 1970s. At the same time we are confronted by a new wave of biological determinism. Genetics has become a popular science and part of popular culture, and biological explanations of social fates and differences flourish. In a situation where biological determinism dominates in scientific, political, social and cultural discourses and contexts, the critics of science and technology seem to have withdrawn. Even women's and environmental movements, and their critical alliances in science and technology, have stopped responding to biological determinism. What can be the reasons for this silence surrounding biological development? Has the urgency of the problems and challenges with which we are confronted helped to silence the critique during the 1980s? Or has the awareness that nature and reality are constructs paralysed critical discourses? Is it the problem of relativism that has killed off the critiques?

The intention of this anthology is to reopen and reinvent the critical discourses, to put the politics of biotechnology under scrutiny and debate. We will show how urgent it is to take up the concerns and questions of critical traditions in relation to biotechnology. Furthermore, the aim is to generate new questions and challenges which must be confronted in bio-political struggles. New discourses, communities and alliances which bring together and build bridges between old ones are needed in order to confront and answer these new challenges.

Part 1, 'Biotechnology as Culture: (Re)constructions of Biology and Nature', is dedicated to problematizations and (re)constructions of what biological knowledge and nature 'are' and can be, of how we conceptualize the relationship between knowledge and nature. Many of the conflicting points of view which reoccur in controversies over biotechnology rest on differing understandings of nature, scientific knowledge and the relationship between our knowledge and nature. The problem is that these premises are seldom made explicit and opened up for debate. This applies just as much for discussions of biology as for discussions of risk, ethics and politics. Therefore the question addressed in this first section has a bearing on and demands attention from many more people than scientists and science critics alone. A bioethic, and critical political standpoints and policies on biotechnology – whether held by environmental organizations, public authorities or international negotiatiors – require a grasp of such underlying frameworks of understanding, assumptions and values in biotechnological research and development. The question is how to make the politics of knowledge a subject of investigation, and how to integrate such a politics into discussions of biotechnology. This is where the significance of discussing conceptions of knowledge and technology, of problematizing our frameworks of understanding, comes in. If the field of discourses on the roles of science and technology in possible common futures is opened up and admitted *as a field of various comprehensions, a question of values and conceptions of nature (including human nature), knowledge and technology,* the focus is shifted away from questions about truth and validity and towards values, relations and politics for which we must bear the responsibility.

The best and most influential critiques of science and technology as politics grew out of protest movements against militarism, racism, sexism and colonialism. A common concern of these protest movements, relevant and important here, is the fight against biological determinism and reductionism. Against such attempts to reduce complex phenomena and problems to biology and genes, oppressed people and cultures, with their marginalized and subjugated knowledges, have created space for resistance and opposition. The critical traditions have taken their starting point here to deconstruct and challenge the supposedly neutral, objective, non-positioned knowledge productions of modern Western science and technology.

The critique of biological determinism has been a constant concern of women's movements and feminism since the 1970s. It has generated problematizations of science and technology as society and culture, and more complex comprehensions of science and technology as integrated in and integrating for the societies to which they belong. First of all, biological determinism and its legitimizing of patriarchal views on reality, values and social relations led to a problematization and investigation of the significance and roles of the knowledge-producing institutions in social and cultural processes of change, and of conditions for change in general. Work on change is demanding and difficult, and must embrace science and technology as part of the problem. Second, the alliance between the movement and the critique of science and technology involves commitment, morally and politically. The controversies on the science question in feminism have, because of this, become frightening and harrowing for many. None the less, the feminists' struggles with biological determinism, their efforts not to fall into the trap between determinism and relativism, and the challenge of developing ways of making us responsible for our productions of knowledge, have nourished – and continue to nourish – fertile developments in both biological sciences and critiques of science. They have generated alternative interpretations and readings of what we are and what we can become, as well as attempts to constitute more benevolent relations and more viable worlds.

Even if feminist critiques have been focused up to now on women's biology and bodies rather than on green nature, food, agriculture and ecological systems, the attempt to open up discussions of biotechnology as politics and culture will find valuable resources for critique and alternatives here. This is why it has been essential to base the discussions in this collection on a quite extensive sampling of feminist critiques of biological determinism and attempts at alternative readings and constructions of nature and culture.

Part 2, 'Biohazards: Risk in Context', deals with discourses on risk with regard to releases of genetically modified organisms. This is explosive material: risk appears to be a point of crystallization for the greatest challenges this anthology and introduction can shake out of their pages. Problems and challenges in and across biology, ethics and politics are concentrated in discourses on risk. The question of risk in biotechnology carries challenges east and west, and no one can avoid confrontation with questions which explode the frameworks for professional risk analysis and closed scientific discussion, as well as their critiques. Risk demands scientific multi-language skills, or rather a communicative competence across scientific cultures – demanding and difficult conversations and collaborations. Perhaps these are the reasons why critics seem to avoid this field.

Many argue that if they enter into debates on risk, they will be locked in and subject to a discourse where the terms have been drawn up, and drawn wrongly. Controversies over risk in biotechnology do not allow one to question the strategy, the understanding of knowledge and the values involved in scientific and technological knowledge production. They do not permit one to problematize our cultural intercourse with risk as a clinically clean discipline with access only to experts, question how we invest our faith in technological solutions, or problematize the roles of science and technology in developments which have become critical. The argument requires one to look more closely at the question of risk from another angle, and refuse to accept risk as a question of 'environmental engineering' or 'scientific management' of health. Risk is a question of values and politics, in science and technology and in the cultural and social intercourse with technology.[23]

One of the contributions to Part 2 has its basis here, and tries to move the field in the direction of discussing the politics in various discourses on risk. Debates on biotechnology and risk are deconstructed with regard to differing concepts of nature, knowledge and technology, underlying values and implications for political directives. Risk is a field of knowledge where it is evident that the meanings and uses of knowledge are intimately connected, and where the implicit values and conceptions of the relations between knowledge and nature are decisive for the evaluation of biotechnological developments. The argument is that they must be laid open for debate. Risk is not just a question of medicine and biology, biophysical tolerances and the safety of containment in biotechnology research and development. As Les Levidow points out, people's fears in relation to biotechnology contain questions of social justice and economics, conceptions of nature and cultural values. Risk appears to be a question of who we wish to be, and to become; the concept cannot be isolated from ethical and political questions, but must be wide enough for all these concerns.

The other two contributions which are included in this section make ecology the context for discussions on biotechnology and risk. The culture and politics of the distinction between nature and culture are also featured centrally, however, and constructions of knowledge and nature in modern experimental sciences are problematized. The point here is to focus on the need to bring together the concerns and approaches of ecologists, feminists and science critics, and to point out the potential for moving on from critiques which are stuck fast between determinism and relativism.

A multitude of alternative directions exist and operate within the biological sciences, too, and should be brought up and mobilized in order to develop other critiques of biotechnology. It is important to raise the science question, the question of the roles of science and technology in the environmental and developmental crises, in ecological discourses as well as in environmental movements. They must be confronted with and need to include in their theoretical and political strategies the questions and perspectives raised by critiques of science and technology. They should also inspire critical work on biology and biotechnology within feminist discourses and communities, however. Why have feminists only dealt with the question of risk in relation to the female body and reproduction? Nature neither starts nor stops with the human body. When biodiversity and ecology are brought into the centre for discussion, other concerns and questions – on biological boundaries, stability and destabilization – are brought up. What is at stake in biotechnology is to a large extent the question of boundaries, and responsibility for the boundaries we live with. These are challenges which we must hasten to raise.

Feminist critiques have challenged and formed a bulwark against the biological determinism which has naturalized gender hierarchies and other social destinies and arrangements on the basis of biological boundaries and differences. They have tried to come to terms with nature and reality as constructions and representations which are constituted on as well as constitutive for cultural and social relations. 'Nature' is a political category which is used to create differences and boundaries, to separate and integrate, and to determine value. In this situation, to deconstruct and destabilize meanings and boundaries which are effective in our lives seems a good strategy. Trafficking and exploring boundaries have liberated women to look for new forms of subjectivity and relations, more friendly and open, and new ways to think about change. But if we shift our focus to ecologies and biodiversity, we are confronted by other meanings, functions and consequences of boundaries and stability. As such, the question of risk in biotechnology fundamentally challenges debates on nature and reality as social constructions. These seem to have been trapped in dichotomies like nature versus culture, determinism versus relativism, language versus reality. The problem is that representations are not only representations, signs and images. They are constructive and productive in reality, and we have seen that this is nowhere demonstrated so dramatically as in genetics and biotechnology.

One way of challenging the influence of determinism as well as the impotence of the relativist critique is through revisions of our understanding of the organism. The organism has virtually disappeared both in the so-called central dogma in deterministic biology and in studies of science and technology as social constructions. We are left with genes and dead matter – a command and control centre and its material, 'biomass'. According to Vandana Shiva, the prevailing ideology in biology and biotechnology and the critique of science meet here, and paradoxically enough they end up supporting each other. Within constructivist frameworks of understanding, knowledge of biological difference and genetic modification becomes a problem, or perhaps not: they are validated as just another representation, editing or reconstruction of signs and texts. The result is that genetic determinism is given free scope. By focusing on the organism and its ecologies, however, a critique could come closer to an understanding of the materialities and realities of our constructions of knowledge in biotechnology. As Rosalyn Diprose and Robyn Ferrell put it, the admission, and the scrutiny, of reality's constructed nature is only part of the task. We need to explore, deal with and take responsibility for the reality and consequences of our constructions.[24] Representations and fictions are terribly material and productive. The restructuriing of the world through biotechnology becomes acute, not so much as a question of transgressing boundaries, but as one of responsibility for boundaries, and degrees of stability and destabilization.

The question of responsibility is central too in Part 3, 'Bioethics: Knowledge and Ethics as Politics'. How are we to understand the fuss about ethics in the 1980s and 1990s? Bioethics, science ethics, business ethics – in the course of the last ten years ethics has become the new magic formula for science and technology politics which struggle to legitimize their authority against a background of crises and breakdowns in modern worlds and projects. The power and politics in the new biotechnologies seem to have left the scientific communities and political bodies with no direction and guidance. As the critical traditions of the 1970s have abated, the issues of the politics of science and technology have been marginalized and individualized as questions of ethics. For example, the question of patents in biotechnology, with widespread consequences for biodiversity and economic relations between North and South, is inverted into a question of whether it is morally acceptable with patents on life. These questions, in their turn, become institutionalized and professionalized in special committees or commissions of bioethics. In an attempt to keep science straight, ethics and politics are carefully kept apart from knowledge and science. When it comes down to struggling with social and cultural conditions and consequences in biotechnology, we have no way of taking responsibility, collectively, for the ethics and politics in our knowledge.

Rather than presenting answers and solutions to ethical questions, the aim in Part 3 is a discussion of normative bioethics, their conditions, functions and consequences. Current ethical questions and arguments arising from biotechnology will be put aside for a moment. If one takes into consideration the demands on ethics and the roles ethics plays in the biotechnological era, it is urgent that ethics too – since it occupies itself with responsibility and how scientists and technologists can become responsible – should deal with ethical knowledge as culture and politics. This is the theme of Chapter 11.

The question of ethics as politics does not challenge ethicists alone. In the struggle to develop and negotiate through responsible politics and policies regarding biotechnology, representatives for environmental movements, bureaucrats and politicians readily seize on ethical expert help in making difficult decisions. Opening up debates on the politics of knowledge, on the implicit values, assumptions and strategies of all parties and participants in debates on biotechnology, is as urgent here as elsewhere in this book.

The first two contributions represent differing attempts to develop an ethic which embodies the critiques of biology and medicine respectively. Jesper Hofmeyer takes the chronic problem of nature–culture in the modern scientific culture, and attempts at non-deterministic readings and representations of the nature in and around us, as his points of departure. He argues from a biosemiotic approach where nature is understood as creative, as an interpreter and producer of meaning. Against this background, anthropocentric ethical traditions are challenged. Rosalyn Diprose takes up the challenge of making physicians and the discourses on medical ethics responsible for the ethics and politics in genetic knowledge. Genetics is an extremely powerful discursive practice which produces and organizes difference, rather than representing real differences in nature. A 'gen-ethics' which makes sense must be one which goes into the knowledge and takes responsibility for its meanings, relations and applications.

Bringing ethics and critiques of science and technology together also challenges relativism in constructivist studies of science and technology. Studies of science and technology are often criticized for having lost their critical project and becoming professional, for cultivating an academic and relativistic critique. But instead of leaving blasé students of science and technology at peace in their own professionalized meta-discourses discussing only other people's discourses, we are challenging science and technology studies to get on track and relate their reflections to those of biology and ethics. The challenges are queuing up: we are being asked to take responsibility for the breakdowns between science and the world out there; we are struggling with epistemological and political difficulties concerning the reality in or behind our representations and fictions. On the one hand everything is language, on the other hand we have lost the language skills that involve communicating and translating across closed language games and worlds. Can an ethic be possible in this period of confusion of language, or are those right who say that the possibility of an ethic is dead? There seems to be no language, no discourse in which to talk about unity, boundaries, organisms, integrity and intrinsic value, to tackle violence and transgressions of boundaries. Are there any longer discourses in which to talk about what is common, what connects people across differences and problems of translation, what makes collective solidarity action possible? Where should we look for possible ways out of this vacuum? Instead of letting ourselves be paralysed, and withdrawing into comfortable sceptical and relativistic positions in academic space, we must confront these discourses and practices with challenges in biotechnology, and reconstruct them in order to take up risk, ecology and ethics. Can feminist discourses and movements (which have up until now been focused mainly on women's biology and the body), and the environmental movements and their discourses (which have up until now been focused mainly on the natural environment) inspire one another in their critiques of biotechnology? I understand the renewed interest within feminist discourses in the exploration of what our embodiedness can mean, as well as of the organism in ecological discourses, as a wish and an attempt to commit oneself, to find new routes to more benevolent subjectivities, relations and knowledge production(s). Embodiedness signifies here responsibility for meanings and boundaries. Responsibility for constructions and boundaries is yanked back into the centre of the problems.

Part 4, 'Biopolitics: The Political Ecology of Biotechnology', problematizes biotechnology within the discourses on sustainable development and North–South relations. The focus is on the complexity in, and the connections between, questions like biotechnology and biodiversity, biotechnology and patents, and biotechnology and North–South relations. The political ecology of biotechnological research and development – its accounting with regard to ecological and social sustainability, use and management of natural resources, and intercourse with living nature – is tied up with and ties up economic and political relations and institutions. The contributions in Part 4 work through these relations and institutions: biotechnology as realized in concrete and specific social, cultural, historic, economic and ecological contexts. Will biotechnology feed the world, clean up and minimize pollution, promote biodiversity, and oppose deforestation, desertification and climatic change? Or is modern biotechnology fundamentally integrated in the developments which are critical for the possibility of a common future, or of any future at all?

Readers who are unfamiliar with the critical traditions in science and technology studies which the anthology introduces will possibly find it useful to begin with the contributions in this part. This does not mean that the critique of science and technology as politics, as part of the problem and not only a solution, is any less central here. On the contrary, the authority which modern science and technology still enjoy in the West quickly begins to crack when the focus is directed towards 'culture meetings' between modern Western science and technology and the so-called Third World. Biotechnology constitutes the last in a row of meetings like these. Both the conditions and the consequences become so obvious and dramatic: science and technology are politics and culture.

Notes

1   Sejersted, F. & I. Moser (eds) (1992) 'Preface', in *Humanistic Perspectives on Technology, Development and Environment. Papers from a Conference*, TMV Report Series No.3, University Press, Oslo.
2   See, e.g., Sachs, W. (ed.) (1993) *Global Ecology. A New Arena of Political Conflict*, Zed Books, London.
3   See, e.g., conference reports and statements from 'Sustainable Development, Science and Policy', Bergen, 8–12 May 1990, 'International Conference on an Agenda of Science for Environment and Development into the 21st Century' (ASCEND 21), Vienna, 25–29 November 1991, and *AGENDA 21: The United Nations Programme of Action from Rio*, 1992. Exceptions worthy of note are *Women's Action Agenda 21* and the report from the 'World Women's Congress for a Healthy Planet', Miami, 8–12 November 1991.
4   World Commission on Environment and Development (1987) *Our Common Future*, Oxford University Press, Oxford, see, e.g., pp. 8, 43 and 45.
5   *Ibid.*, see, e.g., pp. 16, 44 and 60.
6   For a philosophical defence of internalism and the debate on the status of scientific theories, see, e.g., Lakatos, I. & A. Musgrave (eds) (1970) *Criticism and the Growth of Knowledge*, Cambridge University Press, Cambridge; Laudan, L. (1977) *Progress and Its Problems*, University of California Press, Berkeley; and Bhaskar, R. (1978) *A Realist Theory of Knowledge*, Hassocks, Harvester, England. For the social critique of science and technology see, e.g., periodicals like *Science for the People* in the USA, *Science for People* in Europe, and *Radical Science Journal*. For the history (and a rich bibliography) of the radicalization of science, see Rose, H. & S. Rose (1976) *The Radicalization of Science*, Macmillan, London.
7   Rose, H. & S. Rose (1969) *Science and Society*, Allen Lane & Penguin, Harmondsworth, (1976) *The Political Economy of Science*, Macmillan, London, and (1976) *Ideology of/in the Natural Sciences*, Schenkman, Boston MA.
8   Hessen, B. (1931) 'The Social and Economic Roots of Newton's Principia' in Bukharin, N. *et al.* (eds) *Science at the Crossroads*, Kniga, Moscow. Reprinted with a new introduction by Joseph Needham, London 1971; Bernal, J. D. (1939) *The Social Functions of Science*, Routledge & Kegan Paul, London; Needham, J. (1969) *The Grand Titration*, Allen & Unwin, London.
9   For a defence of sociobiological theories see, e.g., Jensen, A. (1972) *Genetics and Education*, Methuen, London; Goldberg, S. (1975) *On Male Dominance: The Inevitability of Patriarchy*, New York; Wilson, E. O. (1975) *Sociobiology: The New Synthesis*, Harvard University Press, Cambridge MA; and Dawkins, R. (1976) *The Selfish Gene*, Oxford University Press, Oxford. Regarding the critique, the debates and good documentations of these, see Kamin, L. J. (1974) *The Science and Politics of IQ*, Erlbaum, Potomac, MD; Tobach E. & B. Rossoff (eds) (1978) *Genes and Gender*, Gordon Press, New York; Hubbard, R. & M. Lowe (eds) (1979) *Genes and Gender 2: Pitfalls in Research on Sexual Gender*, Gordian Press, New York; Hubbard, R., M. S. Henifin & B. Fried (1979) *Women Looking at Biology Looking at Women*, Schenkman, Cambridge and (1982) *Biological Woman – The Convenient Myth*, Schenkman, Cambridge; Gould, S. J. (1981) *The*

(1981) *The Mismeasure of Man*, Norton, New York; Rose, S. (ed.) (1982) *Against Biological Determinism*, Allison & Busby, London; Lewontin, R. C., S. Rose & L. J. Kamin (1984) *Not in Our Genes. Biology, Ideology and Human Nature*, Penguin, London; Kevles, D. K. (1985) *In the Name of Eugenics. Genetics and the Uses of Human Heredity*, Knopf; Hubbard, R. (1990) *The Politics of Women's Biology*, Rutgers, New Brunswick; Rose, H. (1992) 'Victorian Values in the Test-Tube: The Politics of Reproductive Science and Technology' in Sejersted, F. & I. Moser (eds) (1992) *op.cit.*, and (1992) 'Feminist/Gender Studies of Science: An Overview of the Field' in *Genus, teknik och naturvetenskap – en introduktion till kvinnoforskning i naturvetenskap och teknik*, FRN, Stockholm.

10 See Rose, H. (1992) *op. cit.*, for a view of and introduction to feminist critiques of science and technology. The bibliographies in Rose's writings are very rich. In my history of lessons and experiences, and the presentation of theoretical and political resources to problematize science and technology, I am indebted to Hilary Rose. Other feminist science critics who inspire my work and to whom I remain indebted theoretically and politically include Rosi Braidotti (1991) *Patterns of Dissonance*, Polity Press, Cambridge, (1994) *Nomadic Subjects*, Columbia University Press, New York; Brita Brenna, Tarja Cronberg, Jane Flax (1990) *Thinking Fragments*, University of California Press, Berkeley; Elisabeth Gulbrandsen, Donna Haraway (1984) 'Primatology is Politics by Other Means' in Bleier, R. (ed.) (1986) *Feminist Approaches to Science*, Pergamon Press, New York, (1989) *Primate Visions: Gender, Race, and Nature in the World of Modern Science*, Routledge, New York, (1991) *Simians, Cyborgs and Women. The Reinvention of Nature*, Free Association Books, London; Sandra Harding (1986) *The Science Question in Feminism*, Cornell University Press, Ithaca; Ruth Hubbard (1990) *The Politics of Women's Biology*, Rutgers, New Brunswick; Evelyn Fox Keller (1985) *Reflections on Gender and Science*, Yale, New Haven, (1992) *Secrets of Life, Secrets of Death. Essays on Language, Gender and Science*, Routledge, New York; Carolyn Merchant (1980) *The Death of Nature: Women, Ecology and the Scientific Revolution*, Harper and Row, New York; and Vandana Shiva (1989) *Staying Alive: Women, Ecology and Development*, Zed Books, London and Kali for Women, New Delhi, (1991) *The Violence of the Green Revolution. Third World Agriculture, Ecology and Politics*, Zed Books, London and Third World Network, Penang.

11 See the contributions here of Evelyn Fox Keller and Ruth Hubbard.

12 See Haraway, D. (1984) *op. cit*; (1986) *op cit.*, (1989) *op cit.*, (1991) *op cit.*, and here, for a feminist critique of relativism and discussions of the political-theoretical possibilities of constructivism.

13 See, e.g., Hubbard, R. & E. Wald (1993) *Exploding the Gene Myth*, Beacon Press, Boston MA, and Nelkin, D. (1993) 'Promotional Metaphors and Their Popular Appeal' in *Public Understanding of Science*, 2.

14 Haraway, D. (1984) *op.cit.*, (1989) *op.cit.*, (1991) *op.cit.*, and here; Hubbard, R. (1990) *op.cit.*, Keller, E. F. (1983) *A Feeling for the Organism. The Life and Work of Barbara McClintock*, W. H. Freeman and Company, New York, and especially Chapter 8; 'Between Language and Science: The Question of Directed Mutation in Molecular Genetics' in (1992) *Secrets of Life, Secrets of Death. Essays on Language, Gender and Science*, Routledge, New York.

15 See Shiva (1989) and (1991) *op. cit.* and (1992) 'The Seed and the Earth: Bio-
    technology and the Colonisation of Regeneration' in *Development Dialogue* 1–2,
    Dag Hammarskjold Foundation, Uppsala, and here.

16 See, e.g., Castillo, G. T. (1990) 'The Fine Print in Sustainable Global Food
    Supply: Some Micro Scenarios' in *Sustainable Development, Science and Policy.
    The Conference Report*, Bergen, 8–12 May 1990; Fowler, C. & P. Mooney (1990)
    Shattering. Food, Politics, and the Loss of Genetic Diversity, University of Arizona
    Press, Tucson; and Perlas, N. (1993) 'The Seven Dimensions of Sustainable
    Agriculture', paper presented at the Second Asian Development Forum, 22–27
    February 1993, Xavier University, Cagayan de Oro City, Mindanao, Philippines.

17 See Rose, H. & S. Rose (1976) *op.cit.*

18 See Young, R. M. (1985) *Darwin's Metaphor: Nature's Place in Victorian Culture*,
    Cambridge University Press, Cambridge, and Donna Haraway's contribution
    here for a discussion of the problem field.

19 For feminist discussions of the possibilities in science and technology as culture
    and politics – as possibilities for responsibility – see, e.g., Haraway, D. (1984)
    op.cit., (1991) *op.cit.*, and here, as well as Butler, J. & J. W. Scott (eds) (1992)
    Feminists Theorize the Political, Routledge, London (especially Flax, J. (1992)
    'The End of Innocence'); and Braidotti (1991) and (1994) *op. cit.*.

20 Keller, E. F. (1992) *op.cit.*, p. 9.

21 See, e.g., Brown, L. (1990) 'Feeding the World in the Nineties' in *Sustainable
    Development, Science and Policy. The Conference Report*, Bergen, 8–12 May 1990;
    Hobbelink, H. (1991) *Biotechnology and the Future of World Agriculture*, Zed
    Books, London, and here; and Perlas, N. (1994) *Overcoming Illusions about
    Biotechnology*, Zed Books, London, and Third World Network, Penang, and here.

22 See notes 12, 14 and 18.

23 See, e.g., Rose, H. (1992) *op.cit.*, Sachs, W. (ed.) (1993) *op.cit.*, Achterhuis, H.
    (1992) 'Human Safety and the Technological Project' in Sejersted, F. & I. Moser
    (eds) *op.cit.*

24 Diprose, R. & R. Ferrell (1991) 'Introduction' to *Cartographies. Poststructuralism
    and the Mapping of Bodies and Spaces*, Allen & Unwin, NSW, Australia.

PART I

Biotechnology as Culture:
(Re)constructions of Biology and Nature

Human Nature

RUTH HUBBARD

The ambiguity of the term biology is at the heart of questions about what scientists do when they try to examine nature. We use the term to denote what scientists tell us about organisms and also the living experience itself. When I speak of 'my biology', I usually mean the ways I experience my biological functions, not what scientists tell me about them. I can also use the word to denote the scientific discipline, as in 'I am studying biology.' This confusion about what we mean by biology reflects ambiguities about the conditions between scientific descriptions of the world and the phenomena scientists try to describe. We need to be aware of these ambiguities when we think about human nature because it does not describe real people. It is an abstraction, or reification, a normative concept that incarnates (in the literal sense of enveloping in flesh) historically based beliefs about how people should behave.

Biologists' descriptions of human nature are imbedded in the ways we study organisms. Most scientists accept the notion that nature can best be described in levels of organization that extend from ultimate particles, via atoms and molecules, to cells, tissues, and organs, to organisms considered individually, and then on to groups of organisms (that is, societies). Biology is concerned with the range of levels from atoms and molecules through organisms, and also with the relationships between different organisms over time (evolution) and space (animal behaviour and ecology). Some biologists study organisms by taking them apart, while others observe whole organisms in the laboratory or the field. Yet, in the current view, these levels do not have equal prestige and are not credited with equal explanatory power. Most biologists, as well as chemists and physicists, believe that the 'lower' levels, such as atoms and molecules, are more 'basic' and have intrinsically greater explanatory power. As I have shown elsewhere, molecular biologists have described genes (which are molecules) as keys to the 'secret of life' or blueprints of the organism. I have criticized the Human Genome Initiative, which has been organized to determine the composition and sequence of all the genes on the human chromosomes, for its faith in the superior explanatory power of the 'lower' levels, its reductionism.

Reductionism operates across levels. Reductionists believe that by studying individuals we will come to understand how societies operate and that a better understanding of organs, tissues, and molecules will teach us how organisms (and hence societies) function. For this reason they explain the existence of crime on the basis of a 'criminal personality' and believe that criminals behave as they do because they have diseased brains, too much or too little of certain hormones or other critical substances, or defective genes. So, reductionism is a bottom-up, hierarchical theory.

The converse is sometimes called holism. Some people base it on a similar analysis that accepts hierarchies of levels, but they assign superior explanatory power to the 'higher' levels, the organism as a whole or even the organism in its surroundings. At present, this is a less popular system of explanation among scientists but one that carries considerable weight among practitioners of alternative methods of healing, such as massage and acupuncture, and among some feminists and environmentalists. They see reductionist ways of conceptualizing how organisms function and live in nature as a threat to people and our environment because these treat specific points of interest as though they could be isolated from the context in which they are embedded.

Biodeterminism is a form of reductionism in that it explains the behaviour of individuals and characteristics of societies in terms of biology. Feminists know it best in the form of Freud's notorious statement that 'biology is destiny'. In previous discussions, we have encountered biodeterminist explanations for the obvious differences in women's and men's access to social, economic and political power. Among them were Darwin's descriptions of the effects of sexual selection on the social behaviours of females and males. Biodeterminism also inspired nineteenth-century comparisons between the sizes of men's and women's brains and between brains of men of different races, which was held unequivocally to prove the superiority of Caucasian men over men of other races and over all women.

A good deal of present-day research into the causes of social and behavioural differences between women and men relies on reductionist explanations that draw on hypothetical differences in hormone levels of female and male foetuses or on hypothetical genes that favour spatial skills, mathematical ability, competitiveness and aggression in men and domesticity and nurturance in women. But the most pervasive and comprehensive of present-day biodeterminist theories is sociobiology, which has as its project 'the systematic study of the *biological basis* of all social behaviour' (Wilson, 1975, p. 4; my italics).

Sociobiological Models of Human Nature

Sociobiologists claim that it is possible to identify the fundamental elements of human nature by the fact that they characterize all people, whatever their cultural or historical differences, and selected animals as well. Once supposedly universal traits have been identified – for example, male aggression and female nurturance – sociobiologists argue that their very universality is evidence that they are adaptive.

The term adaptive has a special meaning in this context. It implies that the traits in question are inherited unchanged by successive generations and that individuals who exhibit them leave more descendants than other individuals do. In this way, the genes for more adaptive traits come to outnumber the genes for less adaptive ones until the more adaptive traits become universal. Sociobiologists argue that we try to do the things that help spread our genes about, and behaviours that let us do that most effectively become universal. Prominent among such traits among males, they say, are behaviours that lead them to inseminate as many females as possible, hence promiscuity; among females, behaviours that optimize their ability to spot, and attach themselves to, genetically well-endowed males and to take good care of their offspring, hence fidelity and nurturance.

Sociobiologists believe that women's disproportionate contributions to the care of their children and homes are biologically programmed because women have a greater biological 'investment' in children than men have. For this belief they offer the following rationale: an organism's biological fitness, in the Darwinian sense, depends on producing the greatest possible number of offspring who themselves survive long enough to reproduce. The number of offspring who reproduce determines the frequency with which an individual's genes will be represented in successive generations. Following this logic a step further, sociobiologists argue that women and men must adopt basically different strategies to maximize opportunities to spread genes into future generations.

As we have seen in the preceding chapter, the calculus goes as follows: eggs are larger than sperm, and women can produce many fewer of them in a lifetime than men can sperm. Hence, women are said to be the 'scarce resource'. Also, each egg that develops into a child represents a much larger fraction of the total number of children a woman can produce, hence of her total 'investment' and 'reproductive fitness', than a sperm that becomes a child does of a man's 'investment' and 'fitness'. Furthermore, women 'invest' nine months of pregnancy in each child, whereas men's procreative efforts are complete once they ejaculate. For these reasons, women must be more careful than men to acquire genetically well-endowed sex partners, who will also be good providers and will help women make their few investments (read, children) mature. Thus, from the seemingly innocent asymmetries between eggs and sperm flow such major social consequences as female fidelity, male promiscuity, women's disproportional contribution to the care of children, and the unequal distribution of labour by sex.

Such explanations ignore the fact that human societies do not operate with a few superstuds and that stronger and more powerful men, in general, do not have more children than weaker ones do. In theory, men could indeed have many more children than women can; but in most societies roughly the same number of women and men engage in producing children, although not in taking care of them. These kinds of biodeterminist theories are useful to people who have a stake in maintaining present inequalities, but they cannot help us explain social and economic realities.

There is no reason to believe that females expend more energy (whatever that means) on the biological components of procreation than males do. Females indeed produce fewer eggs than males do sperm, and, among mammals, females gestate embryos; but it is not obvious how to translate these facts into expenditures of energy. Is it reasonable to count only the energy required to produce the few sperm that actually fertilize eggs or should one not count the total energy males expend in producing and ejaculating semen (that is, sperm plus spermatic fluid) in a lifetime, however one might calculate that?

There are other puzzles. Does it make sense to describe the growth of a foetus inside its mother's womb as an investment of her energy? True, the metabolism of a mammalian embryo is part of a pregnant female's metabolic functions. As she eats, breathes, and metabolizes, some of the food and oxygen she takes in gets used by the growing embryo. But why does that represent an investment of her energy? An embryo that grows in an undernourished woman is a drain because it will use her body for its growth, but well-nourished, healthy women often feel energized by their pregnancies and have no trouble living normal, active lives. They have even been known to compete in Olympic events.

To speak of the foetus as a drain on a pregnant woman's energies is reminiscent of the way physicians in the nineteenth century spoke of menstruation as requiring 'energy' when they argued that girls who taxed their brains by becoming educated would not be able to have children when they grew up.

Sociobiological explanations that posit differences in the energy women and men invest in procreation to account for the fact that most men take less responsibility for the care of their children than do most women have a similar, superficial ring of scientific plausibility. But there is no way to specify the variables, much less to do the necessary calculations, to turn such waves of the hand into scientific statements.

Richard Dawkins (1976) takes sociobiological reductionism to its extreme by asserting that an organism is merely a gene's way of making more genes. He claims that everything organisms do they do out of self-interest because organisms are only living manifestations of 'selfish genes' engaged in the process of replicating themselves. But one of the problems with this kind of formulation is that genes do not replicate themselves. Nor do eggs or sperm. Even many organisms do not reproduce themselves – at least not organisms that procreate sexually, such as people and most other animals sociobiologists discuss. In sexual procreation, individuals with different genetic make-ups produce other individuals who are genetically different from both their parents and from each other. These differences have made it difficult for biologists to know how to analyse the ways in which even simple Mendelian traits, which involve differences in one gene, become established in a population. When it comes to the ill-defined behaviours that sociobiologists label selfishness, aggression or nurturance, there is no rigorous way to determine that they are transmitted biologically, or how they become established in populations.

Human sociobiology allows far too much leeway for equating traits that are observed in different cultures and under different historical circumstances. By calling different behaviours by the same name, sociobiologists make it appear as though they represented universal traits, especially when they go on and attribute the 'same' traits to animals. In this way, everything from sharp business practices and warfare, to the roughhousing of toddlers and young animals, to interactions scientists observe among animals in the field, in zoos, or in crowded laboratory cages becomes 'aggression'. The term *rape*, which in ordinary speech refers to the violent, sexualized assertion of power men impose on unconsenting women and occasionally on other men, is used by sociobiologists merely to mean a way for males to spread their genes around. As a result, sociobiologists have described what they choose to call rape among birds, fishes, insects, and even plants (Barash, 1979). Contexts and cultural meanings are erased, and all that is left are reified traits, rendered universal because a variety of behaviours are called by the same name.

Because people are biological organisms, there are similarities between some of the ways animals and people behave. But the variety of animal behaviours is so great that one can ascribe evolutionary significance to any human behaviour if the criterion is merely that some animals behave that way. That brings me to a crucial problem for scientific attempts to interpret in evolutionary terms relationships among the behaviours of different kinds of animals or of animals and people.

Ordinarily, when biologists try to understand whether anatomical similarities between different species are of evolutionary and hence genetic significance, they distinguish between two kinds of resemblances: analogies and homologies. Analogous traits are examples of what biologists call convergent evolution – different evolutionary pathways that provide similar solutions to similar biological or environmental problems. Examples of analogous structures are the wings of bats, birds, and insects, or the eyes of mammals, insects, and octopus or squid. Although they look similar and serve the same function – in our example, flight or vision – they have evolved independently and are not related genetically. Traits that share a common evolutionary and genetic basis are called homologous. Their common descent often is not obvious on superficial inspection. It must be deduced by careful, systematic examination of the paleontological record. Examples of homologous structures are the scales of reptiles and the feathers of birds. Although they look different, they serve similar functions (covering, insulation); most important, they can be shown to have a common ancestry.

To establish lines of biological inheritance, analogies are irrelevant. One must look for homologies, which usually requires culling the fossil record. But behaviour leaves no fossils. There are only observations of how contemporary animals (including people) act and interpretations of what their behaviour signifies. This kind of inspection offers much leeway for postulating connections and lines of descent on which to base hypotheses about why particular groups of people and animals behave in similar ways, but no solid information.

Interactive, Dialectical and Complementary Models of Nature

I want to turn to a fundamental criticism of the hierarchy-of-levels analysis of nature, whether it ends up being interpreted in a reductionist or holistic manner – that is, bottom-up or top-down. To get away from reductionism and futile arguments about whether nature or nurture is more significant in shaping behaviour, a number of scientists have stressed that, obviously, both genetics and environment are important. But more than that, genetic and environmental effects cannot be separated. According to the simplest model, the effects are additive. On the basis of this kind of model psychologists like Arthur Jensen (1969) and Richard Herrnstein (1971) have argued that 80 per cent of intelligence is inherited and 20 per cent is due to environment.

Other scientists point out that this formulation is overly simplistic; that nature and nurture interact in ways that cannot be quantified that easily because they are not additive but act simultaneously and affect each other.

For example, Richard Lewontin (1974) has pointed out that we can assess the individual contributions of genetic and environmental factors that act jointly only under strictly controlled conditions that permit the experimenter to change one variable at a time. On the basis of such experiments scientists can construct graphs, called norms of reaction, that describe how specific changes in each variable affect the phenomenon under observation (such as the growth of a plant in various types of soil or in the same soil but under various conditions of moisture, temperature, or cultivation).But such norms of reaction do not permit one to predict the response of different varieties of the same organism even when grown under identical experimental conditions, or the reactions of a single variety under conditions that one has not measured. In other words, norms of reaction illustrate the complexity of the interrelationships but cannot be used to describe the real world in which changes do not occur one variable at a time or in controlled or controllable ways.

Lewontin, Rose and Kamin (1984), as well as Lynda Birke (1986), argue that this kind of interactive model, although less limited than the simple, additive ones, is still too static. Lewontin and his colleagues propose a dialectical model that acknowledges levels of organization, such as the ones I have enumerated, but makes none of them more fundamental than any other. None 'causes' or 'determines' another. Rather, all of them are related dialectically and mutually draw on, and modify, the changes that may be produced at any particular level. What is more, the properties at a particular level cannot be deduced from properties observed at the other levels because all the levels are related dialectically. One cannot predict the physics and chemistry of water from the properties of hydrogen and oxygen atoms. Nor can one predict the structures and functions of proteins from the properties of the amino acids of which they are composed, and even less from the properties of the atoms that make up the amino acids. Such predictions are impossible not because we do not know enough about atoms or amino acids but because new properties emerge when atoms or amino acids come together in different combinations, and these properties must be discovered empirically. The same goes for the relationships between organisms and their genes, or between societies and the individuals who live in them.

I like to call this process transformationism, an awkward term but one that expresses the fact that biological and environmental factors can change an organism so that it responds differently to other, concurrent or subsequent, biological or environmental changes than it would have done otherwise. Simultaneously the organism transforms the environment, which, of course, includes other organisms.

We can visualize this kind of dialectical interaction, or transformation, by thinking about the interplay between biological and cultural factors that affect the ways boys and girls grow up in our society. If a society puts half its children in dresses and skirts but warns them not to move in ways that reveal their underpants, while putting the other half in jeans and overalls and encouraging them to climb trees and play ball and other active outdoor games; if later, during adolescence, the half that has worn trousers is exhorted to 'eat like a growing boy', while the half in skirts is warned to watch its weight and not get fat; if the half in jeans trots around in sneakers or boots, while the half in skirts totters about on spike heels, then these two groups of people will be biologically as well as socially different. Their muscles will be different, as will their reflexes, posture, arms, legs and feet, hand–eye coordination, spatial perception, and so on. They will also be biologically different if, as adults, they spend eight hours a day sitting in front of a visual display terminal or work on a construction job or in a mine. I am not saying that one is more healthful than the other, only that they will have different biological effects. There is no way to sort out the biological and social components that produce these differences, therefore no way to sort nature from nurture, when we confront sex differences or other group differences in societies in which people, as groups, do not have equal access to resources and power and hence live in different environments.

Recently, some of us have begun to use yet another model to look at the different levels of organization, one that draws on Niels Bohr's principle of complementarity. Bohr proposed complementarity as a way to think about the fact that light and other electromagnetic radiation can be described as bursts of particles (quanta), and also as waves spreading out from a point source. Classical physicists argued over which they really were. Bohr and the other quantum theorists asserted that they were both, and by complementarity Bohr meant that they were both at all times, not sometimes one, sometimes the other. Which description is appropriate depends on the instruments an observer uses to examine the radiation: observed with a photoelectric cell, light is a random succession of packets of energy (quanta); observed with a diffraction grating or a prism, light is composed of waves.

Complementarity provides a fruitful model for integrating the different levels of organization we can use to describe living organisms. The phenomena we observe at the subatomic, atomic, molecular, cellular, organismic or societal levels are all taking place simultaneously and constitute a single reality. It is an outcome of Western cultural history and of the history of professionalization that we have developed separate academic disciplines to describe these levels as though they were different phenomena. In fact, the only reason we think in terms of these levels is that we have developed specialities that draw distinctions between them. But the distinctions are not part of nature. Physicists and theoretical chemists, who calculate energy levels in atoms and molecules, do not have access to more fundamental truths than have molecular biologists, who study the structure and sequence of genes on the chromosomes. Nor are the descriptions molecular biologists provide more fundamental than those of biologists who study cells or organisms. Biologists do not probe deeper realities than anthropologists and historians, just different ones. The fact that academic professionals value the explanatory power of these disciplines differently tells us more about the history and sociology of professionalization and about the alliances different academic disciplines have been able to forge with economic and political power than about nature.

Problems with the Concept of Human Nature

It is questionable whether the concept of human nature means anything. People's 'nature' can be described only by looking at the things they do. To try to abstract, or reify, a human essence from the ways in which different groups of people have grappled with issues of survival in the range of geographical, ecological, and demographic settings that our species has populated is a dubious enterprise because what people interpret as 'natural' depends on their experience and viewpoint and is not likely to be agreed on by individuals with different backgrounds or interests. Margaret Mead (1949) pointed out years ago that societies with different, even opposite, sexual divisions of labour all believe that women's and men's tasks – whatever they are – follow from differences between women's and men's nature.

Prime among the traits sociobiologists believe to be inherent in our nature, as I pointed out before, is selfishness, because that is what supposedly gets us to perpetuate our genes in the first place. A variant of selfishness is altruism – the kind that benefits the altruist in the end (something like 'I'll scratch your back if you'll scratch my children's'). Then there are territoriality and a tendency toward establishing dominance hierarchies. These traits entered descriptions of animal behaviour around the beginning of the First World War, when a pecking order was first noted among barnyard chickens, a not very 'natural' population. There are also the supposedly sex-differentiated characteristics of male aggressiveness and competitiveness and female coyness and nurturance that follow from the assumed asymmetry in our reproductive interests that I questioned previously (the fact that males produce a lot of sperm in a lifetime, whereas females produce relatively fewer, larger, and hence 'more expensive' eggs). E. O. Wilson (1978) includes in human nature the various behaviours that make sexual relationships between women and men emotionally satisfying, such as fondling and kissing; religious and spiritual aspirations that generate the need to believe in something beyond oneself; and the incest taboo. (Apparently Wilson is unaware of the feebleness of this taboo, considering the widespread occurrence of sexual abuse in families, especially of girls by their fathers, brothers, uncles, and even grandfathers.) He acknowledges cultural influences but insists that biology contributes a 'stubborn kernel' that 'cannot be forced without cost' (p. 147).

Because sociobiologists posit that 'stubborn kernel' of biological traits, honed over eons of evolution, their human-nature theories are conservative. They portray as natural the competitive and hierarchical capitalist societies in which men dominate women and a small, privileged group of men dominates everyone else. But competition and dominance hierarchies are not characteristic of all human societies, and there is no reason to believe that biology determines the ways different societies are constructed. On the contrary, people can undergo substantial physical as well as psychological changes as a result of major political and economic transformations in their societies. For example, rationing and other social policies the British government enacted during the Second World War resulted in a generation of people from working-class backgrounds who were healthier and looked significantly different from their parents. People who participate in major political or personal changes that drastically alter the ways they live often experience simultaneous changes in the ways their bodies function – changes in their ability to work and concentrate, in sleep and eating patterns, muscle mass, shape and strength, body weight, skin colour and texture, and many other physical characteristics. It is not that changes in our way of life cause our biology to change. All the changes are interconnected. We change. Women who have participated in the women's liberation movement are well aware that such changes can occur in our 'natures' as well as in our lives.

References

Barash, D. (1979), *The Whispering Within*, Harper & Row, New York.

Birke, L. (1986), *Women, Feminism and Biology*, Methuen, New York.

Dawkins, R. (1976), *The Selfish Gene*, Oxford University Press, Oxford.

Herrnstein, R.J. (1971), 'I.Q.' in *Atlantic Monthly*, 228 (3) (September), pp. 43–64.

Jensen, A.R. (1969), 'How much can we boost IQ and Scholastic Achievement?' in *Harvard Educational Review*, 39 (Winter), pp. 1–123.

Lewontin, R.C. (1974), 'The Analysis of Variance and the Analysis of Causes' in *American Journal of Human Genetics*, 26, pp. 400–11.

Lewontin, R.C., S. Rose and L.J. Kamin (1984), *Not in our Genes*, Pantheon, New York.

Mead, M. (1949), *Male and Female*, Dell, New York.

Wilson, E.O. (1975), *Sociobiology: The New Synthesis*, Harvard University Press, Cambridge.

Wilson, E.O. (1978), *On Human Nature*, Harvard University Press, Cambridge.

CHAPTER 3

Genes as Causes

RUTH HUBBARD

Genetics is the systematic description of hereditary mechanisms, but to a large extent it is also a reading into nature of the ideologies of hereditarianism and individualism that were dominant during the period when it was invented. Hereditarianism dominated the social thinking of Spencer and the other Social Darwinists and was evident in the novels of Dickens, George Eliot and Thackeray, as well as in the scientific thinking of Francis Galton and the eugenicists.

This ideology has been the impulse behind a great deal of genetic experimentation in the expectation that genetics can be useful for purposes of social and genetic engineering. For example, H. J. Muller ([1913] 1962) wrote near the start of his scientific life:

> The intrinsic interest of these questions [about heredity] is matched by their extrinsic importance, for their solution would help us to predict the characteristics of offspring yet unborn and would ultimately enable us to modify the nature of future generations.

This goal is echoed by many present-day advocates of genetic engineering. For example, the American theologian Joseph Fletcher (1974, p. 4) writes:

> The intention of genetic engineering is to locate and alter the genes which cause defects in superior people.... Discoveries like genetic coding make the breakthrough of old-fashioned hard technologies seem like child's play.

Nineteenth-century biologists were interested in exploring the intrapersonal 'causes' of what Galton termed 'hereditary genius' and of numerous less desirable attributes they considered equally innate, such as 'pauperism'. They hypothesized that these characteristics were mediated by a hereditary substance inside cells, which different writers denoted by different names. Galton called it 'stirp', Karl Nägeli 'idioplasm', and August Weismann 'germ plasm'. Some of them assumed that the genetic substance that is transmitted to successive generations is made up of particles, which Darwin called 'gemmules', Weismann 'ids', Hugo De Vries 'pangenes', and W. Johannsen 'genes' – the name that stuck. The concepts or things represented by these various terms were not the same. But the fact that all of them were invented to denote hypothetical hereditary particles suggests that there was a strong ideological need to assume the existence of material substances, often particles, located within individuals, that transmit traits from one generation to the next. And their invention predates what can legitimately be called a science of heredity – that is, genetics.

Gregor Mendel, who is quite properly credited as the father of genetics, had a more limited goal than that of these biologists. In his classic paper in 1865, Mendel does not go beyond formally designating 'characters' (observable traits). He suggests only once that these might be correlated with hypothetical 'factors' inside his pea plants. Other scientists assumed that observable traits and the ways they are passed on to, or changed between, successive generations must be associated with material substances within the organism. For example, the German embryologist August Weismann wrote in 1893 (p. 11): 'The phenomena of heredity among higher organisms are connected with a definite substance . . . localized . . . in the nuclear substance of the germ cells.'

Although chromosomes were observed shortly after the turn of the century, genes continued much longer as purely theoretical constructs. But the materialist and reductionist impulse that led physicists to describe matter in terms of atoms and, later, subatomic particles led biologists to assume quite early that inheritance is mediated by intracellular, hereditary particles. As the American geneticist Thomas Hunt Morgan explained in 1926 (p. 1): 'In the same sense in which the chemist posits invisible atoms and the physicist electrons, the student of heredity appeals to invisible elements called genes.'

After the rediscovery of Mendel's laws around 1900, his 'factors' became the genes. During the following decades the hypothetical genes became concrete objects – pieces of chromosomes – and finally, in 1953, molecules of double-stranded DNA. But it would be well to keep in mind that the geneticist L. J. Stadler admonished as late as 1954 that 'our concept of the gene is entirely dependent on the occurrence of gene mutations', that is, on changes in inherited traits. This important point is worth exploring further.

What made it possible for Mendel and the later geneticists to establish formal laws of heredity and explore the mechanism of inheritance experimentally is the fact that traits can change from one generation to the next, not that they stay the same. Changes are what made it possible to sort and name specific traits out of the overall similarities that get passed on from one generation to the next. The British geneticist J. B. S. Haldane put it this way (1942, p. 11):

> Genetics is the branch of biology which is concerned with innate differences between similar organisms. . . . Like so many other branches of science, genetics has achieved its successes by limiting its scope. Given a black and a white rabbit,

the geneticist asks how and why they differ, not how and why they resemble one another.

Johannsen, the man who coined the word gene, also invented the terms *phenotype* and *genotype* to distinguish an organism's outward appearance, which he called its phenotype, from hypothetical, correlated internal factors, its genotype. These two terms have often been used as though the genotype determines the phenotype, even though many scientists have stressed that phenotypes are generated by an ongoing, complex and mutual interplay between genotypes and environments. When by genotype one means genes, then the environment includes not only what happens outside the organism but also the many metabolic reactions that go on in cells and between them. Therefore I want to stress from the start that nothing in the concept of factor, gene or genotype necessarily implies a causal line from it to characters or traits, as the quotation from Fletcher (p. 38 above) would suggest.

Genes (DNA) differ from one another in their base sequence. Because the differences among them are quite specific, genes introduce specificity when they interact with other molecules. But specificity is also imparted by other molecules, among them RNA (which is another type of nucleic acid involved in translating the molecular properties of genes into traits), proteins, and even some carbohydrates and lipids (which are a class of fats). Many of the processes that take place in organisms and during the interactions in which organisms engage their environments can mediate specificity.

To repeat, hereditarianism, the belief in the biological inheritance of socially important traits, was part of all the major trends in nineteenth-century thought. It was fundamental to the thinking of the conservative followers of Thomas Malthus, to liberal beliefs in meritocracy and to evolutionist hopes for human betterment. The scientific question was how traits (characters) were passed from one generation to the next. That the answer was found in hypothetical particles was not surprising at a time when scientists demonstrated that matter and energy consist of particles and that particles carry diseases. In fact, similar fallacies are involved in trying to explain how bacteria 'cause' disease and how genes 'cause' traits. In both cases, the power of the particles is exaggerated, while the contributions of the systems in which they operate are undervalued or ignored. This belief in the superior explanatory power of the smallest elements in a system is reductionism, which we have discussed previously.

What Mendel's laws can and cannot tell us has been explained in a book published collectively by a group of French biologists who call themselves Agata Mendel (1980). (They invented Agata by analogy to Virginia Woolf's story in *A Room of One's Own* about the life of Shakespeare's imaginary sister, Judith.) This book raises important issues that are usually overlooked and I want to go over them in some detail.

Mendel's Laws

As I have said, Mendel's laws, which are basic to modern genetics and molecular biology, are about change and difference, not about likeness. But so urgent is our need to explain why 'like father, like son' that experiment after experiment is interpreted as though we could.

Mendel devised his experiments to explain certain regularities observed when dissimilar individuals are crossed to produce hybrids. He chose for his experimental organism the sweet pea (Pisum) because it fulfilled certain basic conditions: it exhibits characters which 'stand out clearly and definitely' and do not differ in a 'more or less' way (Mendel, [1865] 1950, p.4). In other words, he specifically selected differences in kind rather than of degree – qualitative, not quantitative, differences. He eventually selected seven pairs of characters, an example being round, smooth seeds as against angular, wrinkled ones.

A simple convention governs the way successive generations are denoted in Mendelian genetics. P_1 signifies the parent generation, which produces the first generation of offspring, called F_1. Successive generations of offspring, produced by breeding members of the preceding generation together, are called F_2, F_3, etc. In other words, the P_1 generation produces the F_1 generation, F_2 produces F_3, and so on.

Mendel first made sure that both parental lines (P_1) bred true, and that crossing the P_1 plants produced the same kind of hybrid (F_1), no matter which parent strain provided pollen and which eggs. He also took care to select pairs of characters whose hybrid (F_1) closely resembled one of the P_1 strains rather than looking like a mixture of the two parental lines. He called 'those characters which are transmitted entire, or almost unchanged in the hybridization ... dominant, and those which become latent in the process recessive' (p. 8). He explained that he used the term recessive because although such characters 'withdraw or entirely disappear in the hybrids, [they] nevertheless reappear unchanged in their progeny' (p. 8).

Mendel established his laws by examining four successive generations: P_1, F_1, F_2, and F_3. He showed that when the F_1 hybrids are bred with each other, in the F_2 generation 'there reappear together with the dominant characters, also the recessive ones ... in the definitely expressed proportion of three to one' (p. 9). He then showed that those F_2 plants that exhibited the recessive trait bred true, like the recessive P_1 plants, and continued to breed true for however many generations he bred them. But the F_2 plants that exhibited the dominant character divided into two groups: two-thirds behaved like the F_1 hybrid and one-third bred true, like the dominant plants in the P_1 generation. He therefore concluded that the appearance of a 3:1 ratio in the F_2 generation resulted from what was in fact a 1:2:1 ratio, in which one part behaved like the dominant P_1 plants, two parts like the hybrid F_1 (which looked like the dominant P_1 plants but didn't breed true), and one part like the recessive P_1 plants.

Although he denoted the dominant pure line as *A,* the recessive as *a,* and the hybrid as *Aa,* he used these symbols as formal representations that were not meant to signify something inside the plant that caused or produced the character. He departed from the descriptive use of the term *character* at only one place, when he assumed the presence of identical *factors* in the pure lines and the hybrids in order to explain that hybrids (*Aa*) can give rise both to pure *A* and pure *a* lines.

(R. A. Fisher has suggested that Mendel, who was trained in mathematics and physics, probably had his theory of hybridization worked out before he began the extensive, painstaking series of breeding experiments (Olby, 1966). It is plausible that Mendel planned his experiments as decisive tests of a worked-out hypothesis rather than that his vast accumulation of data, collected over seven years, led him to his laws.)

Following the rediscovery of Mendel's paper just after the turn of the century, the new geneticists soon transmuted his hypothetical factors into genetic particles, or genes, that were located on chromosomes and said to cause traits by their chemical action. The nature of this action was not specified until mid-century, after the chromosomes, hence genes, had been shown to contain the bulk of a cell's DNA. The structure of DNA was elucidated in 1953, which made it possible to explain how DNA is copied when cells divide and to explore some of its other chemical activities. During this half-century, the laws by which Mendel formally described how hybrids can give rise to differences were imperceptibly and without conscious intent interpreted as though they described how like characters are passed from parents to offspring.

The fact that the pattern of inheritance of an observable, qualitative difference between two organisms of the same species can be described by Mendel's laws has led scientists since Mendel to assume that the difference is mediated by different forms of the same gene, called *alleles.* But this assumption is not equivalent to saying that the gene, in any of its allelic forms, generates or causes the character in question. Nothing we have learned since Mendel's time about how genes function justifies the conclusion that genes cause traits or control development. They make significant contributions to both, but so do lots of other substances, including other genes.

Let us take hemoglobin, the protein that gives blood its red colour and carries oxygen around the body. Normal and sickle-cell hemoglobin are a pair of characters whose inheritance follows Mendel's laws, with normal hemoglobin dominant over sickle-cell hemoglobin. These two kinds of hemoglobin molecules are known to differ by a single amino acid. (Amino acids are the small molecules of which the much larger proteins are built.) The difference can be mediated by a change, a mutation, in a single base pair in the DNA sequence, or gene, involved in hemoglobin synthesis. It is correct to say that, all other things being equal (which they never are outside of controlled laboratory experiments), the difference in the two forms of DNA exerts a decisive influence during the synthesis of the two forms of hemoglobin. It is not correct to assume that either gene causes one or the other form of hemoglobin to be synthesized.

Hemoglobin synthesis, like the synthesis of any other complex molecule, involves a battery of reactants and energy sources that must come together at the appropriate times and under appropriate conditions, among them appropriate genes (DNA). If the DNA in the 'hemoglobin gene' is changed, a different hemoglobin will be formed. Or perhaps hemoglobin will not be formed at all if the change in the DNA is too great or of the wrong sort. But if one of the other genes that must get into the process is changed, or a critical concentration of one of the essential small molecules, or one of the enzymes, or the temperature, or the pH, or . . . , normal hemoglobin also may not be formed. Indeed the cell, or even the organism, may not survive at all.

Take another familiar Mendelian character – the Rh blood antigen, which is present in Rh positive people (Rh+), but lacking in Rh negative ones (Rh–). The Rh+ trait is dominant over Rh– and, by inference from Mendel's laws, one can assume that the difference involves two forms of one gene. This assumption in no way allows one to conclude that the 'Rh+ gene' causes Rh antigen to be formed or that it directs its synthesis.

The point to stress is this: in a complex system of reactions, such as protein synthesis, which requires many components and conditions that must work together in non-additive ways and that often are interdependent, it is wrong to single out any one substance or event as the cause.

DNA as Information

Some biologists insist on the primacy of DNA, while granting that the biosynthesis of a protein, such as hemoglobin or the Rh antigen, is complex and requires interactions among many molecules, subcellular structures and processes. They argue that it is appropriate to assign a commanding role to DNA because it contains the information that imparts specificity. But as Barry Commoner (1968) pointed out, the enzymes involved in the synthesis of RNA and DNA, which, like all enzymes, are proteins, also impart specificity. He concluded 'that the biological specificity of inheritance originates in no one molecule but in a complex circular network of molecular interactions in which various DNA, RNA and protein agents participate'. Questioning the workability of genetic engineering, he went on to say:

> If . . . the specificity transmitted in inheritance is determined by a multimolecular system vastly more complex than a DNA molecule, any promise to control inheritance by chemical manipulations of DNA is likely to be illusory.

Most molecular biologists, if pressed, grant that there are multiple sources of specificity and control in biosynthetic systems and that the critical control points undoubtedly change over time. Despite this admission, they give primacy to DNA because they insist that information usually passes in only one direction, from DNA to RNA to protein. But the whole point of a complex metabolic system is that at one time or another all the parts must talk to one another.

Donna Haraway (1979) has pointed out that at the end of the Second World War integrated ways of thinking about cellular interactions and relationships inside organisms, such as those Walter B. Cannon (1939) expressed in his book *The Wisdom of the Body,* were replaced by analogies from information theory. This was when 'feedback circuits' and 'information flow' entered biology. The reasons for this change undoubtedly included the wartime flow of biologists into operations research and the post-war flow of disillusioned physicists into biology.

These kinds of changes in outlook brought into genetics ways of thinking about information, coding, and control that are considerably more mechanistic, reductionist, and hierarchical than biochemical thinking was before the war.

In the late 1950s, molecular biologists formulated what Crick called the Central Dogma – that genes act by virtue of the fact that DNA defines the structure of RNA, which in turn defines the composition and structure of proteins: in shorthand, DNA → RNA → proteins. At that time, scientists assumed that the base sequence of a gene (DNA) completely specifies the sequence of amino acids of the protein in whose synthesis it participates (or, as they would say, 'for which it codes'). In addition, they assumed that the amino-acid sequence of a protein determines its three-dimensional structure and, by implication, its function. Hence, it seemed logical that the shape of hemoglobin, its colour, and the way it transports oxygen in the blood all are determined by 'the hemoglobin gene'.

We now know that this dogma is not true. In organisms other than bacteria, the base sequence of a gene (DNA) is not translated literally into the amino-acid sequence of the protein in whose synthesis it participates. Some portions of the DNA template are not used at all, while others are placed into new juxtapositions. These events are mediated by enzymes, proteins that function in all cells. How the information is introduced that tells the cell what parts of the DNA to translate, and in what sequence, is only partly understood. With sufficient determination, it will no doubt be possible to prove that in some ultimate sense also this set of metabolic reactions is mediated by genes (DNA). We do know that the message encoded by DNA can be changed while it is translated into RNA and that proteins (hence further genes) are involved in all these processes. Therefore many genes must be involved in mediating every trait, irrespective of whether its transmission from one generation to the next follows the relatively simple pattern described by Mendel's laws or whether its transmission follows a more complicated pattern and hence is difficult to predict or describe.

Most traits geneticists study, and which biologists and other people think about, are of this complex sort. Many of them vary continuously, such as height. For these kinds of characters, called *quantitative traits,* reductionist explanations involving master molecules are clearly inappropriate.

Let me repeat: 'information' is not a good metaphor for what DNA contributes to protein synthesis. But even if it were, we would not be entitled to conclude that DNA controls or programmes the many different ways in which proteins participate in the structure and functioning of organisms, not to speak of controlling or programming the complex characteristics of individuals and species.

How Genes Do and Do Not Function

Let us come back to genetics. I have said that the fact that a change in a gene registers as an observable difference in a character in no way implies that the gene controls or programmes the character, only that it is one of the many components essential for the character to exist. I have now explained why this is so at the molecular level. But it is important to understand the genetic point because if we understand that the idea of genetic programming or control is based on a misinterpretation of how genes function, we can begin to understand why Mendel's laws can describe the transmission of only a few inherited traits and why some inherited traits follow Mendel's laws only some of the time.

Most traits do not follow Mendel's laws, and many are quantitative, not just present or absent. But often when a Mendelian pattern cannot be assigned, yet there is reason or inclination to believe the trait is inherited (which is conventionally taken to mean innate), the trait is said to be polygenic – that is, 'controlled' by so many genes that the Mendelian yes/no pattern gets washed out. The assumption that many genes are involved when one will not explain the observation was criticized in the early days by Morgan (1909), who warned:

In the modern interpretation of Mendelism facts are being transformed into factors at a rapid rate. If one factor will not explain the facts, then two are invoked; if two prove insufficient, three will some times work out.

Morgan and his colleagues (1915, p. 210) also pointed out 'that a single factor may have several effects, and that a single character may depend on many factors'.

All traits are polygenic in the sense that they are produced by many interacting, and often mutually regulating, processes that involve many enzymes and substrates, and therefore many genes. Occasionally, these relationships operate in such a way that changes in one particular gene are expressed as observable changes in the organism. But that does not mean that this gene causes the trait it affects. It is fortunate for geneticists that some of these changes follow Mendel's laws because these rare situations have made it possible to observe the transmission of this class of inherited traits among successive generations and to deduce information about the activities of genes.

One of the problems here is that the concept of the gene is used quite loosely. Genes are invoked to explain the origin of specific traits as well as of major structures and functions of organisms. They are called upon to programme the orderly transformations during development and ageing. And they are said to be decisive for slow, cumulative changes during evo-lution and species formation. Much of this speculation rests on assertions that are not based on observations. Often the appropriate experiments cannot be designed or even envisaged.

The identification of the gene as the double helix of DNA has increased the confusion. When a cell divides, the genes are duplicated, so that each daughter cell ends up with an identical set of genes. The beauty of the DNA structure is that one strand of the double helix serves as the template for the synthesis of its partner, so that DNA replication is quite straightforward. Unfortunately, this mode of reproduction of DNA has been accepted as a metaphor for the reproduction of likenesses between parents and offspring. But the replication of DNA is not a proper model for the inheritance of traits because the only thing that is copied in this way is DNA itself. Agata Mendel writes (p. 260):

> What the complementary relations between thymine and adenine, and between guanine and cytosine explain, is that when a gene reproduces, an exact copy of the original is reproduced. If for one reason or another the gene is changed (which corresponds to a change in the base sequence), it is the changed form which will be copied during reproduction. Therefore what is in fact explained is that a *difference* in a gene will give rise to *differences* in its descendants [my translation].

I want to stress also that genes do not reproduce and DNA does not replicate itself, as they are sometimes said to do. Their reproduction or replication happens as part of the metabolism of living cells. Even if we understand in detail how DNA is synthesized and replicated in cells, this information cannot tell us how the replication of genes is translated into the transmission of traits from one generation to the next.

The diversity of living organisms, as well as the differentiation of cells and tissues during embryological development, results from an ongoing dialectic between the production of likeness and difference. By studying spontaneous and induced mutations, geneticists can learn about some of the intracellular correlates of difference (the genes); they cannot find out how likeness is produced.

That has been the task of embryologists. But embryology as well as genetics has been forced into the same reductionist paradigm. At present, molecular biologists try to study development by way of developmental genetics, which involves the production and analysis of so-called developmental mutants, organisms which exhibit an inherited defect that makes their development stop at one or another specific stage. This study of mutants can elucidate some of the sequences or steps that occur during normal development, but it cannot reveal what causes the individual steps or controls their spatio-temporal patterning (Wright, 1979). Agata Mendel jokes that molecular biologists tend to reason like a child who, because turning the knob on the television set makes the picture appear, concludes that the knob causes or programmes the picture, and then goes on to the next, more absurd, step of trying to understand how television works by chemically analysing the knob.

The reemergence of eugenics in the form of genetic engineering is the most recent stage in the drama of genes as determinants or causes. Its promise today is the same as was Muller's in 1913: to predict the characteristics of the unborn and modify them according to plan. Fletcher (1974) rhapsodizes:

> Insect societies are stable (stagnant?) for millennia because they are shaped by genetic transmission over which insects have no control. Unlike the locked-in bugs, men [sic] are at last able creatively to shape their own lives – genetically as well as culturally. When genetic therapy and surgery reach at last the goals already on their drawing boards we will have control over the quality of the infants to be born even *before* conception. . . . All of this means we have entered upon positive or *direct* eugenic control, and that we have surmounted the inadequacy and errors of negative control by selective mating.

By now it should be clear that I do not think this biocratic dream can be realized by manipulating genes because it exaggerates the control genes exert over metabolism and development. But the issue is not just whether genetic engineering and gene therapy will work in practice. The promise that people will be improved by manipulating our genes has an ideological impact, whether or not it can be done.

For more than a century people have been assured on scientific authority that the causes of our most serious personal and social problems reside within us. Now they are told that scientists soon will be able to cure all manner of ills – from sickle-cell anaemia to manic depression and schizophrenia – by replacing 'bad genes' with 'good' ones. The fact that, under the direction of foreign genes, bacteria can be made to produce chemicals they would not produce normally (for example, human insulin or interferon) is cited as proof. But to engineer bacteria to make a specific product is not comparable to changing the genetic make-up of multicellular organisms or even of some of their cells and tissues. Bacteria do not provide proper models for the way genes participate in the functions of multicellular organisms, where patterning and control involve large numbers of interacting metabolites and pathways as well as interactions between cells and tissues and between the organism and its environment. Genes are only part of this story, and their roles are not sufficiently well understood to predict what will happen if one or another of them is changed, replaced, or even just moved from one position to another on the chromosomes. In fact, many molecular biologists believe that oncogenes – genes involved in cancerous growths – may be ordinary genes that are running amok because they somehow got into the wrong place.

The various attempts scientists have made to get genes they have inserted into multicellular organisms ('gene therapy') to do something have failed so far. Although molecular biologists have been able to make genes (DNA) induce bacteria or isolated cells, grown in tissue culture, to produce chemical products, when they have introduced genes into organized tissues or whole living organisms, the genes so far have been silent.

Sequencing the Human Genome

The reductionist belief in genes as causes has encouraged molecular biologists to undertake the gigantic project of trying to determine the base composition and sequence of the DNA (in other words, of the genes) in all 23 human chromosomes. In another place I look at some of the political and ethical questions raised by this project and its exaggerated emphasis on genes. For now let us look at some scientific problems with the Human Genome Initiative.

We can begin by asking why anyone would want to undertake the herculean task of trying to identify and sequence the fifty to a hundred thousand genes estimated to make up the human genome and the approximately three billion nucleotide bases of which they are composed. The grandiose, reductionist reply offered by James Watson (1989) and a number of other molecular biologists is that this project will at last tell us what it means to be human – despite the fact that we seem to share 99 per cent of our genes with the chimpanzees. (Or perhaps their very point is that when scientists have sequenced all the genes for humans and chimpanzees, they will at last be able to tell us apart.) A more modest claim is that having the complete DNA sequence will enable medical scientists to diagnose, and eventually cure, large numbers of genetically based diseases. Both claims are firmly grounded in the assumption that genes cause traits and, therefore, that the more genes we can characterize, the more we will know about how organisms function.

This is the wrong way to look at the situation. The fundamental question that needs to be answered is how the different cells in multicellular organisms come to assume quite different functions despite the fact that they all have the same genes. As I pointed out previously, the problem of differentiation lies at the heart of the way complex organisms develop from a fertilized egg, one single cell. Molecularly inclined embryologists try to explain this differentiation by saying, for example, that the cells in the different tissues become different from one another even though all of them contain the same complement of DNA because in different types of cells different genes get activated at different times. But that explanation begs the question by merely shifting the presumption of genetic 'control' to a different level.

There is a historical reason why molecular biologists – the scientists who try to explain gene function in terms of the replication of DNA and its translation into the language of proteins – may not be conceptually in tune with the problem of differentiation. Their ways of thinking have developed out of working with bacteria and with viruses, called *bacteriophage* or simply *phage,* that can infect bacteria. Phage have only a few genes, and their job is to enter bacteria and get them to make more phage. Although bacteria are metabolically more complicated than phage, they do not need to cope with the problem of turning into cells that are as different from each other as nerve, muscle, liver, and kidney cells, or producing anatomical structures as different as a hand and an eye. Reductionist thinking, although limited, may yield useful answers when applied to phage or bacteria. But detailed information about our genes can answer only a limited range of questions about complicated creatures like ourselves.

This is not to say that some of these questions are not of scientific interest and not worth asking. But they could be asked much more conveniently with, say, fruit flies (*drosophila*). Scientists understand the genetics of fruit flies in considerable detail. *Drosophila* has only four pairs of chromosomes in its cells instead of our 23 pairs, and the locations of many genes on its chromosomes are known fairly accurately. What is more, the variability in the sequence of bases within genes has been studied extensively, so that scientists are beginning to have a sense of how different DNA sequences within a gene and different gene combinations are expressed, or not expressed, in different traits.

By studying the genetic map of fruit flies at the molecular level it should be possible to get some insight into the relationships between specific DNA sequences and specific anatomical or physiological characteristics of the whole organism. So, mapping the DNA sequence of *drosophila,* where we have so much genetic information and can do controlled genetic experiments, might make sense. But even here it would be more informative to look in detail at a few genes and compare their composition and the ways they function in many different individuals than to map all the genes of one or a few individuals.

The point of looking at a specific gene in a lot of different individuals is to try to differentiate coincidental correlations between base sequences and the appearance of a specific trait from those that are functionally related. For example, scientists have observed a number of different base sequences within a specific gene in *drosophila* without being able to see any difference in the trait with which the gene is associated. Yet some of these sequences also occur in individuals that, in fact, look different. Unless these scientists had analysed a sufficiently large number of similar and different-looking individuals, they would have drawn the false conclusion that some of these base differences are responsible for the observable differences in the trait.

This sort of detailed analytical work cannot be done with people. Yet it would be necessary if one wanted to know what significance to attach to any particular base, or indeed gene, sequence. But we have 23 pairs of chromosomes with many millions of genes on each, so the job of associating specific base sequences with specific traits is much more difficult than in *drosophila.* What is more important is that experimental work can be done ethically on only a limited number of people because there must be good reason to believe that it will benefit the individuals in question. One could try to get permission to collect a minute amount of tissue from huge numbers of people, say, by asking them to open their mouths and taking a tiny scrape off the inside of their cheeks. But because these people would not be well characterized genetically, and it would be ethically improper so to characterize them, the molecular information that could be obtained would be of little analytical value.

Anyway, the genome project is not intended to give us information about genetic diversity, which I am contending we would need in order to know what significance to attach to any specific DNA sequence. It is intended to produce the complete DNA sequence of the 23 chromosomes for a human 'prototype', which would be a composite of chromosomal regions obtained from the cells and tissues of different people.

The scientific significance of this laborious and expensive effort is as questionable as was the scientific significance of putting a man on the moon. But it has a similar, heroic appeal. The problem is that, quite aside from the waste of resources – both money and scientific personnel – the human genome project will have unfortunate practical and ideological consequences because it will increase the mythic importance our culture assigns to genes and genetic inheritance.

References

Cannon, W.B. (1939), *The Wisdom of the Body*, Norton, New York.

Commoner, B. (1968), 'Failure of the Watson-Crick Theory as a Chemical Explanation of Inheritance' in *Nature,* 220, pp. 334–40.

Crick, F.H.C. and J.D. Watson (1954), 'The Complementary Structure of Deoxyribonucleic Acid' in *Proceedings of the Royal Society*, A223, pp. 80–96.

Darwin, C. (n.d.), *The Origins of Species* [1859] and *The Descent of Man* [1871], Modern Library Edition, New York.

Fletcher, J.F. (1974), *The Ethics of Genetic Control*, Doubleday, Garden City, New York.

Fletcher, J.F. (1980), 'Knowledge, Risk and the Right to Reproduce: A Limiting Principle' in A. Milunsky and G.J. Annas (eds) *Genetics and the Law II*, Plenum, New York.

Galton, F. (1883), *Inquiries into Human Faculty*, Macmillan, London.

Haldane, J.B.S. (1942), *New Paths in Genetics*, Harper and Brothers, New York.

Haraway, D. (1979), 'The Biological Enterprise: Sex, Mind and Profit from Human Engineering to Sociobiology' in *Radical History Review*, Spring/Summer, pp. 206–37.

Mendel, A. (1980), *Les Manipulations Génétiques*, Editions du Seuil, Paris.

Mendel, G. (1865) (1950), *Experiments in Plant Hybridisation*, translation prepared by the Royal Historical Society of London, with notes by W. Bateson. Harvard University Press, Cambridge.

Morgan, Th. H. (1909), 'What are "factors" in Mendelian Explanations?' in *American Breeders Association*, 5, p. 365.

Morgan, Th. H., A.H. Sturtevant, H.J. Muller, and C.B. Birdges (1915), *The Mechanisim of Mendelian Heredity*, Henry Holt and Co., New York.

Muller, H.J. [1913] (1962), 'Principles of Heredity' in H.J. Muller (ed.), *Studies in Genetics,* University of Indiana Press, Bloomington.

Olby, R.C. (1966), *Origins of Mendelism*, Constable, London.

Stadler, L.J. (1954), 'The Gene', in *Science*, 120, pp. 811–19.

Watson, J.D. (1968), *The Double Helix*, Atheneum, New York.

— (1989), quoted in Pamela Zurer, 'Panel Plots Strategy for Human Genome Studies' in *Chemical and Engineering News*, January, 9, p. 5.

Watson, J.D. and F.H.C. Crick (1953), 'A Structure for Deoxyribose Nucleic Acid' in *Nature* 171, pp. 737–8.

Weismann, A. (1893), *The Germ Plasm*, Charles Scribner's Sons, New York.

Wright, B. (1979), 'Causality in Biological Systems' in *Trends in Bio-chemical Sciences*, 4, pp. N110-11.

Fractured Images of Science, Language and Power: A Post-Modern Optic, or Just Bad Eyesight?*

EVELYN FOX KELLER

Almost four centuries ago, Francis Bacon put forth a vision of a kind of knowledge, a veridical reading of the Book of Nature that would enable the translation of knowledge to power, and thus restore man's proper dominion over nature. In the intervening centuries, Bacon's rhetoric of dominion served simultaneously to describe and to foster the growth of a social institution that succeeded in transforming that vision into material reality. In the late twentieth century, modern science has come into its maturity, producing technologies next to which Bacon's own vision seems modest. None of the early architects of modern science ever anticipated a day when men would acquire the kind of control over nature that would enable them, should they so choose, to destroy the human species, or, if not destroy it, shape its future according to their fantasies of a personal best. With a few exceptions, it was not until the twentieth century that men dared to dream of the power over life and death that is today enabled by modern physics and promised by modern biology.

Yet, just as such dreams appear on the verge of realization, their founding mythology has, for many, lost all credibility. In the late twentieth century, we can no longer appeal to a veridical reading – not of Nature, nor even of more ordinary texts – to explain what has made such realization possible. Instead, we have learned to read that very mythology for its particular forms of intentionality and subjectivity – expressing a will to knowledge that is itself socially constituted, born of relations of power, and siring a discourse with the power to transform those relations. In this new reading of the relations between science and nature, we have begun to unravel the insidious power of discourse to generate its own forms of truth, to shape the future of human bodies not through genetics, but through politics. Transducing the project of 'dominating nature' into a metaphor, genetics itself comes to be seen more as a construct that is simultaneously excrescence and

*Originally published in *Poetics Today* 12(2): 227–43 (1991). A longer version of this argument has appeared under the title, 'Physics and the Emergence of Molecular Biology', *Journal of the History of Biology* 23(3): 390–409 (1990).

vehicle of particular forms of power relations between speaking subjects than as the founding essence of human nature, that is, having more to do with social than with chemical mechanisms. In a word, we have become post-modernists.

Yet there is a striking irony in the fact that, at the very moment when the Baconian equation between knowledge and power has come to assume such ominous proportions, the basic facts of its conspicuous force have receded from view; that it is at this point in history that so much of our collective attention has shifted instead to a different equation between knowledge and power, away from its material force and towards the discursive mechanics of knowledge. This inattention to material consequences is not so much the subject of this chapter, as it is the object of my concerns. The basic problem, put as succinctly as I know how, is this: if classical scientific realism must be rejected (as I agree it must), and if contemporary analytics take the domain of power, and hence of knowledge, to be the purely social body, then we are left with no way of understanding how it happened that what began as a socially constituted dream has been able to insinuate itself into material reality, inducing the objects of a non-discursive regime to behave as reflections of our own purely discursive regime. To put it yet more bluntly, we are left entirely unable to account for the material and techno-logical efficacy of those domains of modern science that have what Foucault calls a 'high epistemological profile' unless we take that efficacy as unprob-lematic – a move that is, in my view, tantamount to granting the veridicality of classical scientific realism.

To avoid this retreat, I suggest that it is necessary to reexamine the question of the *forms* of scientific theory (cf. Hacking 1987), only this time in simultaneous and dual relation to the subjects they speak for and the objects they speak to. Scientific theories, I want to argue, may be thought of as tools; like ordinary tools, they reflect in their very form the agency and intentionality of their makers. In the forms of theory, one can see not only the discourses they embody, but also the structures facilitating their adequacy in meeting the goals for which they have been designed. Good theories are theories that work, that facilitate the kinds of action for which they are intended. They enable an 'us' to act in and on the world in ways that a 'we' deems desirable. As such, they reflect both the subjectivity of human objectives and the objects of human action. And because the forms of human objectives and the objects of their actions are so variable, so too should be the forms of theory available to us, even of theories that 'work'. In other words, although scientific theories cannot be understood as faithful reflections of either culture or nature, perhaps they can be understood as good enough reflections of the forms of interaction that speaking and desiring social actors seek to implement with that mute but nonetheless responsive world of actors we call nature – representing, in short, neither nature 'as it is', nor even some unquestioned and unquestionable notion of instrumentality, but rather a network of intentionality, consequentiality, and the relations between them that determine even the meaning of instrumentality. To speak of intentionality is immediately to invoke a world of social actors embedded in relations of social and material power, but to speak of consequentiality, where the objects of our actions are prelinguistic, is to invoke a different kind of world – a world of material things that, once called forth (that is, named), become subject to more mundane forms of physical power.

Ultimate Particles of Life: Muller and Schrödinger

In an effort to illustrate the conjoint workings of intentionality and consequentiality, of social and material forms of power, I want here to locate a small but critical episode of recent scientific history within this general framework. In particular, I want to recapitulate an aspect of the early history of a scientific movement that, over the last few decades, has grown to transform the very meaning of biological science. I am referring, of course, to molecular biology;[1] my particular focus is on its early conceptual and social relations to physics.

I begin by identifying the critical shifts in twentieth-century biology that can be attributed to molecular biology:

1   Relocation of the essence (or basis) of life. The locus of vital activity was now to be sought neither in the physical-chemical interactions and structures of the organism-niche complex, of the organism itself, nor even of the cell, but rather, in the physical-chemical structure of one particular component of the cell; namely, in the genetic material, or, more exactly, in the gene.[2]

2   Redefinition of life. From the complex of characteristics of living organisms that have historically been employed to define life (for example, growth and development, reproduction, irritability), life came to be redefined by molecular biologists as the 'instructions [or information] encoded in the genes' or, more simply, as a code, or 'code-script'. As J. D. Bernal put it 22 years ago, 'Life is beginning to cease to be a mystery and becoming . . . a cryptogram, a puzzle, a code.'[3]

3   Recasting of the goals of biological science. One popular description of the distinctiveness of biological science since the end of the nineteenth century is cast in terms of the shift from an observational science to an

experimental one. This shift might alternatively be expressed as a shift in aim from representation to intervention (or from description to control). But the shift that I think can fairly be attributed to molecular biology is a more subtle one: it is not so much from representation to intervention, but from intervention in the larger and indirect sense of the term appropriate to the aspirations of most late nineteenth-century and early twentieth-century biological science to the particular conception of intervention or control that promises effective mastery over the processes of making and remaking life.

I suggest that these three shifts can be taken as definitional of the conceptual transformation represented by molecular biology. They occurred in parallel, and in mutual interdependence. H. J. Muller, an early advocate of all three of these shifts, articulated their interconnections unambiguously. His argument for the gene as the basis of life, and mutation as the central problem of biology, was from the start framed in terms of the promise that 'a control of [mutation] might obviously place the process of evolution in our hands'.[4] J. D. Bernal's quote (above) goes on in a similar vein: 'Life is ... becoming ... a cryptogram, a puzzle, a code *that can be broken, a working model that sooner or later can be made*' (italics mine).[5] This essay examines the particular role that physics and physicists played in facilitating these shifts.

A great deal, almost certainly too much, has been made of the importance of physics and physicists in the emergence of molecular biology, especially of their contribution of technical and cognitive skills. But here I want to argue that physics and physicists provided a resource of far greater import for the success of molecular biology than any particular skills: namely, they provided social authority. That authority was, of course, acquired in the first place through the formidable displays of technological and instrumental power issuing from physics itself, but this initially technical authority soon became available for deployment far beyond the domain of their technical triumphs; it became, in short, an authority that could be called upon for the essentially social process of reframing the character and goals of biological science. This borrowing proceeded in a variety of ways – first, through the borrowing of an agenda that was seen as looking like the agenda of physics; second, by borrowing the language and attitude of physicists; and, finally, by borrowing the very names of physicists.

Indeed, even the borrowing of purely technical expertise, ostensibly in the name of making biology 'better', was instrumental in reframing biology, in making it different. And in all this borrowing – of agenda, of language, attitude, names, technique – the material underpinning of the social power of twentieth-century physics, and physicists, lay in close view, evoking in some at least the hope that that the technological prowess of physics, too, could be borrowed. In short, I am arguing that the intersection of physics and early molecular biology provides an illustration of the conjoint workings of the Baconian and the Foucauldian equations between knowledge and power: that is, of the social and material dimensions of the knowledge/power nexus.

To make this argument, I want to review two moments in the prehistory and early history of molecular biology. First, I want to explore the vision of H. J. Muller, a classical geneticist rightly claimed as a major forerunner of molecular biology; and then, more briefly, to consider the influence of the physicist Erwin Schrödinger.

Born in 1890, Muller is known to biologists for his work with T. H. Morgan in establishing the chromosomal basis of inheritance and, particularly, for his development of the techniques of X-ray-induced mutagenesis in 1927, for which he was later awarded the Nobel Prize. But his primary importance to the history of biology may well lie in his early and forceful advocacy of a programme for biological science premised on all three of the shifts I have attributed to molecular biology. For my purposes, however, his real interest lies in the clarity of his vision and in its explicit dependence on a parallelism with current developments in physics.[6]

In the year 1916 – just five years after Rutherford's discovery of the atomic nucleus, fifteen years after the observation of spontaneous transmutation of elements, and three years before the first artificial transmutation was induced – Muller, a new Ph.D, drew attention in a public address to the

> curious similarity which exists between two of the main problems of physics and of biology. The central problem of biological evolution is the nature of mutation, but hitherto the occurrence of this has been wholly refractory and impossible to influence by artificial means, tho' a control of it might obviously place the process of evolution in our hands. Likewise, in physics, one of the most important problems is that of the transmutation of the elements, as illustrated especially by radium, but as yet this transmutation goes on quite unalterably and of its own accord, tho' if a means were found of influencing it, we might have inanimate matter practically at our disposal, and would hold the key to unthinkable stores of concentrated energy that would render possible any achievement with inanimate things. Mutation and Transmutation – the two keystones of our rainbow bridges to power (quoted in Carlson 1971: 160–1).

And five years later he wrote: 'It is not physics alone which has its quantum theory. Biological evolution too has its quanta – these are the individual mutations' (ibid., p. 161). By 1926, Muller was ready to formulate the strong form of his argument for 'The Gene as the Basis of Life'. In a closely reasoned polemic, Muller here argued that the gene can be viewed as, in effect, a biological atom; it is that entity which is solely responsible for maintaining physiological and morphological properties, for the evolution of higher life forms, for growth and variation. On these grounds, he inferred that the gene must be temporally as well as logically prior to all living forms. For the key to 'penetrating' these fundamental units of life, he concludes, we must look to the study of mutations. His somewhat rhapsodic language is worth noting:

> The secret of this immutable (but mutation-permitting) autocatalytic arrangement of gene parts may perhaps be reached first by an upward thrust of pure physical chemistry, or perhaps by biologists reaching down with physico-chemical tools through the chromosome, the virus, of the bacteriophage. . . . The beginning of the pathway to the micro-cosmic realm of gene-mutation study thus lies before us. It is a difficult path, but with the aid of the necromancy of science, it must be penetrated.
>
> We cannot leave forever inviolate in their recondite recesses those invisibly small yet fundamental particles, the genes, for from these genes. . . there radiate continually those forces, far-reaching, orderly, but elusive, that make and unmake our living worlds (Muller 1926: 200–2).

Only one year later, Muller succeeded in his quest. Employing not alpha rays, but X rays, he found a way to induce mutagenesis. Just eight years after Rutherford's success in inducing artificial transmutation, and eleven years after articulating his own ambitions for establishing the keystone to that other 'rainbow bridge to power', he published a paper entitled, appropriately enough, 'The Artificial Transmutation of the Gene'. Using essentially the identical tool that Rutherford had used, he had found a handle on those forces, 'radiating' from the gene, 'that make and unmake our living worlds'. 'In conclusion', he wrote,

> the attention of those working along classical genetic lines may be drawn to the opportunity, afforded them by the use of X rays, of creating in their chosen organisms a series of artificial races for use in the study of genetic ... phenomena. . . . Similarly, for the practical breeder, it is hoped that the method will ultimately prove useful. The time is not ripe to discuss here such possibilities with reference to the human species (Muller 1927: 87).

Muller was now in a position to meet physics, and physicists, eye-to-eye. He had a theoretical conception of the relation of the gene to living organisms directly paralleling the relation of the atom to inanimate matter, with a technology to match. Now it might be possible to close the gap. However, his assessment of American capitalism persuaded him that the United States was not ready for his ambitious programme to improve upon the blind, 'trial and error' mechanism of natural selection (Muller 1935: 45) and 'refashion [the living world] to man's own advantage' (Muller 1935: 70), and he emigrated to the Soviet Union. In 1936, at the physics section of the meeting of the USSR Academy of Sciences, he made his pitch to physicists to join forces with him and his colleagues in the 'conquest over matter, space, life, mind, and the other hitherto inscrutable riddles of existence' (Muller 1935: 48–9). 'The evidence... indicates', he begins, 'that it is in the tiny particles of heredity – the genes – that the chief secrets of living matter... are contained.' These genes – he calls them the 'ultimate particles of life' – 'have properties which are most unique from the standpoint of physics' – indeed, 'so peculiar are [they] ... that it may well be that an elucidation of them may throw light not only on the most fundamental questions of biology, but even on fundamental questions of physics as well' (Muller 1936: 214).

Two properties in particular stood out as demanding explanation, and also as promising new insights into both physics and biology: the problem of 'specific auto-attraction of like with like' (that is, the alignment of chromosomes), and the problem of 'auto-synthesis' (that is, replication). It is through these two mechanisms that the gene becomes 'a modeller... an active arranger of material... after its own pattern'. Noting the analogy to crystallization, he notes also a crucial difference in the magnitude of specificity that needs, here, to be preserved in replication: 'Each of these [thousands of different] genes has to reproduce its own specific pattern out of the surrounding material common to them all.' Only a 'fundamental feature of gene structure' can explain this feat. 'It is this', he concludes, 'which lies at the bottom of both growth, reproduction, and heredity.'[7] He even suggests that a fruitful line of approach 'might be through the study of X-ray diffraction patterns' (such as carried out by Astbury) – more specifically, he suggests that physicists attempt X-ray diffraction studies of the viral substance identified by Stanley, which, he infers, 'represents a certain kind of gene'.[8] He concludes: 'The geneticist himself is helpless to analyse these properties further. Here the physicist as well as the chemist must step in. Who will volunteer to do so?'

Muller's plea went unheeded, and for the most part, unheard. True, it was delivered in the Soviet Union. But the fact that it was also (and promptly) published in the *Scientific Monthly* suggests other factors as well. One such factor is that physicists were, in the late 1930s, otherwise occupied. But I would argue also that Muller, being a mere biologist, lacked the authority either to command the attention of physicists themselves, or to persuade other biologists to a programme that most biologists of the time found totally alien. Eight years later, a remarkably similar plea was reissued – not by a biologist, this time, but by a physicist known worldwide for his role in the development of quantum mechanics. In 1944, Erwin Schrödinger, apparently entirely unaware of Muller's arguments, published his own speculations about the basis of life in a slim volume entitled *What Is Life?* that echoed many of the same thoughts. This work did not fall on deaf ears; indeed, it has been described as the *'Uncle Tom's Cabin* of the revolution in biology that ... left molecular biology as its legacy' (Stent 1968: 392).

Like Muller, Schrödinger quickly identifies the chromosome fibre as 'the most vital part of the organism' (1944: 4), as 'the material carrier of life' (1944: 5). Indeed, his basic argument about the role of the gene as the basis of life – that the distinctive characteristics of living organisms reside in the fidelity of transmission of genetic information – repeats virtually all of Muller's arguments, sometimes even in almost identical language. He, like Muller, suggests that one should look to the study of mutation for the key to understanding both the structure and mechanism of genes, remarking that

> The significant fact [of mutations] is the discontinuity. It reminds a physicist of quantum theory.... He would be inclined to call ... mutation theory, figuratively, the quantum theory of biology (Schrödinger 1944: 36).

For the most part, however, Schrödinger's language is different from Muller's, as are his theoretical tools: where one speaks of code, or code-script, the other speaks of 'pattern'; where one points to the mechanism of auto-synthesis and auto-attraction as the heart of the dilemma of life, the other points to the uncanny reliability of the 'production of order from order' and the evasion of the laws of statistical thermodynamics. But perhaps the most significant difference between the two is to be found in Schroedinger's total silence on the question of practical consequences. He does not envision moulding the evolutionary future of the human race; rather, he speaks only of his 'keen longing for unified, all-embracing knowledge'.

Schrödinger does not, in fact, solve the problem he identifies as the central problem of life, and it is well known that the details he does have to offer on gene structure were based on an already discredited work of Max Delbruck's (in fact, discredited by Muller himself).[9] In retrospect, one would have to say that Schrödinger not only did not solve the problem of life, but that the particular 'paradox' he identified as lying at the heart of this problem effectively dissolved in the face of subsequent developments. Nor can his book be said to have provided any actual suggestions for further research that proved to be useful. As Max Perutz has written, 'A close study ... has shown me that what was true in his book was not original, and most of what was original was known not to be true even when it was written' (1989: 231). Nonetheless, the influence the book had on the subsequent course of molecular biology is undeniable. It has been credited by most of the physicists who turned to molecular biology after the war as a critical if not decisive factor in their move to biology (Stent, Wilkins, Crick, Benzer, etc.). In addition, many of the biologists who came to star in the molecular revolution – Watson, Luria, Hershey, Jacob – have also cited the influence of this book. The question that needs answering is, what kind of influence?

Such physicists as Stent, Benzer and, before them, Delbruck were excited by the promise of new laws; others, like Crick, were lured by the promise of a 'foundation of certainty' grounded in already established laws. Almost as if countering Niels Bohr's contention of natural limits to our capacity to understand the fact of life directly, Crick writes that his own motivation was 'to try to show that areas apparently too mysterious to be explained by physics and chemistry, could in fact be so explained' (Olby 1970: 943). For this, Schrödinger's book was nothing if not supportive. As Crick himself remarked,

> Its main point was one that only a physicist would feel it necessary to make, but the book...conveyed in an exciting way the idea that, in biology, molecular explanations were just around the corner. This had been said before, but Schrödinger's book was very timely (quoted in Perutz 1989: 216).

It was indeed. In fact, timing may provide us with the key to understanding how it was that Schrödinger's legacy depended so little on the utility of any of his particular biological arguments and so much on disciplinary politics. To physicists, he promoted the idea that at least one area of biology was worthy of their talents (that is, genetics), at a time when many were seeking just such an alternative. As Jacob has written,

> After the Second World War, many young physicists were shocked by the military use made of atomic energy. Some...moreover, were dissatisfied by the direction taken in...nuclear physics....Just to hear one of the leaders in quantum mechanics asking 'What is Life?'...was enough to fire the enthusiasm of certain young physicists and to bestow some sort of legitimacy on biology. Their ambition and interest were limited to a single problem: the physical basis of genetic information (Jacob 1973: 259–60).

The Second World War provided a powerful impetus for some not-so-young physicists as well – most notably, perhaps, Leo Szilard, arguably an even more important influence on the actual development of molecular biology than either Schrödinger or Bohr. All these physicists shared the disciplinary and intellectual habits of the world they had left behind – habits that led them to frame biological problems in the particular terms they could understand, in the terms that could lead to what they could recognize as a 'solution'. Szilard was explicit about what he believed he brought to biology: 'not any skills acquired in physics, but rather an attitude: the conviction which few biologists had at the time, that mysteries can be solved'. Life (development, reproduction, etc.) was not a problem that could be 'solved'; the physical basis of genetic information was.

To biologists whose own ambitions (either personal or intellectual) resonated with such a stance, the authority of these physicists provided an invaluable resource in promoting just that transformation of attitude and mind-set in their own profession that Muller had earlier sought but had been unauthorized to effect. Indeed, it was precisely this transformation – this relocation and redefinition of life – that Watson and Crick depended upon for success in their quest for 'the secret of life', and which their success, in turn, did so much to cement. Let me explain.

Elucidating the Mechanism: Watson and Crick

The story of Watson and Crick invites the interest it does – be it in film, autobiography, or history of science – not simply because of the 'greatness of their discovery', but also because of their particularly unlikely casting as scientific heroes. In one of the most perceptive early accounts of this story, Donald Fleming poses for

> himself the double question of why Crick and Watson blithely conceived of their research in these provocatively unfashionable terms [that is, as the quest for the secret of life] and what fed their expectations of victory.... How had they come to form these superbly arrogant ambitions, unbuttressed by any truly compelling evidence and offering total defiance to contemporary standards of good taste in biological discourse (Fleming 1968: 152–5).

Fleming's answer is that it was above all Schrödinger's imprimatur, along with that of Szilard and Delbrück, that permitted and legitimated such a conception. As Watson himself recalls, 'from the moment I read Schrödinger's *What Is Life?* ... I became polarized toward finding out the secret of the gene' (Watson 1966: 239).

In my version of the story, Watson and Crick were not unlikely, but in fact rather ordinary scientific heroes. Like all good scientists, they made use of the resources that were available to them, in the process adapting their aims to fit. They drew on certain disciplines – especially crystallography, physical chemistry and biochemistry – as well as on certain individual crystallographers, physical chemists and biochemists for crucial technical information and concrete assistance in employing these borrowed tools to decode the structure of DNA. But they drew on modern physics, and physicists, for the authority to license the formulation of their quest and, even more importantly, the representation of their accomplishments. The question is not so much about their ambitions but about the scope of their success. It is not even about their claim for a mechanism of genetic replication, or even for a physical basis of genetic information, but rather the claim that that mechanism is 'the secret of life'. For the plausibility that this claim acquired, the authority of modern physics was critical, not only for Watson and Crick, but also for the larger cultural transformation of biology that had already to have begun for such a claim to find general acceptance.

Given this representation of the secret of life as the mechanism of genetic replication, the elucidation of that mechanism inevitably led to the conclusion that life itself was not complex, as had been thought, but simple – indeed simple beyond our wildest dreams. The only secret of nature was that there were no secrets, and now that secret was out.[10]

This larger transformation – of language, of focus, of methodology, of the very definitions of what constitute legitimate questions and adequate answers – is what I take to be the hallmark of molecular biology. Born in the conceptual shifts I named at the start of this essay, nourished by multiple kinds of success (or power) – at first only in physics, but eventually in biology as well – it soon gathered enough momentum to reset the future course of biology. In its wake, it left the ratification of an entire set of new beliefs: belief in the absolute adequacy not simply of materialism, but of a particular kind of (linear, causal) mechanism; belief in the incontrovertible value of simplicity; belief in the unitary character of truth; and, finally, belief in the simultaneous equations between power and knowledge and between virtue and power. From the vantage point of this new constellation of beliefs, the older biology (and many of the older biologists) became objects of disdain; they had lacked, above all, an understanding of scientific progress. Francis Crick's complaint about fencing ['stab, stab, stab, but no penetration'][11] was intended to apply to biology.

In its early stages, this transformation drew at one and the same time on the politics of the disciplines, and on more global politics of knowledge. No one in the late 1940s and early 1950s could ignore just how much power at least some kinds of knowledge could deliver. To quote Crick again, 'We [knew] how to blow ourselves up, but we still [didn't] know how we reproduce ourselves' (BBC film).[12]

But it may well be that the very shock of the atomic bomb made both physicists and biologists peculiarly reticent about the general issue of technological/instrumental goals in science. Without question, the horror of Nazi experiments in eugenics made that particular word unspeakable and the idea behind it virtually unthinkable. The fact is that the particular agenda that had been so clear to Muller was, after the Second World War, nowhere in oral or written evidence. Indeed, there was virtually no mention of any practical consequences of a new approach to biology, at least not until the war on cancer. One might say that there didn't need to be. The technological prowess that underwrote the authority of physicists after the Second World War was perhaps too much in evidence, and too worrisome, to need or want to mention. The attraction of a science of life over a science of death was palpable; in like terms, so was the attraction of pure over applied science.

But the technological potency of scientific knowledge has never depended directly on styles of scientific rhetoric, and despite the silence of early molecular biologists on these issues, it is precisely this – the enormous technological and social power promised by modern molecular biology – that engages our concern today. In a word, I am saying that that power should come as no surprise.

The reason that the technological prowess of molecular biology is not a surprise is simple: in the first place, it *was* anticipated; in the second place, I am suggesting that its pursuit was written into the genetic programme as it has evolved over the past fifty years – not into the sequence of nucleotides, but into the forms of knowledge that biology, following physics, has taken as norm. As Muller dimly intuited so many years ago, theories that structure our understanding in terms of linear causal chains – that posit ontological cores as master molecules, blueprints, or 'central offices' – serve to focus our attention on equally linear chains of consequences. With life relocated in genes, and redefined in terms of their informational content, the project of 'refashioning life', of redirecting the future course of evolution, is recast as a manageable and do-able project. Or, to put it differently, the kind of theory that would provide a workable guide for such a project is precisely a theory that focuses on the causal relations between identifiable and controllable elements. Other processes, less identifiable, and less controllable, are bracketed in the double name of intellectual economy and technological efficacy. In this way, the very meaning of knowledge – what counts as knowledge – is shaped by a tacit instrumental mandate, perhaps even when that mandate has been forgotten.

Over the past 35 years, the world according to molecular biology has become progressively more complex, revealing intricacies and convolutions undreamt of in the central dogma of 1953. And as molecular biology has moved into the domain of developmental biology, the inadequacies of the core concept of the genome as a master programme or blueprint have become especially visible. Nevertheless, the momentum behind this basic view remains powerful – powerful enough to maintain an effectively single-minded focus on the (as it were, autonomous) force of genes, even in the face of an increasing awareness of the complexities of genetic organization. Today's dramatic growth in the technology of nucleotide sequencing and genetic mapping works to further catalyse this earlier momentum, in fact, carrying us right into the human genome project. Growing out of the past, such a project points our way into the future. Drawing simultaneously and conjointly on the material and social dimensions of the knowledge–power nexus, it works to realize the ambitions that fuelled its development in the first place. Finally, we are in a position to fulfil Warren Weaver's early dream of 'a new science of man' and even (though most biologists still prefer not to talk about it) to realize Muller's dream of reshaping the future course of human evolution. We are in this position not simply because we have developed sufficient technological wherewithal, but also because those with the technical expertise have acquired the concomitant political and social power to implement, or sell, the goals appropriate to that technology. When Watson was invited to direct the new National Institute of Health Office of Human Genome Research, a programme that is currently being hailed as the 'Manhattan Project' of the life sciences, he confessed that the appeal of 'starting with the double helix and going up to the double helical structure of man' was undeniable. I am suggesting not only that the double helix provided the first rung of Watson's ladder to man, but also that DNA is itself a ladder that has 'always already' pointed to man, with a directionality, intentionality, and a particular kind of interventional capability built into its original conception.

A seemingly perverse juxtaposition – between the history of the unfolding of molecular biology and a story from another time, and another place, that engaged Foucault's attention – might serve to close this chapter, if only to underscore what makes these stories different. In 1836 a Norman peasant, Pierre Riviere, was convicted of murdering his pregnant mother, his sister, and his brother. What captured Foucault's interest here was the memoir Riviere left, a memoir written before his fatal act. Foucault writes:

> Pierre Riviere was the subject of the memoir in a dual sense; it was he who remembered. . . . He contrived the engineering of the narrative/murder as both projectile and target, he was propelled by the working of the mechanism into the real murder. And, after all, he was the author of it all in a dual sense; author of the crime and author of the text (Foucault 1975: 209).

The case file that Foucault assembled, he says, gives us

> a key to the relations of power, domination and conflict within which discourses emerge and function, and hence provide[s] material for a potential analysis of discourse (even of scientific discourses) which may be both tactical and political, and therefore strategic (1975: xi–xxii).

By contrast, an adequate analysis of scientific discourses with the high epistemological profile of molecular biology requires recognition of a crucial difference between these two stories – namely, the fact that between the projectile and target of molecular biology lies another world, not of human actors nor even of human construction, but of material things, available to be called forth by the names we give them, but constrained in their responses by their own laws of behaviour. The trick that has given modern science so much of its power is the recognition of the need to actively engage this material – above all, to engage it in ways that permit an effective arrangement of its constituents into an instrument that enables the projectile to meet its predesignated target. Perhaps it is the choice of target that we need to examine most of all.

Notes

1 According to popular usage, molecular biology begins with the identification of DNA as the material basis of genetics, although numerous authors have argued for an expanded (and earlier) usage to include the biological and chemical study of DNA, RNA and protein (see, for example, Kendrew 1967; Abir-Am 1985). I would suggest, however, that it is from classical genetics that the clearest and most important lines of continuity can be traced. Accordingly, I use the term here to refer to the study of molecular structure and the activation of genetic information residing in DNA.

2 It should be noted that this move distinguishes molecular biology (as well as its antecedent traditions in classical genetics) from other reductionist research agendas in twentieth-century biological science: that is, from programmes that have sought the physical-chemical basis of biological phenomena in different kinds of structures and processes located, for example, in the cell, in the organism, or in organism–environment interactions. In other words, the shift that I am identifying with the molecular revolution represents the selection of one particular theoretical orientation among a number of others that would also qualify as reductionist in the usual sense of the term

3 Renato Dulbecco (1987: 17); Bernal (1967: 13). For a historical overview of earlier definitions of life, see Hall (1969); Smith (1976); and for a discussion of the particular redefinition of life attributable to molecular biology, see Yoxen (1982).

4 Quoted in Pauly (1987: 179).

5 It is important here to distinguish the particular ambitions associated with molecular biology from more general aspirations toward control and intervention in biological science. Just as most biological scientists were committed to some form of materialism by the end of the nineteenth century, so too had their efforts already both aimed at and resulted in visible technological consequences. These consequences, however, had been of a different order than those both envisioned, and now virtually promised, by molecular biology – directed more to maintenance and regulation than to the creation, or imitation, of life.

6 To frame Muller's thinking, a few historical markers might be helpful: 1896, radioactivity discovered; 1900, rediscovery of Mendelian 'factors' (particulate genetic elements); 1901, spontaneous transmutation of elements observed by Ernest Rutherford and Frederick Soddy (so named by Soddy in 1901); 1902, identification of nuclear chromosomes as the site of genetic factors; 1909, coinage of the term 'gene'; 1911, Rutherford's discovery of the atomic nucleus; 1919, Rutherford induces the first artificial transformation.

7 A more complete excerpt reads:

> Each gene, reacting with the ... surrounding material ... exerts such a selectively organizing effect upon this material as to cause the synthesis, next to itself, of another molecular or super-molecular structure, quite identical in composition with the given gene itself. The gene is, as it were, a modeller, and it forms an image, a copy of itself ...; it is an active arranger of material ... after its own pattern. The analogy to crystallization hardly carries us far enough in explanation of the above phenomenon when we remember that there are thousands of genes ... having different patterns, in every cell nucleus, and that each of these genes has to reproduce its own specific pattern out of surrounding material common to them all. When ... a sudden change in the composition ('pattern') of the gene takes place, ... a 'mutation', then the gene of the new type ... now reproduces precisely the new pattern. This shows that the copying property depends upon some more fundamental feature of gene structure than does the specific pattern which the gene has.... It is this fact which gives the possibility of biological evolution and which has allowed living matter ultimately to become so very much more highly organized than non-living. It is this which lies at the bottom of both growth, reproduction and heredity (Muller, 1936: 211–12).

8 The proximity to Watson and Crick's actual endeavour should be noted.

9 Indeed, Schrödinger's argument seems to build not towards a solution, but rather to a refutation of Niels Bohr's earlier contention of an inherent barrier to understanding the secrets of life – a barrier he claimed to be predicted by an extension of the principle of complementarity. In other words, I am suggesting that a proper understanding of Schrödinger's contribution requires reference to Bohr's earlier (and opposing) bid for a conceptual unification of biology with physics. Bohr had argued that 'We should doubtless kill an animal if we tried to carry the investigation of its organs so far that we could tell the part played by the single atoms in vital functions.' He therefore concluded:

> In every experiment on living organisms there must remain some uncertainty as regards the physical conditions to which they are subjected, and the idea suggests itself that the minimal freedom we must allow the organism will be just large enough to permit it, so to say, to hide its ultimate secrets from us. On this view, the very existence of life must in biology be considered as an elementary fact, just as in atomic physics the existence of the quantum of action has to be taken as a basic fact that cannot be derived from ordinary mechanical physics (Bohr 1958: 9).

In contrast, the central point for Schrödinger seems to be that living matter is distinctive from inanimate matter only in being *too* lawful, in its apparent excess of order; far from constituting a barrier to our understanding, quantum mechanics is precisely the branch of physics that can resolve this paradox. In closing, he writes:

> we seem to arrive at the ridiculous conclusion that the clue to the understanding of life is that it is based on a pure mechanism, a 'clock work'.... But please do not accuse me of calling the chromosome fibres just the cogs of the organic machine – at least not without a reference to the profound physical theories on which the simile is based ... the single cog is not of coarse human make, but is the finest masterpiece ever achieved along the lines of the Lord's quantum mechanics (Schroedinger 1944: 91).

10 There is no doubt that the triumph of the double helix would have had major

significance no matter how it had been described, but its particular representation allowed molecular biologists an assumption of scientific hegemony heretofore unfamiliar in biology. Having solved the problem of life – as Monod put it, 'in principle if not in all details' – there was no longer room for doubt, for uncertainty, for questions unanswerable within that framework, even for data that would not fit, or for another conception of biology. A science that had historically been characterized by diversity – perhaps like the life it presumed to study – became, if not totally monolithic, very close to it. Molecular biology became synonymous with scientific biology.

11 From the recent film version of this story, *The Race to the Double Helix,* for which Francis Crick served as adviser.

12 An earlier remark of Crick's linked the problem of reproduction with sub-atomic physics in terms strikingly reminiscent of Muller's own associations. In a 1968 interview with Robert Olby, he turned to the question of how 'the egg form[s] the organism' and said: 'If you look at the problem in its full horror, it's like Rutherford surveying the atom at the beginning of sub-atomic physics' (quoted in Judson, 1979: 209).

References

Abir-Am, P. (1985), 'Themes, Genres and Orders of Legitimation in the Consolidation of New Scientific Disciplines: Deconstructing the Historiography of Molecular Biology' in *History of Science*, 23, pp. 73–117.

Bernal, D.J. (1967), 'Definitions of Life' in *New Scientist*, 3 January, pp. 12–14.

Bohr, N. (1958), 'Light and Life', in *Atomic Physics and Human Knowledge*, John Wiley and Sons, New York.

Carlson, E.A. (1971), 'An Unacknowledged Founding of Molecular Biology: H.J. Muller's Contribution to Gene Theory, 1910–1936', in *Journal of the History of Biology*, 4, pp. 149–70.

Crick, F.H.C. (1981), *Life Itself*, Simon and Schuster, New York.

— (1970), 'Central Dogma of Molecular Biology' in *Nature,* 227, pp. 561–3.

— (1957), 'On Protein Synthesis' in *Symposium of the Society of Exp. Biology*, 12, pp. 138–63.

Delbruck, M. (1946), 'Discussion', in *Cold Spring Harbour Symposium*, 11, p. 154.

— (1970), 'A Physicist's Renewed Look at Biology: Twenty Years Later', in *Science*, 168, p. 1312.

Dulbecco, R. (1987), *The Design of Life*, Yale University Press, New Haven, CT.

Fleming, D. (1968), 'Emigre Physicists and the Biological Revolution' in *Perspectives in American History*, 2, p. 155. Harvard University Press, Cambridge, MA.

Foucault, M. (1975) (ed.), *I, Pierre Riviere, Having Slaughtered My Mother, My Sister, and My Brother*, Penguin, New York.

Hacking, I. (1987), 'Weapons Research and the Form of Scientific Knowledge' in *Canadian Journal of Philosophy*, supp. vol. 12, pp. 237–60.

Hall, T.S. (1969), *Ideas of Life and Matter*, 2 vols, University of Chicago Press, Chicago.

Jacob, F. (1973), *The Logic of Life*, Vintage, New York.

Judson, H. (1979), *The Eighth Day of Creation: Makers of the Revolution in Biology*, Simon and Schuster, New York.

Kendrew, J. (1967), 'How Molecular Biology Started' in *Scientific American*, 216, pp. 141–3.

Muller, H.J. (1927), 'Artificial Transmutation of the Gene' in *Science* LXVI, No. 1699, pp. 84–7.

— (1929), 'The Method of Evolution' in *Scientific Monthly*, 29, p. 505.

— (1929), Presented before the International Congress of Plant Sciences, Section of Genetics, Symposium on 'The Gene', Ithaca, New York, 19 August 1926. Published in Proceedings International Congress of Plant Sciences, I, pp. 897–921.

— (1935), *Out of the Night*, Vanguard Press, New York.

— (1936), 'Physics in the Attack on the Fundamental Problems of Genetics', in *Scientific Monthly*, 44, pp. 210–14.

Olby, R. (1970), 'Francis Crick, DNA and the Central Dogma' in *Daedalus*, Fall, pp. 938–87.

Pauly, P. (1987), *Controlling Life*, Oxford University Press, New York.

Perutz, M. (1989), *Is Science Necessary?* E.P. Dutton, New York.

Schrödinger, E. (1944), *What is Life?* Cambridge University Press, Cambridge.

Smith, C.U.M. (1976), *The Problem of Life*, John Wiley and Sons, New York.

Stent, G. (1968), 'That was the Molecular Biology, That Was' in *Science*, 160, pp. 390–5.

Watson, J.D. (1968), *The Double Helix*, Atheneum, New York.

Yoxen, E.J. (1982), 'Giving Life a New Meaning: The Rise of the Molecular Biology Establishment' in *Sociology of the Sciences*, 6, pp. 123–43.

CHAPTER 5

Otherworldly Conversations, Terran Topics, Local Terms*

DONNA HARAWAY

Therefore the Lord God sent him forth from the garden of Eden, to till the ground from whence he was taken. So he drove out the man; and he placed at the east of the garden of Eden Cherubims, and a flaming sword which turned every way, to keep the way of the tree of life (Genesis, 3, 23–24; Robert Young, *Darwin's Metaphor, Nature's Place in Victorian Culture*, p. 3).

Nothing is ultimately contextual; all is constitutive, which is another way of saying that all relationships are dialectical (Robert Young, *Darwin's Metaphor, Nature's Place in Victorian Culture*, p. 241).

Animals are not lesser humans; they are other worlds. (Barbara Noske, *Humans and Other Animals*, p. xi).

Although, of course, I longed in the normal human way for exploration, I found my first world oddly disconcerting. . . . It is only in circumstances like these that we realize how much we ourselves are constructed bilaterally on either-or principles. Fish rather than echinoderms. . . . It was quite a problem to get through to those radial entities (Naomi Mitchison, *Memoirs of a Spacewoman*, pp. 19, 20, 23).

Nature is for me, and I venture for many of us who are planetary foetuses gestating in the amniotic effluvia of terminal industrialism and militarism, one of those impossible things characterized in a talk in 1989 in California by Gayatri Spivak as that which we cannot not desire. Excruciatingly conscious of nature's constitution as 'other' in the histories of colonialism, racism, sexism, and class domination of many kinds, many people who have been both ground to powder and formed in European and Euro-American crucibles nonetheless find in this problematic, ethno-specific,

---

* A meditation on Naomi Mitchison, *Memoirs of a Spacewoman* (London: The Women's Press, 1976, copyright 1962); Barbara Noske, *Humans and Other Animals: Beyond the Boundaries of Anthropology* (London: Pluto Press, 1989); and Robert M. Young, *Darwin's Metaphor: Nature's Place in Victorian Culture* (Cambridge, England: Cambridge University Press, 1985).

long-lived, and globally mobile concept something we cannot do without, but can never 'have'. We must find another relationship to nature besides reification, possession, appropriation, and nostalgia. No longer able to sustain the fictions of being either subjects or objects, all the partners in the potent conversations that constitute nature must find a new ground for making meanings together.[1]

Perhaps to give confidence in its essential reality, immense resources have been expended to stabilize and materialize nature, to police its/her boundaries. From one reading of Genesis 3, 23–24, it looks as if God established the first nature park in the neolithic First World, now become the oil-rich Third World, complete with an armed guard to keep out the agri-culturalists. From the beginning such efforts have had disappointing results. Efforts to travel into 'nature' become tourist excursions that remind the voyager of the price of such displacements – one pays to see fun-house reflections of oneself. Efforts to preserve 'nature' in parks remain fatally troubled by the ineradicable mark of the founding expulsion of those who used to live there, not as innocents in a garden, but as people for whom the categories of nature and culture were not the salient ones. Expensive projects to collect 'nature's' diversity and bank it seem to produce debased coin, impoverished seed and dusty relics. As the banks hypertrophy, the nature that feeds the storehouses 'disappears'. The World Bank's record on environmental destruction is exemplary in this regard. Finally, the projects for representing and enforcing human 'nature' are famous for their imperial-izing essences, most recently replicated in the Human Genome Project. It seems appropriate that a core computer project for storing the record of human unity and diversity – GenBank, the US depository for DNA sequence data – is located in the national laboratories at Los Alamos, New Mexico, site of the Manhattan Project and a major US weapons laboratory since the Second World War.

So, nature is not a physical place to which one can go, nor a treasure to fence in or bank, nor an essence to be saved or violated. Nature is not hidden and so does not need to be unveiled. Nature is not a text to be read in the codes of mathematics and biomedicine. It is not the 'other' who offers origin, replenishment and service. Neither mother, nurse, lover, nor slave, nature is not matrix, resource, mirror, nor tool for the reproduction of that odd ethnocentric, phallogocentric, putatively universal being called Man. Nor for his euphemistically named surrogate, 'the human'.

Nature is, however, a *topos,* a place, in the sense of a rhetorician's place or topic for consideration of common themes; nature is, strictly, a common-place. We turn to this topic to order our discourse, to compose our memory. As a topic in this sense, nature also reminds us that in seventeenth-century English the 'topick gods' were the local gods, the gods specific to places and peoples. We need these spirits, rhetorically if we can't have them any other way. We need them in order to reinhabit, precisely, *common* places – locations that are widely shared, inescapably local, worldly, enspirited: in a word, topical. In this sense, nature is the place to rebuild public culture.[2]

Nature is also a *trópos,* a trope. It is figure, construction, artifact, movement, displacement. Nature cannot pre-exist its construction, its articulation in heterogeneous social encounters, where all of the actors are not human and all of the humans are not 'us', however defined. Worlds are built from such articulations. Fruitful encounters depend on a particular kind of move – a *trópos* or 'turn'. Faithful to the Greek, as *trópos* nature is about turning. Troping, we turn to nature as if to the earth, to the tree of life – geotropic, physiotropic. We turn in the hope that the park police, the Cherubims, are on strike against God and that both swords and plowshares might be beaten into other tools, other metaphors for possible conversations about inhabitable terran otherworlds. Topically, we travel toward the earth, a commonplace. Nature is a topic of public discourse on which much turns, even the earth.

Less grandly, I turn to a little piece of this work of world-building – telling stories. When I grow up, or as we used to say, after the revolution, I know what I want to do. I want to have charge of the animal stories in the *Readers' Digest,* reaching twenty or so million people monthly in over a dozen languages. I want to write the stories about morally astute dogs, endangered people, instructive beetles, marvellous microbes and co-habitable houses of difference. With my friends, I want to write natural history at the end of the Second Christian Millennium to see if some other stories are possible, ones not premised on the divide between nature and culture, armed Cherubims, and heroic quests for secrets of life and secrets of death.[3] Following Ursula LeGuin, and inspired by some of the chapters in the evolutionary tales of woman-the-gatherer, I want to engage in a carrier-bag practice of story telling, in which the stories do not reveal secrets acquired by heroes pursuing luminous objects across and through the plot matrix of the world. Bag-lady story telling would instead proceed by putting unexpected partners and irreducible details into a frayed, porous carrier bag. Encouraging halting conversations, the encounter transmutes and reconstitutes all the partners and all the details. The stories do not have beginnings or ends; they have continuations, interruptions, and reformulations – just the kind of survivable stories we could use these days. And, perhaps, my beginning with the transmogrification of LeGuin's 'Carrier-Bag Theory of Fiction'[4] to the bag-lady practice of story telling can remind us that the lurking dilemma in all of these tales is comprehensive homelessness, the lack of a common place, and the devastation of public culture.

In the United States story telling about nature, whatever problematic kind of category that is, remains an important practice for forging and expressing basic meanings. The profusion of nature television specials is a kind of collective video-Bridgewater Treatise, producing secularized natural theology within late capitalism. A recent visit to the San Diego Zoo confirmed my conviction that people reaffirm many of their beliefs about each other and about what kind of planet the earth can be by telling each other what they think they are seeing as they watch the animals. So I would like to begin my meditation on these books by Robert Young, Barbara Noske and Naomi Mitchison with a few stories to reveal some of the investments I bring to reading their books.

Ducks, Enzymes and Shaggy Dogs: Inter-Specific Tales

A few years ago I was visiting my high-school friend, who lived with her husband and three sons aged 16, 14 and 11 near Milwaukee, Wisconsin. Periodically throughout the weekend, the two older boys teased each other mercilessly about a high-school dance coming up; each boy tried to get under his brother's skin by queer-baiting him relentlessly. In this middle-class, white, American community, their patent nervousness about dating girls was enacted in 'playful' insults about each other's not-yet-fully-consolidated gender allegiances and identities. In confused, but numbingly common moves, they accused each other of being simultaneously a girl and a queer. From my point of view, they were performing a required lesson in compulsory heterosexuality in my culture and theirs. I found the whole scene personally deeply painful for many reasons, not least the profoundly poor manners and disrespect the parents allowed, knowing the gay, lesbian, and bisexual make-up of my life, family and community. My world is sustained by queer confederacies. Lacking courage and feeling disoriented, late in the weekend I told my friend what I thought was happening. Shocked at me, she said the boys were much too young to be taught anything about homosexuality and homophobia, and in any case what they were doing was just natural. Despite the fact that I was the godmother of the older boy, I culpably shut up, leaving his moral education to the proven sensibilities of his milieu.

Later that day, knowing my interest in another kind of nature and hoping to heal our dis-ease with each other by a culturally appropriate, therapeutic trip 'outside civilization', my friend and her husband took me to a beautiful small lake in the wooded countryside. With high spirits if little zoological erudition, we began talking about some ducks across the lake. We could see very little, and we knew less. In instant solidarity, my friend and her husband narrated that the four ducks in view were in two reproductive, heterosexual pairs. It quickly sounded like they had a modest mortgage on the wetlands around that section of the lake and were about to send their ducklings to a good school to consolidate their reproductive investment. I demurred, mumbling something about the complexity and specificity of animal behaviour and society. Meanwhile, I, of course, held that the ducks were into queer communities. I knew better; I knew they were *ducks*, even though I was embarrassed not to know even what species. I knew ducks deserved our recognition of their non-human cultures, subjectivities, histories, and material lives. They had enough problems with all the heavy metals and organic solvents in those lakes without having to take sides in our ideological struggles too. Forced to live in our ethno-specific constructions of nature, the birds could ill afford the luxury of getting embroiled in what counts as natural for the nearby anglo community.

Nonetheless, furious at each other, both my friends and I were sure we were right in our self-interested and increasingly assertive stories about the ducks. After all, we could *see* what they were doing; they were right across the lake; we had positive knowledge about them. They were objects performing on our stage, called nature. They had been appropriated into our shamefully displaced struggle, which belonged where earlier in the day we were too chicken (!?) to put it – directly over the homophobia, compulsory heterosexuality, and commitments to normalizing particular kinds of families in *our* lives. We avoided building needed, contested, situated knowledges among ourselves by – once again, in ways historically sanctioned in middle-class, anglo cultures – objectifying nature. More sophisticated scientific accounts of animal behaviour published in the best technical journals and popularized in the most expensive public television series patently do much the same thing. But not always; sometimes, rarely and preciously, we – those of us gestating in techno-scientific media – manage to tell some very non-innocent stories about, and even with, the animals, rather than about our 'natural' selves. Meanwhile, I'm still sure I was more right than my friends about those ducks, whoever they were. And, while queer-bashing remains a popular sport, I still feel the pain and know my complicity in the natural development of those particular boys.

A second story: once upon a time, early in graduate school in biology in the mid-1960s, I was tremendously moved, intellectually and emotionally, by an ordinary lecture on the enzymes of the electron transport system (ETS). These biological catalysts are involved in energy-processing in cells complicated enough to have elaborate, internal, membrane-bound organelles (little organs) to partition and enlarge their activities. Using new techniques, the process was being studied experimentally *in vitro* in structural-functional complexes of membrane sub-units prepared from the cellular organelles, called mitochondria. The membrane sub-units were disassembled and reassembled to be analysed by both electron microscopy and biochemistry. The result was a stunning narrative and visual imagery of structural-functional complexity of the type that has always made biology, including molecular biology, a beautiful science for me. The apparatus of production of these written and oral accounts and visual artifacts was rigorously analytical and biotechnical. There was no way around elaborate machine mediations, complete with all their encasements of dead labour, intentional and unintentional delegations, unexpected agencies, and past and present, pain-fraught, socio-technical histories.

After the lecture, on a walk around town, I felt a surging high. Trees, weeds, dogs, invisible gut parasites, people – we all seemed bound together in the ultra-structural tissues of our being. Far from feeling alienated by the reductionistic techniques of cell biology, I realized to my partial embarrassment, but mainly pleasure, that I was responding *erotically* to the connections made possible by the knowledge-producing practices, and their constitutive narratives, of techno-science. So, who is surprised: when were love and knowledge not co-constitutive? I refused, then and now, to dismiss the specific pleasure experienced on that walk as epistemological sado-masochism, rooted in alienation and objectifying scientific reductionism or in ignorant denial of the terrible histories of domination built into what we politely call 'modern science'. I was *not* experiencing a moment of romantic post-modern rapture in the techno-sublime. Machine, organism, and human embodiment, all were articulated – brought into a *particular* co-constitutive relationship – in complex ways that forced me to recognize a historically specific, conjoined discipline of love, power, and knowledge. Through its enabling constraints, that is, through lab practice in cell biology, this discipline was making possible – unequally – particular kinds of subjectivity and systematic artifactual embodiments, for which people in my worlds had to be responsible.

This knowing love could not be innocent; it did not originate in a garden. But neither did it originate from *expulsion* from a garden. Not about secrets – of life or death – this knowing love took shape in quite particular, historical-social intercourse, or 'conversation', among machines, people, other organisms, and parts of organisms. All those feminists like me still in the closet – that is, those who have not come out to acknowledge the viscous, physical, erotic pleasure we experienced from disharmonious conversations about abstract ideas, auto repair, and possible worlds that took place in local consciousness-raising groups in the early 1970s – might have a thrill of self-recognition in thinking about the electron transport system. Our desires are very heterogeneous, indeed, as are our embodiments. We may not be ducks; but, as natural-technical terran constructs, we are certainly ETs.

And a final story: when Alexander Berkman and Sojourner Truth, my lover's and my half-labrador mutts, were just over a year old, we all went to obedience training together in a small town in northern California. Although we had discoursed on dog training from library books for a year, none of us had ever before been to obedience training, that amazing institution domesticating people and their canine companions to agree to cohabit particular stories important to civic peace. It was late in our lives together to seek institutionalized obedience training. One of us already showed signs of criminality, or at least bore the marks of a shared incoherent relation to authority, of the kind that could result in mayhem and legally mandated death sentences for dogs and nasty fines for people. That is, one of us seemed intent on murdering con-specifics in any and all circumstances, and the rest of us were handling the situation badly.

In some important situations in the 1980s in California, we four didn't seem to speak the same language, either within or across species boundaries. We needed help. So, with a motley assortment of other cross-specific pairs of mammals, of types that had shared biological and social histories for a couple of tens of thousands of years, we entered a commercial pedagogical relationship with the dog, Goody-goody, and her human, Perfection, who seemed to have mastered the political problem of paying consequential attention to each other. They seemed to have a story to tell us.

In her discussion of the language games of training, Vicki Hearne invoked Wittgenstein's injunction, 'to imagine a language is to imagine a form of life'.[5] A professional trainer and an incurable intellectual, Hearne was looking for a philosophically responsible language for talking about the stories inhabited by trainers and companion animals like dogs and horses. She was convinced that the training relationship is a moral one that requires the personhood of all the partners. But, although Hearne did not affirm this point, the moral relationship cannot rely on a shared *anthropomorphic* personhood. Only some of the partners are people, and the form of life the conversants construct is neither purely canine nor purely human. Further, personhood is only one local, albeit historically broadly important way of being a subject. And, like most moral relationships, this one cannot rely on ignorance of radical heterogeneity in the commitment to equality-as-sameness.

Certainly, however, in the training relationship animals and people are constructing an historically specific form of life, and therefore a language. They are engaged in making some effective meanings rather than others. Hearne's moral universe had such premises as: dogs have the right to the consequences of their actions; and: biting (by the dog) is a response to incoherent authority (the human's). She envisioned certain civil rights, like those enjoyed by seeing-eye dogs and their people, for other dogs and people who had achieved superb off-lead control.

I quibble about discussing this matter in terms of people's control of the dogs, not out of a fetishized fear of CONTROL, and of naming who exercises it over whom, but out of a sense that my available languages for discussing control and its directional arrows mis-shape the forms of attention and response achieved by serious dogs and trainers. By *mis-shape,* I do not mean *mis-represent,* but, more seriously, I mean that the language of uni-directional 'human control over dog' instrumentally is part of producing an incoherent and even dangerous relationship that is not conducive to civil peace within or across species. A convinced sceptic about the ideologies of representation anyway, I am not interested in worrying too much about the accurate portrayal of training relationships. But I am very much concerned about the instrumentality of languages, since they are forms of life.

Sojourner, Alexander – the canine reincarnation of the lover of Emma Goldman and the anarchist who shot Frick in the 1880s Pullman railroad strike – Rusten and I were serious about training, but we were very unskilled. We should have met Vicki Hearne, but at that point we had her only in the *New Yorker.* We needed more on-the-ground skill. Instead, we blundered into an appalling conversation that makes those heterosexually construed ducks look untouched by human tongues. As long as you didn't listen to the English that Perfection used to explain to the other humans what was happening, but attended only to the other semiotic processes, like gesture, touch and unadorned verbal command, Goody-goody and Perfection had a pretty good story for lots of ordinary events in inter-specific life. But, like lots of sheltered folk, they weren't good with anarchists and criminals; they relied, or at least Perfection did, on escalating force and languages of stripped-down subjugation. The result was stunning escalation of the potential for violence with our dog. The conversation was going quite wrong. We later met some trainer humans and social-worker dogs who taught us how to work on reliable obedience in challenging circumstances – such as the mere existence of other dogs in the world. But, our first encounter with obedience training posed in stark terms the fact that forms of inter-specific domestic life can go very wrong.

My growing suspicions that our incoherence was only increasing in this particular attempt at training reached their apogee near graduation time, when Goody-goody and Perfection demonstrated how a human could examine any spot on a dog's body if necessary. This exercise could be crucial in emergencies, where pain and injury to the dog could put both human and animal at risk. The class was very attentive. While Perfection was touching Goody-goody in every imaginable place, opening and closing orifices, and generally showing how few boundaries were necessary when trust and good authority existed, the conversants seemed to me to be involved in a complex intercourse of gesture, touch, eye movement, tone of voice, and many other modalities. But, while grasping a paw and holding it up for our view, what Perfection was saying to us went something like this: 'See this paw? It may look like Goody-goody's paw, but it's really my paw. I own this paw, and I can do anything I want with it. If you are to be able to do what you see us doing, you too must accept that form of appropriation of your dog's body.'

It was my opinion that day, and still is, that if Perfection had really acted on her explicit words, Goody-goody and she would have achieved nothing. Their other conversation belied the discourse she provided the students. If my lover and I had been better at attending to that other conversation, we might have been able to get further on our needed communication with Alexander and Sojourner on difficult subjects. We were actually very good at the physical examination language game. In our harder task, the one involving our dog's tendency to con-specific murder, with his sister aiding and abetting, we were deterred by mis-shaping words that Perfection did not follow in her relations with Goody-goody, but did impose in both physical and verbal relationships with at least some other dogs and people. Maybe she just had that trouble with criminals, anarchists, and socialists. That population is, it must be said, quite large. Unpromisingly, my household went to obedience-training graduation wearing 'question authority' buttons. We had not yet built a coherent conversation, inter- or intra-specifically, for the crucial subject of authority.

Robert Young: *Darwin's Metaphor*

My opening stories have been about three forms of life and three conversations involving historically located people and other organisms or parts of organisms, as well as technological artifacts. All of these are stories about demarcation and continuity among actors, human and not, organic and not. The stories of the 'wild ducks in nature', of the 'reductive' methodologies and the ETS in cell biology, and of the problem of 'discourse' between people and companion species collectively raise the problems that will concern us for the rest of this essay, as we turn to Young, Noske, and Mitchison. Is there a common context for discussion of what counts as nature in techno-science? What kind of topic is the 'human' place in 'nature' by the late twentieth century in the worlds shaped by techno-science? How might inhabitable narratives about science and nature be told, without denying the ravages of the dedication of techno-science to militarized and systematically unjust relations of knowledge and power, while refusing to replicate the apocalyptic stories of Good and Evil played out on the stages of Nature and Science?

In *Darwin's Metaphor: Nature's Place in Victorian Culture,* a richly textured, scholarly, and politically passionate book that collects a series of still vitally important essays written across the 1970s on the nineteenth-century British debates on 'man's place in nature',[6] Robert Young depicts the structure and consequences of the broad, common cultural context within which intellectuals' struggle over the demarcation between 'man', God, and nature took place. The twentieth-century phrase 'science *and* society' would not have made much sense to the participants in the earlier debates, for whom the parts were not two pre-constituted, oppositional entities, *science* and *society,* held apart by a deceiving conjunction. The phrase *should* not make sense in the 1990s either, but for different reasons than those that pertained in Darwin's world. My debased goal of writing the animal stories for the *Readers' Digest* should be seen in the context of a very different social scene for the nineteenth-century contestation of shared meanings and inhabitable stories. In those halcyon days, I might have aspired instead to have written for the *Edinburgh Review*.

Young's fundamental insistence is that probing deeper into a scientific debate leads inexorably to the wider issues of a culture. If we inquire insistently enough – if we actually take doing cultural studies seriously – 'we may learn something about the nature of science itself, and thereby illuminate the way societies set agendas in their broad culture, including science, as part of the pursuit of social priorities and values' (p. 122). For Young, if one wishes to follow the nineteenth-century debates which he is exploring and, more generally, to engage any important issues in the history of science as culture, to sequester the scientific debate from the social, political, theological, and economic ones is to falsify all the parts and 'to mystify oppression in the form of science' (p. 192).

In the 1970s Young's reference for these arguments was the debate over 'internalist versus externalist' approaches to the history of science that exercised scholars throughout the decade. Can science be understood to have 'insides' and 'outsides' that justify separating off 'contents' of scientific 'discovery' from 'contexts' of 'construction'? All of Young's essays are rigorous, principled objections to the dichotomy as scholarly obfuscation and political mystification. In 1991, I would still be hard put to recommend a more richly argued invitation to and enactment of politically engaged, holistic, scholarly work than Young's 1973 essay, reprinted in *Darwin's Metaphor,* 'The Historiographic and Ideological Contexts of the Nineteenth-century Debate on Man's Place in Nature'. I found in the 1970s, and still find, that Robert Young's cogency about the need to confront the content of the sciences with a non-reductionistic, social-historical analysis and to avoid easy answers to the relations of science and ideology is indispensable to all my projects as a critical intellectual. That cogency is certainly indispensable to understanding science *as* culture, rather than science *and* culture. As he put it – much earlier than those now cited in science studies for injunctions that sound similar, but lack Young's crucial political edge – 'Nothing is ultimately contextual; all is constitutive, which is another way of saying that all relationships are dialectical' (p. 241). Following a Marxist tradition, especially in the work of Georg Lukács, 'whose analysis of reification provides the tools for looking more closely at the ways in which science has been used for the purpose of reconciling people to the status quo', Young builds his book around the premise that 'nature is a social category' (p. 242). I will come back to this indispensable and highly problematic assertion.

Young's general view of the nineteenth-century debate is that its questions were not allocated to specialist disciplines, but were deeply embedded in a shared (although class-differentiated) cultural context, for which the relation of God and His creation, that is, theism and the fate of natural theology, was the organizing centre. For example, the fine structure of Darwin's scientific discourse on 'selection' shows that theological and philosophical issues were constitutive, not contextual. The common intellectual context of the debate about 'man's place in nature' from the early 1800s to the 1880s took shape in a widely read periodical literature, in which theological, geological, biological, literary, and political questions were complexly knotted together. The debate about 'man's place in nature' was not an integrated whole, but a rich web. The threads were sustained by a material apparatus of production of a common culture among the intelligentsia, including potent reading, writing, and publishing practices.

Through the 1870s and 1880s, the break-up of the common intellectual context through specializations and disciplinizations familiar to an observer from the late twentieth century was reflected by – and partly effected by – a very different structure of writing and publishing practices. As Young put it, 'The common intellectual context came to pieces in the 1870s and 1880s, and this fragmentation was reflected in the development of specialist societies and periodicals, increasing professionalization, and the growth of general periodicals of a markedly lower intellectual standard' (p. 128). Thus was born my desire to write for *National Geographic, Omni* and, to return to the deepest shame and hope for an academic used to audiences of a few hundred souls, the *Readers' Digest,* or even *The National Enquirer.*

But if there has been a disruption in one context – and its constitutive literary, social, and material technologies – Young notes a stream of continuity from the early nineteenth to the late twentieth century that is fed by the very specializations in practice and the literary debasements which he describes: current biotechnology, perhaps especially genetic engineering and the profusion of genome projects to appropriate an organism's DNA sequences in a particular historical form – one amenable to property and commodity relations – must be seen as, in significant part, the 'harvest of Darwinism' that has reshaped biological culture at its roots. 'The current context for reflecting on these matters is a period in which biotechnology is harvesting and commercializing the long-term fruits of Darwinism and making commodities out of the least elements of living nature – amino acids and genes' (p. 247). 'Darwinism provides the unifying thread and themes from Malthus to the commodification of the smallest elements of living nature in genetic engineering. With this set of interrelations go the social forms of technocracy, information processing, and the disciplines that are recasting how we think of humanity in terms of cybernetics, information theory, systems theory, and "communication and control"' (p. xiii).

So, our 'common context' is not theism – the relations of a creator God to His product – but constructivism and productionism. Constructivism and productionism are the consequences of the material relocation of the narratives and practices of creation and their ensuing legal relations onto 'man' and 'nature' in (how else can I say it?) white capitalist heterosexist patriarchy (hereafter WCHP, an acronym whose beauty fits its referent). The nineteenth-century debate about the demarcation between God's creative action and nature's laws, and so between man and nature, mind and body, was resolved by a commitment to the principle of the uniformity of nature and scientific naturalism. In the context of the founding law of the Father, nature's *capacities* and nature's *laws* were identical. Narratively, this identification entails the escalating dominations built into stories of the endless transgressions of forbidden boundaries – the erotic *frisson* of man's projects of transcendence, prominently including techno-science. 'Science did not replace God: God became identified with the laws of nature' (p. 240). God did not interfere in his creation, not even in those previously reliable reservoirs for His action called biological design and mental function. But the deep European, monotheist, patriarchal, cultural commitment to relating to the world as *made, designed,* and structured by the prohibitions of law remained. A recent element in the stories, *progress* was inserted into the body of nature and deeply tied to a particular kind of conception of the uniformity of nature as a *product.* By the late twentieth century, very few cracks, indeed, are allowed to show in the solid cultural complex of WCHP constructionism.

In March 1988, Charles Cantor, then the head of the US Department of Energy's Human Genome Center at the Lawrence Berkeley Laboratory, made these matters clear in his talk at the National Institute of Medicine, 'The Human Genome Project: Problems and Prospects'. In the context of explaining the different material modes of existence of various kinds of genetic maps (genetic linkage maps, physical maps stored in libraries, of

Yeast Artificial Chromosome (YAC) libraries or 'cosmid libraries', and database sequence information existing only in computers and their print-outs), Cantor noted why having the physical maps mattered so much: 'You own the genome at this point.' I wanted Cantor to exlore further the socio-technical relations of physical libraries to sequence data; this exploration would show us something about the late twentieth-century 'common context' for demarcation debates between 'nature', 'man', and, if not God, at least the supreme engineer. The 'realization' of the value of the genome requires its full materialization in a particular historical form. Instrumentalism and full constructivism are not disembodied concepts. To *make* and store the genome is to appropriate it as a specific kind of entity. This is historically specific human self-production and self-possession or ownership.

The long tradition of methodological individualism and liberty based on property in the self comes to a particular kind of fruition in this discourse. To patent something, one must hold the key to making it. That is what bestows the juridical right of private appropriation of the product of no longer simply given, but rather fully technically replicated, 'nature'. In the Human Genome Project, generic 'man's place in nature' really does become the universal 'human place in nature' in a particular form: species existence as fully specified process and product. The body is matrix, superfluous, or obstructive; the programme is the prize. As the mutated, but still masculin-ist, heroic narrative unfolds, the relation between sex and gender is one of the many worlds that is transformed in the concrete socio-technical project now under way in Europe, Japan, and the United States.

Like toys in other games, 'genes "R" us', and 'we' (who?) are our self-possessed products in this apotheosis of technological humanism. There is only one Actor, and we are It. Nature mutates into its binary opposite, culture, and vice versa, in such a way as to displace the entire nature/culture (and sex/gender) dialectic with a new discursive field, where the actors who count are their own instrumental objectifications. Context is content with a vengeance. Nature is the programme; we replicated it; we own it; we are it. Nature and culture implode into each other and disappear into the resulting black hole. Man makes himself, indeed, in a cosmic onanism. The nineteenth century transfer of God's creative role to natural processes, within a multiply stratified industrial culture committed to relentless constructivism and productionism, bears fruit in a comprehensive biotechnological harvest, in which control of the genome is control of the game of life – legally, mythically, and technically. The stakes are very unequal chances for life and death on the planet. I honestly don't think Darwin would have been very happy about all this.

Let us return to Young's affirmation of Lukács's proposition that nature is a social category. In the face of the implosion described above, that formulation seems inadequate in a basic way. In the Marxist radical science movement of the 1970s, Young formulated the problem in these terms:

> In the nineteenth century, the boundaries between humanity and nature were in dispute. On the whole, nature won, which means that reification won. It is still winning, but some radicals are trying to push back the boundaries of reifying scientism as far as they can, and a critical study of the development of the models which underlie reifying rationalizations may be of service to them as they begin to place science in history – the history of people and events (p. 246).

I would rather say not that 'nature' won, but that the man/nature game is the problem. But this is a quibble within my analysis so far; Young and I are united in identifying crucial parts of the structure of 'reification'.

To oppose reification, Young appealed to a Marxist modification of the premise, 'Man (i.e., human praxis) is the *measure* of all things' (p. 241). But, deeply influenced by the practices of an anti-imperialist environmentalism that joins justice and ecology, and of a multi-cultural feminism that insists on a different imagination of relationality – both social movements that took deep root after Young wrote this essay – I think human praxis formulated this way is precisely part of the problem. In 1973, Young sought a theory of mediations between nature and man. But nature remained either a product of human praxis (nature's state as transformed by the history of people and events), or a pre-social category not yet in relation to the transforming relation of human labour. What nature could not be in these formulations of Marxist humanism is a social partner, a social agent with a history, a conversant in a discourse where all of the actors are not 'us'. A theory of 'mediations' is not enough. If 'human praxis is the measure of all things', then the conversation and its forms of life spell trouble for the planet. And, less consequentially for others but dear to my heart, I'll never get to have a coherent conversation with my anarchist mongrel dog, Alexander Berkman. In Lukács's and Young's story in the 1970s, nature could only be matrix or product, while man had to be the sole agent, exactly the masculinist structure of the human story, including the versions that narrate both the planting and the harvest of Darwinism.

Barbara Noske : *Humans and Other Animals*

We are in troubled waters, but not ones utterly unnavigated by European craft, not to mention other traditions. Animism, however, has a bad name in the language games I need to enter as a critical intellectual in techno-science worlds, and, besides, animism is patently a kind of human representational practice. Though efforts to figure the world in lively terms pervade Hermeticism in early modern Europe, and some important radical and feminist work has tried to reclaim that tradition, there is not really much help for us in that history, I fear. Nevertheless, I think we must engage in forms of life with non-humans – both machines and organisms – on livelier terms than those provided by harvesting Darwinism or Marxism. Refiguring conversations with those who are not 'us' must be part of that project. We have got to strike up a coherent conversation where humans are not the measure of all things, and where no one claims unmediated access to anyone else. Humans, at least, need a different *kind* of theory of mediations.

It is that project that enlivens Barbara Noske's book, *Humans and Other Animals: Beyond the Boundaries of Anthropology*. Noske thoroughly warps the organizing field of humanist stories about nature and culture. Her situation as a radical Western intellectual in the late 1980s, when animal rights movements, environmentalism, feminism, and anti-nuclearism restructure the intellectual and moral heritage of the Left, stands in historical contrast to Young's a decade earlier. Noske's discussion of Darwinism is much poorer scholarship than Young's fine-grained analysis, but she has her finger on a key political-epistemological-moral problem that I don't think the Young of those essays could broach. If he had broached the trouble in our relationship with other organisms in the way Noske does, he certainly could not have resolved the issue as she does.

Noske is consumed by the scandal of the particular kind of object status of animals enforced in the Western histories and cultures she discusses. In Marxist formulations, reification refers to the re-presentation to human labourers of the product of their labour – that is, of the means through which they make themselves historically – in a particular, hostile form. In capitalist relations of production, the human activity embodied in the product of labour is frozen, appropriated, and made to reappear as It, the commodity form that dominates and distorts social life. In that frame, reification is not a problem for domestic animals, but, for example, for tenant farmers, who objectify their labour in the products of animal husbandry and then have the fruit of that labour appropriated by another, who represents it to the worker in a commodity form. But, more fundamentally, the farmer is represented to *himself* in the commodity form. The paradigmatic reification within a Marxist analysis is of the worker *himself*, whose own life-making activity, his labour power, is taken from him and represented in a coercive commodity form. He becomes It. Noske is after another sense of objectification. For her, the Marxist analysis cannot talk about the animals at all. In that frame, animals have no history; they are matrix or raw material for human self-formation, which can go awry, for example, in capitalist relations of production. Animals are not part of the *social* relationship at all; they never have any status but that of not-human, not subject, therefore, object.

But, the kind of 'not-subject, not-human, therefore, object' that animals are made to be is also not like a status occupied by women within patriarchal logics and histories. Feminist analysis that either affirms or resists women's identification with animals as nature and as object has not really gotten the point about animals either, from Noske's provocative point of view. In an important stream of anglo-feminist theory, woman as such does not suffer reification in the way the Marxist describes the process for the worker.[7] In masculinist sexual orders, woman is not a subject separated from the product of her life-shaping activity; her problem is much worse. She is a projection of another's desire, who then haunts man as his always elusive, seductive, unreliable 'other'. Woman as such is a kind of illusionist's projection, while mere women bear the violent erasures of that history-making move. There is nothing of her own for her to reappropriate; she is an object in the sense of *being* another's project.

The kind of objectification of animals that Noske is trying to understand is also not like the history of racial objectification in the West, although the status of slavery in the New World came dizzyingly close to imposing on the enslaved the same kind of *animal* object status borne by beasts, and by nature in general within colonizing logics. In African-American slavery, for example, slaves *were* fully alienable property. Slave women were not like white women – the *conveyers* of property through legitimate marriage.[8] Both slave men and women *were* the property itself. Slave women and men suffered both sexual and racial objectifications in a way that transformed both, but still the situation was not like that of non-human animals. Slave liberation depended on making the *human* subjecthood of the slaves an effective historical achievement. In that history-remaking process, what counts as human, the story of 'man', gets radically recast.

But no matter how recast, this human family drama is not the process of reestablishing the terms of relationality that concerns animals. The last thing they 'need' is human subject status, in whatever cultural-historical form. That is the problem with much animal rights discourse. The best animals could get out of that approach is the 'right' to be permanently represented, as lesser humans, in human discourse, such as the law – animals would get the right to be permanently 'orientalized'. As Marx put it in another context and for other beings, 'They cannot represent themselves; they must be represented.' Lots of well-intentioned, but finally imperialist ecological discourse takes that shape. Its tones resonate with the pro-life/anti-abortion question, 'Who speaks for the foetus?' The answer is, anybody but the pregnant woman, especially if that anybody is a legal, medical, or scientific expert. Or a father. Facing the harvest of Darwinism, we do not need an endless discourse on who speaks for animals, or for nature in general. We have had enough of the language games of fatherhood. We need other terms of conversation with animals, a much less respectable undertaking. The point is not new representations, but new *practices,* other forms of life rejoining humans and not-humans.

So, in the human–animal relationship gone awry, the analogy to other objectifications, so often invoked in radical discourse, breaks down systematically. That is the beauty of Noske's argument. There is *specific* work to be done if we are to strike up a coherent form of life, a conversation, with other animals. 'It may all boil down to a form of anthropocentric colonizing, where everything and everyone is still being measured by a human and Western yardstick. In the context of our law systems, animals are bound to appear as human underlings. However, animals are not lesser humans; they are other worlds, whose otherworldliness must not be disenchanted and cut to our size, but must be respected for what it is' (Noske, p. xi, punctuation corrected). Great, but how? And how especially if there is no *outside* of language games?

Trying to get a grip on this matter, Noske achieves four things that I value highly. First, she starts out by formulating the *historicity* of all the partners in the stories. Animals have been active in their relations to humans, not just the reverse. Domestication, a major focus of Noske's discussion, is paradigmatic for her argument. Although an unequal relationship, domestication is a two-way matter. Domestication refers to the situation in which people actively force changes in the seasonal subsistence cycles of animals to make them coincide with particular human needs. Emphasizing the active aspect and the changing and specific ecologies of both species, the definition Noske uses insists on an historically dynamic continuum of human–animal relations of domestication. From this point of view, capture, taming, and reproductive isolation are relatively recent developments.

Second, in her analysis of contemporary factory-animal domestication, Noske formulates a very useful concept, the 'animal-industrial complex'.[9] Animals are forced to 'specialize' in one 'skill' in a way that would chill the harshest human labour-process deskillers. 'The animal's life-time has truly been converted into "working-time": into round-the-clock production' (p. 17). The design of animals as laboratory research models is one of the most extreme examples of domestication. Not only has the animal been totally *incorporated* into human technology; it has *become* a fully designed instance of human technology.

Noske doesn't discuss genetic engineering, but her argument would readily accommodate those intensifications of reshaping the animals (and humans) to productionist purposes – as, indeed, from the point of view of dominant narratives about the human genome initiative, humans themselves are the reading and writing technologies of their genes. Nature is a technology, and that is a very particular sort of embodied social category.

'We' (who?) have become an instance of 'our' (whose?) technology. The 'Book of Life' (the genome in the title image used by the NOVA television programme *Decoding the Book of Life,* 1988) is the law of life, and the law is paradigmatically a technical affair. Noske agrees with the Dutch philosopher Ton Lemaire that this full objectification of nature could only be complete with the full autonomization of the human subject. Autonomy and auto-maton are more than aural puns. Fully objectified, we are at last finished subjects – or finished *as* subjects. The world of autonomous subjects is the world of objects, and this world works by the law of the annihilation of defended selves imploding with their deadly projections.

Here, Noske, Young, and I are very much in the same conversation. The notion of the 'animal-industrial complex' makes it easy to discuss some of the crucial issues. The consequences of these forms of relating rest on humans and animals, but differently. At the very least, it must be admitted that 'animal exploitation cannot be tolerated without damaging the principle of inter-subjectivity' (p. 38). Here we are getting to the heart of the matter. What is inter-subjectivity between radically different kinds of subjects? The word *subject* is cumbersome, but so are all the alternatives, such as agent, partner, or person. How do we designate radical otherness at the heart of ethical relating? That problem is more than a human one; as we shall see, it is intrinsic to the story of life on earth.

Noske's third achievement is, then, to state unequivocally that a coherent conversation between people and animals depends on our recognition of their 'otherworldly' subject status. In a discussion of various culture concepts in anthropology and in biology, Noske notes that both traditions can only see animal behaviour as the outcome of mechanisms. They cannot take account of the animals' socially constructing their worlds, much less con-structing ours. Biology, in particular, does not have the methodological equipment to recognize 'things socially and culturally created and which in turn shape the creators' (p. 86). In her final chapter, 'Meeting the Other: Towards an Anthropology of Animals', Noske describes the history of Western writing about 'wolf children', very young children believed to be somehow lost from human communities, raised by other social animals, and then found by people. She is interested in how to hear the stories of and about animal-adopted children. So she asks if, instead of asking if people can 'de-animalize' the children by restoring, or teaching for the first time, fully human language, we can instead ask what kind of social thing happened when a human child acquired a specific *non-human* socialization? She imagines that the children did not become human, but they did become social beings. Even in stories of less extreme situations, such as the tales of US, middle-class, professional homes that contain young apes and human children, the children experience animal acculturation, as well as the reverse. For Noske, these situations suggest not so much human–animal communication, as animal–human communication. None of the partners is the same afterwards.

Noske's fourth achievement for me was her use of Sandra Harding's *The Science Question in Feminism* to shift the focus to 'the animal question in feminism' (Noske, pp. 102–16). Noske insists that some feminists' positive identification with animals, including their embracing our own femaleness, and other feminists' resistance to such supposed biological essentialism, are both wrong-headed as long as the terms of the troubled relationship of 'women and nature' are seen within the inherited, ethnocentric subject/object frame that generates the problem of biological reductionism. Noske argues for a feminist position *vis-à-vis* animals that posits continuity, connection and conversation, but without the frame that leads inexorably to 'essentialism'. Essentialism depends on reductive *identification,* rather than ethical *relation,* with other worlds, including with ourselves. It is the paradox of continuity *and* alien relationality that sustains the tension in Noske's book and in her approach to feminism. Once the world of subjects and objects is put into question, that paradox concerns the congeries, or curious confederacy, that is the self, as well as selves' relations with others. A promising form of life, conversation defies the autonomization of the self, as well as the objectification of the other.

Naomi Mitchison: *Memoirs of a Spacewoman*

Science fiction offers a useful writing practice within which to take up Noske's arguments. Published in an explicitly feminist context by The Women's Press in London in 1985, *Memoirs of a Spacewoman* was the first SF novel written by Naomi Mitchison. The story of space exploration, told from the point of view of a woman xenobiologist and communications expert named Mary, was first copyrighted in 1962, when the author was 63 years old and in the midst of a rich career as a national and international political activist and writer. Her references in the 1960s were to a different generation of women's considerations of science and politics than that represented by her later publishers and readers. Daughter of the important British physiologist, J. S. Haldane, and sister of one of the architects of the modern evolutionary synthesis, J. B .S. Haldane, Mitchision could hardly have avoided her large concerns with forms of life. She came, in short, from the social world that produced the Darwins and the Huxleys, those familial arbiters of authoritative terran and otherworldly conversations. Sexual experimentation; political radicalism; unimpeded scientific literacy; literary self-confidence; a grand view of the universe from a rich, imperialist, intellectual culture – these were Mitchison's birthright. She wrote that legacy into her spacewoman's memoirs.

Foregrounding the problem of imperialism, which was the silent, if deeply constitutive, axis in Victorian debates on 'man's place in nature', Mitchison set her xenobiologist a most interesting task: to make contact with 'otherworlds', adhering to only one serious restriction in the deployment of her psychological, linguistic, physical, and technological skills – non-interference. Knowledge would not come from scientific detachment, but from scientific connection. Exploring her garden of delights, spacewoman Mary had to obey only one little restriction. 'Contacts' could take any number of forms – linguistic, sexual, emotional, cognitive, mathematical, aesthetic, mechanical, or, in principle, just about anything else. Erotic fusions, odd couplings and curious progeny structure the humour and the serious inquiry of the novel. Communication, naturally, is inherently about desire; but there's the rub. How could conversation occur, in any form, if the rule of non-interference were to be strictly interpreted? The question of power cannot be evaded, least of all in 'communication'. This was the moral problem for Mary's world: 'Humans were beginning to run out of serious moral problems about the time that space exploration really got going' (Mitchison, p. 16). But no more.

The rule of non-interference wasn't strictly interpreted, of course; so the story could continue. The delicate shades of interference turned out to be what really mattered narratively. 'The difficulty seems to be that in the nursery world we take ourselves for granted as stable personalities, as completely secure. Impossible that we should ever deviate, that interference should ever be a temptation' (p. 19). Every explorer found out otherwise rather quickly. So, the imperative of non-interference constituted the law, the symbolic matrix within which subjects could be called into position for 'conversation'. To obey the founder's law is always impossible; that is the point of the tragi-comic process of becoming a social subject webbed with others. Not to eat of the tree of life in Mitchison's book is not to know the necessary, impossible situation of the communicator's task. Communication, even with ourselves, is xenobiology: otherworldly conversation, terran topics, local terms, situated knowledges. 'It all works out in the end. But the impact of other worlds on this apparently immovable stability comes as a surprise. Nobody enjoys their first personality changes' (p. 19). Neither, presumably, do those with whom contact is made.

In Althusser's sense, in *Memoirs of a Spacewoman* subjects are interpellated, or hailed, into being in a world where the law is not the policeman's 'Hey, you!' or the father's 'Thou shalt not know', but a deceptively gentler moralist's command, 'Be fruitful and multiply; join in conversation, but know that you are not the only subjects. In knowing each other, your worlds will never be the same.' Interference is static, noise, interruption in communication; and yet, interference, making contact, is the implicit condition of leaving the nursery world.

> Although, of course, I longed in the normal human way for exploration, I found my first world oddly disconcerting.... It is only in circumstances like these that we realize how much we ourselves are constructed bi-laterally on either-or principles. Fish rather than echinoderms....It was quite a problem to get through to those radial entities (pp. 19, 20, 23).

The subject-making action – and the moral universe – really begins once those bilateral and radial entities establish touch. And that's only the beginning: 'I think about my children, but I think less about my four dear normals than I think about Viola. And I think about Ariel. And the other' (p. 16).

But, what if we went back to another beginning, to the early days of living organisms on Terra a few billion years ago? That seems a good place to end this meditation on natural conversation as heterogeneous intercourse. Might those yuppie Wisconsin ducks have a legitimate queer birthright after all, and might there be a respectable material foundation to my sexual pleasure in mitochondrial respiratory enzymes? Using Lynn Margulis and Dorion Sagan's *Origins of Sex: Three Billion Years of Genetic Recombination*[10] as my guide, I will tell a concluding story very different from Cantor's version of the human genome project or corporate biotechnology's harvest of Darwinism. As elsewhere, biology in my narrative is also a rich field of metaphors for ethno-specific cultural and political questions. My bag-lady version of Margulis and Sagan's authoritative account of the promiscuous origins of cells that have organelles[11] is about metaphor work. Doing such work is part of my vocation to prepare for my job at the *Readers' Digest* after the revolution. I think this kind of metaphor work could tell us something interesting about the metaphor tools we (who?) might need for a usable theory of the subject at the end of the second Christian millennium.

Consider, then, the text given us by the existence, in the hindgut of a modern Australian termite, of the creature named *Mixotricha paradoxa,* a mixed-up, paradoxical, microscopic bit of 'hair' (*trichos*). This little filamentous creature makes a mockery of the notion of the bounded, defended, singular self out to protect its genetic investments. The problem our text presents is simple: what constitutes *M. paradoxa*? Where does the protist[12] stop and somebody else start in that insect's teeming hindgut? And what does this paradoxical individuality tell us about beginnings? Finally, how might such forms of life help us imagine a usable language?

M. paradoxa is a nucleated microbe with several distinct internal and external prokaryotic symbionts, including two kinds of motile spirochetes, which live in various degrees of structural and functional integration. All the associated creatures live in a kind of obligate confederacy. From Margulis and Sagan's 'symbiogenetic' point of view, this kind of confederacy is fundamental to life's history. Such associations probably arose repeatedly. The ties often involved genetic exchanges, or recombinations, that in turn had a history dating back to the earliest bacteria that had to survive the gene-damaging environment of ultra-violet light before there was an oxygen atmosphere to shield them.

> That genetic recombination began as a part of an enormous health delivery system to ancient DNA molecules is quite evident. Once healthy recombinants were produced, they retained the ability to recombine genes from different sources. As long as selection acted on the recombinants, selection pressure would retain the mechanism of recombination as well (p. 60).

I like the idea of gene exchange as a kind of prophyllaxis against sunburn. It puts the heliotropic West into perspective.

Protists like *M. paradoxa* seem to show in mid-stream the ubiquitous, life-changing association events that brought motile, oxygen-using, or photo-synthetic bacteria into other cells, perhaps originally on an opportunistic hunt for a nutritious meal or a secure medium for their metabolic transactions. But some predators settled down inside their prey and struck up quite a conversation. Mitochondria, those oxygen-using organelles with the interesting respiratory enzymes integrated into membrane structures, probably joined what are now modern cells in this way.

> With the elapse of time, the internal enemies of the prey evolved into microbial guests, and, finally, supportive adopted relatives. Because of a wealth of molecular biological and biochemical evidence supporting these models, the mitochondria of today are best seen as descendants of cells that evolved within other cells (p. 71).

The story of heterogeneous associations at various levels of integration repeated itself many times at many scales.

> Clones of eukaryotic cells in the form of animals, plants, fungi, and protoctists seem to share a symbiotic history.... From an evolutionary point of view, the first eukaryotes were loose confederacies of bacteria that, with continuing inte-gration, became recognizable as protists, unicellular eukaryotic cells.... The earliest protists were likely to have been most like bacterial communities.... At first each autopoietic [self-maintaining] community member replicated its DNA, divided, and remained in contact with other members in a fairly informal manner. *Informal* here refers to the number of partners in these confederacies: they varied (p. 72).

Indeed, they varied.

So, speaking as a multi-cellular, eukaryotic, bilaterally symmetrical confederacy – a fish, in short – I want to learn to strike up interesting intercourse with possible subjects about livable worlds. In nineteenth-century bourgeois US law, such sexually suspect doings were called criminal conversation. Mitchison's spacewoman understood: 'Although, of course, I longed in the normal human way for exploration, I found my first world oddly disconcerting. . . .'

Notes

1 Katie King. 1990. *Conversations*. Book prospectus, University of Maryland, Women's Studies Program.

2 Here I borrow from the wonderful project of the journal *Public Culture,* Bulletin of the Center for Transnational Cultural Studies, The University Museum, University of Pennsylvania, Philadelphia, PA 19104. In my opinion, this journal embodies the best impulses of cultural studies.

3 Evelyn Fox Keller. 1990. 'From Secrets of Life to Secrets of Death'. In *Body/Politics. Women and the Discourses of Science,* eds Mary Jacobus, E. F. Keller, Sally Shuttleworth (New York: Routledge), pp. 177–91.

4 Ursula LeGuin. 1989. 'The Carrier-Bag Theory of Fiction'. In *Women of Vision,* pp. 1–11.

5 *Adam's Task: Calling Animals by Name* (New York: Knopf, 1986), p. 4.

6 In his preface to the 1985 reprinting of his essays, Young gives his justification for not dealing with the language of the pseudo-universal, 'man', in his revisions: 'I cannot resolve the question of gender in these essays: 'man's place in nature' was the rhetoric of the period, and 'he' had characteristic resonances which it would be anachronistic to expunge, and this set the style' (p. xvii). I disagree not with Young's decision to keep 'man' and 'he', but with the absence of sustained discussion of precisely what *difference* the 'characteristic resonances' and the 'style' made to nineteenth-century discourse and to Young's discourse. Feminist demands are not to expunge offensive material, but to require precise analysis of how the unmarked categories work – and how we continue to inherit the trouble. That analysis could not proceed if the problem were made harder to see by covering up 'man' with a euphemistic and anachronistic 'human'. Some of Young's most important discussions, for example, in the essay on 'Malthus and the Evolutionists', originally published in 1969, before recent feminist theory could have made a difference, by the mid-1980s merited at least a footnote on how feminist analyses require a restructuring of historical understanding of the debates about natural theology, human perfection and evolution. Minimally, Malthus's argument against Godwin's version of future human perfection through the complete transcendence of need, especially sex, and Malthus's doctrine on the private ownership of women and children in the institution of marriage were intrinsic to the establishment of a constitutively self-invisible masculinist discourse in natural theology. Similarly, in 'Natural Theology,

Victorian Periodicals, and the Fragmentation of a Common Context', I waited for some discussion of how the processes of specialization and publication fundamentally restructured the gender fabric of the practice of evolutionary biology. The 1985 postscript to that essay might have been a place to say something about how feminist theory makes one rethink the issues of 'common context' and 'fragmentation'. I also think Young should have revised some of his notes, especially for 'The Historiographic and Ideological Contexts of the Nineteenth-Cenutry Debate on Man's Place in Nature', themselves a real treasure for which I remain in his debt politically and professionally, to take better account of feminist theory in the field. It is because his notes are otherwise so exhaustive that I am critical of the very thin attention to feminist reformulations of science studies debates (see note 174.2 on p. 273; here would have been an oppportunity). Bob Young's notes helped train me in the history of science; that's why I am disappointed in this aspect of his revisions for the 1985 book. The unexamined commitment to masculinism in the chief texts of the history of science to which Young reacted at Cambridge remained present in too much of the radical science movement and its literatures. The same commitment to masculinism is evident in the canonized texts of the current social studies of science orthodoxy, e.g., the important books by Steve Shapin and Simon Schaffer, *The Leviathan and the Air-Pump* (Princeton: Princeton University Press, 1985) and by Bruno Latour, *Science in Action* (Cambridge: Harvard University Press, 1987). This trouble must not be allowed to persist in the movement to address science as culture, in which Young is a creative leader.

7   I am indebted here to Catharine MacKinnon, 'Feminism, Marxism, Method, and the State: An Agenda for Theory', *Signs* 7,3 (1982): pp. 515–44.

8   Here I rely heavily on Hazel Carby, *Reconstructing Womanhood* (New York: Oxford University Press, 1987), and Hortense Spillers, 'Mama's Baby, Papa's Maybe: An American Grammar Book', *Diacritics* 17, 2 (1987): pp. 65–81.

9   To my mind, on this subject as elsewhere in her interesting and rich book, Noske makes sweeping generalizations and does not ask carefully enough how her claims should be limited or modified. Her discussion of the history of 'objectifying' Western science is particularly stereotypical in this regard. Other discussions, like those about the history of primate behavioural studies, are much better. But these issues are quibbles in relation to the fundamental and synthetic project of her book, which remains unique in green (environmentalist), red (socialist), purple (feminist), and ultra-violet (scientific) literatures. Noske's book is firmly located in critical conversation with social movements and with natural and social sciences on the tricky problem of anthropocentrism.

10 New Haven: Yale University Press, 1986.

11 Such cells are called *eukaryotes;* they have a membrane-bound nucleus and other differentiated internal structures. *Prokaryotes,* or bacteria, do not have a nucleus to house their genetic material, but keep their DNA naked in the cell.

12 A protist is a single-celled, eukaryoyic micro-organism, such as the familiar amoeba. Plants, animals, and fungi descended from such beginnings.

PART 2

Biohazards:
Risk in Context

The Limits of Experimental Knowledge: A Feminist Perspective on the Ecological Risks of Genetic Engineering

REGINE KOLLEK

Micro-organisms are categorized into four groups, according to their risk potential for humans, animals or plants (WHO, 1979a, 1979b). The safety measures which must be applied when handling these micro-organisms are related to the degree and type of risk associated with each respective group. The classification of micro-organisms is, therefore, conducted on the basis of known levels of safety and danger, reflecting longstanding empirical proof, and is not, therefore, based on theoretical considerations. This concept has been applied to work with organisms which have been altered by means of genetic engineering. Here, a manipulated organism is in principle classified on the basis of the host organism and the transplanted gene, that is according to the additive model (Kollek, 1988a, p. 113, 1988b). It is questionable, however, whether this concept, which is characteristic of conventional biotechnology, can be applied to work with genetically engineered organisms. Nevertheless, it is accepted widely by legislative and executive bodies. Since the risks of genetic engineering will affect all of us, it is necessary to scrutinize whether it is an adequate basis for the evaluation of the risks associated with genetically engineered organisms.

The Epistemic Background of Experimental Science

According to the traditional ideal of scientific inquiry, reality should be perceived by the researcher during the process of research as correctly, completely, and objectively as possible. Methodological rules and standardized processes are designed to optimize this process of perception. Some of these basic rules were defined in 1630 by the French philosopher René Descartes. They were designed to guide theoretical or other approaches to mathematical phenomena in the pursuit of knowledge (Descartes, 1972). Although Descartes later reflected critically on the epistemic significance of these rules, they represented for a long time, and to a certain extent even today, the basis of scientific methodology.

The first rule asserts that it should be the goal of scientific studies to orientate perception in such a way that it can generate objective knowledge about all existing objects and phenomena (Descartes, 1972, p. 3). In other words, conclusions drawn by means of scientific logic and methodology can be claimed to be true and objectively given. The second rule prescribes that only those objects or phenomena should be subjected to scientific inquiry which can be approached by scientific means (Descartes, 1972, p. 5). This rule defines the domain of scientific inquiry, but by defining the sphere which can be perceived by scientific means, it implicitly also defines the phenomena which are relevant to the scientist. Phenomena which can not be approached or examined by scientific methods are not recognized as fields where knowledge can possibly be acquired.

The first two rules outline the scope of science. In his fourth rule Descartes points out the necessity of methods for the acquisition of systematic knowledge, and goes on to explicate this in the fifth rule. The most important task of methods is the classification of phenomena in order to reveal relevant characteristics (Descartes, 1972, p. 16). One must adhere to this principle if complex phenomena, intricate circumstances or hypotheses are to be subjected to scientific examination. They must be reduced step by step to simpler phenomena, processes, or interactions. On the basis of knowledge about the most simple elements of a phenomenon it should then be possible to reconstruct them by reconstructing the process of reduction.

Descartes designed these rules in order to solve problems of mathematics and physics. Furthermore, it was his intention to rationalize scientific discourse and to confront the widespread practice of wild speculations about natural phenomena with a systematic search for truth. In the further development of science, this approach also prevailed in other disciplines, where it was applied to analysing complex problems and to systematizing empirical phenomena. The systematic analysis of repeatedly observed phenomena or events – such as the appearance of comets or the distribution of flower colours after cross-breeding of red and white pea plants – led to the definition of rules and principles which were believed to influence and control those natural phenomena.[1]

At the beginning of the seventeenth century Francis Bacon, considered to be the other founder of modern science, propagated the experiment for the better understanding of natural phenomena. His methodological proposal was rapidly successful because many natural phenomena and events are of tremendous complexity, so that their underlying principles cannot be discovered by observation alone. Furthermore, in the course of an experiment, objects can be withdrawn from the real world, examined under controlled conditions and also exposed to specific factors and influences. Hence, effects could be studied which were not previously visible. By thus abstracting from preceding environmental relations, knowledge could be increased and new possibilities of controlling and manipulating objects could be tested. These procedures still form a relevant part of experimental science today. They promote the 'invention of new skills' with which it might be possible to reveal the hidden and secret parts of nature. For Bacon, this was the central objective and the path which should be taken by humankind (mankind) in order to rule the universe (Bacon, 1970, p. 415). Science or, more specifically, the acquisition of new knowledge and new products by way of new skills and methods, was in Bacon's eyes also control over nature, which conferred social and political power on those who had this knowledge and those skills at their command.[2]

One principle of the proposed experimental methods was and is to examine the properties of physical objects under controlled conditions. This principle was later also applied to cellular and molecular biology. Following the paradigm of theoretical and methodological reduction of complex phenomena to ever more simple elements, experimental approaches in molecular biology concentrate on the elucidation of molecular mechanisms within cells and the genetic base for these mechanisms. Here again, through the exclusion of preceding contextual relationships, objects and phenomena are stripped of seemingly superfluous, unnecessary or undesired complexities which hinder the identification of the 'real nature' of the object or process in question. Thus, contextual relationships themselves are not the object of scientific inquiry. The 'loss of meaning' which results from the theoretical and experimental process of abstraction in molecular biology is substantiated by the difficulties in explaining certain empirical or experimental phenomena using reductionist interpretations. Before some examples of such phenomena are outlined, a short introduction into the characteristics of genetic engineering techniques will be given.

The Characteristics of Genetic Alterations Using Genetic Engineering Techniques

Genetic engineering generally involves the excision of individual genes or sections of chromosomes from a particular genome; they are transferred into a different cell and, thus, a different genomic background. In this way it is possible to overcome the barriers which normally limit the arbitrary cross-breeding of organisms of different species. This is precisely the characteristic feature of a species, that is, that only members of a species can be crossed with each other and that it is ordinarily impossible with individuals of another species. Nevertheless, there are exceptions to this rule and hybrids between species are possible, although normally between closely related species (for example, mules). It is also possible to use genetic engineering to overcome the barriers which limit the exchange of genetic material where bacteria are concerned (compatibility of groups, differences in the structure of the cell wall, ecological divisions). Since several different changes can be effected using this method within a relatively short period of time, a time-lapse effect is created relative to normal evolutionary processes.

In contrast to the mechanisms which are assumed to form the basis of natural evolution, manipulations performed in the field of genetic engineering make possible (1) practically any number and type of changes in the relations between neighbouring genes, that is, in the genetic context of a particular gene; (2) an exchange of genes between different species which in terms of its qualitative and quantitative characteristics goes far beyond what is observed within the framework of natural mechanisms; and (3) a reduction in the time required for the development of new species or breeds compared to conventional breeding methods or evolution itself. Finally, it is possible with the help of this range of methods – possibly for the first time in the history of life – to design and synthesize new genetic material, for which older, related predecessors of this genetic material do not necessarily have to exist.

Parameters related to space, time, biology and natural history which influence the characteristics of individual organisms as well as the way they interact with other organisms, and which have proven themselves to be useful, perhaps even necessary, to life on earth, are therefore altered by genetic engineering techniques (Kollek, 1989, p. 19). Organisms are being created with genetic information and characteristics which they previously did not possess. It is precisely this novelty which is the basis of the potential usefulness of genetically engineered organisms and which makes genetic engineering and its products so interesting for a whole range of possible applications. And it is precisely the novelty outlined above which contains the risk: in the case of deliberate or accidental release of new forms of life, nature which developed of its own accord must cope with this new form of nature which has been invented. Negative ecological consequences could result from these interactions.

Controversial Concepts in the Relationship between Genotype and Phenotype

In order to understand the relationships between changes in the genetic material induced by the techniques of genetic engineering (recombinant DNA technology) and this risk potential, it is necessary to analyse the factors and procedures which are involved in the generation of risk. In this perspective, one concept appears to be of special significance: that of a solely genetically based biology as represented by deterministic concepts. The question is, whether or not such an understanding of organisms is sufficient to explain known phenomena or whether in fact other or additional conditions and factors must be postulated. If the characteristics of (non-human) organisms are to a great extent or even entirely based on genetic mechanisms, then one must conclude, on this logic, that changes in such characteristics which can be induced through experimental gene transfer will be, in principle, predictable.

The term *gene* was first used in 1909 by the Danish plant breeder W. Johannsen to refer to an element of the heritability of traits. He also used the term *phenotype* for all of the traits which become visible in the life of an individual organism, defining this phenotype as the result of the inter-action between inherited traits and the environment. For Johannsen it was particularly important that the phenotype, which he saw as the visible form and spectrum of behavioural patterns influenced in part by the environ-ment, be clearly distinguished from the genotype or the hereditarian type. However, under the influence of the school of thought promoted by Thomas Morgan (the prominent US geneticist), he changed this concept two years later, defining the genotype as the sum of all genes leading directly to the realization of the phenotype (Jahn, Lother and Senglaub, 1985, p. 472). Apparently, however, Johannsen remained divided in his understanding of the mechanisms of heredity of phenotypes and their material bases. Despite the fact that he retracted the concept of the phenotype as being influenced by environmental factors in 1911, he wrote in 1913:

> On the one hand we thus have the essence of all genes – the genotype – as the basic constitution of the organism. On the other hand we have the environment, the 'conditions of living' – and the often extremely complex interaction between the genotype and the environment which result in the actual individual traits of each organism (Jahn, Lother and Senglaub, 1985, p. 473).

Thus, from the very beginning of genetics, there were different concepts of the relationship between genotype and phenotype. In the course of time, however, the concepts of traits and genes changed more and more. Today in molecular genetics the concept of a gene refers to a segment of the DNA which can have regulatory functions or can be translated into a protein. However, in spite of the elucidation of the molecular structure of many chromosome segments, our knowledge of the structure and the biochemical make up of DNA or of a specific protein does not allow us to infer which biological function a particular protein will have in the cell or how the activity of that protein will affect organs or the interaction between different organisms. Two examples from cellular and molecular biology will be discussed here (in the terms of biochemistry and molecular biology) to illustrate this point.

Position Effects

As a result of evolutionary processes, all organisms are genetically related to one another in some specific way. Therefore, some organisms which are not closely related phylogenetically nonetheless have similar or identical nucleic acid sequences or functional genes. For example, a particular enzyme, an isomerase, can be found in bacteria as well as in yeast cells, insects and mammals. This enzyme, as found in these various species, has extensive homologies in the amino acid sequences, as well as in its biochemical properties. More careful examination shows, however, that proteins with identical or similar biochemical properties do not automatically also have similar biological functions. This specific protein, as found in the fruit fly, apparently catalyses the folding of a pigment which is involved in vision, whereas the protein found in mammalian life forms seems to be involved in the regulation of the maturation of immune cells. This means that one enzyme (and the relevant gene) can influence very different biological phenomena with a different ecological relevance, depending on the genetic, cellular or phylogenetic context in which it is found (Fischer *et al.*, 1989; Shieh *et al.*, 1989; Takahashi *et al.*, 1989).

The second example illustrating the contextual relevance of genetic information is from the area of cancer research. The processes which lead to the transformation of a cell into a cancer cell are extremely complex. According to the present status of experimental and theoretical work, certain proteins, the products of so-called oncogenes, are involved in cooperation with other genes in the stepwise transformation of a cell into a cancer cell. In many cases oncogenes are derived from genes which participate in the regulation of growth and differentiation processes. The influence of their gene products on physiological processes in the cell can change under certain circumstances, that is, when (a) the nucleic acid sequence of such DNA segments is modified by natural mechanisms or through genetic engineering manipulations, or (b) more important here, when these sequences are introduced into a different chromosomal environment with the help of such mechanisms. In both cases the specific cell is thus transformed into a premalignant or malignant form (Bishop, 1987).

These examples show that the biological effect of the gene is changed when it is introduced into a different chromosomal environment. The biological function of a gene and/or the respective gene product is thus influenced not only by its sequence but also by its specific location within a particular chromosomal and cellular context. Genetic studies on the fruit fly *Drosophila* have shown that there is a concrete relationship between the spatial arrangement of the genetic material and its functional activity. The resulting effects were described by Sturtevant, an American geneticist, as position effects in the 1920s (Sinnott, Dunn, and Dobzhansky, 1958, pp. 379–80). The term stands for an empirical concept which enables cytogeneticists to describe phenomena observed on the phenotypical level and which have been localized by means of chromosomal studies. It has also been introduced into molecular genetics but both molecular geneticists and cytogeneticists have been unable to postulate a theoretical explication of this term. To date, there is no comprehensive theory capable of describing the relationships between the functional effect of a gene and its spatial arrangement within the genome. The fact that such position effects exist means as a consequence that the biological significance of a gene is not sufficiently described solely by its nucleic acid sequence, nor that of a protein by its amino acid sequence, but that rather the relevant topographical data, that is, at least the chromosomal and cellular context, must also be taken into consideration. We must also assume that the time scheme of the activation of a gene can also be influenced by its spatial arrangement within the chromosome. In order to understand the biological (that is, cellular, physiological and ecological) function of a gene, the biochemical description must be complemented by one which considers spatial and temporal factors. In contrast to the amino acid sequence of proteins, these factors are not or, in the case of position effects, only indirectly coded in the DNA. Thus they cannot be deduced from the structure of individual genes.

Epigenetic Phenomena

Phenotypes, however, are influenced not only by their genes and their chromosomal and cellular context, but also by their extracellular surroundings and the general environment. Although somatic cells – that is, those cells which form organs and the different kinds of tissue within an organism – with few exceptions all have the same DNA structure, morphologically they differ extremely. According to the interpretation of cell biology, this morphological variance which gives each type of cell a particular identity results from the stable interaction between the genome and its direct surroundings (its so-called micro-environment). During cultivation under experimental conditions, cells of differentiated tissues increasingly lose their differentiated functions. The stable inheritance of the differentiated state of a cell thus depends upon the specific organization of the tissue in the environment, that is, on the epigenetic context (Rubin, 1988). (A similar principle holds for embryonal development.) The DNA and its direct surroundings (that is to say the genetic and cellular context) are not changed. They are the same in both cases. The stability or the loss of the differentiated state thus is not influenced by changes in the structure of the genetic material of the cell, but rather by spatial and temporal interactions of the cells.

All these findings show that a reductionist and deterministic approach, according to which DNA is the sole driving force of cellular and developmental processes, is not sufficient to explain the transmission and realization of biological information in an adequate manner, nor is it capable of describing fully the phenotype of a cell or an organism.

Reduction of Contexts and Risk: The Price of Abstraction

The examples discussed in the previous sections show that the biological significance of genetic information is to a great extent dependent on contexts, and that a gene or a gene product may have different biological meanings in different contexts. Ignoring contexts which are defined as not being relevant for a particular area of research is, on the one hand, the prerequisite for the success and efficiency of this strategy and, on the other hand, a prerequisite for the manipulation of the research object. Since these contexts are not the object of laboratory research, the knowledge that is acquired is not relevant or at least not sufficient to controlling these objects under conditions other than those found in the laboratory or in production units. That is, it is not knowledge about the practical conditions of use. The limits of control are thus reached when the objects have been experimentally transformed and are again confronted with complexity and contingency. This is exactly what happens when genetically engineered organisms are created and then put to practical use.

The principle of genetic engineering manipulations is to transfer genes from one organism to another. These genes enter a new genetic context and the products resulting from them enter new cellular and thus also epigenetic and ecological environments. It is not possible to determine beforehand whether these gene products will be of specific significance in these new contexts or whether they will interact with other gene products already present in the cell. In contrast to the possibility of evaluating or predicting the possible behaviour of already existing organisms, there is to date very little empirical experience for such predictions with regard to the interactions of genetically altered organisms with the environment. Such interactions cannot be (completely) deduced from the behaviour of such organisms under controlled conditions, since they will be realized only in confrontation with the open environment. This process of interpretation is decisive in determining whether these modified objects will die off, be integrated without causing deleterious effects for their surroundings or, in fact, cause problematic interactions, damage, or catastrophies. The efficiency of this strategy of experimental manipulation under controlled conditions is thus tied to the loss of predictability in the environment. Not every genetically engineered modification will increase the risk potential of a specific organism. The problem, however, is to elucidate which manipulations will have which consequences. Uncertainty and risk are thus the price which must be paid for the total accessibility and control of these living objects in the laboratory.

In the actual practice of risk assessment, it is often assumed that a recombinant organism does not pose a higher risk than the original host organism, plus the specific risk potential of the foreign gene which has been introduced (BMFT, 1986). Such a classification is thus based on the addition of the characteristics of the host organism and those of the transferred gene, the so-called 'additive model' (Kollek, 1988a, p. 113; 1988b). According to this view, the characteristics of an organism are seen as the result of the sum of its genes. The addition of a specific gene causes, at most, the addition of the traits coded for by the transferred gene. According to this understanding, the gene is a carrier of information which is independent of the organism or the specific genetic background: that is, the gene is the carrier of context-independent information. Seen from this perspective, one cannot expect that organisms would develop surprising or unknown traits through the transfer of genes with known nucleic acid sequences.

However, although there are cases which can possibly be described in an additive fashion, the examples discussed above show that many biological phenomena cannot be adequately described with this model. Such a model can, at best, be used as a base for risk assessment in cases in which complexity and the interconnections of different contexts are limited, that is when only endogenous (intracellular) but not exogenous (extracellular) contexts, such as interactions with other cells or organisms, are involved. This is, for example, the case when manipulated organisms are found in controllable surroundings with a low level of variation, for example, within the physical containment of a biotechnological production unit. Such a perspective becomes problematic, however, when complexity and interactions are great (Duerr, 1988, p. 87), such as when transgenic cells or organisms are deliberately or accidentally released into the environment and when the biological effects of the transferred genes unfold in epigenetic and ecological contexts.

The risk of the introduction of experimentally modified organisms thus stems from the fact that no certain prediction can be made as to how information which has been changed on the genetic level will influence levels of higher complexity or, in other words, change the network of inter-correlated functions. An analysis of risks which arise as a result of genetic transfer, both for the organism itself and for the environment with which it interacts, must therefore consider the contextual dependencies of genes, tissues and organisms as part of the research strategy.

Approaching the Meaning of Context[3]

We have seen that the significance of a biological structure is not only the result of the physico-chemical characteristics of its elements, but also of the spatial and temporal relationships to other elements and structures. The context of a gene, a protein, or a cell also influences biological significance. However, we have not yet described in more detail what the concept of context actually means and how it is defined.

The example of embryonal development shows that contexts not only reflect a difference of perspective between the organizational levels of life (chromosome, cell, organ, etc.), but also differences in the establishment of patterns in dependence on space and time. It is not just that the direct sur-roundings lend significance to individual parts in the sense of functionalistic interactions. Rather, the continual development of an object in time creates a precondition for its interaction with other objects at specific points in time. Environment and time are thus not only the prerequisite and the framework for the unfolding and development of the inherent potential of a particular object, but also influence the object itself.[4] Within this process of change they produce a specific spatial and temporal structure.

The characteristics of biological objects are thus, at least to a certain extent, relative. They must be described in relationship to the elements of a particular surrounding and against the background of a particular develop-mental history of the components involved, that is to say, within a particular context. A context, however, does not define the structural and functional interaction of different elements in the sense of a construction plan, nor does it contain the information for the structuring of biological (or social) units. Instead, the concept of context is to be understood as one of a 'framework which creates significance'.[5] A context therefore represents the possibility of interpreting the significance of an object or of an empirical observation in or for a particular situation. In this sense context is clearly a theoretical concept which does not correspond to a biological (or social) structure, independent of the organizational level of life forms to which it refers, although such structures may be an element of a particular context.

The Limits of Experimental Knowledge

In describing the characteristics of genes it is therefore essential that one consider their context and the existing relationships to other genes and biological interactions. If these are not considered as part of the analysis, false statements about the characteristics of the object studied, in this case a gene, may result. Knowledge which is acquired experimentally is therefore at first relevant to the conditions under which particular phenomena were observed or measured. This means that what is studied in the laboratory under experimental conditions is not nature as such but more precisely specific parts or aspects of nature which can be studied or tested under specific laboratory conditions.

Following this analysis, we realize that the part of nature studied has actually been recreated in an artificial world. What we learn by laboratory experiments does not represent knowledge about nature, but rather knowledge about an experimentally manipulated nature. Scientific statements are thus relevant only for this manipulated nature and for that which can be grasped through scientific methodology and the technical instruments which have been employed. They do not apply to the behaviour of the object of study in the world outside the laboratory. Furthermore, different methods describe the object of study from different perspectives and thus produce different images of reality. The answers we receive are dependent on the questions asked. The methods used are both the megaphone and the hearing aid of the scientific researcher.

This problem can be illustrated through the analogy of a fisherman who uses a net with a mesh of two inches. Because he only catches fish which are larger than two inches in diameter, he could conclude that fish are always larger than two inches. In a similar situation, a scientist would formulate a law of nature. Hans-Peter Duerr (1988, p. 71) has offered a new interpretation of this parable which was originally formulated by the English astrophysicist Sir Arthur Eddington (1939). Duerr relates the parable to our limited ability to recognize nature with scientific, in this case experimental, laboratory methods. In his eyes, the net symbolizes the reduction of reality in changes in the quality of perception caused by our scientific point of view.

Theories used as a background for developing questions about nature and the methods that are intended to help in answering these questions have emerged in historical and social contexts. They are thus not neutral in their relationship to reality. Put in a different way, science can be seen as a social undertaking of human beings who act in accordance with specific laws which have developed in a specific historical context and are subject to social change. These laws structure the framework of experience and action by scientists. This structuring is effective with the help of different mechanisms, among them for example specific lines of questioning, special technical instruments, patterns of action and of perception, as well as a specific language and a body of knowledge which accumulates in the course of time. These mechanisms stabilize what Thomas Kuhn has called a paradigm. A paradigm can be defined as a system of laws which determines what kind of questions are acceptable, which strategies of answering these questions are considered scientifically acceptable and which are not. A paradigm defines a framework within which normal science takes place (Kuhn, 1967). This also means that there are no singular truths about nature, but rather that that which is observed is influenced by the questions asked and the structural instruments which are used.

This short view of the history, the prerequisites and the preconditions which have determined the development of science in the past, and continue to influence it today, show that we can only expect to have a transient view of natural phenomena and natural objects. It is determined by science and those who do science in two different ways: first through the manipulative interventions which are necessary to carry out an experiment (for example, most of the living organisms are dead or in some way manipulated in the course of study), and second through the questions and instruments which have brought to our consciousness exactly this and no other image of nature.

This does not mean that we cannot achieve a close approximation of an understanding of reality through systematically searching and asking questions, complemented by historical and practical experience, so that we are capable of building instruments and production units which function. The interpretation of science as a creator of instrumental knowledge as it is formulated here does not question its powerfulness, its precision, or its successes with regard to the construction of new effects and products. Scientific thought is most successful 'where the interactions between different components are weak, where the whole comes close to being understandable as the sum of its parts thought in isolation', that is, in closed systems where only a limited number of factors have an effect. 'Scientific thought becomes problematic, however, wherever networks are strong and complexity is great' (Duerr, 1988, p. 87).

Experiments in Reality

Scientists learn in a laboratory that their objects of study behave according to existing theories. This is not surprising since theories have been formulated on the basis of laboratory experience. Scientists, but also many other people, tend not only to apply the principles found under such conditions to a specific experimental system, but also to consider them to be valid in other contexts. The impression is thus created that knowledge developed in closed systems under controlled conditions has unlimited validity in open systems as well. This conclusion is neither founded in theoretical considerations, nor always confirmed by practical experience. It becomes particularly significant when we attempt to predict the results of interventions in the natural environment on the basis of laboratory experiments.

The aim of laboratory experiments is to create conditions which are as constant or controllable as possible. In the environment this is not feasible; the factors of influence (temperatures, humidity, the flow of substances, the variety of specific species, etc.) change constantly. These changes may follow certain regular principles but can hardly be predicted exactly. Rare occurrences (earthquakes, hurricanes, flooding, droughts, volcanic eruptions, etc.) are always possible. Since the characteristics of living organisms in the environment are also defined by their relationships to other living and non-living elements of the environment, it must be expected that they will behave in relation to these environmental parameters. In particular in the case of genetically engineered organisms not previously found in the environment, exact predictions about their behaviour and thus about specific risk potential cannot be made. This is beyond the theoretical and experimental borders of the laboratory. In the confrontation between primary, evolutionary nature and this secondary, synthetic nature uncertainties and risks emerge which can no longer be grasped and described with the theories of experimental science (Bonß, Hohlfeld and Kollek, 1989).

Here the limits in the scope and validity of scientific statements and theories are reached, at least in those cases in which they have been formulated predominantly on the basis of laboratory experiments. Today there is intensive work in progress aimed at finding theoretical models for the behaviour of open changing systems capable of development. But although it may be possible to develop such models, which describe actual or real relationships and their dynamics better than those models which are developed on the basis of closed systems, the scope of statements made on the basis of such models is also limited in principle. The reasons for these limits are based on the fact that it is impossible, for theoretical and practical reasons, to predict all possible events and to calculate the probability of their realization.

In contrast we are confronted today with a situation in which genetically modified organisms are being released into the environment. At present the numbers of different modified organisms which are to be released will be relatively small. The problem of predictability of their behaviour in the environment will become even more significant when large-scale application of such products takes place in the future. By often failing to explicitly point out the theoretical and practical problems of predictability, scientists mask the experimental nature of such releases and the fact that the knowledge necessary to understand and describe risks can only be won through such experiments. However, release experiments, like any other, can fail. In some cases, the organisms will not be able to establish themselves in the environment, in others they may cause irreversible and large-scale damage. It is questionable whether such experiments will be reversible in every case: in other words, whether the consequences of scientific curiosity will themselves be reversible. In contrast to chemical substances, these laboratory products can reproduce and change further in the environment. Since the outcome of such releases into the environment cannot be exactly predicted, they are in fact experiments in the environment and with the environment (Krohn and Weyer, 1989).

Conclusions

By deliberately (or accidentally) releasing laboratory products into the environment, experimental science abandons the ground on which it is, on the basis of its own experience, capable of making valid statements and reliable predictions. Even after consulting ecologists, population biologists and other scientific disciplines which contribute to the contemporary understanding of real world biological phenomena, it is difficult to legitimate such unreliable and risky experiments on the basis of the goals of scientific research alone. Therefore, they are often declared to be the application of reliable knowledge in the pursuit of goals, the benefits or necessity of which it is hard to doubt. In connection with the deliberate release of genetically manipulated organisms, the main goals are named as contributions to the solution of the worldwide problems of hunger and environmental pollution.

But such experiments in the environment are not only about solutions to important global problems. Rather, they are also about specific interests of scientific research and the broadening of the sphere of activity and influence of science. Scientific experts are supposed to be the ones with the power to define which are the adequate strategies for solving social and political problems. In this process, these global problems are defined according to well-known patterns which make the application of genetic engineering methods appear essential. The problems themselves are defined in such a way that only the desired methods appear applicable. In this way, scientists hold fast to the second Cartesian rule according to which, 'one should only deal with such objects, for which our power of knowledge clearly is sufficient to produce reliable and indubitable knowledge about their nature' (Descartes, 1972, p. 5). By proceeding in this fashion, science confronts society with risks and dangers which society has a right to reject. This is not a question of a limitation of the right to freedom of research, but rather a question of the limits of experimental science and its statements about reality, about the limits of science itself.

Several feminist scientists have drawn our attention to these limits of scientific knowledge. They have analysed the consequences which result from the lack of self-reflection within science and the application of additive models as a basis for describing human nature. For example, in her study on women, feminism and biology Lynda Birke criticizes the ascription of the social phenomenon of 'male dominance' to hormone levels, thus reducing it to a simple biological cause. She points out that there is no scientific evidence for the assumption that biology and environmental influences can simply be added to each other, and she rejects the hypothesis that we can thus find out about the biological base of human nature by varying the superstructure. She continues:

> Such additive models of human nature are common, but they are fundamentally flawed in one major respect: they do not readily allow for the possibility that the biology itself might be influenced by the superstructure. That such two-way influences can indeed operate is part of the argument proposed against the additive model (Birke, 1986, p. 44).

According to Birke's analysis, the existence of women's subordination is likely to be seen as the product of invariable biology. Implicit in this is the idea that biology is somehow primary and that on to this the accretions of the social and cultural context can be added. '"Gender", according to this additive view, emerges first from the action of biological factors, be they genes or hormones or whatever; and second from the actions of various social factors, such as learning about gender-differentiated behaviour' (Birke, 1986, pp. 53–4). The problem with the additive model is that it ignores other factors of influence, like parental and social expectations and the interactions with the environment, which occur at all stages of development and provoke new patterns of interaction.

When Birke's analysis is compared with the one on the risks of genetic engineering presented in this chapter, important parallels become visible. Although both perspectives recognize the relevance of biology, they reject explicitly biological determinism (Birke, 1986, p. 54) and oppose the concept of a linear relationship between genotype (biochemistry) and phenotype (behaviour). These parallels indicate that there is an intimate correlation between those concepts which are used to describe the nature of non-human organisms and those describing human nature. To elucidate the 'secret patriarchal substance' (Ruebsamen, 1983) of scientific conceptualizations of nature, it is therefore necessary to focus analysis on the methodological approach to nature and the deductions founded on this basis.

Notes

Acknowledgement. I would like to thank Paula Bradish for convincing me that I should write this article, and for her help in translating it into English.

1 For a detailed description of the Cartesian ideas and their historical context, see the work of Carolyn Merchant (Merchant, 1980, pp. 192–215). A psychoanalytic analysis of the Cartesian masculinization of thought was done by Susan Bardo (Bardo, 1986, pp. 439–56).

2 For a detailed analysis of Baconian thought and politics see the work of Evelyn Fox Keller (Fox Keller, 1986).

3. The idea of applying the concept of contextualism to the analysis of molecular genetics originates in my practical experience in molecular genetics. The theoretical explication was done in cooperation with my collcagues Rainer Hohlfeld and Wolfgang Bonß (Bonß, Hohlfeld and Kollek, 1989). The work of Gregory Bateson helped us to specify our thoughts (Bateson, 1983).

4 This aspect was also pointed out by Lynda Birke for the development of humans (Birke, 1986, p. 53). It is discussed in more detail in thc final section of this article.

5 In linguistics, the term context means the relationships of a word or a sentence (grammatical context), or the situation in which a sentence is used and understood (pragmatic context).

References

Bacon. Francis. Quoted in Bernal, J. D. (1970). *Wissenschaft,* Vol. 2. Hamburg: Rowohlt Taschenbuch Verlag.

Bardo, Susan. (1986). The Cartesian masculinization of thought. *Signs,* 11, pp. 439–56.

Bateson, Gregory. (1986). *Ökologie des Geistes.* Frankfurt am Main: Suhrkamp.

Birke, Lynda. (1986). *Women, Feminism and Biology. The Feminist Challenge.* New York: Methuen.

Bishop, J. Michael. (1987). The molecular genetics of cancer. *Science,* 235, pp. 305–11.

BMFT (Bundesminister für Forschung und Technologie) (1986). *Richtlinien zum Schutz vor Gefahrendurch in-vitro neukombinierte Nukleinsäuren.* vom 28. Mai. Bonn: BMFT.

Bonß, W., Hohlfeld, R. and Kollek, R. (1989). Risiko und Kontext, Zum Umgang mit den Risiken der Gentechnologie. Unpublished manuscript.

Descartes, René. (1972). *Regeln zur Ausrichtung der Erkenntniskraft.* Felix Meiner Verlag, Hamburg.

Duerr, Hans-Peter. (1988). Naturwissenschaft und Wirklichkeit. Der Beitrag naturwissenschaftlichen Denkens zu einem möglichen Gesamtverständnis unserer Wirklichkeit. In Mueller, Helmut A. (ed.), *Naturwissenschaft und Glaube*. Bern: Scherz, pp. 68–87.

Fischer, G., Wittmann-Liebold, B., Lang K., Kiefhaber, T. and Schmid, F. X. (1989). Cyclophilin and peptidylprolyl cis-trans isomerase are probably identical proteins. *Nature*, 337, pp. 476–8.

Fox Keller, Evelyn. (1986). *Liebe, Macht und Erkenntnis*. München: Carl Hanser Verlag.

Jahn, I., Löther, R. and Senglaub, K. (1985). *Geschichte der Biologie*. Jena: VEB Gustav Fischer Verlag.

Kollek, Regine. (1988a). Gentechnologie und biologische Risiken – Stand der Diskussion nach dem Bericht der Enquete-Kommission 'Chancen und Risiken der Gentechnologien'. *WSI-Mitteilungen*, 88 (2), pp. 105–15.

Kollek, Regine. (1988b). 'Ver-rückte' Gene. Die inhärenten Risiken der Gentechnologie und die Defizite der Risikodebatte. *Aesthetik und Kommunikation*, 18 (69).

Kollek, Regine. (1990). The contained use of genetically modified micro-organisms: problems of safety. In *Proceedings of the European Workshop on Law and Genetic Engineering*. Bonn: BBU Verlag.

Krohn, Wolfgang and Weyer, Johannes. (1989). Gesellschaft als Labor. Die Erzeugung von Risiken durch experimentelle Forschung. *Soziale Welt*, 40 (3), pp. 349–73.

Kuhn, Thomas S. (1967). *Die Struktur wissenschaftlicher Revolutionen*. Frankfurt am Main: Suhrkamp.

Merchant, Carolyn. (1980). *The Death of Nature. Women, Ecology and the Scientific Revolution*. San Francisco: Harper and Row.

Rubin, Harry. (1988). Molecular biology running into a cul-de-sac? *Nature*, 335, p. 121.

Ruebsamen, Rosemarie. (1983). Patriarchat – der (un-)heimliche Inhalt der Naturwissenschaft und Technik. In Pusch, Luise, (ed.), *Feminismus, Inspektion der Herrenkultur*. Frankfurt am Main: Suhrkamp.

Shieh, B.-H., Stamnes, M. A., Seavello, S., Harris, G. L. and Zuker, S. C. (1989). The ninA gene required for visual transduction in Drosophila encodes a homologue of cyclosporin A-binding protein. *Nature*, 338, pp. 67-70.

Sinnott, E. W., Dunn, L. C. and Dobzhansky, T. (1958). *Principles of Genetics*. New York: McGraw-Hill.

Takahashi, N., Hayano, T., Suzuki, M. (1989). Peptidylprolyl cis-trans isomerase is the cyclosporin A-binding protein cyclophilin. *Nature*, 337, pp. 473–5.

WHO (World Health Organization). (1979a). Safety measures in microbiology; the development of emergency services. *Weekly Epidemiological Record*, 20, pp. 151–6.

WHO (World Health Organization). (1979b). Safety measures in microbiology; minimum standards of laboratory safety. *Weekly Epidemiological Record*, 44, pp. 340–2.

CHAPTER 7

Error-Friendliness and the Evolutionary Impact of Deliberate Release of GMOs

CHRISTINE VON WEIZSÄCKER

In technology assessment the words 'chance' and 'risk' frequently highlight the controversies. The word 'chance' is derived from the Latin *cadentia*, the falling of the dice, meaning lucky throw. 'Risk' is also derived from a Latin root, *risicare,* to navigate dangerous rocks, meaning to dare and to incur danger. Both words together characterize the two sides of situations involving specific exposure to the vicissitudes of an open-ended, unpredictable and indeterminable future. We should appreciate this one point on which the opposing camps are in agreement, a rare enough island of consensus in the sea of controversies.

If we say 'chance' we want to stress that the future contains the possibility of good luck. If we use the word 'risk' we want to imply the possibility of bad luck. One of our problems is that we do not know the future.

Another problem is that there is no impartial objective judgement on which luck is which. Good and bad luck cannot be defined irrespective of the biased hopes and interests of the people involved in the game. There is no law of nature proving that it is always and for all players true that to throw a six in dice is best. One man's good luck can be another's misfortune. I wish that the discussions on how to throw the dice and how to steer clear of rocks, even invisible underwater ones, were not muted by certain experts pretending to be able to perform the impossible: to judge chances and risks objectively. The implementation of the 'Liberty of Active and Creative Formation of Opinion' (*Meinungserarbeitungsfreiheit,* coined by R. Ueberhorst) cannot flourish in a situation where technology is thought to develop inexorably and only according to its inherent laws, and where the withdrawal of public support from certain technologies is considered a futile gesture, since someone else will certainly serve the allegedly immutable 'technological progress'.

The words 'risk' and 'chance' are also indicative of the different sides in the controversy, the two typical camps outlined below.

The 'New Chances – Old Risks' Camp

Members of this camp present the chances as new, stimulating, promising quick and huge success according to precise plans. The risks, on the other hand, are considered to be as ancient and unavoidable as of old. Thus they point out:

- that genetic changes for the benefit of human beings are old hat because they were always induced by traditional breeding;

- that there have always been gene transfers between species in nature, though admittedly their incidence is unknown and probably very small;

- that no-one has ever nervously protested against the use of biotechnology for making beer, bread or yogurt. Why all the fuss now?

Professor Hubert Markl, president of the Deutsche Forschungsgemeinschaft (German Research Association) has commented in this respect. 'The greatest risks in genetic engineering lie in the release of panic scenarios.'

The 'Old Chances – New Risks' Camp

The members of this camp claim that the chances of new technologies will probably be no more hope-inspiring or straightforward than the consequences of earlier technological progress. The examples of modern medicine and agriculture show that actual success very often lags far behind the success in banishing hunger and disease originally claimed. In fact, medicine and modern agriculture have sometimes even been counterproductive. Therefore members of this camp assume that new technologies will fall short of their promises in the same old way. The risks, on the other hand, are seen as new and alarming. They point out:

- that the argument that nuclear energy is not dangerous merely because radioactive decay also occurs in nature is far from conclusive, because it omits all quantitative aspects;

- that if genetic engineering applies mechanisms that occur in nature, this cannot be considered an automatic safeguard either;

- that the historically new pace of development, scope and commercialization of modern advanced technologies do contribute to a qualitatively new level of risk.

This camp could be characterized by a sentence from the writer Friedrich Dürrenmatt: 'The more complete the plans become, the more effective is the hand of fate.'

How Can Evolution Theory Contribute?

The discussion on the evolutionary impact of deliberate releases of GMOs is bang in the middle of the crossfire between these two camps. Evolution theory can perhaps contribute in two ways:

1 Potential long-term effects can be recognized and undesirable ones can therefore be avoided.

2 The long history of evolution and the successful survival and differentiation of an increasing number of species could be of exemplary interest for dealing successfully with a future full of surprises, and could serve as a model for many aspects of future technological strategy in an admittedly open-ended, unpredictable future. (Please recall the consensus mentioned above.)

Let me first return to the line of argument of the 'New Chances – Old Risks' camp. Indeed, there is nothing fundamentally new in influencing the course of evolution. *All genetic changes in every organism* are theoretically capable of causing major changes in the course of evolution. Consider the evolutionary ping-pong match that has taken place between algae and fungi, which ultimately resulted in their symbiosis in the form of lichens. Lichens are ecological pioneers and their existence induced changes in the biosphere.

Cultural changes in the interaction between man and his environment have always had a potential influence on the course of evolution as well, and will continue to do so. For example, the many interrelationships between people (English and Irish, rich and poor), the potato and the potato blight have influenced the ecology and social structure of Ireland to this very day. Even the setting-up of nature reserves to protect the natural environment from human influence is a difficult *cultural* achievement which has its effects on evolution. Apparently, we cannot help playing a role in evolution due to the unavoidable fact that we are players and not alien spectators in the game.

Up to this point I have followed the arguments of the first camp. When they start to conclude, however, that in view of the general human influence on evolution there is no need for special discussion of the consequences of genetic engineering, I can no longer agree. Nor am I happy with the argument that genetic engineering is particularly safe because it is a biological discipline and because biologists know best about nature. Specialized knowledge in one area of biology is not in itself sufficient, I feel, for technology assessment. To make matters worse, there is an evident lack of intensive collaboration between genetic engineers and their biologist colleagues specializing in ecology and evolution. Moreover, there is a great disparity in number and funds.

Anyway, evolution will continue and humans will continue to exert their influence on it. So we will have to look for criteria for assessing the *direction* of these influences. In a first naïve but reasonable guess we believe, for example, that afforestation offers a better evolutionary perspective than forest destruction with resultant desertification. Let us forget for the moment what the desert rat thinks about such an assumption. But even such simplified assumptions confront us already with a difficult question: if the destruction of ecosystems and their inherent evolutionary potential is so easy, while the reconstitution of a rich ecological balance, if possible at all, takes centuries or at least decades, why has evolution not failed long ago? Does the vulnerability of ecosystems not suggest the idea of replacing these complex, vulnerable, unpleasantly unmanageable ecosystems by a simple, robust, foolproof and altogether more convenient human design? Before doing that, however, we would be well advised to screen the body of scientific knowledge for well-founded theories about the probability of future success. Therefore, I would like to take you on a short excursion into the history of biology.

The dispute between Lamarck and Darwin in the middle of the nineteenth century ended with the disappearance of teleological concepts from the theory of evolution. Since that time evolution has not been discussed in terms of its ends, only in terms of its means. Biologists refrain from claiming to know what is 'good' or 'bad' evolution. Terms such as 'natural selection' and 'survival of the fittest' are descriptive, not moral terms.

Outstanding biologist that he was, Darwin knew a lot about the implicitly favourable ecological framework for the working of natural selection. He knew the significance of the geographical isolation of the Galapagos Islands for the story of differentiation and speciation he had to tell about the finches, later named after him. And in a letter written to Professor Asa Gray in 1887 his keen understanding of ecological interaction of species is evident: 'We can prove experimentally that a piece of land is more productive if it is sown with many different species and genus of grass, than if it is sown with two or three only.' Modern breeders take the exactly opposite line. They prefer to produce one single and optimal variety. Thus modern agricultural philosophy, even without its accentuation by genetic engineering, contradicts Darwin's comments and lands us with two further questions:

1 What happens in the long term to 'the piece of land' and the 'many different species and genus of grass'? Do they change or disappear? Is their disappearance harmful? How should the loss of species and varieties be included in an overall appraisal?

2 How is the 'best grass' to be defined at all? What is the most relevant criterion? The yield in biomass, the economic yield, the reliability of harvest under fluctuating weather conditions, the sustainability in terms of soil fertility, the taste preferences of the grazing animals, or the aesthetic preferences of the landscape gardener? Is not one of the qualities of the 'best grass' that it can provide the basis for future grass evolution under changing external conditions?

Darwin wisely used the term 'survival of the fittest' – and not the term 'survival of the best'. The term 'fitness' immediately raises the question of the context of an organism in relation to which 'fitness' can be shown. I shall pursue this by introducing the example of locks and keys. In order to find out which is the best key, all available keys must be tried out in the lock that we want picked. The arguments in favour of genetic engineering and deliberate release lie in the speeding up of the search process, the production of new keys where no old key fits the lock one has in mind, and the quick exclusion of unnecessary keys. Even if we agree so far, we have to take care that the fate of the discarded keys and the choice of the locks to be picked are adequately discussed. There may be problems with the restriction of the scope of experience and criteria and with the choice of short-sighted priorities with regard to the locks to be picked.

To understand the ecological and evolutionary realities better, we must exchange a static for a highly dynamic model. We must try to imagine keys and locks which are all flexible and changeable and which – to make matters even more complicated – can both compete and cooperate with each other: a confusing nightmare for the key service, and nevertheless a brilliant concept for establishing fitness, or matching, between locks and keys. What the genetic key service wants to do has apparently been running of its own accord for a long time, the biological keys and locks found today being the successful results of a long process of co-evolution.

Classically, biologists approached every biological phenomenon, even if it was one that looked absurd at first glance, with the assumption that there must be a good reason for its existence. This was a successful guiding principle. For this reason classical biologists are sad that, with modern bio-technological facilities, improvements are often sought before an attempt has been made to establish if and in what way the existing organism is fit and well balanced. If such an assessment is systematically forgotten, there will be a huge risk in the deliberate release of what is, perhaps irrationally and ideologically, considered superior.

In a highly dynamic key–lock model over a number of generations, the definition of fitness becomes of necessity a tautology. Neo-Darwinism dropped all attempts at defining present fitness, but had it that the fit were those whose descendants were still around. This marked a great step forward, entailing as it did the abandonment of Social Darwinism, which had abused the authority of science to state whose genes, lifestyle, technology, economy or moral code were superior. Needless to say, Social Darwinists tended to assume that it was their own genes which were superior. This alleged superiority expressed itself in inhuman atrocities. But was that just immoral, or also bad biology?

Let us return once more to innocent locks and keys. I have already mentioned that Charles Darwin spotlighted the role of selection in the evolutionary process (*On the Origin of Species by Means of Natural Selection*, London 1859). The selection of suitable keys, however, is only part of the problem. Selection by definition entails a reduction rather than an increase in variance. Selection alone cannot explain the increase in the number of species, the increase in the complexity of organisms, and the increase in the complexity of their interactions. To pick unknown locks, of which the future is one, we need a whole bunch of keys. At the level of evolution the problem shifts from mere optimization, which, as we have seen, is difficlt enough, to the production and maintenance of numerous future options.

How Are Biological Options Produced and Maintained in Nature?

In biological evolution new options arise through accidental mutations. Experiments with the mut-gene, amongst others, have shown that the mutation rate of an organism is adjusted to the rate of change in the environment of that organism. Regulated speed of change reduces the danger that parts of a co-evolving system may drop out of the common process and thereby cause major disturbances. Mutations are shuffled within the populations by recombination. The continual process of trying out ever new combinations of mutations ultimately may result, and often has resulted, in several 'errors' and 'weaknesses' combining to a new 'strength' and 'success'. Almost all mutations start off being errors, faults and weaknesses and they reduce actual fitness. When dinosaurs roamed the earth who would have put his Cretacean money on mutants with porous bones, dwarf stature and a funny tendency to flap their front extremities? We would probably all have backed conventional dinosaur evolution with teeth, armour plating and giant growth. In doing so we would have missed the major evolutionary step which led to birds. Economic and scientific betting behaviour has a tendency to be rather conventional.

How to Live with Errors

If to date the fate of mutants and oddities in biology has not been essentially dependent on our betting behaviour, it could now become so. Up to now new bunches of biological keys were being created continuously in large gene pools, protected from instant natural selection by a whole array of biological mechanisms. Prominent amongst these is genetic recessivity: in organisms with a double set of chromosomes one experimental gene can be towed along through many generations by its fit parallel gene. Another such mechanism is the strict compartmentalization of the biosphere. Isolation through geographical, molecular and behavioural barriers protects organisms from having to take part in a quasi 'non-stop international high-performance elimination race'. In terms of long-term evolution it is not only the selection of the fittest which matters, but also the survival of the less fit for opening up future options. Only in this way has it been possible to prevent today's fitness from becoming tomorrow's cul-de-sac.

With the introduction of deliberate release of GMOs we are faced by a dilemma to which there is no easy solution:

1 The massed and rapid introduction of GMOs, undertaken deliberately and hence systematically focusing on specific interests, would appear to call for careful central control. Yet realistically central control, paying due respect to the justified demand for a high level of protection, can be achieved only for a few fully standardized organisms. The high costs and time involved can only be repaid through massive and international releases.

2 A small number of standardized products with high development costs and wide distribution will inevitably lead to further genetic erosion – that is, to further losses of genetic richness and variance. This will affect wild species, have an additional impact on soil organisms, and narrow down the *in situ* genetic base of crops and domestic animals. In other words, future options will be lost irretrievably. For evident quantitative reasons, stockpiling in germplasm banks and cultivation in a few test fields cannot solve the problem, even if the access to these stockpiles of biological and cultural heritage were regulated in a fairer way.

The dilemma is thus that strict state control and accurate Environmental Impact Assessment, which we urgently need, could endanger biological variance, which we also urgently need. Are the benefits so guaranteed, and is the search for alternative solutions so futile, that consciously inviting such a tragic situation is justified?

I have spoken so far of mutants and errors. But is error the right word for something which has great evolutionary significance and is therefore protected by biological mechanisms? Lewis Thomas said in 1979: 'Biology needs a better word than "error" for the driving force in evolution. But perhaps "error" will do after all if we consider that it comes from an old root meaning to wander about looking for something.'

For the open future which we allude to when using words like 'chances' and 'risks', strategies will be required to deal with uncertainties. It is doubtful that the future will make itself 'known and predictable' just for the sake of the European Community. Let me quote an evolutionary law formulated by Ronald Fisher in 1930: 'The rate of increase in fitness of any organism at any time is directly proportional to its variance in fitness at that time.' In other words, streamlining evolution is hampering evolution.

I coined the term 'error-friendliness' to describe a unique combination of qualities in living organisms. They are error-tolerant, from repair-genes via wound healing to child rearing. They are error-prone, from mutations up to the behavioural art of curiosity. They use errors in new and cooperative ways. Long-term success lies in the combination of these elements. Neither error production alone nor robustness alone will do. Error-friendliness is complementary to Darwinian fitness. They are opposites but nonetheless both indispensable for survival. While fitness represents the history of an organism in its environment, error-friendliness points to the future. It is, if I may say so, the biological betting system (cf., e.g., Ernst and Christine von Weizsäcker, 'How to Live with Errors. – On the Evolutionary Power of Errors', *Journal of General Evolution,* New York, 1987).

How to Protect Options

Together, fitness and error-friendliness allowed the co-evolution of eco-systems within a framework of high biodiversity, adapted rate of change, and the maintenance of barriers.

Genetic engineering, however, advocates itself by claiming a much higher rate of change, and the construction of organisms optimized in accordance with narrow, short-term market criteria. Part of its case is the removal of biochemical barriers between species, a world-wide distribution which breaks down geographical barriers and speeds up the destruction of indigenous ecosystems. These aims fundamentally contradict the frame-work of an error-friendly evolution, especially for more complex and long-lived species like human beings and most of their domestic plants and animals. There is a strong hint that we may be in for more than just a few minor accidents. Uniform, quick and massive success may in fact be the real disaster, a disaster that does not yet shed its shells and does not show up in a few petunia releases. Even after massive releases the consequences might not be proven beyond doubt until decades later. Biodisasters may cry out for quick remedies, which again will mean genetic manipulation, this time without conscientious Environmental Impact Assessment because of lack of time. This is where a vicious circle may start.

Before we land ourselves in such a vicious circle I propose several topics for inclusion in the discussion:

1 How can we assess the number and evolutionary importance of biological options which this technology will replace and destroy? (Biological Error-friendliness.)

2 How can we guarantee that other attempts at solving the problems which genetic engineering proclaims to be able to solve will have an equal chance in terms of personnel and funds? What could be the incentives for the production of many different and multidisciplinary alternative scenarios? This would be the basis for real choice. (Technological Error-friendliness.)

3 How can we ensure that the political discussion of aims, objectives and priorities takes in the voices of all different interests and concerns involved? How can the interests of future generations and of people living in other areas of the globe be represented fairly?

CHAPTER 8

The Greening of Biotechnology: GMOs as Environment-Friendly Products

LES LEVIDOW AND JOYCE TAIT

The prospect of a world transformed by biotechnology evokes strong feelings, be they fears of catastrophe or hopes for the ultimate human harnessing of natural forces. The consequent debate on risk regulation is as much about containing fears as about preventing environmental harm (Shackley, 1989). This chapter explores the conflicts of value involved in the expression and containment of such fears, particularly regarding the intentional release of genetically manipulated organisms (GMOs).

In the USA, West Germany and Denmark, there has been much opposition to the experimental release of GMOs into the environment. Britain has had little protest, perhaps partly because it has a long-standing regulatory procedure, incorporating diverse views about how the environmental risks should be conceptualized, assessed and regulated. Various public statements offer an opportunity to analyse the value conflicts which surround the issue and to consider the likely future of the debate, in Britain and more widely.

In Britain, prospective releasers have cooperated with procedures for a proactive risk regulation (Tait and Levidow, 1992). Such an approach anticipates and thus averts any environmental harm, including new kinds of potential harm, for which there may be no prior scientific evidence. Industry and government acceptance of proactive regulation has provided an opening for critics of biotechnology to raise wide-ranging concerns, both within and beyond environmental risk assessment, in effect stretching its terms to encompass those of technology assessment.

At stake is not simply a choice of administrative procedures but also the approach to dealing with environmental impacts: what kinds of previous experiences, and therefore what kinds ot facts, should be considered most relevant for anticipating the effects of GMO releases? What would count as adequate knowledge for dealing with ecological uncertainties? What would be the most likely, and acceptable, effects on agriculture?

As we argue here, the controversy involves metaphors which convey either alarming or reassuring views of biotechnology, comparing the effects of GMO releases to other experiences. In particular, industry has portrayed GMOs as precisely programmed, evolutionary extensions of naturally efficient organisms that will reduce the need for harmful chemical inputs in agriculture. Such a portrayal seeks to facilitate the eventual transition from current trial releases to large-scale releases of GMOs: the organisms will become 'environment-friendly' products, reliably kept under benign control. Yet that reassurance has been challenged by various critics, with different implications for proactive risk regulation. Surveying the controversy, this chapter will analyse various participants' public statements as clues to the contending values that they bring to bear.

First we will explore three contentious metaphors for conceptualizing GMOs, and suggest how they converge in portraying GMO products as environment-friendly. Then we will discuss implications for the control and public acceptance of biotechnology.

Contentious Metaphors

As sociologists of science have argued, each social group defines risk according to its world view (for instance, Wynne, 1982; Douglas and Wildavsky, 1982; Thompson, Ellis and Wildavsky, 1990). Value judgements are involved in describing the breadth of risk assessment warranted, and even in selecting the concepts that inform an apparently technical risk assessment. In risk debates more generally,

> Some words imply disorder or chaos, others certainty and scientific precision. Selective use of labels can trivialize an event or render it important; marginalize some groups, empower others; define an issue as a problem or reduce it to a routine (Nelkin, 1985, p. 20).

Such labels also suggest conceptions of nature itself, each with different implications for how, or how well, it can be known and controlled.

Such language is not merely arbitrary, or incidental to the science. As Barry Barnes has argued (1985, pp. 92–3),

> The whole history of science is a story of the extension of empirical knowledge from one context to another by analogy . . . scientists will be liable to become enthusiasts for their own favoured analogies . . . .

Moreover, metaphors have been integral to conceptions of nature – not simply in presenting science, but also in constituting its object of study, which science in effect constructs.

For example, living nature has been variously invested with social concepts such as pathogenic invasions, a division of labour, competition and, more recently, computer codes. Similarly, in psychology, the human mind has been invested with hydraulic and cybernetic metaphors (Leary, 1990). Almost by definition, such metaphors imply ways for scientific knowledge to exercise a human yet naturally based control.

However, such legitimation has often been contentious, particularly in the case of genetically modified organisms. The GMO debate abounds with culturally resonant metaphors about nature being out of control – or under control of different kinds. In parts of the popular imagination, biotechnology is feared as a violation of nature, which may then go out of control. Some environmentalists have warned us against opening a Pandora's box of transgenic organisms (Wheale and McNally, 1990), which may detonate an ecological 'time bomb' (Hatchwell, 1989). Describing pollen transfer as a possible 'escape route for genes, taking them beyond their intended home', a science journalist has used metaphors of rampant, dangerous sexuality: 'illicit partners' enjoy 'the delights of sex', through 'saturation bombing' (Young, 1989). All these phrases suggest ominous results of new genetic combinations out of control.

The controversy also concerns the kind of control to be exercised: beneficent or sinister? Logically speaking, this concern presumes that GMOs do remain under someone's control, for better or for worse. At the same time, the scenario of nature running out of control may also serve as a subconscious metaphor for institutional forces beyond public control: 'Perhaps we see the increasingly powerful, autonomous, comprehensive, yet arguably less visible social forces controlling our lives as more threatening even than those of the supernatural' (Wynne, 1980, p. 285). Fears of a sinister control envisage nature being exploited for purposes benefiting the few at the expense of the many, for example, as yet another means for multinational corporations to enhance their control over agriculture worldwide.

Such fears may be contained or displaced by a language of benign control. By deploying metaphors from computer programming, biotechnologists suggest that their molecular-level intervention will make GMOs' behaviour even more predictable than the products of earlier techniques. While those techniques improved strains of useful organisms by directed selection from natural variation, industry suggests that GMOs offer similar or greater improvements, embodying a precision control while retaining proximity to natural processes. In order to draw out such meanings, we analyse how such rhetoric lends GMOs a natural, benign legitimacy, through three metaphors in particular: software, evolution (vs revolution), and efficiency. Not merely rhetorical, these metaphors express industry's practical reconstruction of nature in mechanical terms.

GMOs as Reprogrammed Software

In a survey on the public understanding of science, less than half the respondents associated DNA with living things, and 7 per cent associated it with computers (Durant *et al.*, 1989). Although 'incorrect', such associations have great metaphorical relevance for industry's reduction of life to programmable chemicals. Through a computer metaphor, life becomes reducible to a universal genetic 'code' which can be read, copied and edited.

By isolating and manipulating molecular-level components, control over living things will be enhanced, as industrial chemists have demonstrated with chemical 'building blocks'. Molecular intervention is seen as the reprogramming of life, in a manner analogous to running software on a computer. To ensure that a gene is expressed only where intended, scientists construct what they describe as genetic 'cassettes'. Ed Dart of ICI plc, speaking on television, has compared this cassette technique to a 'Lego kit' (BBC, 1990, p. 5), a more mechanical analogy.

At a major conference on the intentional release of microbial GMOs, some speakers portrayed GMOs as preferable to traditional alternatives, because 'genetic engineering produces alterations that are often simpler and more easily understood than changes produced by other techniques: as a result their properties may be more predictable' (Sussman *et al.*, 1988, p. 205). In this view, recombinant DNA offers greater safety. Another speaker noted agreement with the OECD statement that 'genetic changes from rDNA techniques will often have inherently greater predictability compared with traditional techniques, because of the greater precision that the rDNA technique affords to particular modifications' (Sussman *et al.*, 1988, p. 290; OECD, 1986, p. 31).

Such confidence arises from the mechanical reductionist world view that informed the founders of molecular biology in the 1930s: 'The molecular biology schema purports to describe all organisms as self-assembling, self-maintaining, self-reproducing, information-processing machines' (Yoxen, 1981, p. 69). De-emphasizing natural history models of nature, this approach looked to molecular-structural explanations for natural characteristics, a Meccano view geared to the strip-mining of nature (Yoxen, 1983, pp. 34–5).

However, the computer metaphor for DNA is contentious, especially where genetic engineering crosses species barriers. Some people view DNA as sacred, as the 'essence of life', whose molecular recombination transgresses the unity of living things and thus threatens disaster (F&FS, 1989). Similarly, the World Council of Churches sees 'the integrity of creation' being threatened by the mechanistic world view of biotechnology (WCC, 1989, p. 5).

These ethical objections resonate with the anti-mechanistic concerns of some who have engaged in the debate at a scientific level. The expression of eukaryote DNA has been described as regulated by 'jumping genes', mobile elements of the genome. Some critics of biotechnology have appropriated the metaphor 'jumping genes' in a contrary sense, viewing the genome as a homeostatic ecosystem in continuous flux (Wheale and McNally, 1988, pp. 93–6; 1990, p. 4). In that view, the use of vectors to recombine DNA may disrupt the genome, with unpredictably dangerous consequences; thus they dispute even the most modest reassurances about predictably enhanced control through molecular-level intervention.

Mark Williamson (1988), an ecologist member of the risk-regulation body, the Advisory Committee for Releases into the Environment, and of its predecessor, the IISC, has argued that precise genetic changes do not guarantee precise prediction of ecological characters, for several reasons. Genes have pleiotropic effects; a particular gene may turn out to interact with others, altering characters of ecological importance. Moreover, 'the distinction between a crop and a weed is very narrow'; it depends upon poorly understood genetic and environmental differences (Williamson *et al.*, 1990). Indeed, a slight change in its environment can turn an innocuous organism into a pest.

Such differences of scientific opinion undermine any straightforward application of the OECD's recommendation that predictions of GMOs' behaviour be based on 'knowledge gained from the extensive use of traditionally modified organisms for agriculture and the environment generally' (OECD, 1986, p. 41). Indeed, many ecologists ask whether the products of traditional breeding techniques are less relevant precedents for GMOs than the introduction of 'exotic' (non-native) species, some of which have displaced native species. As Williamson has noted, 'the probability of an invasion succeeding is small, while the risk from a successful invasion is large'.

Even when a GMO is derived from an organism already well character-ized in a particular environment, it remains unclear what type or degree of genetic change would warrant calling it a 'non-native' organism. According to the Royal Commission on Environmental Pollution,

> Even if the release were into the native environment, the unmodified organism might well be adapted through natural selection to survive in that environment and the genetic manipulation might, possibly deliberately, upset the ecological balance that normally helped to limit the population growth of the unmodified organism (RCEP, 1989, p. 21).

Thus the software metaphor has been implicitly contested by those who adopt a more holistic approach, emphasizing the interactions between component parts and their often profound influence on the behaviour of the system as a whole.

The structure of the British regulatory system implicitly categorizes GMOs along with introduced non-indigenous organisms, some of which have unexpectedly become pests. When the Advisory Committee on Releases to the Environment (ACRE) was created in 1990 to assess applications for GMO releases, its remit also included 'other novel organisms'. The concept of a GMO as a reprogrammed genome, therefore reliably kept under control, may be belied by the risk assessment procedure, at least initially.

At the same time, the case-by-case scrutiny may help overcome any suspected similarity between a GMO and a non-indigenous organism. For example, some official guidelines emphasize that small-scale field trials 'should not be considered analogous to uncontrolled introductions of foreign plants into entirely new environments' (OECD, 1990, p. 17), though that assurance leaves open the question of larger-scale releases.

Evolution vs Revolution

In the 1970s, when new biotechnology firms were seeking large injections of venture capital, enthusiasts proclaimed that this new technology would transform our way of life, suggesting analogies to both the industrial and information revolutions (Tait et al., 1990). Although some promoters have continued those revolutionary proclamations (Taverne, 1990), today such language is more likely to be used by science journalists, in the form of futuristic phrases like 'brave new botany' (Buck, 1989). Generally, promoters of biotechnology have come to reserve the language of total novelty for more selective occasions, such as in arguments for extending patent rights to GMOs, or in appeals for public funds (CEC, 1991, p. 2; Stewart, 1989).

In public discourse, the promoters' language has largely shifted from biological revolution to evolution (Shell, 1989). In the closing address to a scientific conference, a speaker concluded that microbial GMOs 'are more analogous to domesticated organisms . . . that have been bred for man's use' than to wild species (in Sussman et al., 1988, p. 296). Sir Hans Kornberg argued that recombinant DNA simply builds upon 'the ancient cornerstones of modern agriculture' in order to give us 'precise genetic changes' (Sussman et al., p. 3).

That evolutionary comparison is also put by ICI Seeds (1989, p. 3): 'For centuries biotechnology has been used in the development of products – the conversion of barley to beer for instance'. Thus the term 'biotechnology' is stripped of its novelty by projecting it back into the familiar history of beer-brewing, yoghurt-making and selective breeding. Similar language has been adopted by the two UK government departments responsible for risk regulation of GMO releases: 'Often it [biotechnology] is little more than an extension of the traditional drive to develop better strains of plants and animals and to use the properties of micro-organisms in useful processes, like the production of bread, wine and cheese' (HSE and DoE, 1989).

Parallel with the rhetorical shift from revolution to evolution, we have seen the genetic alteration itself renamed. Until recently, official documents and regulatory bodies have tended to adopt the term genetic 'manipulation', sometimes used interchangeably with 'engineering'. There were no explicit differences in intended nuance when 'engineering' was used by the Royal Commission on Environmental Pollution (RCEP, 1989) and 'manipulation' by the Department of the Environment (DoE, 1989), although the RCEP document gave more emphasis to environmental risks.

Meanwhile, since its first proposal for a Deliberate Release Directive, the European Commission (CEC, 1988) had been using the term genetic 'modification'. In December 1989, the term 'modified' became officially enshrined in Britain with publication of the Environmental Protection Bill (HC Bill 14). And in June 1990 the body regulating the contained use of GMOs, the Advisory Committee on Genetic Manipulation (ACGM), had the last word of its name changed to 'modification'. What is the underlying significance of these changes?

Since the 1970s 'genetic engineering' has served as a colloquial term suggesting a potentially omnipotent physico-chemical approach to biology and to life itself. For many people, this implies a transgression of nature, by reducing life to interchangeable parts. That perceptual problem has been acknowledged by Derek Burke, Vice-Chancellor of the University of East Anglia: 'There is a perception out there that "genetic engineering" is a nasty foreign technique, which is disturbing the natural world, which is producing things which shouldn't exist, and which should be resisted' (NEAD, 1989a, p. 32).

For many, the term 'manipulation' seemed no more reassuring than 'engineering'. The World Council of Churches (1982) has questioned the ethics of 'manipulating life'. More recently the National Consumer Council has noted that both genetic 'engineering' and 'manipulation' have a sinister ring (Straughan, 1989, p. 34). By contrast, the term 'modification' presents the organisms as *merely* modified, a modest evolutionary step.

Thus the rhetorical shift can be understood partly as a response to public fears about novel organisms degrading the environment and/or industry controlling human destiny. The new language forms part of an attempt to overcome people's doubts over whether the effects of GMO releases will be adequately controlled – that is, reliably predictable and socially beneficial. In that sense, complementing the software metaphor, the 'evolution' metaphor rhetorically places nature under benign control.

Yet, not merely rhetorical, such language expresses an industrial investment in living matter, whereby nature becomes anthropomorphized as a 'selective breeder'. In the late eighteenth-century concept of evolution, such personification of nature held an ambiguous meaning, with the possible implication that nature 'could do something as conscious as select' (Williams, 1980, p. 73; compare with Young, 1985). Extending that metaphor, now breeders and bioengineers appear to discover genetically based properties, such as wealth and efficiency. When biotechnology is presented as the precise evolutionary extension of natural qualities, it entails an unacknowledged choice regarding how to construct nature.

Wealth-creation Metaphors

The language of 'wealth creation' has been prominent in statements promoting biotechnology, and in a consultative document issued by the Department of the Environment (DoE, 1989). A market definition of wealth also underlies the term 'efficiency' when denoting the maximum short-term extraction of a particular raw material from an organism. That meaning is implied when ICI (1989) describes its biotechnology programme as 'giving nature a nudge towards greater efficiency'; likewise when Derek Burke describes agriculture as being 'driven faster and more efficiently' by biotechnology (NEAD, 1989a, p. 33).

In this way, a modern commercial criterion of efficiency is attributed to natural selection and/or selective breeding; then genetic modification is seen as enhancing that natural quality through a careful molecular-level control. Paradoxically, biotechnology is presented as safe and benign because it allows us to nudge along, improve upon, the evolutionary process. Thus industry's green rhetoric portrays biotechnology, in effect, as a benign controlled evolution.

A different concept of wealth guides those who defend land-race (indigenous) varieties for their genetic diversity, as against the tendency for certain hybrid seeds and plant GMOs to reduce biodiversity. As Kamal Ibrahim has argued, 'The maintenance of genetic variation within and between these land-race populations is also enhanced by the diverse uses the farmers make of their crops' (NEAD, 1989b, p. 10). His argument implicitly defines efficiency as making the best overall use of plants for local people's needs, as well as keeping considerable genetic diversity available for the future. This concept of wealth implies a diverse, socially shared benefit.

Controversy persists even when wealth is defined in terms of food production. On one side, for example, a trade magazine article has praised new agrochemicals for helping food production to keep pace with increasing population. It went on to claim, 'Now it appears to be the turn of biotechnology, which is so often castigated as an enemy of the environment, but which in reality will be the saviour of the human race and its environment' (Mabbett, 1989, p. 9).

Predicting worse food shortages in the future, ICI's Keith Pike has declared biotechnology to be essential for averting Third World famine: 'New varieties of wheat were the key to India's successful green revolution, and improved varieties of all crops will be the most reliable and environmentally acceptable way to secure the world's future food supplies.' As well as reducing dependence on agrochemicals, he has argued, biotechnology will improve agriculture for 'feeding the world' (Pike, 1989, p. 6; NEAD, 1989b, p. 1).

Critics of the green revolution have argued that it made farmers more dependent upon expensive inputs and dispossessed many of them, who became less able to buy the revolution's products. Rice and high-protein pulses were displaced from fields by more expensive wheat. As a result of these changes, it is argued, 'The poor often end up with no land and no money to buy food, trying to eke out a living on marginal land or in the cities' (NEAD, 1989b, p. 33). Hence the paradox of more food and more hunger.

Under these circumstances, biotechnology is seen as leading to yet more dispossession. Herbicide-resistant seeds, for example, could increase farmers' chemical and financial dependence. Although seeds designed for less hospitable conditions could benefit regions with poor agriculture, those same seeds could also displace yet more farmers. Questioning predominant models of development, the World Council of Churches has warned that biotechnology carries a 'potential for even swifter and more widespread deprivation of humanity and damage to the environment in the Third World' (WCC, 1989, p. 28).

Responding to such concerns, Derek Burke has argued, 'That's a political problem. You must not blame scientists'. From his perspective, biotechnology firms need feel obliged only to help increase food production; it is for governments to take steps to guarantee that broad social benefits follow (NEAD, 1989a, p. 33). However, others have argued that current R & D priorities run contrary to the directions that would be needed to benefit Third World farmers as a whole (NEAD, 1989a, pp. 38–9). From this perspective, socio-economic factors are not merely external conditions that affect the distribution of benefits; more profoundly, they become embedded in a choice of research strategy that lends itself more readily to applications benefiting the multinational corporations.

Industry's notion of efficiency has been challenged by the Genetics Forum (1989): 'We are concerned that attempts to use genetic engineering to achieve levels of efficiency in agriculture comparable to those of mechanical and chemical systems in industry may result in the "chemical treadmill" being replaced by a "genetic treadmill".' They criticize industry for taking a short-term view of efficiency, in which genetic designers solve new problems by intensifying the sorts of interventions that created the problems in the first place.

Thus, the future direction of agriculture as a whole is at stake in the controversy. Proponents of biotechnology are promoting certain assumptions about both the means and ends of agriculture when they invoke 'wealth creation' and 'efficiency'. In contrast, for those who conceptualize such terms (if at all) as broadly ecological and social processes, some chemical and/or genetic interventions themselves become short-sighted forms of efficiency, even forms of environmental damage.

'Environment-friendly' Products

So far we have surveyed three metaphors for GMOs – as a reprogrammed genome, as a modest evolutionary extension. and as an enhanced natural efficiency. By portraying biotechnological creations as rooted in natural or familiar processes, these metaphors support industry's claim to be developing environment-friendly products. Such products include microbes for cleaning up waste, microbial pesticides, and seeds designed to require relatively less harmful herbicides or fewer pesticides. Of all the prospective products, the most controversial are herbicide-resistant crops, intended to substitute a single, broad-spectrum herbicide for the present cocktail of selective herbicides which distinguish between a particular crop and weeds.

As Britain's largest seeds merchant, ICI Seeds has defended herbicide-resistant crops as environment-friendly on behalf of the entire biotechnology industry. The firm's booklet, *Herbicide Tolerant Plants*, sets out to show 'that even such a simple effect ... has much to offer .... The general concept of herbicide tolerance ... is not new .... Such natural variation within species has always existed'; what biotechnology offers is the opportunity to transfer the selectivity from the herbicide to the crop species. Moreover, it is argued, 'By encouraging the development of more efficient systems of integrated weed control, the cost of food production will be contained at the present low levels' (Bartle, 1991, pp. 2, 8, 12).

Conceptually, then, the promise to reduce chemical inputs rests upon a precise genetic reprogramming of a modest, single-gene evolutionary modification offering enhanced efficiency, along the lines of the metaphors which we discussed earlier. In response to suspicions that the new seeds are intended to boost sales of the related herbicide, Ed Dart of ICI Seeds has emphasized that 'our herbicide-resistant targets are not ICI herbicides' (BBC, 1990, p. 14). For ICI in particular, the new seeds advance an ambitious strategy based on gene-mapping technology: 'In the medium term, a set of single-gene resistances to broad-spectrum herbicides will enable the farmer to benefit from crop-weed selectivity through genetics rather than chemistry' (Dart, 1988. p. 9).

The promise of precision-controlled benefits has met a suspicious reception. Some concerns involve ecological uncertainties and complexities; these include the difficulty in predicting whether the herbicide resistance might spread to weedy relatives of the crop, or whether more widespread use of a particular herbicide will increase selection pressure for resistant weeds (Genetics Forum, 1989). Indeed, given that weeds have already evolved resistance to some new herbicides, crop protection specialists are advising farmers to mix newer herbicides with older, more toxic ones in order to avert that evolution (Brosten, 1988). Such advice – cited by some critics – may undermine industry's predictions that their new seeds will 'reduce the dependence on herbicides which have already given cause for concern' (Bartle, 1991, p. 11).

Beyond the concept of risk as accident, the World Council of Churches has described the prospect of increased herbicide usage as an ominous example of 'intended effects' (WCC, 1989, p. 25). In ethical terms, a researcher for the National Farmers Union has declared that herbicide resistant crops run 'against the spirit of nature' (cited in Girling, 1990). Such products are seen as highlighting the role of biotechnology in perpetuating the sort of agricultural systems which require intensive corrective intervention, as well as its role in precluding alternative methods of crop protection, in favour of an endless genetic-chemical treadmill. From that viewpoint, herbicide-resistant crops epitomize more general problems applicable to other GMO products, even where they promise to replace chemical inputs entirely.

In summary, critics anticipate an ethical violation of nature bringing unforeseeable consequences, and/or a commercial manipulation of nature pushing agriculture further down an already misguided route. It is not simply a question of whether nature will go out of control, or come under a sinister control. It is also a question of how nature should be conceptualized, even reconstructed, as in the stated aim of 'stimulating the industrialization of agriculture in Europe' (GIBiP, 1990, p. 56). Thus the controversy entails a conflict of values which could not be resolved simply by a technical risk assessment as conventionally done.

Control of Biotechnology

The emerging UK regulatory system is not designed to adjudicate different concepts of agricultural practice, much less different concepts of the 'natural'. Nevertheless, as a proactive system, it is intended to anticipate, and thus prevent, any environmental harm caused by the deliberate release of GMOs. Even those who downplay the risks favour such regulation, if only in order to establish clear rules for commercial competition, and to allay public fears.

Proposed releases of GMOs, currently at the stage of small-scale experiments, are assessed by ACRE. As announced in an April 1990 press release, the new committee's brief encompasses 'all aspects of the safety' of such releases. That remit seems unlikely to include, for example, the eventual effects of herbicide-resistant crops upon herbicide usage, much less the effects of agricultural changes upon people's living and working environment in the broadest sense.

The committee's formal role is to advise on human and environmental risk, thus far understood as direct effects of the GMO. However, its remit and powers can be exaggerated. For example, a science journalist described ACRE's chairman, John Beringer, as 'clerk-of-works' to the New Creation: 'Like Noah, his committee stands at the gangplank of the ark, punching out tickets to the future' (Girling, 1990, p. 42).

That journalistic flourish highlights a gap between the likely extent of regulation and possible public expectations for such regulation. Public confidence may depend upon ACRE being seen as independent of industry, and also upon the handling of issues beyond ACRE's remit. Regulators seek to distinguish their proactive approach to GMO regulation from the reactive approach taken to the nuclear industry in the 1970s, yet they may find themselves similarly perceived as 'those who, through fact-finding rituals, pretend not to choose our future but to make it safe' (Wynne, 1982, p. 172).

Such stakes have been implied by the Director General of Britain's Health and Safety Executive, John Rimington: 'The really important ethical question concerns the business of human beings messing about with too much power – the Faustian question' (CBC, 1990, p. 8). Indeed, the risk regulation effectively serves as a surrogate means of containing unease about the institutional forces involved, as much as about the GMOs themselves.

Industry's power to choose our future will depend partly upon shaping public perception to accept its innovations as a benign control. Although few people will attempt to comprehend the technical details, most will grasp metaphors derived from the science, as well as those from science fiction. Indeed, the latter distinction can become unclear on both sides of the debate. As one biotechnology enthusiast has claimed, 'if we have the imagination and resources, there is almost no biological problem we cannot solve' (Taverne, 1990, p. 4). That fantasy of benign technological omnipotence has been encouraged by the prospect of selectively transferring genes, which 'encode life's processes' (Taverne, 1990).

Of course, the use of metaphor is as old as language itself. By describing nature or technology in familiar, graspable terms, metaphor can be more effective than overt argument as an ideological weapon. Like other major areas of public discourse and commercial activity, biotechnology has given rise to a variety of vivid metaphors which contend for influence. When industry, government, civil servants, public interest groups and (perhaps to a lesser extent) scientists deploy such language, they do so with such purposes in mind. Whichever metaphors prevail in public perception will affect the acceptance of biotechnology, and perhaps in turn the extent of regulation.

Assessing Need

Given concerns which go beyond criteria formally considered by a technical risk assessment, there have been calls on the government to create an additional public body for assessing prospective GMO products (Genetics Forum, 1989). By applying wide-ranging criteria, this would in effect broaden the notion of proactive risk regulation. However, the terms of the debate have so far tended to separate out environmental, economic, ethical and social aspects of product effects, rather than broaden the definition of environmental risk assessment, as might be appropriate for assessing the indirect (even if 'intended') effects of herbicide-resistant crops on herbicide usage.

A potential precedent has been set in the case of non-therapeutic veterinary medicines, such as bovine somatotrophin (BST). Public disapproval – more than scientific evidence of real risks – led the European Parliament's Environment Committee to recommend against licensing them. Subsequently, pressures have been exerted to make explicit the socio-economic considerations involved, the 'fourth hurdle'.

Industry has been concerned that the European Commission may apply the fourth hurdle to biotechnology in general. As Britain's Bio-Industry Association has warned, 'Clearly, the final decision on whether a product licence should be granted may become largely political ... we are concerned that this will pose a serious threat to the competitiveness of the European biotechnology industry' (BIA, 1989, p. 3).

Rejecting calls for a broadened risk assessment for GMO products, the

European Commission declared that it would not consider social costs and benefits (CEC, 1989), as if that settled the question of broader criteria. More recently, in response to industry pressure, the Commission has ambiguously suggested that only 'exceptional cases' will warrant consideration of socio-economic aspects (CEC, 1991, p. 9).

Attempting to keep the question closed, the European biotechnology industry has insisted that product regulation should 'assess only safety, quality and efficacy for man and the environment, on the basis of objective scientific criteria' (SAGB, 1990, p. 13). For government to impose criteria of economic effects would threaten democracy: 'Indeed, economic renewal through innovation is the motor force of democratic societies' (SAGB, 1990, p. 15). From industry's standpoint, social need should be determined by the free choice of consumers in the market. And that is only natural, given the metaphors of market efficiency invested in nature itself.

Britain's Opposition MPs have rhetorically asked whether industry should remain free to pursue whatever technological advances are feasible, regardless of any ethical constraints. As a Liberal Democrat mused, if bio-technology makes it possible to play God, then the government's deference to market mechanisms means 'that the free market is God' (Hansard, 6 March 1990, p. 955).

Rejecting an amendment to create an Ethics Commission within the Environmental Protection Bill, the Minister of State for the Environment and Countryside said that 'It has always been easy for me to handle that by separating ethics from the environment and the environment from patents' (Hansard, 6 March 1990, p. 971). That statement illustrates how even a formal consideration of ethical aspects could turn out to relegate them to a compartment separate from safety issues, which would then remain defined narrowly, so as not to consider socio-economic sources of environmental harm.

Many organizations in Britain, as well as some members of ACRE, have proposed that the committee be supplemented by a Public Biotechnology Commission, or a Genetic Modification Commission. If such a body were given official legitimacy, it might gain the authority to erect a fourth hurdle, even to challenge the official dichotomy between purely technical risk assessment and wider concerns. Such scenarios may have deterred government from accepting proposals that it create such a commission.

If there is no explicit way to consider social, economic and ethical aspects of environmental safety, then either they will remain implicit within the current procedure for assessing environmental risk, or they will be integrated (if at all) behind closed doors in a department of state – or both. For example, a separate safety assessment of particular pesticides and crops would substitute for a more wide-ranging assessment of whether or not a new GMO crop would bring about an environmentally desirable change in chemical use. In any case, the conflicts of value underlying potential public unease would remain unresolved, or even unclearly formulated.

Public Acceptance

The intentional release of GMOs is already becoming a test case for control over the direction of new technology, as well as for industry's wider campaign to win acceptance as the purveyor of environment-friendly products. Noting public fears that biotechnologists are perpetrating something 'unnatural', a Cabinet Office advisory committee has suggested using the counter-argument that biotechnology could provide a more 'natural' process or product, for example, by helping reduce chemical usage in agriculture (ACOST, 1990, p. 23). In that vein, a television advertisement for 'Green Science from Schering Agriculture' claims that it has 'maximum regard for the grower, the environment and the consumer' (BBC, 1990, p. 13).

According to industry's reassuring portrayal, biotechnology modestly reprogrammes nature to make it serve social needs more reliably and efficiently, as manifest in market demand for environment-friendly products. Such a portrayal seems intended to deflect demands from public pressure groups that assessment of GMO products be extended to wide-ranging criteria of environmental, ethical, economic and social implications. Will the putative greening of biotechnology overcome public suspicion? Industry's green perspective, which represents nature as a state that can be emulated or recreated by scientific product development, stands at odds with more radical versions of environmentalism. This latter perspective, often with religious or metaphysical undertones, presents nature as a fragile, vulnerable system, constantly under threat from chemical agents out of control. It remains to be seen whether the frequent repetition of industry's green rhetoric will reinforce radical environmentalism or undercut it (Green and Yoxen, 1990, p. 493).

Through natural metaphors implying precise, benign control, a sophisticated public-relations language is downplaying the complex ecological issues that face the risk assessors. Given that the government is carrying out a high-profile, nominally proactive approach to risk regulation, industry's rhetorical greening of biotechnology may heighten public unease, rather than assuage it. If it ignores the wider concerns we have surveyed here, the regulatory regime could be seen as providing industry with the appearance of a proactive approach without the substance.

With the aim of reconciling conflicts of value, regulatory procedures could formally encompass wider public concerns, including the content and context of biotechnology. By drawing out the protagonists' values, as indicated by the metaphors they adopt, such a procedure could help to resolve underlying differences. By enriching and deepening the debate, it could make the resulting technology more socially resilient. Equally, it could have the opposite effect of clarifying unresolvable conflicts of value about nature, risk and society. Such are the stakes involved as various protagonists attempt to shape the scope and public accessibility of risk regulation for GMO releases.

References

ACOST (1990), *Developments in Biotechnology* (Cabinet Office, Advisory Council on Science and Technology/HMSO, London).

Barnes, B. (1985), *About Science* (Blackwell, Oxford).

Bartle, I. (1991), *Herbicide-Tolerant Plants: Weed Control with the Environment in Mind* (ICI Seeds, Haslemere, Surrey).

BBC (1990), *Horizon:* Guess What's Coming to Dinner, 12 February (Broadcasting Support Services, London, transcript).

BIA (1989), *BIA Bulletin,* 1, November–December (Bio-Industry Association, London).

Brosten, D. (1988), 'Low-dosage resistance', *Agrichemical Age*, 32, pp. 12, 28.

Buck, K. (1989), 'Brave new botany', *New Scientist*, 3 June, pp. 50–5.

CBC (1990), *The Impact of New and Impending Regulations on UK Biotechnology* (Cambridge Biomedical Associates, Cambridge).

CEC (1988), *Proposal on a Council Directive on the Deliberate Release to the Environment of Genetically Modified Organisms*, Brussels, COM (88) 160 final – SYN 131, 16 May.

CEC (1989), *Communication from the Commission to the Parliament*, SEC (89) 2091 final – SYN 131, 6 December, in European Parliament Session Documents, Series C 3-228/89.

CEC (1990), *Council Directive on the Deliberate Release to the Environment of Genetically Modified Organisms*, 9644/89 ENV 200 SAN 128 PRO-COOP 164, 29 March.

CEC (1991), *Promoting the Competitive Environment for the Industrial Activities Based on Biotechnology within the Community* (Commission of the European Communities, Brussels) 19 April.

Dart, E. (1988), *Development of Biotechnology in a Large Company* (ICI External Relations Department, London).

DoE (1989), 'Environmental protection: proposals for additional legislation on the intentional release of genetically manipulated organisms', Consultation Paper, Department of the Environment, June.

Douglas, M. and A. Wildavsky (1982), *Risk and Culture: An Essay on the Selection of*

Technological and Environmental Dangers (University of California Press, London/ Berkeley).

Durant, J, J. Evans and G. Thomas (1989), 'The public understanding of science', *Nature*, 6 July, pp. 11–14.

F&FS (1989), *Some Ethical Aspects of Biotechnology* (Farming and Food Society, London).

Genetics Forum (1989), Submission of Evidence to the RCEP, typescript, March.

GIBiP (1990), 'The green industry biotechnology platform', *Agro-Industry High-Tech*, 1, December, pp. 55–7 (Teknoscienze, Milano).

Girling, R. (1990), 'Why life will never be the same again', *Sunday Times magazine*, 13 May, pp. 34–51.

Green, K. and E. Yoxen (1990), 'The greening of European industry: what role for biotechnology?', *Futures*, June, pp. 492–5.

Hansard (1990), Standing Committee H, House of Commons, proceedings of session 3, committee stage of Environmental Protection Bill, 6 March.

Hatchwell, P. (1989), 'Opening Pandora's box: the risks of releasing genetically engineered organisms', *The Ecologist*, 19 (4) (July–August), pp. 130–6.

HC Bill 14 (1989), *Environmental Protection Bill* (HMSO, December).

HSE and DoE (1989), *Biotechnology and Genetically Modified Organisms: The Proposed New Controls* (Health & Safety Executive and Department of the Environment, London, December).

ICI (1989), *Annual Report 1988*, London.

Leary, D.E. (ed.) (1990), *Metaphors in the History of Psychology* (Cambridge Univesity Press, Cambridge).

Mabbett, T. (1909), 'Sowing the seeds of biotechnology', *Agriculture International*, 41 (1 & 2), pp. 7–9 (Agraria Press, Horley, Sussex).

NEAD (1989a), *Food Matters*, special feature 1 (NEAD/Farmers Link, 3840 Exchange Street, Norwich NR2 1AX).

NEAD (1989b), *Food Matters*, special feature 2.

Nelkin, D. (ed.) (1985), *The Language of Risk: Conflicting Perspectives on Occupational Health* (Sage, London).

OECD (1986), *Recombinant DNA Safety Considerations* (Organization for Economic Co-operation and Development, Paris).

OECD (1990), Good Developmental Practices for Small-Scale Field Research with Genetically Modified Plants and Micro-organisms (OECD, Paris, March).

Pike K. (1989), *Feeding the World* (ICI Seeds, Haslemere, Surrey).

RCEP (1989), *Thirteenth Report: The Release of Genetically Engineered Organisms to the Environment* (Royal Commission on Environmental Pollution, Chair: the Rt Hon. the Lord Lewis of Newnham, Cm720, HMSO, July).

SAGB (1990), *Community Policy for Biotechnology: Priorities and Actions* (CEFIC, Brussels).

Shackley, S. (1989), 'Regulation of the release of genetically manipulated organisms into the environment', *Science and Public Policy*, August, pp. 211–23.

Shell (1989), 'Biotechnology: risks and rewards', management brief, October (available on request).

Stewart, W. (1989), 'Science policy: the future of agricultural and food R & D',

Hannah Research Institute Yearbook (Hannah Research Institute, Ayr, Scotland).

Straughan, R. (1989), *The Genetic Manipulation of Plants, Animals and Microbes: The Social and Ethical Issues for Consumers* (National Consumer Council, 20 Grosvenor Gardens, London SW1).

Sussman, M. *et al.* (eds) (1988), *The Release of Genetically Engineered Micro-organisms* (Academic Press, London).

Tait, J. J. Chataway and S. Jones (1990), 'The status of biotechnology-based innovations', *Technology Analysis and Strategic Management* 2 (3), pp. 293–305.

Tait, J. and L. Levidow (1992) 'Proactive and reactive approaches to risk regulation: the case of biotechnology', *Futures.*

Taverne, D. (1990), *The Case for Biotechnology* (Prima Europe, London).

Thompson, M. R. Ellis and A. Wildavsky (1990), *Cultural Theory* (Westview Press, Boulder, CO).

WCC (1982), *Manipulating Life: Ethical Issues in Genetic Engineering* (World Council of Churches, Department on Church and Society, Geneva).

WCC (1989), *Biotechnology: Its Challenges to the Churches and the World* (World Council of Churches, Geneva).

Wheale P. and R. McNally (1988), *Genetic Engineering: Catastrophe or Utopia?* (Harvester, London).

Wheale, P. and R. McNally (1990), *The Bio-Revolution: Cornucopia or Pandora's Box?* (Pluto, London).

Williams, R. (1980), 'Ideas of nature', in Raymond Williams, *Problems in Materialism and Culture* (Verso, London) pp. 67–85.

Williamson, M. (1988), 'Potential effects of recombinant DNA organisms on ecosystems and their components', in J. Hodgson and A. M. Sugden (eds), *Planned Release of Genetically Engineered Organisms* (*Tibtech*, 6 (4), *Tree*, 3 (4), April) (Elsevier, Cambridge) pp. S32–5.

Williamson, M. J. Perrin and A. Fitter (1990) 'Releasing genetically engineered plants: present proposals and possible hazards', *Tree*, 5, pp. 417–19.

Wynne, B. (1980), 'Discussion paper on J. Conrad', in J. Conrad (ed.), *Society, Technology and Risk Assessment* (Academic Press, New York/London) pp. 281–8.

Wynne, B. (1982), *Rationality and Ritual: The Windscale Inquiry and Nuclear Decisions in Britain* (British Society for the History of Science).

Young, R.M. (1985), *Darwin's Metaphor: Nature's Place in Victorian Science* (Cambridge University Press, Cambridge).

Young, S. (1989), 'The great escapes', *Guardian*, 20 October.

Yoxen, E. (1981), 'Life as a productive force: capitalizing the science and technology of molecular biology', in L. Levidow and R. M. Young (eds), *Science, Technology and the Labour Process*, vol. 1 (CSE Books, London) pp. 66–122 (reissued by Free Association Books, 1983).

Yoxen, E. (1983), *The Gene Business: Who Should Control Biotechnology?* (Pan, London, reissued by Free Association Books, 1986).

PART 3

Bioethics:
Knowledge and Ethics
as Politics

Biosemiotics and Ethics

JESPER HOFFMEYER

Hume's Guillotine

When David Hume in 1740 pointed out his intuition that, logically, an analysis of what is in this world can never, no matter how accurate it may be, lead to any inference as to what ought to be, in a way he only uncovered the logical consequence of the triumphant Newtonian paradigm. Contrary to the spiritual and obliging medieval universe, the new image of nature as composed of passive particles governed by universal and eternal natural laws was, of course, incapable of sustaining human feelings of belonging to or having a relationship with nature. Neither logically nor emotionally can a nature which has been deprived of all traces of true creativity, and thus also deprived of any capacity for malconduct, appear as a precept for human free choice. The Newtonian universe leaves human beings in an alien world from which no obligations can be deduced.

The adoption by philosphers of 'Hume's Guillotine' meant that morality and nature were compartmentalized as separate and unrelated phenomena in European philosophy. The 'fallacy' of drawing inferences from natural science to ethics, however, has been an extremely popular one among scientists. And the reason presumably is that a ban on making such inferences has absurd consequences in post-Darwinian times. For if the human species has not been created through a miracle it must be a result of organic evolution. It follows that at some time in the hominid prehistory precisely that thing must have happened which is now considered a logical impossibility: nature, without assistance we presume, became the source of human beings, 'is' became 'ought'.

Since, for good reasons, true creativity cannot arise in the middle of a universe in which creativity does not already exist, there remain logically only two options for the scientific understanding of human evolution. Either the creativity of human beings is itself an illusion, or the world, contrary to the classical physical image, was creative even before human creativity appeared.

Faithful to its deep reductionist propensity, biology has in this century generally proceeded along the first of these avenues. The attempts at explaining the human 'behavioural phenotype' through reference to bio-chemical or genetic mechanisms are countless. Bio-anthropology, ethology and socio-biology have traditionally adopted a reductionist strategy and most researchers in these areas have certainly been remarkably insensitive to the peculiarities of human social and mental existence. In general, the synthetic theory of organic evolution has been seen as a sufficiently legitimizing metatheory underneath the reductionist endeavours. Mind has been considered an epiphenomenon of the big brain.

In recent years attempts at solving the paradox through the alternative explanatory strategy – by ascribing real creativity to pre-human nature – have been multiplying. An important premise for this line of research has been the work of Ilya Prigogine and his collaborators on the thermo-dynamics of irreversible systems.[1] The biologically important result of this work was the recognition that even relatively simple non-biotic systems can eventually experience a succession of genuinely non-deterministic steps leading to increased order. This means that structure may arise through a process which can only be grasped through a description of its actual and unique historical trajectory.

Although these insights do not explain the creation of specific biological organization, they lend credibility to the view that evolutionary creativity is a genuine phenomenon which does not contradict accepted physical principles. Many researchers in this area are motivated by the defects of the reductionist programme vis-à-vis major problems of the natural foundation of modern society. While nobody should deny the triumphs of the reductionist programme in science, it has nevertheless become increasingly clear that big, important, and perhaps chronic lacunae remain in the basic scientific knowledge of modern civilization. Parallel to our progressive mapping of the total human genome, for instance, the feeling inevitably arises that our lack of a fundamental key to the understanding of the human being as a bio-psycho-social creation makes such knowledge dangerous. The nature–nurture conflict has been of central concern to society for a century, and yet no real progress has been noted in this respect. Rather, the received view of this problem has undergone waves of change which only too obviously reflect change in general political sentiment. Why does this problem persistently escape scientific clarification?

In general, the existence of this kind of void in our understanding reflects a considerable social confusion with respect to current challenges. It is remarkable, moreover, that these areas of confusion almost invariably are also areas where strong interactions between natural and cultural factors are involved (examples include the environmental crisis, the sphere of technological problems, and psychosomatic diseases). What is at stake seems to be a chronic inability of our scientific culture to cope with the culture–nature interface. Our social ability to invent creative solutions to some of the most threatening challenges of our time has become paralysed. Apparently, the Cartesian dualism between body and mind, being and signifying, nature and culture, has brought us to a blind alley. Paradoxically, in the middle of its apparent victory, reductionism suffers a defeat: it has left us with an inflamed relationship to nature, an inflamation to which it does not itself suggest any cure. It seems justified, therefore, now to pose the question of how humankind belongs to nature in a non-reductionist way. The evolutionary genesis of human signification inevitably raises the question of natural signification. No longer should this question be prohibited in science.

The Vision of Biosemiotics

I wish to suggest a model (Figure 1) according to which environmental, technical, and psychosomatic problem areas are always seen as interrelated and, in this interrelationship, as deeply dependent on their common anchoring in the general semiotics of life, the sphere of biosemiotics.

The basic idea implicit in the model is that an eventual transcendence of dualism, and thus the establishment of a fruitful programme of research into our knowledge lacunae, will presuppose the development of a semiotic, or sign-theoretic, perspective on the dynamics of nature. 'Sign' should be understood here as a triadic unit (Figure 2) according to the tradition from the American scientist and philosopher Charles Sanders Peirce (1839–1914). The semiotic perspective implies that natural entities and processes should be analysed as interconnected webs of sign relations, shaking hands, so to say, throughout nature and between levels in the hierarchical scale stretching, along the spatial dimension, from the single cell to the biosphere or, along the semantic dimension, from pheromone signalling to the human psycho-neuro-immuno-endocrine system.

The development of a modern biosemiotics goes at least as far back as the German biologist Jakob von Uexküll who, in 1926, established his Institut fur Umweltsforschung at the University of Hamburg. By the term *umweltsforschung* von Uexküll meant 'research into the phenomenal worlds, selfworlds or subjective universes, i.e., the worlds around animals as they perceive them'.[2]

Although the thoughts of Jakob von Uexküll had very little direct impact on the further development of biology in this century, he deeply influenced Konrad Lorenz and thus indirectly contributed to the foundation of ethology as a scientific discipline.[3] It is little wonder that ethology would be the branch of biology most open to a semiotic perspective. The communicative aspect of animal behaviour, after all, is hard to overlook. As Thomas A. Sebeok has observed, ethology is 'hardly more than a special case of diachronic semiotics'.[4] But again, among ethologists there is no widespread awareness of the roots of their discipline in the age-old tradition of semiotics. This disregard for the fruitful potential of the semiotic tradition may well reflect tacit pressure from the scientific society to conform to established explanatory ideals. For ethology to gain respect among the core disciplines of biology it had to prove its credibility through strict adherence to the classical causal scheme, leaving out dubious reference to concepts implying the existence of subjects sticking to the objects under investigation.[5]

This is probably the reason why the creation of a modern scientific biosemiotics had to be initiated outside the core disciplines of biology. What was needed was not just a more open-minded ethology, for if semiotic reasoning was deemed acceptable the whole of biology would become involved.[6] In 1963 Thomas A. Sebeok, reflecting on zoology from the viewpoint of a linguist, recognized that the study of animal interaction deals far more explicitly with signs than does linguistics and he accordingly suggested that the study of animal interaction be called 'zoo semiotics'. In the following decades Thomas A. Sebeok has energetically continued his efforts to integrate the study of life processes into the general framework of semiotic theory, while gradually during the 1970s and 1980s a diverse range of studies have contributed to this aim (the most recent account of the status of the field may be gained from Sebeok and Umiker-Sebeok).[7]

In its most radical implication the emergent vision of biosemiotics entails a paradigm in which signification is the key concept for the study of life and in which organic evolution is understood as the natural history of signification and 'semiotic freedom'.[8]

The temptation among biologists to introduce anthropomorphic concepts in their explanations is an old one. After all, the only place to go for models of the purposeful behaviour of living systems would be the cultural sphere of the human being. And ever since the Watson-Crick double helix model of the DNA molecule was introduced in 1953 the 'nature as language' metaphor has seemed attractive to many researchers.[9]

The metaphor of language, however, is far too narrow to capture the richness of communication going on at all levels of the life zone. The human linguistic domain is basically dependent on a digital code of phonemes and morphemes, i.e. a code based on discrete symbols with no, or at least no pronounced, resemblance to things symbolized. Although a multitude of analogue codes such as gestures and all sorts of body languages as well as auditory parameters (tempo, rhythm, pitch of the voice) supervenes on the primary digital code, language retains the typical repertoire of digital

Figures

Figure 1: The dualism of nature–culture repeats itself as a dualism between internal human nature and external nature. In the dualistic perspective the question of human evolution poses endless problems. The model suggests that a semiotic understanding of life may serve as a key which opens the door to a unified understanding of the three indicated relations.

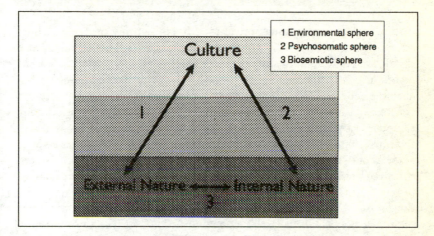

Figure 2: Peirce's triadic understanding of the sign: 'A sign is a something which stands for something else to somebody'; i.e., the sign consists of three links: (a) the primary sign, (b) the object to which the primary sign refers, and (c) the interpretant or key according to which the primary sign refers to the object.

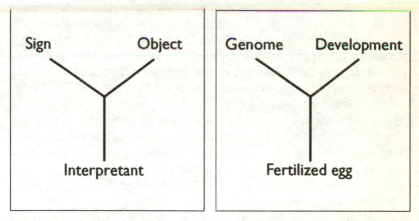

Figure 3: The figure describes ontogenesis (development) as a semiotic relation (as in Figure 2): The genome does not just determine the developmental processes. Rather it should be seen as a set of signs, and as such the genome will have to be interpreted by the fertilized egg as referring to that process.

codes:[10] the *distance* between the words spoken and what is spoken about makes possible (1) a *freedom of combination* (natural laws do not impose constraints on the content of spoken language), (2) *sharing* (objectivity in the sense of intersubjectivity), (3) *memory* (sentences have the capacity to fix past experiences into schemata that are easy to retail, albeit only as concepts), and (4) *meta messages* (messages about messages, such as self-referential denials).

These characteristics of digital codes are not at all typical of the codes through which communication among living entities proceeds. Thus, according to Anthony Wilden,[11] the human species is the only one to use digital communication in any systematic way; members of all other species communicate in the analogue (even the dance of bees is based on an analogue code, as Wilden convincingly shows).[12] Also, most communication processes inside the organism seem to be based on modulation of continuously varying parameters such as levels of hormones or antibody molecules in the body fluids, or saturation of receptor sites at the cellular surfaces of tissues. At one level, however, digital communication is a very decisive element of life on earth, namely the genetic level, the transmission of hereditary messages or instructions between generations. This communication is based on the digital sequential code of DNA consisting of four molecular groups normally abbreviated to A, T, C and G (referring to the names of the involved nucleotide bases). For example, the human genome (the totality of the human genetic material) consists of some 3 billion of these units ordered in a highly complex sequence which is unique to each human individual. And, as is now well known, the fertilized human egg is normally capable of constructing the child by reading the instructions contained in this DNA-message (the egg has nowhere else to go for learning how to do this). If one gene were compared to one word, the human genome would be like several very thick books.

The metaphor of nature as language therefore depends on and underscores a 'DNAistic' view of nature in which the transmission of hereditary instructions coded as DNA plays the all-dominating role, while other communication processes are seen as derived processes essentially predetermined by the genome. In spite of the seemingly anthropomorphic character of language competence this view is utterly reductionistic. As has previously been shown,[13] it is legitimized through an objectivistic conception of the term 'information' which is understood simply as a property of the gene. Conceived of as genes, information can be exchanged and selected through the neo-Darwinian schemes. By identifying the hereditary message with a set of instructions each corresponding to a given segment of the DNA molecule, it became possible to treat the dynamics of messages in terms of the dynamics of molecules.

This explanatory scheme, however, presupposes that there is no need for the hereditary messages to be interpreted, or in other words that instructions are independent of context. This is hardly the case, even at the level of the individual cell, less so at the level of tissues, and still less so at the level of an individual organism. Furthermore, genetic instructions should be analysed in the proper time perspective, that of evolutionary change. In this perspective genetic instructions are continuously changed and recombined in new functional patterns. These changes reflect necessities imposed by structural and functional constraints on the reshaping of embryos (a reshaped animal presupposes a reshaped embryo). The biological meaning (reading) of given genetic instructions thus definitely changes in response to changed genetic contexts in the growing embryo. And the coordination of, say, 80,000 functional genetic instructions working in synchrony during embryonic development is not itself genetically coded. Coordination depends on a reciprocal fit between the genetic 'manual' and the autonomous properties of a multitude of growing and differentiating tissues.

Code Duality and Self-Reference

Considerations like these lead me to suggest[14] that rather than seeing DNA as the director of life tirelessly ruling all processes both inside and in between organisms and ecosystems on this earth, we should adopt a view in which DNA is only one part of a game, the other part being the analogue version of the living system (the organism). In this view the role of DNA is rather like that of a library in which detailed information about life has been written down and stored. The individual organism, or embryo, would be then like a reader relentlessly searching through its internal library for necessary information about how to proceed. Furthermore, according to this view DNA should be considered no more in charge of the life processes than books on the shelves of a library are held to be in charge of the social process. In human life, we normally consider digital codes such as for example the text on this page to be passive, while individuals of flesh and blood – the analogue codes – are conceived as active. We have every reason, likewise, to consider a fertilized egg or a growing embryo as an active part which somehow manages to translate or interpret the passively waiting genomic messages.

Inside every known organism there exists a kind of self-description made in the digital code of DNA. In the process of sexual reproduction this self-description, or rather half of it, is mixed with another (half) digital self-description in a small template cell, thereby producing the fertilized egg.

The return to the analogue sphere is possible because this template cell (and only this cell) perpetuates the spatial organization of the cell, the cytoskeleton, from generation to generation and contains the cues necessary for understanding the mixed self-descriptions, reading them as a detailed set of instructions for constructing the organism. The possession of this principle of code duality[15] – the unending chain of codings and recodings shuffling the message back and forth between the analogue and digital form of representation (organism and DNA) – is in my view the best possible definition of life.

Of course, underneath this whole conception there is a hidden supposition, that individual biological entities, cells, tissues, organisms, populations, species, ecosystems or even the biosphere are intentional subjects engaged in semiotic acts of interpretation. Do we have any right to think so?

Answering no to this question routes us directly back to dualism. But how can we possibly answer yes? I think the key to this problem is self-reference. The essence of code duality is the existence inside any organism of a self-description in digital code. The crucial point is that this description is far from being a total description. Understanding it presupposes a cellular interpreter which can provide for indispensable material and spatial cues to the 'text' without which its 'meaning' becomes inaccessible (Figure 3). The combination of individual mortality and semiotic survival through the messages contained in the genotype pool (better: the genomorph)[16] of the population results in that unending chain of *semi-faithful self-referential loops*,[17] which we call organic evolution.[18]

Due to the evolutionary process, living systems differ from non-living systems in a way which is very important for the present discussion: inanimate nature is bound to 'remember' anything which happens until wind, water or life processes have eventually erased the tracks. For instance, the surface of the moon is still covered with nearly ineradicable scars from meteoric fall-out in the distant past. Here is no oblivion. In contrast, all living systems have selective mechanisms for the incorporation of the present into the future. Due to extinction (biological oblivion) and modification every species represents, literally incarnates, a very selective genomic memory of its own phylogenetic history right back to the beginning of life. The hereditary messages carried in the genotype pool of present species represent conserved experiences of how to construct individuals capable of managing survival and reproduction under the ecological niche conditions of ancestors. In addition to this, the more brainy species have developed short-time memories intended for selective conservation of individual life history in a coded form.[19]

But this temporality, the ability of living entities to 'incorporate the present into the future' seems to be very close to modern conceptions of what constitutes a self. For instance, David Polkinghorne says: 'Self, then, is not a static thing or a substance, but a configuration of personal events into an historical unity which includes not only what one has been but also anticipations of what one will be.'[20] This whole question has been discussed in more depth elsewhere.[21] Here I can only repeat my conclusion that we may consider living systems as subjects in this restricted sense, that they are temporal beings capable of distinguishing and acting upon selective features of their surroundings and participating in the evolutionary incorporation of the present into the future.[22]

Having established that much, I hope to have also legitimized the use of the anthropomorphic concept of signification in the context of pre-human nature. Living systems select their environments, they fill in signification, they interpret life events in terms of their own future. That is the core of semiosis.

Biosemiotics and Environmental Evaluation

At a very general level biosemiotics suggests a view of nature which runs counter to the prevailing belief in simplicity. Living systems, studied at whatever level, consist of historical and unique entities organized in obedience to a logic of semiotic functionality. The biosemiotic view implies that the neo-Darwinian ambition of reducing the majestic process of organic evolution to the chance outcome of an aimless mechanism of natural selection among competing individuals or genotypes is too simplistic. Rather, cells, tissues, organisms, populations and ecological systems should be seen as informationally highly self-dependent – or autopoietic[23] – entities responding to external messages in ways not specified by the messages themselves, but by an internal organization, or historical individuality, of the entity in question. Evolution concerns survival and eventual enrichment of patterns of semiosis rather than survival of organisms or genotypes. Signs, not genes, are the basic units of life.

From an environmental point of view this shift in the view of nature is certainly a very urgent matter, since it dethrones the authority of those simplistic assumptions which have for such a long time legitimized the technological violation of the internal dynamics of living systems on this planet. To change people's minds and inner values is always a slow process, but it may become even slower or impossible if educated people do not understand the full depth of the necessary change. Thus, one may well worry about the long-term success of environmental education if it is offered inside a paradigmatic view of nature which supports the rationality of that homogenizing and simplifying human practice which is the very core of the ecological crisis.

The discussion of the concept of complexity may illustrate this point. Environmentalists have generally considered ecological complexity to be of positive value and logically, at least, complexity would seem to be the opposite of simplicity. But the problem with this concept may well be that our scientific tradition has tended to treat it in a simplifying way, through definition in quantitative terms.

This may be the reason why Daniel McShea can conclude his recent study of complexity as an evolutionary parameter by pointing out, that although it is conventional wisdom that complexity increases through evolution, almost no empirical evidence for any such trend exists.[24] As one of the sceptics, the paleontologist George Simpson, declared as early as 1949: 'It would be a brave anatomist who would attempt to prove that recent man is more complicated than a Devonian ostracoderm.'[25]

Although complexity remains an ambiguous term there is some consensus now that the structural or morphological complexity of a system (biological or otherwise) is a function of the number of its different parts and the irregularity of their arrangement.[26] But seen from the biosemiotic point of view it is hardly surprising that such a general concept, which is insensitive to the peculiarity of living entities, fails to capture the essential character of organic evolution. I have suggested that rather than complexity we should consider the capacity which I termed semiotic freedom,[27] 'the depth of meaning an individual or a species is capable of communicating' as a possible candidate for a systematically increasing parameter in evolution. The concept of 'semiotic freedom' is related to the concept of logical depth.[28] Informally, we can explain logical depth as the number of steps in the deduction or causal path connecting a thing with its plausible origin. The underlying idea is that complexity or meaning depends, not on the length of a message, but on the work spent in producing it, not on the information contained in the message, but on the calculation time needed for throwing away superfluous information.

The development of this and the related concept of thermodynamic depth reflects a growing and much-needed recognition of the insufficiency of traditional information theory vis-à-vis the problems of intentionality of living systems and of human beings in particular. In pointing to the importance, for production of meaning, of the work done in getting rid of irrelevant and therefore distracting kinds of information, these concepts contribute to our understanding of what should be meant by meaning. As such they may also illustrate an important aspect of the term 'semiotic freedom'. However, one should be careful not to conclude that life dynamics can be captured through objectivistic (and simplifying) parameters. Semiotic freedom would have to be understood not as a quantifiable measure but as a quality to be only provisionally ranked through informed consensus or negotiation.

Environmental technology, research and policy should reflect the inner workings of nature, not the workings of mechanisms invented in the laboratory in order to account for life through objective formulas. This is very much a question of research ethics and research policy. We all prefer quantitative statements because they make the choice between decisions so much clearer. But if it can be shown that the continued failure of suggested quantitative parameters reflects a deep logic of the object under study, living nature, the most honest thing to do after all is to turn to other strategies. In all its vagueness the proposed parameter of 'semiotic freedom' offers interesting potentialities in environmental evaluation. The resilience of the semiotic interplay inside an ecosystem may well show up upon closer analysis to be the most decisive factor of all in the fate of the system. And probably ecological disaster would be an objective disaster at least in this sense, that it would imply a loss of semiotic freedom. Thus, a title like 'The Silent Spring' would contain a much more pointed message than perhaps anybody suspected at the time.

Biosemiotics and the Question of Moral Subjects

In recent decades there have been many attempts to extend the conception of moral status to include non-humans. The recognition that biological entities should count as semiotic entities may have implications for this discussion of the moral standing of non-human living beings.

Traditionally, it was assumed that inherent value can only be ascribed to 'moral agents' – subjects which have, in some sense, free will and reason, or at least practical reason. But this criterion implies that mentally retarded or brain-damaged persons, for example, as well as normal minors and embryos, will not be said to have inherent value and thus to count as moral subjects. This means that such persons are not protected by moral duties which are binding for other moral agents. Many philosophers therefore, have claimed that 'moral persons' should be accorded inherent value. A moral person can be understood as a subject who has the capability of being a moral agent regardless of whether this capability is realized as an ability or not.[29]

Now, in order to bring at least mammals under the protection of moral duties, there have been several attempts during the last few decades at establishing less exclusive criteria for being a moral person.[30] Or, alternatively, it has been suggested that the class of moral subjects extends far beyond the class of moral persons, and that inherent value may be ascribed to this broader category in such a way that other moral agents are bound by direct moral duties towards all such moral subjects.[31]

Jon Wetlesen has suggested that we make an 'analogical extension of moral standing to all moral subjects' based on the capacity of self-determination which he links to Spinoza's notion of conation. 'Each individual strives to persevere in its being', as Spinoza says – that is, each being strives to maintain its structural and functional characteristics. This determined striving or conation is inherent in the nature of each real individual being, according to Spinoza. And this can be taken as a ground for the ascription of inherent value and moral standing.[32]

Wetlesen goes on to extend the concept of the individual along Spinoza's lines to include also 'supra-individual wholes':

> When we talk about atoms, molecules, organs, organisms, species-populations, ecosystems, the biosphere, the ecosphere, planetary systems, galaxies etc., some or all of these entities could possibly be understood in terms of Spinoza's notion of an individual, provided it could be attributed an individualized striving. And in that case, we should have a ground for ascribing inherent value to it, and include it in the class of objects which are moral subjects and have a moral standing.[33]

In this way Wetlesen transcends not only anthropocentric ethics but also biocentric ethics, ending up in an ecocentric ethical position.

From the point of view of this chapter the question of analogical extension may be posed in a different way which nevertheless leads to similar conclusions, except for the idea of extending moral status beyond the biosphere.[34] Here the core property of life, as stated above, is the principle of internal self-mapping or code duality. This 'survival through mortality' would be the equivalent of Spinoza's perseverance or conation. Considered as a striving toward maintenance of structural and functional characteristics, the principle of code duality nevertheless is only semi-faithful, allowing for errors or deviations to occur. And it is exactly because of this semi-faithfulness that the interplay of interpretative processes at different levels (egg, organism, gene pool, lineage, ecosystem) looping into each other establishes a generative substratum for the evolutionary process. It is only in the context of this overall evolutionary setting that 'present becomes incorporated into future', and only in this context should primitive organisms be considered as genuine subjects. Thus, the single amoeba in isolation is not a subject, it only becomes a subject when understood as part of an evolutionary project. If by analogical extension we are allowed to include any genuine subjects in the class of moral subjects, then primitive organisms like amoebas should be considered moral subjects *at the level of the species*, whereas individually they are not moral subjects.

In more highly differentiated species where a nervous system has evolved things get more complicated. Animals at this level not only possess the genetic representations of their phylogenetic past, but in addition to this they also have more or less well-developed immunological and neural representations – *umwelts* – of their environments based on their own individual past, their life history. Through the possession of an *umwelt* the organism becomes involved in quite a new way of anticipation. While genetic anticipation cannot reflect events of individual life history, the possession of *umwelts* makes this kind of anticipation a latent possibility. At some point of the evolutionary process this new semiotics of learning has reached a perfection such that one must ascribe subjectivity not only to the species but to the single organism. And accordingly, based on the principle of analogical extension, it would seem reasonable to judge such organisms as moral subjects in their own right.

A Biosemio-anthropology

We must now return to the problem of Hume's position on normative propositions. We still have to answer the question why the kind of analogical extension suggested above should be considered ethically legitimate. Why, in other words, should the eventual possession of the property of subjectivity in the sense used in this text be a sufficient reason for including a given entity in the class of moral subjects?

While attempting to answer this question I shall sketch a semiotically informed bio-anthropology. This bio-anthropology will posit the human need for identification as an existential need which every human individual must satisfy for the sake of her/his own mental survival. I shall further claim that this need for identification is buried in the drama of human self-consciousness and existential alienation. Briefly stated, this drama derives from the fact that the human species may be defined as the kind of animal in which a separation has appeared between individual life history and phylogenetic history. Not one but two stories are then at work in the mind and body of the human being. Self-realization or individuation consists in bringing together these two seemingly independent stories into one narrative which can assure one's belonging to a human community as well as to nature.

My argument is that the most extraordinary novelty in human evolution is the appearance of a new system of code duality based on reshuffling of mental content back and forth between codes of 'inner reality', or phenomenal worlds, and codes of language. In accordance with the evolutionary trend toward increased semiotic freedom many species have developed long life histories and the capacity for learning. We must assume that such animals have also aquired more or less elaborate *umwelts* or phenomenal worlds. But none of them have developed this strange digital system for the representation of internal mental states which is human language.

When considering the problem of how language evolved the surprising fact is that it very probably did not at first develop as a means for communication. The linguist Noam Chomsky has forcefully argued 'that either we must deprive the notion "communication" of all significance, or else we must reject the view that the purpose of language is communication'.[35] The same conclusion has been reached by the philosopher Karl Popper.[36] And Gregory Bateson[37] has pointed out that if language in any sense were an evolutionary replacement for non-verbal communication, we would have expected the older devices 'to have undergone conspicuous decay'. But clearly, they have not only not done that, but have in history become even more intricately elaborated in humans, so much so, indeed, that our skills in this respect exceed by far anything that any other animal is capable of displaying (a ballet or symphony, for example). Bateson concludes that language on the one hand and our repertoire of non-verbal communicative contrivances on the other must serve totally different functions.[38]

On the basis of evidence from several different fields Thomas Sebeok has concluded that 'language – or more precisely grammar – as a mute primary modelling system lodged in the brain, began, very likely, to emerge about 3 million years ago, in the australopithecine hominids'. Speech, on the other hand, is a much younger phenomenon: 'One must assume that speech encoding and speech decoding abilities, i.e., the production of language in a vocal mode in linear form, and its corresponding auditory reception, were developed and somewhat refined by about 300,000 years ago.'[39] Therefore, people experienced their world in a syntactical manner for one or two million years before they actually began talking to each other. Sebeok has explained the power inherent in this syntactically based modelling system by comparing it to the use of tinkertoy or lego which enables the child to construct infinite kinds of buildings: 'humans have evolved a way of modelling *their* universe in a way that not merely echoes "what is out there", but which can, additionally, dream up a potentially infinite number of *possible worlds*'.[40] In comparison the animal modelling system might perhaps be likened to the picture lottery principle.

One very important characteristic of a syntactic model of the world is the digital principle. Signs have to be discrete (like lego pieces) and should ideally not depend on the character of the thing signified. A very fundamental and difficult question then is: how can such a code arise from analogue predecessors?

According to Anthony Wilden's thorough analysis of the analogue–digital distinction the essence of a digital distinction is to introduce gaps into continuums.[41] Biologically speaking, for instance, the hand does not contain 5 digits but rather 4 gaps between fingers: during ontogeny cells in the growing embryo are selectively comitting suicide in the areas between what is later to become fingers. Digital distinction, therefore, in its most original sense was in fact an introduction of gaps into the continuous plate of the early hand. Wilden suggests that the idea implicit in producing this gestalt of digitalized distinction is represented in language by the word 'not': 'Boundaries are the conditions of distinguishing the "elements" of a continuum from the continuum itself. "Not" is such a boundary.... "Not" is a rule about how to make either/or distinctions themselves.'[42]

One of the most interesting suggestions as to how something like the concept 'not' may possibly appear at all was given by Gregory Bateson. He refers to the nip as used among monkeys in the so-called 'play'. The message of a nip, he says, is: 'I will not bite you'. That is, the opposite of the final message is worked through to reach a *reductio ad absurdum* which can then be the basis of mutual peace, hierarchic precedence, or sexual relations.[43] But, as he adds, 'These are cumbersome and awkward methods of achieving the negative.' The nip, after all, is still just an iconic message, a narratively signified presence of absence.

Somehow our remote ancestors may have managed to do a thing which no animal would do: to internalize the whole play sequence, imagining it without actually doing it. That is, a ritualized sequence of actions based on a reciprocal relationship became transformable to a mental sequence. But doing such a thing seems to presuppose the ability of internalizing not only 'the other' but in fact one self as 'an other' – the mental ability of *putting one self in somebody's place* which, as we shall see, is a very decisive step in human evolution.

Ritual, and thus social existence, must have been a very important factor behind the evolution of this capacity. Richard Leakey and Roger Lewin have suggested[44] that the creation of a 'food-sharing economy' was the essential step which marked off the line of our hominid ancestors from the apes. The essential element in this sharing economy is that both sexes participate in the procuring of food, each contributing a different component to the common meal (respectively meat and vegetables). According to Leakey and Lewin by far the most important skill in modern hunter-gatherer cultures consists in the ability to make in the brain an effective mental map of the surroundings, and a map with features that alter *in time*. Hunters and gatherers have to know where and when to search for a whole range of food items. It would seem, therefore, that from the moment the hominids began sharing their meals, there would have been an enormous survival-premium on the ability to communicate (non-verbally at first) such mental maps. But the necessary precondition for this is the production in individual minds of socially shared patterns or gestalts.

This is where ritual comes in: to collectivize the *umwelts* of individual group members. Communication via rituals may have helped to fix our ancestors' world in shared patterns which gradually became internalized. Thus, as Bateson proposed, perhaps 'the simple negative arose by intro-jection or imitation of the *vis-à-vis,* so that "not" was somehow derived from "don't".... This step would immediately endow the signals – be they verbal or iconic – with a degree of separateness from their referents, which would justify us in referring to the signals as "names". The same step would make possible the use of negative aspects of classification.'[45]

The appearance one and a half million years ago of the beautiful tear-drop shaped handaxe that is the hallmark of the Acheulian culture might be taken as a first fossil indication of this ritualized and in fact aesthetic mind.[46] 'The conceptualization involved in manufacturing these impressive symmetrical objects is of a different order from that involved in making simple core tools with sharp edges,' write Leakey and Lewin.[47] However, 'The point is that there is virtually no job that can be done with the implements in the well-developed Acheulian tool-kit that cannot equally well be performed using the essential random but effective products of enthusiastically crashing two stones together'.

This, of course, raises the question of why formalized and ordered technology emerged at all. The answer that Leakey and Lewin offer to this question turns upside down our traditional understanding of the relation between the development of technology and intelligence. 'As rules and customs developed for controlling the social and practical organizational problems of operating a successful gathering and hunting economy, those rules and customs impinged on the elaboration of material technology too.'[48] Thus, stone tool manufacture became more formalized: 'not because economics demanded it, but *because that was the way our ancestors' minds were working:* structure was stamped on social dynamics and on material technology'.[49]

It seems safe to conclude that at this time, if not before, evolution had finally managed to create animals with an *umwelt* based on the principle of syntax. The development of spoken language, however, was still far away. The fit between coding devices and decoding devices necessary for communication by the help of sequential auditory signs is no simple thing. As Sebeok has pointed out, it is far from effective even today (most of the time most of us do not fully understand what other people tell us) and evolution certainly has had a hard job in producing this marvellous system in the first place.[50]

But if, as we said above, the capacity for denial, for conceiving the 'not', presupposed the prior appearance of a capacity for putting oneself in somebody's place, then this capacity was very probably already present among *Homo erectus* populations living more than a million years ago. At least latently, therefore, the drama of existential alienation was with us before we could talk about it. In fact, the evolution of speech presupposed a certain kind of alienation, the 'separateness' involved in 'naming' to which Bateson alluded, although it may well be that *Homo erectus* did not subjectively experience any drama of alienation.

For the latent drama of loneliness, of not belonging to the natural world, to be experienced subjectively the sphere of language would probably have to establish itself at a new supra-individual level, as it finally did through the development of speech. Speech is an emergent property in the sense that its supra-individual character implies the creation of a new kind of 'semiotic freedom' not contained in or deducible from the initial conditions, the original syntactical modelling system or *umwelt,* from which it emerges. As we have seen, through speech a new self-referential loop based on code duality unfolds itself, thereby making up for cultural evolution.

This liberation of an anthroposemiotic subject supervening upon the original biosemiotic hominid subject produced a deep split in human identity. Being suspended in the code duality of language we have become alien to our participation in the code duality of life. Our individual life history has become separated from our phylogenetic history. Or, as I said: 'Not one but two stories are at work in the mind and body of the human being.' The only way to transcend this split – this loss of natural belonging – is through our deeply buried capacity for putting oneself in somebody's place. For this capacity makes it possible for humans to identify with the environment in the sense of Arne Naess, the 'spontaneous, non-rational, but not irrational, process through which the interests of another being are reacted to as our own interest or interests'.[51]

Since my claim in this section has been that our evolutionary capacity for identification is connected to our ancestors' introjection of ritualized patterns of relationship, we should be perfectly capable of identifying not only with other human beings but with any entity which might occupy a similar position to ours in the bio-logics of nature. I should think, then, that our natural propensity for identification would include all other *umwelt*-builders in the broadest sense of that term, even species of lower-level organisms lacking neural systems but which, *qua* species, nevertheless create a kind of (genomic) *umwelt* through their evolutionary incorporation of ecological niche conditions into the future. As Gregory Bateson observed: 'Is our reason for admiring a daisy the fact that it shows – in its form, in its growth, in its colouring, and in its death – the symptoms of being alive? Our appreciation for it is to that extent an appreciation of its similarity to ourselves.'[52]

If this is so, identification is a cure for our existential split: at the symbolic level it reconciles our two inner subjects, the anthroposemiotic and the biosemiotic self. In our body, of course, Psyche and Soma necessarily meet and continuously interact in the production of our actual lives.[53] Not only mental but physical health, self-realization or individuation, presuppose the production of a narrative through which our two all too separate stories can become one.

We should now be in a position to answer the question posed at the beginning of this section. Species of lower organisms are moral subjects for the very same reason we are ourselves: we cannot neglect their inherent value if we are to construct a true life-healing narrative, that is, if we are to individuate. Refusing to identify implies the surrender to our own alienation.

To surrender may be fully legitimate, of course. But the point is, that legitimization actually *is* required, for example by referring to contradictory interests. Neither should these considerations support the idea that identification is an everything or nothing phenomenon. We certainly are much more deeply connnected with other human beings, with whom we share not only the phylogenetic code duality but also a cultural code duality, than we are to any other living systems on the earth. I only claim that all living systems deserve to be considered as moral subjects, but some of them more so than others. I should like to suggest 'semiotic freedom' as a parameter which might eventually be used for grading among moral subjects.

Finally, the question is: have I managed to derive through these steps a normative conclusion from descriptive premises? It would indeed seem that I have, but this was only possible because normative premises were built into the descriptive premises: semiosis seems to presuppose intentions of some sort, 'evolutionary intentions' so to say. Obviously, by admitting interpretative processes to be a core phenomenon of life in general, we were able to show that living creatures should be considered as genuine subjects at least at the species levels. And this was very probably the way our ancestors conceived of nature. We could therefore claim that other living creatures did occupy positions in the logic of our ancestors' environments, which from the very beginning of language evolution made them natural objects for identification. If my thesis is valid, and human morality springs from the existential need for identification, it follows that the suggested kind of analogical extension from human beings to other living beings (or species) is valid as well.

But again, a norm has in fact been present from the very beginning of this analysis. In a way this is the case even for the Newtonian premise that no intentions are present in nature: prohibiting norms is also a kind of norm. Only, this particular prohibiting norm cannot explain the existence of norms, and thus it fails to justify its own existence.

Notes

1 Ilya Prigogine, *From Being to Becoming* (San Francisco: Freeman, 1980).

2 Thure von Uexküll, 'Introduction: Meaning and Science in Jacob von Uexküll's Concept of Biology', *Semiotica* 42 no. 1 (1982): p. 1.

3 Konrad Lorenz, 'The Comparative Method in Studying Innate Behaviour Patterns', *Symposia of the Society for Experimental Biology* 4 (1950): pp. 221–68. Konrad Lorenz, *King Solomon's Ring. New Light on Animal Ways* (London: Methuen, 1952). Nicolaas Tinbergen, *The Study of Instinct* (Oxford: Clarendon Press, 1951).

4 Thomas A. Sebeok, *Contributions to the Doctrine of Signs* (Lisse: Peter de Ridde, 1976), p. 156.

5 Jesper Hoffmeyer, 'Semiotic Aspects of Biology: Biosemiotics'. In Roland Posner, K. Robering and T. A. Sebeok (eds), *Semiotics: A Handbook of the Sign-Theoretical Foundations of Nature and Culture* (Berlin: Gruyter, forthcoming).

6 *Ibid.*

7 Thomas A. Sebeok and Jean Umiker-Sebeok (eds), *Biosemiotics: The Semiotic Web 1991* (Berlin: Mouton de Gruyter, 1992).

8 Jesper Hoffmeyer, 'Some Semiotic Aspects of the Psycho-Physical Relation: The Endo-Exosemiotic Boundary'. In Sebeok and Umiker-Sebeok (1992), pp. 101–23.

9 A critical discussion of the use of the nature-as-language metaphor is given in Claus Emmeche and Jesper Hoffmeyer, 'From Language to Nature: The Semiotic Metaphor in Biology' *Semiotica* 84 no. 1/2 (1991): pp. 1–2.

10 Jesper Hoffmeyer: 'The Constraints of Nature on Free Will'. In Viggo Mortensen and R. C. Sorensen (eds) *Free Will and Determinism* (Aarhus: Aarhus University Press, 1987), pp. 188–200. Jesper Hoffmeyer and Claus Emmeche, 'Code Duality and the Semiotics of Nature'. In Myrdene Anderson and Floyd Merell (eds), *On Semiotic Modeling* (New York: Mouton de Gruyter, 1991), pp. 117–66.

11 Anthony Wilden, *System and Structure* (New York: Tavistock, 1980).

12 *Ibid.*, p. 167.

13 Hoffmeyer and Emmeche, 'Code-Duality and the Semiotics of Nature'.

14 Hoffmeyer, 'The Constraints of Nature on Free Will'. Hoffmeyer and Emmeche, 'Code-Duality and the Semiotics of Nature', pp. 125 ff.

15 Hoffmeyer, 'The Constraints of Nature on Free Will'.

16 Hoffmeyer and Emmeche, 'Code-Duality and the Semiotics of Nature', pp. 155 ff.

17 Douglas R. Hofstadter, *Gödel, Escher, Bach: An Eternal Golden Braid* (Middlesex: Penguin Books, 1979).

18 Hoffmeyer, 'Some Semiotic Aspects of the Psycho-Physical Relation'. The dynamic capabilities of code dualism have been discussed in Hoffmeyer and Emmeche, 'Code-Duality and the Semiotics of Nature'.

19 Jesper Hoffmeyer, 'Some Semiotic Aspects of the Psycho-Physical Relation'.

20 Donald Polkinghorne, *Narrative Knowing and the Human Sciences* (Albany: SUNY Press, 1988), p. 150.

21 Jesper Hoffmeyer, 'Some Semiotic Aspects of the Psycho-Physical Relation'.

22 *Ibid.*, p. 101.

23 Humberto Maturana and Fransisco Varela, *Autopoiesis and Cognition. The Realization of the Living* (Dordrecht: Reidel, 1980).
24 Daniel W. McShea: 'Complexity and Evolution: What Everybody Knows', *Biology and Philosophy* 6 (1991): pp. 303–21.
25 Citation from McShea: 'Complexity and Evolution: What Everybody Knows', p. 320.
26 McShea: 'Complexity and Evolution: What Everybody Knows', p. 304.
27 Hoffmeyer, 'Some Semiotic Aspects of the Psycho-Physical Relation', p. 109.
28 Charles Bennet, 'Logical Depth and Physical Complexity'. In Rolf Herken (ed.), *The Universal Turing Machine. A Half-Century Survey* (Oxford: Oxford University Press, 1988), pp. 227–57.
29 Jon Wetlesen, 'Who has Moral Standing in the Environment?' Paper prepared for the Conference *Ethics and Environment: The Dimensions of Dialogue*, Centre for Development and Environment, University of Oslo, 1992.
30 For example, Tom Regan, *The Case for Animal Rights* (Berkeley: University of California Press, 1983).
31 Louis G. Lombardi, 'Inherent Worth, Respect, and Rights', *Environmental Ethics* 5 no. 3 (1983): pp. 257–70. P. V. Taylor, *Respect for Nature. A Theory of Environmental Ethics* (Princeton: Princeton University Press, 1986): pp. 133 ff, 147 ff, 261. Jon Wetlesen, 'Who Has Moral Standing in the Environment?', p. 12.
32 Jon Wetlesen, ' Who Has Moral Standing in the Environment?', p. 17.
33 *Ibid.*, p. 19.
34 Wetlesen later modified his own view on this question (personal communication).
35 Noam Chomsky, *Rules and Representations* (New York: Columbia University Press, 1980), p. 230.
36 Karl Popper, *Objective Knowledge: An Evolutionary Approach* (Oxford: Clarendon Press, 1972), p. 121.
37 Gregory Bateson, 'Redundancy and Coding'. In Thomas A. Sebeok (ed.), *Animal Communication: Techniques of Study and Results of Research* (Bloomington, Ind.: Indiana University Press, 1968). Reprinted in G. Bateson, *Steps to An Ecology of Mind* (New York: Ballantine Books, 1972), pp. 425.
38 *Ibid.*, p. 614.
39 Thomas A. Sebeok, ' The Problem of the Origin of Language in an Evolutionary Frame', *Language Sciences* 8 no. 2 (1986): pp. 169–76.
40 Thomas A. Sebeok. 'Toward a Natural History of Language', *Semiotica* 65 no. 3/4 (1987): pp. 343–58. Here p. 347.
41 Anthony Wilden, *System and Structure*, p. 186.
42 *Ibid.*, pp. 185–6.
43 Bateson, *Steps to An Ecology of Mind*, p. 424.
44 Richard Leakey and Roger Lewin, *People of the Lake* (London: Collins, 1978).
45 Bateson, *Steps to An Ecology of Mind*, p. 425.
46 Hoffmeyer and Emmeche, 'Code-Duality and the Semiotics of Nature' p. 134.
47 Richard Leakey and Roger Lewin, 'The Origins of Human Language', *New Scientist*, 20 September 1979, pp. 894–7.
48 *Ibid.*
49 *Ibid.* Italics added.

50 Sebeok, 'Toward a Natural History of Language', p. 174.
51 Arne Naess, 'Identification as a Source of Deep Ecological Attitudes'. In Michael Tobias (ed.), *Deep Ecology* (San Diego: Avant Books, 1985), pp. 256–70.
52 Gregory Bateson, *Mind and Nature. A Necessary Unity* (New York: Bantam Books, 1979), p. 142.
53 Jesper Hoffmeyer, 'Some Semiotic Aspects of the Psycho-Physical Relation', pp. 118 ff.

CHAPTER 10

A 'Genethics'
That Makes Sense

ROSALYN DIPROSE

This DNA, this double helix, this bare substance of our chromosomal being, source of our sameness, root of our difference.

Fay Weldon, *The Cloning of Joanna May*[1]

To be located in space, which we all are, and to locate others, which we all do, requires embodiment. To be positioned, and to take up a position (even if this involves sitting on the fence) is a question of ethics. 'Ethics' is derived from the Greek word *ethos*, meaning dwelling, or habitat – the place to which one returns. Habitat encompasses habits which, as the product of the repetition of bodily activities, make up one's 'character' – one's specificity or what is properly one's own.[2] To belong to, and project out from an *ethos* is to take up a position in relation to others. This involves comparison, relation to what is different and to what passes before us. Taking up a position, presenting oneself, therefore requires a non-thematic awareness of temporality and location; and the intrinsic reference point for temporality, spatial orientation and, therefore, difference, is one's own body. That location and position are concepts easily interchangeable illustrates the co-incidence of embodiment and ethics which necessarily come together by virtue of our spatio-temporal being-in-the world.

To define ethics in terms of bodily specificity would seem to be at odds with a more modern understanding of ethics. We more usually understand ethics in terms of a universal set of principles which ought to govern behaviour, principles which are formulated and grasped by the rational mind. As these principles claim universality, they evoke an ethics which assumes that behaviour originates in a potentially unified mind housed in a broad, homogeneous habitat.

Despite this emphasis, there are some contemporary accounts of an ethics based on bodily specificity.[3] These variously locate the body as the site of one's habitat or subjectivity – where the body is constituted by a dynamic relation with other bodies in a social context of power, desire and knowledge.

The discrepancy between these two approaches to ethics is not simply a question of etymology. Related to this are different, and usually unacknowledged, understandings of the components which go to make up our spatio-temporal being-in-the-world. The difference pertains to whether we think 'being' is composed primarily of mind or matter; to what we understand by the relation between mind and matter; and to whether we think the world we inhabit is homogeneous or fragmented. Underlying all these questions is some assumption about the meaning of 'in'.[4] An ethics based on universal rational principles assumes that our 'being' is a discrete entity separate from the 'world, such that we are 'in' the world after the advent of both. An ethics of bodily specificity, on the other hand, claims that our 'being' and the 'world' are constituted by the relation 'in'.

Science, that field of knowledge which governs the formulation of the nature of our being and the world we are 'in', assumes the first relation – that our 'being' and the 'world' are primordially distinct. And, as scientific descriptions of the body and the 'world' the body inhabits are thought to hover above both without effect, then ethics is thought to have no place in knowledge.

Despite this distancing and despite a privilege given to an ethics based on universal rational principles, the increasing public scrutiny of the activities of biomedical science suggests a link between science, the specificity of embodiment and ethics. The link is suggestive only. Much of the recent discussion around biomedical ethics does move away from abstract, formal principles, stressing instead individual rights, particular contexts and specific needs.[5] However, the nature of being and individuality is usually assumed in these discussions and rarely is there any analysis of *how* or *why* medicine and science, as modes of knowing, are necessarily ethical. What is even more surprising, given the material of biomedicine, is that rarely is any explicit reference made to the significance of embodiment to biomedical ethics.

David Schenck's paper, 'The Texture of Embodiment: Foundation for Medical Ethics', is a notable exception.[6] Schenck, following Merleau-Ponty, acknowledges that the body is 'our centre of activity in the world'.[7] As we comport ourselves towards the world *through* our bodies then, he argues, our body is not just an instrument by which we express ourselves. Rather, the body *'is literally our selves expressed'*.[8] Biomedical science and medical practice are by nature ethical because they deal with our most intimate and alienating possession – the body as our mode of social expression:

> It is the texture of bodily being that gives to medicine as social practice and medical ethics as social discourse their particular and distinctive features ... .[9]

At the same time, Schenck limits the ethics of medicine to its role of intervention after the texture of the body, its social 'expressiveness', has been rendered incoherent:

> Medicine deals with the *brokenness* of the body The collapse of the body at once invites and necessitates care by others. It *invites* care by virtue of the social expressiveness of the body, the call the injured body makes to unimpaired others [W]hat is given over to others in these moments is that which is most intimate to one's self, most important to one's presence in the world.[10]

Schenck recognizes that the basis of our specific being-in-the-world is our particular embodiment. And he locates medical ethics in the responsibility involved in *repairing* that being-in-the-world. His analysis, therefore, suggests an ethics of difference – one that recognizes the material significance of embodiment to subjectivity. However, the connection he makes between 'being' and 'world' remains unclear and 'in' takes on the status of the copula. It would seem that our 'being', while bodily and habitual, only encounters the 'world' it inhabits after it is constituted. And, as biomedical practices only make the body their object after it is 'broken', they are included in the 'world' that our being encounters. By separating our 'being' from the social discourses and practices which make up the 'world', Schenck's analysis seems to beg the question of *how* the body is the self expressed. What is it, if not something about the 'world', that constitutes the significance of our bodily specificity? What constitutes the habitat/habits which hold together the specificity of our being? While providing an astute analysis of the bodily foundation of medical ethics, Schenck not only leaves these questions unanswered, but seems to contradict the tradition of thought upon which his analysis depends.

Merleau-Ponty, for example, claims that the body, which is the bearer of orientation or position, is not 'in' the world after the advent of both: 'our body is not primarily *in* space: it is of it'.[11] Similarly, Heidegger argues that our being is not 'in' the world in the way water is in a glass. Rather, our 'being-in' is constituted by the context of meaningful relations with which we are involved.[12] We can only 'dwell' in a world, encounter objects within it and be encountered as an object (say, by science) if we are constituted by a set of relations with which we are, thereby, 'familiar'. This familiarity, and the world's significance, is governed by a non-thematic pre-ontological 'understanding' of Being. For Merleau-Ponty, this pre-reflexive understanding resides in the body's orientation activity; for Heidegger, it resides in a history which we cannot control but which presents us as we evoke it at every moment. For both, the objectifying practices which represent our being (including biomedical science) are secondary modes of understanding. But, as such, they do constitute a particular mode of existence – one which marks a border between a human being and the world it inhabits.

If Schenck is to follow this tradition, then he would need to recognize that biomedical science has a role in the constitution of our being as a discrete entity and is not just a mode of reparation of that being.

Biomedical science does not, of course, confess to any constitutive role in the specificity of our embodiment. It does acknowledge a role in the observation and manipulation of that specificity and takes on some responsibility for ensuring that its manipulative function is not socially detrimental. This distinction between the making of the body and its manipulation is maintained by a division between theory and practice. That is, biomedical science claims to 'know', at least potentially, the elements and intricate processes which go together to make up a particular body. It also claims to 'know' in what ways, and for what reasons, bodies differ. This theoretical mode of biomedical science delineates the source of the specificity of our embodied being – a specificity thought to be outside that mode of knowing. On the other hand, biomedical practice can *alter* the texture of the body. Only as this secondary mode of intervention does biomedical science claim a constitutive role – in its ability to modify human matter.

Nowhere is biomedical science more active in its description and manipulation of bodily specificity, and nowhere are the distinctions between observing and doing, theory and practice, fact and value, knowledge and ethics more pronounced, than in the field of genetics. An excursion into the debate about the ethical issues surrounding modern genetics best reveals what is problematic about these distinctions or an ethics aimed at enhancing our being-in-the-world.

Through an increasingly vigorous and public debate about the ethics of genetics, we have been asked to share in the geneticist's competence as well as in the responsibility for the always uncertain consequences of scientific research. The reason why genetics is now thought to require the critical attention of all of us is best summarized in the following terms by one exemplary account: 'Genetics, perhaps more than any other branch of science except brain biology, probes deeply into the identity of individual human beings.'[13] Any account of modern genetics will describe how a cell's genetic content determines its metabolic processes and physical appearance. We are thus given some insight into how and why geneticists think that genes are ultimately responsible for a body's functioning and appearance, and ultimately, therefore, its identity and difference.

These accounts also usually include some critical assessment of the practical application of genetic theory. The potential for designer bodies, or gene therapy – the 'insertion', 'modification' and 'substitution' of genetic material to correct 'defects' – is a common cause for concern. But the application of genetics is not limited to its potential for eugenics. Genetic theory informs a wide range of social and medical practices. It is the condition for the possibility of immunological theory which in turn informs the approach to diseases such as AIDS.[14] Genetics also underscores screening for 'defective' individuals such as the criminal (through 'DNA finger-printing', for example) or a foetus carrying a genetically transmitted disease. Reproductive technology, the development of biological weapons and the selective breeding of flora and fauna for agricultural production all owe their vigour, splendour and status to modern genetics.

Not all genetic practice is considered to be of ethical significance and, even when caution is advised, not everyone agrees.[15] The ethical import of genetics seems to depend, in the first instance, upon the degree to which modification or manipulation of bodily specificity is involved. Why this matters to the guardians of science is usually expressed in the following terms: 'biomedical engineering circumvents the human context of speech and meaning, bypasses choice and goes directly to work to modify the human material itself'.[16] By evoking a distinction between 'social meaning' and matter (which allows the distinction between knowledge, or observa-tion, and intervention), such arguments claim that biomedical manipula-tion can institute an irreversible change to one's habitat. This implies that other vehicles of social change (the 'alteration of meaning' for example) are more flexible. Also, that there is an original and pure mode of being which, presumably, resides outside of 'social meaning' in nature.

Not all genetic practice involves manipulation of matter – sometimes it is just a question of surveillance. But surveillance, or genetic screening, and genetic engineering share a second feature considered to be of ethical import: a certain attitude to difference. Nobody wants to create a chimera (at least no one would admit to this) – the fantastic is considered to be too perverse, too offensive to our sensibilities. Rather, as Leon Kass has suggested, both the supporters and opponents of genetic engineering have, from the time the dream began, 'grounded their hopes and their fears in the same prospect: *that man can for the first time re-create himself*'.[17] This desire to double the self, by reproducing the self or making the other the same, is the target of concern about the role of genetic screening and manipulation in the eradication of difference.

The preservation of diversity is the primary concern expressed by David Suzuki and Peter Knudtson in their account of modern genetics in *Genethics*. They cite numerous examples of applied genetics which 'intentionally' or inadvertently seek to eliminate the expression of difference. The Human Genome Initiative (HGI) – a project aimed at mapping the 100,000 or so genes in the human genome – is a less obvious case in point. HGI expresses the hope of locating all genes responsible for disease, normal metabolic processes and subtle hereditary differences between individuals. With this prospect, Suzuki and Knudtson caution against the possibility of establishing 'wholescale genetic screening programs ... for identifying individuals who harbor genes considered "defective" or "inferior"'.[18] Such programmes, they claim, place too much confidence in a direct causal link between genes and individual behavioural differences, and could result in misguided attempts to normalize and/or isolate individuals considered to be inferior.

There is little doubt that modern genetics lends authority and sophistication to the practices which map and attempt to efface differences. Yet, as the champions of genetics will point out, we have at our disposal more efficient means to 'regulate human behaviour' and minimize the expression of difference.[19] Any sinister use of genetics, they argue, reflects the contamination of science by the ideology governing these other means of regulation. This may be the case. But the defence of genetics here again relies on a distinction between 'social meaning', or a biased interpretation of differences, and differences *per se*. Even Suzuki's and Knudtson's caution implies this distinction by separating theory from practice and then questioning the ability to interpret the meaning and value of observed differences without reference to an unsubstantiated social norm. What supposedly marks 'pure' genetics off from 'other' methods of social regulation, and from the 'bad politics' which may allow its misuse, is that its authority is derived from the claim to know the origin of the expression of difference outside its 'social meaning'. Presumably, then, the ethically correct categorization and manipulation of bodily specificity in the practical application of genetics would involve, not the social evaluation of difference in terms of a social norm, but reference to the origin of difference *per se*.

Implied in these warnings about the evaluation of difference is a claim that this evaluation is relational and therefore should be avoided. But, as Hegel reminds us, identity (in this case, one's bodily specificity) is *produced* through differential relations.[20] To label something or someone defective or inferior relies on the assumption that the 'proper' stands alone. Yet, some notion of the proper as sameness does silently underscore the evaluation of difference with real effects, and it does so by the institution of an interval between the one and the other. What constitutes this interval between entities is also what constitutes the 'in' between one's being and the world. It is what prevents each identity from dissolving into its other (including the subject and object of knowledge). Genetics, by referring to the origin of difference, claims to know the nature of this interval – what lies between entities such that their difference is real. However, it is the complicity of genetics in the *production*, rather than the indifferent description, of this spacing which requires more attention. What I will argue below is that genetic theory is itself a genetic operation – it is involved in the production of difference in the terms of sameness. On the other hand, because the self comes into being in the other, both the subject and object of knowledge are always other than themselves. Hence, the genetic determination of bodily specificity is necessarily deferred.

Genetic theory takes place in a mode of existence which assumes a distinction between the subject and object of knowledge, between the specificity of our bodily being and the discourses which describe that being and make up the world we inhabit. So genetics, at the level of theory, is considered to have a representative rather than a constitutive function in its delineation of the origin and somatic expression of difference. It would seem that genetics, as theory, has no ethics – it does not make the sensory; it makes sense of the sensory. At least its aim is to make sense.

But could genetics make sense in another sense? As a branch of science, genetics promises absolute knowledge or the Truth of Being. Even if incomplete, there is still a promise of more complete and adequate truth. And, lurking within this promise is the same attitude to difference which is of concern in applied genetics. As Emmanuel Levinas claims: 'Without doubt, the finite being that we are cannot in the final account complete the task of knowledge; but in the limit where this task is accomplished, it consists in making the other become the Same.'[21] For Levinas, it is alterity which provokes the desire to know – a claim which seems obvious in the case of genetics. Yet, the subject of knowledge does not simply discover the nature of the interval between entities or between itself and its object. Rather, the subject of knowledge forms and transforms this interval by constituting the other in its own image. We may be sympathetic with the call to responsibility being made by the custodians of science towards the geneticist. But if the formative activity of applied genetics is informed by a similar distribution of difference at the level of theory then perhaps this finger pointing is slightly misplaced.

If 'pure' genetics is a simple re-presentation of the origin and expression of difference then it must uphold its claim to be uncontaminated by 'social meaning' and be devoid of productive effects. But every aspect of genetic theory is informed by the same notion of difference apparent in its practice. This is difference as complementarity, a notion which assumes a preferred identity and where the one and its other appear to stand apart before coming together to make a whole. Genetic theory, in this way, is remarkably reminiscent of the doubling of self of concern in applied genetics. As we accompany the geneticist to the origin of difference we encounter a neat coupling. Beginning with sexual difference we find that the man and the woman each contribute half the complement of chromosomes to be found in the cells of their offspring. These match up into 22 pairs plus two sex chromosomes (identical in females, different in males). Each chromosome consists of a DNA double helix containing two complementary strands which 'are related in much the same way as a photographic print and the negative from which it is made. Each harbors the shadowy image of the other.'[22] And each DNA strand is joined to the other via a series of nucleotide bases which will only link with their opposite.

Described in this way, one would assume that the microscopic distribution of differences mimics sexual difference, or the way in which we map sexual difference at the level of the social – as opposition and complementarity where the negative is the other side of a favoured image. But, according to the geneticist, the production of difference is the other way around: difference as complementarity at the macro-level is an expression of, and stops with, the genetic code. In other words, the genetic code grounds this mirroring effect and is what prevents each identity from dissolving into the other through its determination of difference in and for itself. At least, this is the case in theory. However, in the pathway between the genetic code and its expression there lies another slippery operation of difference and an unsuccessful attempt to contain difference as the other side of sameness. And even the origin of difference, the gene, defies identification in itself.

While the gene is proposed as the origin of meaning, its expression is determined, not by a discrete code as one would assume, but by the order of nucleotide base pairs along the DNA double strand. Nor do contiguous relations alone determine the expression of difference. This sequence must first be replicated or 'transcribed' into the form of a mirror image of itself. This discordant doubling is then reversed: the message carried by the messenger is 'translated' back by specifying the production of its own mirror image. With the appearance of the other of the other, we don't return to the code from which we began: the bases which make up the transfer RNA carry with them the base units of proteins which dutifully assemble according to the order of their nucleotide base hosts – an order prescribed, via a detour through the other, by the 'original' code. With this synthesis of proteins the genetic message is expressed at the microscopic level. But the message must pass through a further symphony of differential relations before difference is orchestrated at the surface of the body. In a mysterious and unknown way the relation between proteins determines the function and shape of cells, the distribution of which determines the function and shape of different parts of the body and, hence, the morphology of the whole.

Even if the geneticist's map were complete, which it is not, the most it could explain is sameness from repetition, not difference. While this description of the origin and expression of difference indicates that the manifestation of the message is always other than itself, there is an attempt to contain the production of meaning within the paradigm of exact translation. This requires insisting, despite all indications to the contrary, upon an integrity between the code and its expression. And such integrity can only be claimed if the code is original, discrete and capable, in its necessary passage through the other, of completely subsuming the other to itself without remainder. The cost of insisting on total incorporation is that diversity, which is the rule rather than the exception, tends to be understood in terms of disruption, breakdown or mutation in the process of transmission rather than as an expression of an absence of integrity in re-production. It is therefore not surprising that difference in 'applied' genetics is understood in the same terms.

At the same time, the geneticist concedes, even within her or his own paradigm, that the expression of the code is never exact, nor is the code original. There is a play of difference which is the condition for the possibility of both the 'original' code and of the oppositional difference operating in its expression. For a start, the gene does not simply appear but is a product of a prior distribution of differences – sexual difference (meosis) and prior DNA replication – and is prone to the uncertainties of both. This uncertainty is acknowledged in genetics but is put down to the limits of knowledge rather than its effect – the effect of a process of signification which divides and disperses entities as it grounds and presents them. The effect of attempting to contain difference within a notion of complementarity also manifests in the inability of genetics to explain adequately the process of DNA transcription and translation without the production of, and reference to, other 'outsides'. For instance, what prior 'message' draws a boundary around base sequences to indicate the beginning and end of a code? Other base sequences ('terminators' and 'promotors') 'which are not expressed', we are told. Who or what recognizes these boundaries so that the process of transcription begins and ends appropriately? Enzymes determine this spacing. Who or what directs the work of enzymes? And there are further differential relations to which this no-longer-original code is referred, all of which are to account for a necessary ambiguity in the expression of meaning: the 'same' code is found in multiple locations; the activity of genes can be affected by the 'geographic location' of other genes; some genes are 'programmed' to be 'nomadic'; most genes are polymorphic and 'hereditary' differences are usually polygenic (invol-ving the interplay of many genes). The spatio-temporal relations which determine the interplay of these different terms are said to be a product of yet another set of 'regulatory mechanisms', but of these 'little is known'.[23]

While the mapping of difference which occurs in applied genetics is meant to be authorized by the truth of the origin of difference, we find that the 'origin' is always other than itself. The geneticist's dream of mapping the play of genes into a seamless whole will remain just that, a dream. This is because genetics does not re-present real differences; it signifies with material effects. As a mode of knowing which divides entities and claims their difference to be original and part of the same, genetics is itself a process of production of origins. This is a mode of production which Jacques Derrida would describe as a spacing which constitutes the interval, necessary for signification, between the two 'things' which that interval produces. It is a process which distributes differences only to ensure that the discrete identity of those differences is deferred. The genetic production of differences, therefore, guarantees the interruption of every self-identity.[24]

The search for the origin of identity and difference, therefore, cannot stop with the gene – an entity which the search itself produces. We are referred beyond genes to mysterious 'regulatory mechanisms' which oversee their production and spatio-temporal distribution. Nor will the origin be found there. As each origin dissolves into its other, we get closer to where we began: to the manifestation of differences at the surface of the body and between bodies, to their socio-political distribution and to the author of that distribution. However, we cannot find an ultimate author or subject of this system of differences either.[25] The geneticist, like the gene, is a placeholder, being also an effect of the same spacing and is, therefore, constituted only in being divided from itself. The body may be the self expressed, as Schenck would put it, but only with a lack of certainty – only by being inscribed in a system of differences which genetics helps to produce and maintain. In other words, we find that both the 'subject' and the 'object' of genetics, the 'world' and one's 'being', are constituted in relation to each other and are, therefore, always other than themselves.

The specificity of embodiment can be almost found in the thick of this genetics and is not indifferent to its terms. The production and manifestation of differences which genetic theory attempts to describe is not outside of that description: genetics is not simply an incorrect re-presentation of real differences. On the other hand, bodily differences cannot be reduced to the gene: genetics does not give us the truth of the origin of specificity. Rather, genetics is one particularly dominant mode of an infinite number of discursive practices which make differences real by the use of categories which produce and organize them through relations on the basis of sameness. The body is the homespun fabric of this process of organization and, as such, it is an almost coherent, but somewhat fragile, effect of power and knowledge.

Genetics is included in what Michel Foucault refers to as biopower: the technologies of power deployed with the emergence of the modern bio-medical and social sciences in the nineteenth century. Without reference to law, and without displaying themselves as power, these sciences divide and assemble the body, evaluate, sort and compare. They thereby transform life by effecting distributions around a norm.[26] The assumption of, and desire for, sameness pervade these sciences of the body. And, as I have argued, this urge to 're-create the self' informs genetic theory as well as its practice. To the extent that the formative function of genetics is disavowed – its function of distributing differences in and between bodies – the body stands alone in the splendour of its presence. This spacing has material effects such that the body appears to stand apart from the 'world' or the discursive practices which constitute it and measure its difference as an apparent afterthought. At the same time, a body's specificity cannot be reduced to this objectification and the gap between our being and the world, which knowledge opens up, cannot be maintained. The origins and causes of being, which are the objects of knowledge, multiply in this gap. Just as the border of the gene disperses into a mirror image which exceeds it at the moment it is assembled, so does the border which marks off the body from the practices which objectify it. The knowledge which effects borders within and between bodies also provides the conditions for the possibility of their 'brokenness'.

If the specificity of embodiment, of one's *ethos* or habitat, is to be found anywhere, it is not in the work of some more archaic 'understanding' of Being, nor in a unified identity which precedes the 'world'. Rather, it lies within the modes of knowing which present us by a spacing which simultaneously marks off as it interrupts every assemblage of self; in between a genetics which determines a body's difference in terms of a norm and the necessary deferment of that determination. One's *ethos* is marked by a *pathos*: by the conflicts and contradictions which are living testimony to the subjection of bodies to normalization; to the impossibility of separating bodies from how they are known; and to the necessary disruption of both poles of this process of identification. It is marked by a somatic expression of difference referring to an 'original' code which cannot be found in and for itself; by a description of the operation of difference which refers to the same 'social meaning' or practice of distributing difference which it is meant to authorize or correct; by a genetics which owes its prestige to locating the source of bodily specificity but confesses only to locating sameness. These contradictions feed off and reinforce the conflicts which mark the specificity of embodiment in applied genetics, both the glamour and shame of which derive from its normative function. Hence, a project such as HGI will, in attempting to map the origin of difference, effect and underscore the effacement of difference.

Attempting to locate a body definitively, or taking up a position by evoking one's own specificity, necessarily involves reference to an 'outside'. Thus, conflict or a fundamental heterogeneity is disavowed at the moment it is produced. One's position is also one's dis-position. Genetics in theory or practice is complicit with this curious mode of production – it makes sense and non-sense, literally. So, medical ethics does not begin with its role in dealing with the 'brokenness' of bodies; nor does 'genethics' begin with the 'misuse' of theory in the practice of effacing differences. Biomedical ethics begins with the formative function of its own modes of knowing which, by mapping what remains other to oneself, are complicit with the constitution and dissolution of borders within and between bodies. Our ways of knowing are dependent upon and multiply differences which we then overlook. And in this production and effacement of different habitats we can locate the conditions for the possibility of what is considered 'unethical' practice. It would seem that biomedical science is an art in all its modes and, as Aldous Huxley claimed in his early warning about genetics, 'art also has its morality'.[27]

Notes

1 Fay Weldon *The Cloning of Joanna May* London: Collins 1989, p. 120
2 For example, 'ethos' is defined by Aristotle as character established through habitual action in *Nicomachean Ethics*, Book 2, Ch. 1. See also Charles Scott's detailed etymology of ethos in 'Heidegger and the Question of Ethics' *Research in Phenomenology* 18, 1988
3 See, for example, the work of Luce Irigaray, particularly *Ethique de la Difference Sexuelle* Paris: Minuit, 1984; Moira Gatens 'Representation in/and the body politic' in this collection and 'Woman and Her Double(s): Sex, Gender and Ethics' *Australian Feminist Studies* 10, 1989; my reading of Nietzsche's ethics in R. Diprose 'Nietzsche, Ethics and Sexual Difference' *Radical Philosophy* 52, 1989; Rosi Braidotti 'The Politics of Ontological Difference' in Teresa Brennan (ed.) *Between Feminism and Psychoanalysis* London and New York: Routledge, 1989, Michel Foucault, particularly *The Use of Pleasure* Robert Hurley (trans.) New York: Vintage, 1985; and Emmanuel Levinas, particularly *Totality and Infinity* Alphonso Lingis (trans.) Pittsburgh: Duquesne University Press, 1969.
4 The meaning of 'Being-in' is Martin Heidegger's question in *Being and Time* John Macquarrie and Edward Robinson (trans.) New York: Harper & Row, 1962, s. 12, pp. 78–86.
5 This kind of ethics of specificity is evoked by H. Tristram Engelhardt Jr in *The Foundations of Bioethics* New York and Oxford: Oxford University Press, 1986 and by various papers in a special issue of *Hypatia* on feminist ethics and medicine, 4: 2, 1989 without reference to the problem of embodiment (with the exception of Susan Wendell's account of disability in the latter).
6 David Schenck 'The Texture of Embodiment: Foundation for Medical Ethics' *Human Studies* 9, 1986.
7 *Ibid.*, p. 44.
8 *Ibid.*, p. 46.
9 *Ibid.*, p. 50.
10 *Ibid.*, p. 51.
11 M. Merleau-Ponty *Phenomenology of Perception* Colin Smith (trans.) London: Routledge & Kegan Paul, 1962, p. 148.
12 Heidegger *Being and Time*, s. 12, p. 79 and s. 18, pp. 114–122.

13 David Suzuki and Peter Knudtson *Genethics: the Ethics of Engineering Life* Sydney: Allen & Unwin, 1989, p. 180.

14 For an account of genetics, difference and AIDS see Rosalyn Diprose and Cathy Vasseleu 'Animation-AIDS and Science/Fiction' in A. Cholodenko (ed.) *The Illusion of Life* Sydney: The Power Institute, 1990. See also Donna Haraway 'The Biopolitics of Postmodern Bodies: Determinations of Self in Immune System Discourse' *Differences* 1: 1, 1989.

15 For documentation of this lack of consensus see D. C. Wertz and J. C. Fletcher (eds) *Ethics and Human Genetics: A Cross Cultural Perspective* Berlin: Springer-Verlag, 1989.

16 Leon R. Kass 'The New Biology: What Price Relieving Man's Estate' in Richard W. Wertz (ed.) *Readings on Ethical and Social Issues in Biomedicine* New Jersey: Prentice-Hall Inc., 1973, p. 62.

17 *Ibid.*

18 Suzuki and Knudtson *Genethics*, p. 336.

19 Bernard Davis, for example, defends the progress that genetics can bring by claiming that the misuse of genetics is no worse than, and merely feeds into, other politically contaminated methods for regulating individuals, 'Prospects for Genetic Intervention in Man' in *Readings on Ethical and Social Issues in Biomedicine*. Charles Birch uses the same distinction between bad politics and scientific exploration of reality slightly differently. He claims that the use of genetics to eliminate real differences is a virtue which rectifies inequalities resulting from the biased evaluation of genetic differences in 'wrong political and social systems'. See 'Genetics and Moral Responsibility' Charles Birch and Paul Abrecht (eds) *Genetics and the Quality of Life* Sydney: Pergamon Press, 1975, p. 8.

20 This idea pervades Hegel's work but a brief account can be found in Hegel's *Logic* William Wallace (trans.) Oxford: Oxford University Press, 1975, s. 119, pp. 171–4. For an account of how Hegel's self/other relation works in regard to sexual difference see Genevieve Lloyd *The Man of Reason: 'Male' and 'Female' in Western Philosophy* London: Methuen, 1984, pp. 70–85.

21 Emmanuel Levinas, *Ethics and Infinity: Conversations with Philippe Nemo* Richard A. Cohen (trans.) Pittsburgh: Duquesne University Press, 1985, p. 91.

22 *Genethics*, p. 52.

23 *Ibid.*, p. 68.

24 For Derrida's most concise account of this operation see Jacques Derrida 'Différance' in *Margins of Philosophy* Alan Bass (trans.) Chicago: University of Chicago Press, 1982. See also chapters by Vicki Kirby and Cathy Vasseleu in this collection for further discussion of the effects of this operation within the discourses of the biological sciences.

25 As Derrida claims, 'subjectivity – like objectivity – is an effect of *différance*'. Hence, there can be no subject of the difference which conditions this distinction. See Jacques Derrida, *Positions* Alan Bass (trans.) Chicago: University of Chicago Press, 1972, p. 28.

26 Michel Foucault *The History of Sexuality*, Volume I Robert Hurley (trans.) New York: Random House, 1978, pp. 135–45.

27 Aldous Huxley *Brave New World* Harmondsworth: Penguin, 1955, p. 7.

CHAPTER 11

Whose Ethics for Agricultural Biotechnology?

LES LEVIDOW

The 'new biotechnology' has evoked hopes and fears for the ultimate human control over nature. Behind claims for hypothetical risks and benefits, there lie value conflicts over how nature may be conceptualized, controlled and even reconstructed for specific human purposes. For bioscience in general, 'conflicts in this area arise from the tension between recognized social values and the unstated values embedded in scientific developments and technical possibilities' (Roy et al., 1991, p. 321). What are these value conflicts?

For agricultural biotechnology, ethics debate has focused upon domesticated animals: as sentient beings, their treatment suggests emotive analogies with people. The case of bovine growth hormone (BGH), designed to increase milk yields, has become a public relations disaster for the biotechnology industry. Perhaps defensively, the industry uses the more technical term, bovine somatotropin (BST), rather than 'hormone'.

According to the agrochemical company, Monsanto, BST is a natural protein supplement which enhances the cow's efficiency. According to its opponents Monsanto is pushing drugs which force cows to work harder on the factory farm and which pollute natural processes. Similar criticism has met attempts at genetically modifying animals so that they produce higher levels of growth hormone. Thus, each side appeals to the 'natural' status of their own social values; either BST enhances a natural efficiency, or BGH transgresses a natural purity.

For the GMO debate, this chapter argues as follows: that conflicting accounts of 'risk' draw upon different cognitive and ethical frameworks; that this informal ethics debate is becoming formalized in explicit 'bioethics' discourses; and these antagonistic discourses serve as political tools for either democratizing or protecting the dominant R & D priorities.

This chapter proceeds in the following order: first, the informal ethics debate around biotechnology R & D priorities; second, antagonistic discourses for defining what is an ethical issue; and lastly, the political role of these discourses. Examples will come mainly from my study of Britain and the wider European Community.

Informal Ethics Debate

Agricultural biotechnology has provoked much debate on how to anticipate unintended effects. At issue is not simply 'acceptable risk', but how to conceptualize risk and the risk-generating system. This section argues that such conflicting accounts are an informal ethics debate on R & D priorities.

Biotechnology as control

Broadly cast, the risk debate concerns whether the biotechnological project should be accepted as progress. Although intensive farming methods have developed for a long time, biotechnologists seek to 'industrialize agriculture' even further (GIBiP, 1990), while critics attack them for aiming 'to convert agriculture into a branch of industry' (Haerlin, 1990). In this way, Green MEPs campaigned against biotechnology as an irrevocable, ominous way forward: GMOs pose 'social and economic risks, as well as risks to our world view and culture' (Rainbow Group, n.d.).

Thus, for some critics, the risk problem goes beyond physically measurable effects, to encompass features which some proponents regard as benefits. This risk perception has been widespread. According to a Dutch opinion survey, for example, many people regard their ethical-cultural values as at risk from biotechnology, seen as a profit-driven force (Sterrenberg, 1992).

Such perceptions have had some basis in the biotechnological project. Its R & D invests nature with metaphors of computer codes, industrial efficiency and a commodity form of wealth (Levidow and Tait, 1991, reprinted as Chapter 8 of this book; also Levidow, 1995a, 1995b). Perhaps somewhat indiscreetly, a British government booklet celebrates biotechnology as a DNA double helix sprouting £5 banknotes (LGC/DTl, 1991, p. 26).

More than a rhetorical overlay, such metaphors guide biotechnology in selecting genes which can increase the market value of products. According to one biotechnologist, the R & D priorities are those of 'value-added genetics' (Lawrence, 1988, p. 32). As the European biotechnology industry acknowledges, 'Agriculture is bound to go for more [high] value-added products' rather than high-productivity products (Anon, 1990).

This biotechnological reconstruction of nature has provoked a 'risk' debate. Fundamentally at issue is whether the potential effects can be analytically divided into distinct risks and benefits. This ethical issue underlies the public debate on hypothetical risks from GMO releases and from eventual products.

In this informal ethics debate, participants have disputed the conceptual status of GMOs – which are variously portrayed as nature under benign control, as nature out of control, and/or as nature under a sinister kind of control. Some arguments appeal to environmental models, such as that of the cornucopian potential of a stable Nature, versus the fragility of an unstable nature threatened by industry. These models express recurrent 'myths of nature', by which protagonists often justify their stances in a technological controversy (Schwarz and Thompson, 1990).

For many proponents, biotechnology will help agriculture to 'feed the world' and to minimize pollution. For example, a Monsanto advertisement depicts maize growing in the desert: 'Will it take a miracle to solve the world's hunger problems?' One scientist advocates inserting herbicide-resistance genes into crops, as 'a moral imperative for world food production' (Gressel, 1992). According to ICI, Britain's largest seeds merchant, herbicide-resistant crops will 'reduce the dependence upon herbicides which have already given cause for concern' (Bartle, 1991, p. 11); here ICI equates reduced quantities with reduced dependence. Through these humanitarian and environmental images, the biotechnology industry seeks ethical legitimacy for its efforts to obtain state subsidy and to minimize regulatory constraints – in particular, to treat GMOs as otherwise normal products.

Moreover, this ethical appeal naturalizes the value system which guides biotechnology R & D. GMOs provide a benign control, thanks to laboratory techniques which can precisely correct genetic deficiencies of crops and biopesticides. According to ICI, biotechnology is 'giving nature a nudge towards greater efficiency', as if the laboratory were simply enhancing natural qualities. An advertisement from Novo Nordisk portrays its bio-pesticides as a green bow-and-arrow, symbolizing a natural kind of clean, surgical strike: 'Fighting for a better world, naturally', goes the green pun. According to another company, GMO biopesticides involve 'an attempt to do better than mother nature in designing improved, more efficacious toxin' (Goodman, 1989, p. 52): an improved form of nature would more safely protect agriculture from untamed nature. With this rhetorical greening, the biotechnology industry celebrates GMOs as a reprogrammed nature: its environment-friendly products will overcome the limits of chemical-intensive agriculture, keep agriculture secure from environmental threats, and fulfil nature's cornucopian potential.

Some sceptics have anticipated GMOs running out of control. Environmentalists, including some ecologists, suggest that apparently innocuous GMOs might cause unintended harm, or even cause an ecological imbalance, by analogy to the harm done by some non-indigenous organisms. They have sought careful experiments which, in effect, test the prospects of GMOs inadvertently disturbing the stability of nature. Yet some models of ecological complexity go beyond the scientific uncertainties which could be meaningfully tested in small-scale field trials.

Some critics have attacked biotechnology in fundamentalist terms. For example, the World Council of Churches criticizes the mechanistic world view of biotechnology which threatens 'the integrity of creation'. According to a researcher for Britain's National Farmers Union, herbicide-resistant crops run 'against the spirit of nature'.

Without idealizing nature, some organizations criticize biotechnology for taking agriculture further down a misguided route. That is, it develops single-gene solutions for problems which derive from a monocultural farming system, designed on industrial models of efficiency (Genetics Forum, 1989). These critics foresee transgenic products intensifying farmers' dependence upon laboratory-based expertise and industrialized inputs; for example, the familiar pesticides treadmill would be replaced or even supplemented by a genetic treadmill. From this perspective, bio-technological control would aggravate the socio-economic dependence and environmental hazards endemic in the wider risk-generating system of intensive monoculture.

Moreover, some critics regard the biotechnological R & D priorities as undermining their own vision of 'sustainable agriculture', which they define primarily as a different relation to nature, rather than as different com-modities.[1] A development NGO has portrayed GMOs mainly as an issue of industrial control over farmers and environmental resources (NEAD, 1989). In its view, any hazards from GMOs depend upon the farming system into which they are put:

> Biotechnology and sustainable agriculture can be complementary, if we start from the [right agronomic] problem, not from a set of techniques that we must apply. But ICI wants to use all these techniques to make a lot of products (Interview, June 1991).

For some environmentalists, such as Greenpeace, GMOs are virtually self-reproducing pollutants, in several senses. That is, culturally speaking, GMOs are genes out of place, an ominous 'reconstruction of nature'. Environ-mentally speaking, GMOs may run out of control, threatening an inherently fragile balance. Agronomically speaking, they may weaken crops, in ways which would require yet more corrective high-tech intervention.

According to the Science Director of Greenpeace in Britain, 'GMO products will be constantly pressurizing the ecosystem. They may not only raise new hazards, but may also intensify harmful processes in agriculture, which has been concentrated in fewer and fewer hands' (Interview, July 1991). In portraying nature and agriculture in this way, Greenpeace could ethically justify its stance of opposing all GMO releases.

Although these images of risk associate GMOs with disorder, they also challenge biotechnological attempts at reordering nature and society. They tend to define intensive monoculture as the risk-generating system, and to define risk more broadly than physically measurable harm. In various ways, critics emphasize a systemic risk from the biotechnological project of treating socio-agronomic problems as genetic problems; some suggest that biotechnology had been directed towards solving the wrong problem – how to sustain intensive monoculture.

By default of any democratic procedure for resolving this strategic question, it is negotiated indirectly, in terms of technical risk. Ethical issues become scientized as technical disputes over systemic disruption, as well as physically measurable harm. Participants argue over whether the proposed biotechnological solutions will remedy or aggravate the damage already caused by industrialized monoculture, e.g. by further exhausting natural resources. As this case illustrates, 'Modernization risks are the scientized "second morality" in which negotiations are conducted on the injuries of the industrially exhausted ex-nature in a socially "legitimate" way, that is, with a claim to an effective remedy' (Beck, 1992, p. 81).

In the case of biotechnology, the risk debate provides an informal technology assessment, as in other recent controversies (Rip, 1986). It also provides an informal ethics debate on the values which drive R & D, whose evaluation necessarily frames how – or even whether – we conceptualize distinct risks and benefits. How, then, do these value conflicts bear upon regulatory agendas?

Regulatory agendas

When the European Community adopted new safety legislation specifically for GMO releases, the official rationale implied an environmental ethics. In the preamble of the EC Deliberate Release Directive, regulators cited the threat of 'irreversible' environmental effects, to justify applying the principle of 'preventive action' (EEC, 1990, p. 15). More than merely preventive, such a rationale was precautionary, by virtue of anticipating hazards not already documented for GMOs, even prior to any consensual cause–effect model for identifying potential harm (Tait and Levidow, 1992). A precautionary approach was encouraged by establishing a process-based administrative system that regulates all products of the genetic modification process – that is, all GMOs; every proposed release requires a prior consent and risk assessment, applying broad ecological criteria.

In preparing the directive, regulators drew selectively upon a 1986 report which they had commissioned. The report regarded 'agriculture and other human-created systems' as particularly vulnerable to disruption by GMO products. It foresaw various hazards – partly by analogy to introduced exotic organisms, and partly by analogy to past agricultural problems, including reduced biodiversity, pathogen invasions, pest resistance and herbicide resistance (Mantegazzini, 1986, pp. 76–80).

Anticipating such agricultural problems from transgenic products, environmentalists had coined the phrase 'genetic treadmill'. This term drew an ominous analogy between GMOs and the chemical treadmill, agricultural practices which had already generated pesticide-resistant pests. However, safety regulation deferred or played down such concerns, which anyway defied meaningful testing and challenged industry's R & D priorities.

Instead, regulators emphasized the genetic novelty of GMOs as a source of greater ecological uncertainty, such as a threat of ecological imbalance or a biological competitive advantage, by analogy to harm already caused by some non-indigenous organisms. With this analogy, regulators could justify a precautionary approach in 'preventive' terms (Levidow and Tait, 1993, p. 200). Associated with a natural analogy, hypothetical hazards of GMOs are conceptually abstracted from the agronomic system and thus from issues of agronomic control. By defining risk as direct physically measurable harm, GMO regulation illustrates a more generate feature of environmental policy, which displaces rather than addresses 'rational anxieties about loss of control' (Grove-White, 1991).

Nevertheless, environmental ethics arise implicitly in the risk assessment procedure, in several ways.

- First, regulators accept the biotechnological reconstruction of nature, now invested with metaphors of computer codes, industrial efficiency and commodities. As an NGO has argued, 'Conventional risk assessment treats nature as a resource to be used and exploited for humans' benefit; this value judgement, however, is presented as the norm of objectivity' (Genetics Forum, interview, September 1991). Moreover, this objectivity anticipates direct harm from the GMO or its inserted genes, but not indirect harm from agricultural practices associated with the GMO product.

- Second, regulators seek adequate evidence of safety for each proposed GMO release. That is, they judge available evidence, seek additional evidence, or set priorities for risk research. In so doing, they judge whether to treat some hypothetical effects as plausible and/or as acceptable. Informally, some advisers also consider the ultimate benefits of a particular release; if doubtful, then they may set more stringent criteria for evidence of safety (according to my research interviews, 1990–1).

- Third, in anticipating hazards, regulators draw upon cognitive frameworks for conceptualizing genetic novelty and the environment. For example, if we conceptualize ecological niches as flexibly dependent upon novel characteristics of organisms, then we can more plausibly expect a GMO to cause some environmental disruption, and so justify biosafety research on ecological uncertainties (for example, Regal, 1986).

If instead we conceptualize niches as fixed characteristics of an environment which shape or limit genetic diversity, then we may regard hypothetical harm as less plausible. In this way, some cognitive framework informs the range of ecological uncertainty deemed relevant to risk assessment (Levidow, 1992).

- Fourth, regulators face judgements on the acceptability of unintended effects: 'So what?' If a GMO release eliminates an entire species, for example, then 'Does it matter?' This semi-rhetorical question was asked publicly by the chairman of Britain's advisory committee (quoted in *ibid*.) The answer to such a question is not simply the final evaluative stage of risk assessment, because it predefines the types of hypothetical hazards which warrant more research (according to Britain's regulatory advisers, interviewed during 1990–1). Similarly, according to a proposed risk assessment procedure, the assessment team should first generate possible consequences, then assess them to decide which ones are unacceptable, and then seek realistic causes for any unacceptable consequences (RCEP, 1991, pp. 11–12). Thus the un/acceptability of a hypothetical outcome would influence efforts to ascertain its plausibility.

Such value judgements arise in a much-debated scenario: if a herbicide-resistant crop transfers its resistance gene to a weedy relative, then the unintended hybrid could become an environmental problem. Regulatory advisers perceive this hypothetical hazard through different cognitive frameworks (according to Britain's regulatory advisers, interviewed during 1990–1). For some, herbicide-resistant weeds would pose a problem only for agriculture, not for the environment, and would be readily controlled by using a different herbicide. By contrast, other advisers conceptually locate agriculture within the environment; in imagining plausible or unacceptable scenarios, they presume no clear boundary between intensive monoculture and the managed semi-natural environment outside it.

The regulatory authority in Britain, the Department of the Environment (DoE), has attempted to anticipate unintended effects from herbicide-resistant crops. In the early 1990s it funded research on whether oilseed rape can form viable hybrids with weedy relatives. By 1993, however, regulators were publicly asking the 'so what?' question, rather than claiming to overcome the environmental uncertainty (Gillespie, 1994, p. 74). The DoE even solicited methods for quantifying the money costs required to remedy hypothetical harm from herbicide-resistant weeds (by switching to a different herbicide, for example). The DoE was now treating the genetic-chemical treadmill as an acceptable, remediable effect.

The issue came to a head in Feburary 1994, when the DoE received a marketing application for herbicide-resistant oilseed rape. Regulatory advisers accepted the applicant's safety arguments, in particular, that the inadvertent spread of herbicide resistance genes would have negligible consequences for environment harm (according to my interviews during 1994–5). Any consequent weed problem 'would be controlled using existing management' – that is, by spraying other herbicides (MacLeod, 1995). Therefore the uncertainty about potential hybridization no longer mattered, at least for herbicide resistance genes. In May 1994 the UK recommended that the European Union grant market approval.

As this example illustrates, environmental values arise in all aspects of risk assessment – not simply when evaluating the acceptability of hypothetical hazards, but also when designing research to clarify their plausibility, when favouring some cause–effect models over others, and when judging evidence of safety. Values guide fact-finding, contrary to the 'rational' stereotype, whereby values enter only in the latter stages of risk assessment. Indeed, as other writers have argued, regulatory systems in general do not follow the official sequence from facts to values, from 'truth seeking' to 'justice seeking' (Salter, 1988, p. 176). Rather, they feature a 'structural interdependence of facts and values' (Schwarz and Thompson, 1990, p. 22; cf. Beck, 1992, pp. 166–8).

In the case of GMO releases, the risk debate originated from conflicts over the 'epistemic plausibility of knowledge-claims' (von Schomberg, 1992, p. 9). Unsurprisingly, these conflicts were extended into the regulatory procedure which was designed to resolve them. Here the value-laden character of 'uncertainty' becomes even more transparent.

In all these ways, the 'risk' arguments are an informal ethics debate. Moreover, the implicit role of environmental ethics could strengthen arguments for greater public participation in safety judgements. Such democratization depends upon undermining the pretence that risk assessment follows the 'rational' stereotype – a pretence which hides most value judgements from public scrutiny.

Formalizing Ethics

If risk assessment is an implicit ethics, then what is the role of an explicit bioethics? Given the pervasive value conflicts around agricultural biotechnology, let us look at how various actors have attempted to formalize ethical issues. Two recent studies exemplify antagonistic versions of bioethics, as they either challenge or accept the further industrialization of agriculture.

In a study commissioned by the European Parliament, the authors identified wide-ranging value judgements as ethical issues. These included the following: the instrumental transformation of nature, the inequitable distribution of risks and benefits, the significance of ecological uncertainty, and the cognitive frameworks involved in risk assessment. For the agricultural system in particular, the authors emphasized economic pressures on the changing role of farmers; they also distinguished between the commercial aims and humanitarian claims of the agro-food industry in developing biotechnology products (GAB/STOA, 1992). In sum, the report used the term bioethics to highlight value choices embedded in R & D and regulatory priorities, which entail an implicit environmental ethics, and which render 'consumer choice' somewhat less than free.

Another bioethics study was commissioned and financed by ICI Seeds (Straughan, 1992). Surveying ethical arguments against biotechnology, the author described them as individual moral feelings which cannot withstand logical ethical scrutiny: for example, there is nothing new in humans 'interfering with nature'. He took such essentialist arguments literally, rather than analyse why people have invoked them to challenge the biotechnological reprogramming of nature. For environmental risk assessment, he acknowledged value judgements in *weighing* risks against benefits, but not in conceptualizing potential harm, much less in dividing effects into distinct risks and benefits. In effect, he relegated bioethics to the marginal terrain of risk–benefit analysis; at most, this would set limits on how society applies biotechnological knowledge, as if it were neutral.

Thus the two reports manifest stark differences over how to define an ethical issue. The GAB report challenged the fact/value and science/ethics distinctions, while the Straughan report served to reinforce them. Likewise, state-sponsored bioethics has policed such distinctions, in attempting to define what is a valid ethical issue – logically prior to defining what is an ethically acceptable activity.

British government

In 1990 some environmentalists proposed that the British government should establish a Public Biotechnology Commission or an Ethics Commission, in order to assess prospective products in terms of environmental benefit and/or socio-economic need. The proposal received support from Opposition members of Parliament during the debate on the Environmental Protection Bill, which mandated safety regulation of GMO releases (Levidow and Tait, 1992, p. 102).

One Member of Parliament argued:

> We can easily imagine the impact that GMOs might have in the hands of self-centred, multinational companies with laser-beam objectives.... It [biotechnology] calls into play the increasingly familiar worries about the moral propriety of mankind playing God ... some people will be able to manipulate life for their own specific purposes' (*Hansard,* 6 March 1990, 952–3).

Another MP warned about 'some people latching on to the idea that we can fix the environment and that GMOs could solve our problems'. A colleague argued that the proposed commission would reassure the public about 'over-commercial objectives and over-rapid development'. Although they emphasized the need for the state to 'draw the line' on permissible applications of biotechnology, their arguments also treated R & D priorities as ethical issues.

The government rejected the proposed commission, with three main arguments. First, the commission would be 'a quango-like body interfering with the actions of the Secretary of State, who is answerable to Parliament and the people'. Second, such a body would obstruct technological advance and thus socio-economic progress. Third, any environmental assessment remained separable from ethical issues. For example, when Opposition members proposed to restrict patent rights on GMOs, the Environment Minister replied, 'We may stray into debating the ethical problem again. It has always been easy for me to handle that by separating ethics from the environment and the environment from patents'.

Thus the British government simply denied that any ethical issues arise in anticipating the environmental effects of GMOs. Yet, paradoxically, it already presumed to treat biotechnology as progress – a stance which the European Commission was to formalize.

European Community

A rhetorical 'objectivity', with its fact/value distinction, has underlain public disputes over biotechnology regulation. When the European Community enacted its process-based legislation for regulating GMO releases, industry publicly attacked the regulatory system for lacking any rational scientific basis and for hindering industrial competitiveness. Industry proposed instead 'product-based' regulation, in at least two sense of the term: classifying each GMO according to its product use, and assessing it according to its inherent product characteristics (SAGB, 1990). This proposal implied that any hazards could be objectively identified by knowing the genetic composition of a GMO, when released into a particular environment; likewise, the proposal could more readily portray risk assessment as objective by restricting the relevant uncertainties to available scientific knowledge.

In response to industry pressure, one year later the European Commission published a report which somewhat fudged the issue of how product-based regulation might replace process-based regulation, though it described them as 'complementary' (CEC, 1991). Perhaps more important, the report separated the following matters: ethical considerations, other value-laden issues, and environmental issues, as handled by safety regulation; thus it conceptually excluded environmental risk from ethics. The report also declared that biotechnology products generally would not undergo a socio-economic assessment: 'As a rule, regulatory decisions have to be based upon objective assessments using clearly identified criteria' (ibid., p. 8). Thus the report reiterated industry's distinction between an objective assessment of product safety and merely subjective views on other issues.

The European Commission report further stated that addressing the ethical challenges of biotechnology would facilitate public acceptance of its benefits (ibid., p. 16). On that basis, the Commission established a Bioethics Committee, whose mission was explained by two speakers at a European Citizens' Audit on Biotechnology in May 1992. According to the EC's Human Rights Coordinator, consumers can decide whether to reject a product on ethical grounds if they have adequate information about it; however, she argued, public fear of biotechnology is not in the interest of industry or the public at large, so the Bioethics Committee would try to correct any misinformation. According to a member of the European parliament, moreover, we must accept 'new mental images' which tend to upset our traditional concepts of nature and human identity (ECAS, 1992, p. 6).

By treating public resistance as ignorant or backward-looking, this version of bioethics may discredit itself. Indeed, even before the Bioethics Committee had reported any specific advice, some MEPs attacked its mission to promote public acceptance of biotechnology: 'Many public interest groups see the Bioethics Committee as a tranquilliser pill for public opinion.... To instrumentalize the ethical debate in this way, by dictating a priori where its findings should lead, is an utterly unethical and unacceptable approach to ethics' (Breyer, 1992, p. 15; cf. Wheale and McNally, 1993, p. 274).

Although the Bioethics Committee has shown no interest in GMOs, it has given advice on 'performance enhancers' in agriculture (see my introduction). It advised 'that the use of BST to increase lactation in cows is ethically unobjectionable, and safe for both humans and animals, provided that the following measures are adopted...'; the measures included a cost-benefit analysis of 'animal discomfort', and labelling of BST-treated milk (Warnock, 1993). The Committee acknowledged no ethical problem in extending models of industrial efficiency to animals, nor in trusting dairy farmers to observe elaborate safeguards, as if these measures could be reliably superimposed upon real-life factory farming. In effect, the Committee divided up the control issues into three distinct realms: technical risk management, free consumer choice, and ethics.

As framed by the European Commission, bioethics compensates for the R & D priority of further industrializing agriculture, while narrowing the realm of ethical debate. Although the Bioethics Committee may recommend setting ethical limits, it also serves to overcome such limits by legitimizing the contentious unstated values of biotechnology (cf. Roy, 1991, p. 321). In so doing, it protects the underlying R & D agenda from ethical challenge.[2]

Whose Ethics?

As this chapter argues, the risk debate on agricultural biotechnology illustrates a more widespread tendency. Risk assessment serves as an implicit ethics, and even as a potential means to democratize industrial development, by default of any other procedure for adjudicating contentious technological choices. 'Risks lie across the distinction... between value and fact', and thus across the distinction between ethics and science (Beck, 1992, pp. 28, 70–1). Moreover, these stereotypical distinctions are either challenged or reinforced by 'bioethics' discourses.

In various ways, critics dispute the official image of GMOs as a benign control. Their discourses highlight links between biotechnological modes of reconstructing nature and reordering society, particularly through R & D priorities which treat socio-agronomic problems as genetic deficiencies.[3] Critics highlight systemic hazards which lie beyond risk regulation and value judgements within it.

By contrast, the state authorities promote an ethics discourse which displaces issues of biotechnological control. These issues become divided into three separate fragments:

- environmental risk assessment, to be determined by objective science;

- socio-economic effects, to be decided by free consumer choice; and

- bioethics, provided by professional experts.

In practice, this state-sponsored bioethics accepts the R & D priorities of biotechnology, as if its knowledge production were neutral. Ethicists may set limits on applying this knowledge, yet also help to overcome such limits. In any case, their bioethics plays the role of compensating for unacknow-ledged value choices made beforehand. Moreover, this approach privileges a small group of specialist 'ethics experts' (Welin, 1993, p. 70); we may well ask whether the anti-democratic effect is incidental or intentional.[4]

In conclusion, antagonistic bioethics discourses become political tools for either broadening or narrowing public debate on agricultural biotechnology. Such discourses serve either to legitimize or to challenge the values which guide R & D priorities. Paradoxically, state-sponsored bio-ethics tends to depoliticize biotechnology, yet the scope of bioethics debate

Notes

1 See similar debates in the USA (Crouch, 1991; Mellon, 1991; Johnson and Thompson, 1991; Levidow, 1991a, 1991b).

2 Subsequently the European Commission proposed to extend its ban on BST, mainly on the grounds that permitting BST would conflict with EC policy to minimize milk surpluses. The Commission noted that the ban was a special case; after all, the scientific advisory committee had reported that BST products satisfy the normal regulatory criteria of safety, efficacy and quality (CEC, 1993). In this way, the Commission reiterated the normal division of control issues.

3 In this respect, we may compare agricultural biotechnology to human genome research, which encourages society to treat more and more health problems as if they were genetic deficiencies (Stemerding, 1993, p. 33).

4 A leading proponent of biotechnology has identified an alliance of critics, including 'bioethperts', who may be pursuing 'self-interested rather than objective arguments' (Cantley, 1992, p. 23). No less self-interested, some bioethperts legitimize rather than criticize biotechnology.

References

Anon (1990) 'Editorial', *Agro-Industry High-Tech* 1(1), pp. 3–4. Milano: Teknoscienze.

Bartle, I. (1991) *Herbicide-Tolerant Plants: Weed Control with the Environment in Mind*. Haslemere, Surrey: ICI Seeds [now Zeneca].

Beck, U. (1992) *Risk Society: Towards a New Modernity*. London: Sage.

Breyer, H. (1993) Committee on Energy, Research and Technology: draft response to Bangemann report [CEC, 1991], December. Luxembourg: European Parliament.

Cantley, M. (1992) 'The evolution of policy for biotechnology in the European Community, 1982–92', in J. Durant, ed., *Biotechnology in Public: A Review of Recent Research* pp. 18–27. London: Science Museum.

CEC (1991) *Promoting the Competitive Environment for the Industrial Activities based on Biotechnology within the Community*. Brussels: Commission of the European Communities.

CEC (1993) Communication from the Commission concerning Bovine Somatotropin. Brussels: Commission of the European Communities, 16 September, COM (93) 331 final.

Crouch, M. (1991) 'The very structure of scientific research mitigates against developing products to help the environment, the poor and the hungry', *Journal of Agricultural & Environmental Ethics* 4(2), pp. 151–8.

ECAS (1992) *Le Citoyen Européen* no. 17: Biotechnologie. Brussels: Euro-Citizen Action Service.

GAB/STOA (1992) *Bioethics in Europe*, report by Gruppo di Attenzione sulle Biotecnologie. Luxembourg: European Parliament, Science & Technology

Action Service.

GAB/STOA (1992) *Bioethics in Europe*, report by Gruppo di Attenzione sulle Biotecnologie. Luxembourg: European Parliament, Science & Technology Options Assessment (STOA).

GIBiP (1990) 'The Green industry biotechnology platform', *Agro-Industry High-Tech* 1 (1), pp. 55–7. Milano: Teknoscienze.

Gillespie, I. (1994) 'Regulation and risk assessment of deliberate release of GMOs in the UK', *Umweltauswirkungen Gentechnisch Veranderter Organismen*, pp. 60–74. Vienna: Umweltbundesamt, proceedings of 1993 conference in Vienna; also 'Hazards: Real and Imagined', unpublished talk from NIAB conference, Cambridge, 25 January.

Goodman, Robert M. (1989) 'Biotechnology and sustainable agriculture: policy alternatives', in J. F. MacDonald, *op. cit.*, pp. 48–57.

Gressel, J. (1992) 'Genetically-engineered herbicide-resistant crops: a moral imperative for world food production', *Agro-Food-Industry Hi-Tech* 3 (6), pp. 3–7. Milano: Teknoscienze.

Grove-White, R. (1991) 'The emerging shape of environmental conflict in the 1990s', *RSA Journal* 139, pp. 437–47. London: Royal Society of Arts.

Haerlin, B. (1990) 'Genetic engineering in Europe', in P. Wheale and R. McNally, *The Bio-Revolution: Cornucopia or Pandora's Box?* pp. 253–61. London: Pluto Press.

Hansard (1990) Standing Committee H, House of Commons, committee stage of Environmental Protection Bill, 6 March.

Holland, A. (1990) 'The biotic community: a philosophical critique of bio-engineering', in P. Wheale and R. McNally, eds, *The Bio-Revolution: Cornucopia or Pandora's Box?* pp. 166–74. London: Pluto Press.

Johnson, G. and Thompson, P. (1991) 'Ethics and values associated with agricultural biotechnology', in B. Baumgardt and M. Martin, eds, *Agricultural Biotechnology: Issues and Choices* pp. 121–37. West Lafayette, Ind.: Purdue University.

Lawrence, Robert H. (1988) 'New applications of biotechnology in the food industry', in *Biotechnology and the Food Supply* pp. 19–45. Washington, DC: National Academy Press.

Levidow, L. (1991a) 'Cleaning up on the farm', *Science as Culture* 2 (4), pp. 538–68. London: Free Association Books.

Levidow, L. (1991b) 'Biotechnology at the amber crossing', *Project Appraisal* 6(4), pp. 234–8.

Levidow, L. (1992) 'What values in the GEMMOs?', in D. Stewart-Tull and M. Sussman, eds, *Regem 2: The Release of Genetically-Engineered Microorganisms*, pp. 10–12. London: Plenum Press.

Levidow, L. (1995a) 'Agricultural Biotechnology as clean surgical strike', in S. Elworthy et al., eds, *Perspectives on the Environment II*, pp. 31–44, London: Avebury, 1995.

Levidow L. (1995b) 'Scientizing security: agricultural biotechnology as clean surgical strike', *Social Text*, 1995, no. 44, forthcoming. Durham, NC: Duke University Press.

Levidow, L. and Tait, J. (1991) 'The greening of biotechnology: GMOs as environment friendly products', *Science & Public Policy 18* (5), pp. 271–80, reprinted in this volume.

Levidow, L. and Tait, J. (1992) 'The release of genetically modified organisms: precautionary legislation', *Project Appraisal 7* (2), pp. 93–105.

Levidow, L. and Tait, J. (1993) 'Advice on biotechnology regulation: the remit and composition of ACRE', *Science and Public Policy 20* (3), pp. 193–209 .

MacDonald, J.F., ed. (1989) *Agricultural Biotechnology at the Crossroads*. Ithaca, NY: National Agricultural Biotechnology Council.

MacLeod, J. (1995) 'Deliberate release and marketing', talk at conference on Genetically Modified Crop Cultivars, National Institute of Agricultural Botany, 2–3 February.

Mantegazzini, M. (1986) *The Environmental Risks from Biotechnology*. London: Pinter.

Mellon, M. (1991) 'Biotechnology and the environmental vision', in J. F. MacDonald, *op.cit.* pp. 66–70.

NEAD (1989) *Food Matters* special features 1 & 2, Norwich: Norfolk Education for Action and Development/*Farmers Link*.

Rainbow Group (n.d., 1988?) 'Deliberate release into the environment of genetically engineered organisms' [leaflet], Brussels.

RCEP (1991) Royal Commission on Environmental Pollution, 14th Report. *Genhaz: A System for the Critical Appraisal of Proposals to Release Genetically Modified Organisms into the Environment*. London: HMSO.

Regal, P. (1986) 'Models of genetically engineered organisms and their ecological impact', in H. Mooney and J. Drake, eds, *Ecology of Biological Invasions of North America and Hawaii* pp. 111–29, New York: Springer-Verlag.

Rip, A. (1986) 'Controversies as informal technology assessment', *Knowledge 8*, pp. 349–71.

Roy, D.J. *et al.* (1991) *Bioscience-Society*. Schering Foundation Workshop proceedings. Chichester: John Wiley.

SAGB (1990) Community Policy for Biotechnology, Brussels: CEFIC.

SALB (1990) *Community Policy for Biotechnology: Economic Benefits and European Competitiveness*. Brussels: Senior Advisory Group on Biotechnology/CEFIC.

Salter, L. (1988) *Mandated Science: Science and Scientists in the Making of Standards*. London: Kluwer.

Schomberg, R. von (1993) 'Political decision-making and scientific controversies', in R. von Schomberg, ed., *Science, Politics and Morality: Decision-Making and Scientific Uncertainty* pp. 7–26. Dordrecht: Kluwer Academic.

Schwarz, M. and Thompson, M. (1990) *Divided We Stand: Redefining Politics, Technology and Social Choice*. London: Harvester.

Stemerding, D. (1993) 'How to deal with the implications of human genome research?', in H Haker *et al.*, eds, *Ethics of Human Genome Analysis* pp. 217–35. Tubingen: Attempto-Verlag.

Sterrenberg, L. (1992) Introduction of Genetically Engineered Organisms into the Environment: the Dutch Discussion, ms. The Hague: NOTA.

Straughan, R. (1992) 'Ethics, morality and crop biotechnology', manuscript available from Zeneca [formerly ICI Seeds], from DG XII/E- 1 or from the author at the University of Reading.

enhancers in agriculture and fisheries', Opinion of the Group of Advisers on Ethical Aspects of Biotechnology, Commission of the European Communities, 12 March 1993.

Welin, S. (1993) 'Some issues in research ethics', *Studies in Research Ethics* 2, pp. 59–75. Goteborg: Centre for Research Ethics.

Wheale, P. and McNally, R. (1993) 'Biotechnology policy in Europe: a critical evaluation', *Science and Public Policy* 20 (4), pp. 261–79.

Acknowledgements

This chapter arises from two related studies, both funded by Britain's Economic and Social Research Council: 'Regulating the Risks of Biotechnology', 1989–91, project number R000 23 1611; and 'From Precautionary to Risk-Based Regulation: the Case of GMO Releases', during 1995–96, project number L211 25 2032.

The chapter is developed from talks presented at two conferences: on 'Science, Discourse and Morality', at Tilburg University, in September 1993; and on 'Ethical Aspects of Biotechnology', co-sponsored by the Centre for Research Ethics, Goteborg, and by the National Committee for Research Ethics in Science and Technology, Oslo, in November 1993. For helpful editorial comments I would like to thank Rene von Schomberg, Soemini Kasanmoentalib, David King, Dirk Stemerding, Ingunn Moser, Mark Sagoff and anonymous referees of the journal *Environmental Values*.

PART 4

Biopolitics: The Political Ecology of Biotechnology

CHAPTER 12

Biotechnological Development and the Conservation of Biodiversity

VANDANA SHIVA

In the dominant paradigm, technology is seen as being above society both in its structure and evolution, in its offering technological fixes, and in its technological determinism. It is seen as a source of solutions to problems that lie in society, and is rarely perceived as a source of new social problems. Its course is viewed as self-determined. In periods of rapid technological transformation, it is assumed that society and people must adjust to change, instead of technological change adjusting to the social values of equity, sustainability and participation.

There is, however, another perspective which treats technological change as a process that is shaped by and serves the priorities of whoever controls it. In this perspective, a narrow social base of technological choice excludes human concerns and public participation. The interests of that base are protected in the name of sustaining an inherently progressive and socially neutral technology. On the other hand, a broader social base protects human rights and the environment by widening the circle of control beyond the current small group.

The emergence of the new biotechnologies brings out these two tendencies dramatically. The technocratic approach to biotechnology portrays the evolution of the technology as self-determined and views social sacrifice as a necessity. Human rights, including the right to a livelihood, must therefore be sacrificed for property rights that give protection to the innovation processes. Ironically, a process based on the sacrifice of human rights continues to be projected as automatically leading to human well-being.

The sacrifice of people's rights to create new property rights is not new. It has been part of the hidden history of the rise of capitalism and its technological structures. The laws of private property which arose during the fifteenth and sixteenth centuries simultaneously eroded people's common rights to the use of forests and pastures while creating the social conditions for capital accumulation through industrialization. The new laws of private property were aimed at protecting individual rights to property as a commodity, while destroying collective rights to commons as a basis of sustenance. The Latin root of private property, *privare*, means 'to deprive'. The shift from common rights to private property rights is therefore a general social and political precondition for exclusivist technologies to take root in society. The scene for such a shift is now being set to allow the emergence of a biotechnical era of corporate and industrial growth.

In the narrow view, science and technology are conventionally accepted as what scientists and technologists produce, and development is accepted as what science and technology produce. Scientists and technologists are in turn taken to be that sociological category formally trained in Western science and technology, either in institutions or organizations in the West, or in Asian institutions miming the paradigms of the West. These tautological definitions are unproblematic if one leaves out people, especially poor people, and if one ignores the cultural diversity and distinct civilizational histories of our planet. Development, in this view, is taken as synonymous with the introduction of Western science and technology in non-Western contexts. The magical identity is development = modernization = Westernization.

In a wider context, where science is viewed as 'ways of knowing' and technology as 'ways of doing', all societies have had their diverse and distinct science and technology systems on which development has been based. Technologies or systems of technology bridge the gap between nature's resources and human needs. Systems of knowledge and culture provide the framework for the perception and utilization of natural resources. Two changes occur in this shift of definition of science and technology – they are no longer viewed as uniquely Western but as a plurality associated with all cultures and civilizations. And a particular science and technology does not automatically translate into development everywhere. Ecologically and economically inappropriate science and technology can become causes of, not solutions to underdevelopment. Ecological inappropriateness is a mismatch between the ecological processes of nature which renew life support systems and the resource demands and impact of technological processes, which can lead to higher withdrawals of natural resources or higher additions of pollutants than ecological limits allow. In such cases they contribute to underdevelopment through the destruction of ecosystems.

Economic inappropriateness is the mismatch between the needs of society and the requirements of a technological system. Technological processes create demands for raw materials and markets, and control over these becomes essential to the politics of technological change.

Lack of theoretical cognition of the two ends of the technological process, its beginning in natural resources and its end in basic human needs, has created the current paradigm of economic and technological development which demands the increasing withdrawal of natural resources and generates the increasing addition of pollutants, while marginalizing and dispossessing increasing numbers from the productive process. These characteristics of contemporary scientific industrial development are the primary causes of current ecological, political and economic crises. The combination of ecologically disruptive scientific and technological systems in terms of resource-use efficiency and capability for basic needs satisfaction has created conditions that increasingly propel society towards ecological and economic instability, in the absence of a rational and organized response to arrest and curtail these destructive tendencies.

The introduction of ecologically and economically inappropriate science and technology leads to underdevelopment instead of development. Modernization based on resource-hungry processes materially impoverishes communities which use those resources for survival, either directly, or through their ecological function. Growth under these conditions does not ensure development for all, but creates underdevelopment for those affected negatively by resource diversion or destruction. Conflicting demands on resources thus lead to economic polarization through growth. The growing extent of popular ecology movements is a symptom of this polarization and a reminder that for many people natural resources play a vital role in survival. Their diversion to other uses or their destruction through other uses therefore creates increasing impoverishment and an increasing threat to survival.

Underdevelopment is commonly projected as a state created by the absence of modern Western science and technology systems. However, poverty and underdevelopment are, more often than not, conditions created by the externalized and invisible costs of resource-intensive and resource-destructive technological processes which support the livelihood of millions.

The experience of all industrial revolutions illustrates how poverty and underdevelopment are created as an integral part of the whole process of contemporary growth and development, in which gains accrue to one section of the society or nation and the costs, economic or ecological, are borne by the rest.

The first industrialization was based on the mechanization of work, with its focus on the textile industry. The second industrialization was based on the chemicalization of processes in agriculture and other sectors, and the emerging third industrialization is based on the engineering of the life process. We can draw some lessons from history about how technological change initiated by a special interest brings development to that interest group while creating underdevelopment for others.

Colonization and the Spinning Wheel

The mechanization of textile manufacture was the leading technological transformation of the first industrial revolution. By the time that technological innovations made their full impact on the British textile industry in the early nineteenth century, England had gained full political control over the resources and markets of its colonies, including India. India until then had been a leading producer and exporter of textiles in the world market. The industrialization of England was based in part on the de-industrialization of India. The development of England was based in part on India's underdevelopment. It is no coincidence that India's independence movement was based in large measure on seeking liberation from the control over Third World resources and people that were part of the process of Europe's industrialization. Two symbols of India's independence struggle were the Champaran *satyagraha* and the *charkha*. The Champaran *satyagraha* was a peaceful revolt against the forced cultivation of indigo as a dye for the British textile industry. The *charkha* or spinning wheel was the technological alternative that created self-reliance instead of dependence, and generated livelihoods instead of destroying them.

While the rapid technological innovations in the British textile industry were made possible only through the prior control over resources and the market, the stagnation and decay of this industry in India was a result of the loss of political control first over the market and later over the raw materials. The destruction of India's textile industry necessitated the destruction of the skills and autonomy of India's weavers. Often this destruction was extremely violent. For instance, the thumbs of the best Bengal weavers were cut off to prevent market competition when Indian hand-woven textiles continued to do better than the British mill products.[1] The impact of the violent manipulation and control of Indian weavers by English merchants was first felt when the East India Company (EIC) became a territorial power by defeating Nawab Sirajuddaula in the battle of Plassi in 1757. Before that, Indian weavers were independent producers and had control over their produce. The EIC replaced indigenous merchants by a 'body of paid servants receiving instructions from them with coercive authority over weavers that none had before. They had virtual monopoly of the market and had effectively exercised control over raw materials and began to extend this control over the weavers' tools. Under the company, weavers had virtually become wage workers on terms and conditions over which they had no control.'[2]

In the context of such erosion of the control of resources and the market, the traditional weavers of India were displaced. There was an exodus out of the weaving trade. New textile technology was imported into India from

England in the mid-nineteenth century by the cotton traders of India who were involved in export of cotton to England. This new group of powerful merchants-turned-mill-owners competed with the handloom weavers for the common market and the raw material base. The establishment of textile mills in Lancashire and later in India deprived the Indian weaver both of the market and the raw material. When American cotton supply to the English textile industry was disturbed by the American civil war, the famous cotton famine of the 1860s broke out and the English instantly reacted by grabbing cotton in India. The cotton famine was transferred to India. A government survey of 1864 gives the following picture of the production and supply of clothing:

> It is evident that the whole population must be far nearer a state of pristine nudity than ever before. Every poor person stints himself to an inconceivable degree in his clothing and every purpose to which cotton is applied. He wears his turban and breach cloth to rags, dispenses with his body clothing and denies himself of his annual renewal of his scanty suit.[3]

There was also the devastating impact of the new textile mills opened in India on the handloom weavers:

> The growth of the industry began to impinge on the market of the handloom industry.... This incursion of the mills into areas hitherto considered the special reserve of the handloom industry had a many-sided effect...and led to unprecedented worsening of the conditions of the handloom weavers.... Actual unemployment was seen as in the statistics of idle handlooms: this was estimated at 13 per cent in 1940 by the fact finding committee (of handlooms and mills).[4]

Gandhi's critique of the industrialization of India on the Western model was based on his perception of the poverty, dispossession and destruction of livelihood which resulted from it:

> Why must India become industrial in the western sense? What is good for one nation situated in one condition is not necessarily good for another differently situated. One man's food is often another man's poison.... Mechanisation is good when hands are too few for the work intended to be accomplished. It is an evil where there are more hands than required for the work as is the case in India.[5]

It was to regenerate livelihood in India that Gandhi thought of the spinning wheel as a symbol of liberation and a tool for development. Power-driven mills were the model of development in that period of early industrialization. However, the hunger of mills for raw materials and markets was the reason for a new poverty, created by the destruction of livelihood either by diverting land and biomass from local subsistence to the factory, or by displacing local production through the market.

Gandhi had said that 'anything that millions can do together, becomes charged with unique power'. The spinning wheel was a symbol of such power. 'The wheel as such is lifeless, but when I invest it with symbolism, it becomes a living thing for me.'[6]

When Gandhi described the *charkha* in 1908, in Hind-Swaraj, as a panacea for the growing pauperism of India, he had never seen a spinning wheel. Even in 1915, when he returned to India from South Africa, he had not actually seen a spinning wheel. But he saw an essential element of freedom from colonialism in discarding the use of mill-woven cloth. He set up handlooms in the Satyagraha Ashram at Sabarmati, but could not find a spinning wheel or a spinner, who was normally a woman. In 1917, Gandhi's disciple Ganga-behn Majumdar started a search for the spinning wheel, and found one in Vijapur in Baroda State. Quite a few people there had spinning wheels in their homes, but had long since consigned them to the lofts as useless lumber. They now pulled them out, and soon Vijapur *khadi* gained a name for itself. And *khadi* and the spinning wheel rapidly became the symbol for India's independence movement. The spinning wheel symbolized a technology that conserves resources, people's livelihoods and people's control over their livelihoods. In contrast to the imperialism of the British textile industry, the *charkha* was decentred and labour-generating, not labour-displacing. It needed people's hands and minds, instead of treating them as surplus, or as mere inputs into an industrial process. This critical mixture of decentralization, livelihood generation, resource conservation and strengthening of self-reliance was essential to undo the waste of centralization, livelihood destruction, resource depletion and creation of economic and political dependence that had been engendered by the industrialization associated with colonialism.

Gandhi's spinning wheel is a challenge to notions of progress and obsolescence that arise from absolutism and false universalism in concepts of science and technology development. Obsolescence and waste are social constructs that have both a political and ecological component. Politically, the notion of obsolescence gets rid of people's control over their lives and livelihoods by defining productive work as unproductive and removing people's control over production in the name of progress. It would rather waste hands than waste time. Ecologically, too, obsolescence destroys the regenerative capacity of nature by substituting manufactured uniformity in place of nature's diversity. This induced dispensability of poorer people on the one hand and diversity on the other constitutes the political ecology of technological development guided by narrow and reductionist notions of productivity. Parochial notions of productivity, perceived as universal, rob people of control over their means of reproducing life and rob nature of her capacity to regenerate diversity.

Ecological erosion and destruction of livelihood are linked to one another. Displacement of diversity and of people's sources of sustenance both arise from a view of development and growth based on uniformity created through centralized control. In this process of control, reductionist science and technology act as handmaidens for economically powerful interests. The struggle between the factory and the spinning wheel continues as new technologies emerge.

Colonization of the Seed

The changes that took place in the textile industry during colonialism were replayed in agriculture after India's independence through the green revolution. Whether we consider the chemicalization of agriculture through the green revolution or its transformation through the new biotechnologies, the seed is at the centre of all recent changes in agricultural production.

All technological transformation of biodiversity is justified in the language of 'improvement' and increase of 'economic value'. However, 'improvement' and 'value' are not neutral terms. They are contextual and value-laden. What is improvement in one context is often regression in another. What is value added from one perspective is value lost from another.

The 'improvement' of the seed is not a neutral economic process. It is, more importantly, a political process that shifts control over biological diversity from local peasants to transnational corporations and changes biological systems from complete systems reproducing themselves into raw material. It therefore changes the role of the agricultural producer and the role of ecological processes. The new biotechnologies follow the path of hybridization in changing the location of power as associated with the seed. As Jack Kloppenburg has stated, 'It decouples seed as "seed" from seed as "grain" and thereby facilitates the transformation of seed from a use value to an exchange value.'[7]

Agricultural research is primarily a means of eliminating barriers to the penetration of agriculture by capital. The most important barrier is the nature of the seed, which reproduces itself and multiplies. The seed thus possesses a dual character that links both ends of the process of crop production: it is both means of production and, as grain, the product. In planting each year's crop the farmers also reproduce a necessary part of that means of production. The seed thus presents capital with a simple biological obstacle: given appropriate conditions the seed will reproduce itself manifold.

The seed has therefore to be transformed materially if a market for seed is to be created. Modern plant breeding is primarily an attempt to remove this biological obstacle to the market in seed. Seed reproducing itself stays free, a common resource and under the farmer's control. Corporate seed has a cost and is under the control of the corporate sector or under the control of agricultural research institutions. The transformation of a common resource into a commodity, of a self-regenerative resource into mere 'input', changes the nature of the seed and of agriculture itself. Since it robs peasants of their means of livelihood, the new technology becomes an instrument of poverty and underdevelopment.

The decoupling of seed from grain also changes the status of seed. From being finished produce which rises from itself, nature's seeds and people's seeds become mere raw material for the production of corporate seed as commodity. The cycle of regeneration of biodiversity is therefore replaced by a linear flow of free germ plasm from farms and forests into labs and research stations, and the flow of modified uniform products as priced commodities from corporations to farmers. Diversity is destroyed by transforming it into mere raw material for industrial production based on uniformity, which necessarily displaces the diversity of local agricultural practice.

Cropping systems in general involve an interaction between soil, water and plant genetic resources. In indigenous agriculture, for example, cropping systems include a symbiotic relationship between soil, water, farm animals and plants. Green revolution agriculture replaces this integration of inputs at the level of the farm with the integration of inputs such as seeds and chemicals. The indigenous cropping systems are based only on internal organic inputs. Seeds come from the farm, soil fertility comes from the farm and pest control is built into the crop mixtures. In the green revolution package, yields are intimately related to purchased inputs of seeds, chemical fertilizers, pesticides, petroleum fuels and intensive irrigation. High yields are not intrinsic to the seeds, but are a function of the availability of inputs. According to the United Nations Research Institute for Social Development (UNRISD) 15-nation study of the impact of the new seeds, the term 'high-yielding variety' (HYV) is a misnomer because it implies that the new seeds are high-yielding in and of themselves. The distinguishing feature of the seeds, however, is that they are highly responsive to certain key inputs such as fertilizer and irrigation. Palmer therefore suggested the term 'high-responsive varieties' (HRVs) in place of HYVs.[8]

As Claude Alvares has said, 'for the first time the human race has produced seed that cannot cope on its own, but needs to be placed within an artificial environment for growth and output'.[9] This change in the nature of seed is justified by creating a framework that treats self-regenerative seed as 'primitive' and as new germ plasm, and the seed that is inert without inputs and is non-reproducible as a finished product. The whole is rendered partial, the partial is rendered whole. The commoditized seed is ecologically incomplete and ruptured at two levels:

1 It does not *reproduce* itself, while, by definition, seed is a a regenerative resource. Genetic resources are thus, through technological transformation, transformed from renewable into non-renewable.

2 It does not *produce* by itself. It needs the help of inputs to produce. As the seed and chemical companies merge, the dependence on inputs will increase, not decrease. And whether a chemical is added externally or internally, it remains an external input in the ecological cycle of the reproduction of seed.

It is this shift from the ecological processes of reproduction to the technological processes of production that underlies both the problem of dispossession of farmers and genetic erosion.

The new plant biotechnologies will follow the path of the earlier HYVs of the green revolution in pushing farmers onto a technological treadmill. Biotechnology can be expected to increase the reliance of farmers on purchased inputs even as it accelerates the process of polarization. It will even increase the use of chemicals instead of decreasing it. The dominant focus of research in genetic engineering is not on fertilizer-free and pest-free crops, but pesticide- and herbicide-resistant varieties. For the seed-chemical multinationals, this might make commercial sense – since it is cheaper to adapt the chemical crop variety to the plant. The cost of developing a new crop variety rarely reaches US$2 million, whereas the cost of a new herbicide exceeds US$40 million.

Herbicide and pesticide resistance will also increase the integration of seeds/chemicals and the multinationals' control of agriculture. A number of major agricultural chemical companies are developing plants with resistance to their brand of herbicides. Soya beans have been made resistant to Ciba-Geigy's Atrazine herbicides, and this has increased annual sales of the herbicide by US$120 million. Research is also being done to develop crop plants resistant to other herbicides, such as Dupont's 'Gists' and 'Glean' and Monsanto's 'Round-Up', which are lethal to most herbaceous plants and thus cannot be applied directly to crops. The successful development and sale of crop plants resistant to brand-name herbicides will result in further economic concentration of the agricultural industrial market, increasing the market power of transnational companies. The farmers will own the land, but the corporation will own the crop in the field, giving instructions by a computer that monitors the progress and needs of a crop grown from genetically programmed seed.

Biotechnology can thus become an instrument of dispossessing the farmer of seed as a means of production. The relocation of seed production from the farm to the corporate laboratory relocates power and value between the North and South; and between corporations and farmers. It is estimated that the elimination of home-grown seed would dramatically increase the farmers' dependence on biotech industries by about US$6 billion annually.

It also becomes an instrument of dispossession by selectively removing those plants or parts of plants that do not serve the commercial interests but are essential for the survival of nature and people. 'Improvement' of a selected characteristic in a plant is also a selection *against* other characteristics which are useful to nature, or for local consumption. Improvement is not a class- or gender-neutral concept. Improvement of partitioning efficiency is based on the 'enhancement of the yield of desired product at the expense of unwanted plant parts'. The desired product is, however, not the same for rich people and poor people, or rich countries and poor countries, nor is efficiency. On the input side, richer people and richer countries are short of labour and poorer people and poorer countries are short of capital and land. Most agricultural development, however, increases capital input while displacing labour, thus destroying livelihoods. On the output side, which parts of a farming system or a plant will be treated as unwanted depends on what class and gender one is. What is unwanted for the better off may be the wanted part for the poor. The plants or plant parts which serve the poor are the ones whose supply is squeezed by the normal priorities of improvement in response to commercial forces.

In the Indian context, plants that have been displaced by plant improvement in the green revolution are pulses and oilseeds, which are crucial to the nutrient needs of people and the soil. Monocultures of wheat and rice spread through the green revolution have also turned useful plants into weeds, as is the case with green leafy vegetables which grow as associates. Herbicide use has destroyed plants useful for the poor, and pesticide use has destroyed the fish culture usually associated with paddy cultivation in the Asian rice farming system. These losses through biodiversity destruction resulting from increasing yields of monocultures are never internalized in the productivity measure of technological change. Instead, both increased inputs and decreased outputs are externalized in measurement of productivity. Productivity is a measure of output per unit input. A typical subsistence farm in an Asian village produces more than 20 crops and supports animals. Individual crops are also multi-purpose. Rice, for instance, is only partially food. The residue after removal of the grain is not a nuisance to be disposed of as it would be on a farm in the developed world. The straw is used to feed work animals, to cook food, or even to help fertilize the field for the next year's crops. The straw and husk are important construction material. Traditional rice varieties produced five times as much straw as grain, and were an important source of food, feed, fuel, fertilizer and housing material.

Plant breeders, however, saw rice only as food and created a science and technology to increase grain yields. Traditional crop varieties, characterized by tall and thin straw, typically convert the heavy doses of fertilizer into overall growth of the plant, rather than increasing the grain yield. Commonly, the excessive growth of the plant causes the stalk to break, lodging the grain on the ground, which results in heavy crop losses. The 'miracle seeds' or 'high-yielding varieties' which started the process of the green revolution were biologically engineered to be dwarf varieties. The important feature of these new varieties is not that they are particularly productive in themselves but that they can absorb three or four times higher doses of fertilizer than the traditional varieties and convert it into grain, provided proportionately heavy and frequent irrigation applications are also available. They also have high susceptibility to insect and pest attacks.

For equivalent fertilization, the high-yielding varieties produce about the same total biomass as the traditional rice. They increase the grain yield at the cost of the straw. Thus while traditional rice produces four to five times as much straw as grain, high-yielding varieties of rice typically produce a one-to-one ratio of grain to straw. Thus a conversion from traditional to high-yielding rice increases the grain available but decreases the straw. Abundance creates scarcity. Output as total biomass does not increase, but the input increases dramatically. High-yielding varieties of wheat, for example, need about three times as much irrigation as traditional varieties. If water is considered a critical input, the productivity of the new seeds is only a third of the productivity of traditional varieties. In terms of water use, the green revolution is clearly counter-productive. Increased irrigation intensity has further costs associated with it in terms of waterlogging and salinity, as the experience in India's Punjab has shown. In other regions such as Maharashtra and Tamil Nadu, the green revolution is causing large-scale mining of ground water. Large-scale desiccation of the regions of the world now supporting the green revolution is thus a real possibility. Abundance again generates scarcity.

The increased water, fertilizer and pesticide use is also counter-productive for the Asian farmer in financial terms. From studies conducted at the International Rice Research Institute, it is estimated that whereas the total cash costs of production for the average Filipino rice farmer using traditional methods and varieties is about US$20 per hectare, the cost rises to US$220 when the new, high-yielding varieties are grown.

The fragmentation of components of the farm ecosystem, and their integration with distant markets and industries, is a characteristic of modern 'scientific' agriculture. The most common justification of the introduction of this system of food production is that it raises agricultural productivity. The high productivity of modern agriculture is however a myth when total resource inputs are taken into account. The social and ecological costs with respect to the manufacture and use of fertilizers, pesticides and labour-replacing energy and equipment are never taken into account, thus rendering the system artificially productive. If the energy used to provide all inputs to modern farming is deducted from the food calories produced, modern agricultural technologies are found to be counter-productive. Whereas at the turn of the century, even in the countries of the north, one calorie of food value was produced by the input of less than a calorie of energy, so that there was a net gain, today 10 calories of energy are used to produce the same one calorie of food value.

The higher productivity and efficiency of industrial agriculture is contextually determined, by selecting those inputs and outputs which suit the endowments of rich people and rich countries. Before we push through new agricultural technologies, it would be wise to pause and look at the other paths that were available for increased production but were never considered. Alternatives in agriculture have been based on conserving nature and people's livelihoods, while improving yields, not on destroying them.

The myth that only chemically intensive, labour-displacing agriculture is productive has recently been challenged by a major study of the National Research Council in the US.[10] The report, *Alternative Agriculture,* shows that besides reducing the health and environmental hazards posed by chemical agriculture, alternative farming systems have economic viability. Traditionally, most evaluations comparing chemical farming to alternative practices have focused principally on the cost and returns of adopting a specific farming method. Fewer studies have considered the impact of alternative farming systems on the economic performance of the whole farm. The committee could find no useful studies of the potential effects of widespread adoption of alternative agricultural systems, and no aggregate studies that compare the costs and benefits of conventional agriculture with successful alternative systems. Most studies have the flawed approach of comparing conventional farming practices with the economic performance of a similar farm, assuming withdrawal of certain categories of farm inputs instead of comparison with a farm using alternatives. The bias in favour of green revolution and chemical agriculture has distorted the assessment and potential of alternative agriculture. However, the new search for alternatives is showing that sustainable farming systems do not have to compromise at the level of productivity and yields.

A case study of the Thompson Farm established yields of 130–150 bushels/acre for corn against the national average of 124 bushels/acre, 45–55 bushels/acre of soya bean against the national average of 40 bushels/acre and 4–5 tons of hay against 3–4 tons/acre of the national average. Similarly, at the Kitamira farm the yield of 35.5 tons/acre of tomatoes was much higher than the country's average.

It is not only countries like the US which are making a shift away from energy- and chemical-intensive agriculture. In India, a decade long experiment with *rishi kheti* or alternative agriculture undertaken at Friends Rural Centre in Rasulia, Madhya Pradesh by Pratap Aggarwal yielded higher returns with indigenous seeds and no external inputs than the green revolution agriculture of HYV seeds and heavy chemical and irrigation inputs which had been practised on the farm previously.[11]

In the Terai region of Uttar Pradesh a local farmer called Inder Singh continued to grow traditional varieties while most farmers shifted to Pant-4, an HYV seed. As intensive irrigation led to a decline in the water table, the thirsty HYVs could no longer be cultivated. Inder Singh's seeds came in useful. Owing to high productivity and low costs of cultivation in terms of fertilizers and water input, a particular variety called Indarasan (named after Inder Singh) spread to cover nearly 50 per cent of the area. During drought years, Indarasan has coped much better than Pant-4, with yields of 32 quintals per acre compared to Pant-4 which has stagnated at 20 quintals per acre under irrigation. Without irrigation the HYV is totally destroyed. The Indarasan variety is also more remunerative in the market, selling at Rs 208 per quintal compared to Rs 175 per quintal for Pant-4.[12]

In the Philippines on 29 May 1986, the MASIPAC Centre (Farmers and Scientists for Agricultural Science Development Centre) was inaugurated in Jaen, Nueva Ecya. The centre's programme is to build an agricultural alternative which is not dependent on capital and external inputs as the green revolution was.[13]

Worldwide examples of successful alternative agriculture exist and are growing, even while they continue to be ignored by the dominant world view of agriculture. And it is these initiatives that carry the seeds of a sustainable agriculture. Blindness to these alternatives is not a proof of their non-existence. It is merely a reflection of the blindness.

Biotechnological Development and the Conservation of Biodiversity

The central paradox posed by the green revolution and biotechnological development is that modern plant improvement has been based on the destruction of the biodiversity which it uses as raw material. The irony of plant and animal breeding is that it destroys the very building blocks on which the technology depends. When agricultural modernization schemes introduce new and uniform crops into the farmers' fields, they push into extinction the diversity of local varieties. In the words of Garrison Wilkes of the University of Massachusetts, it is analogous to taking stones from a building's foundations to repair the roof. And as Brian Ford-Lloyd and Michael Jackson elaborate:

> Current international activities surrounding the genetic resources of plants aim to confront one paradoxical problem. This is that scientists throughout the world are rightly engaged in developing better and higher yielding cultivars of crop plants to be used on increasingly large scales. But this involves the replacement of the generally variable, lower yielding, locally adopted strains grown traditionally, by the products of modern agriculture – the case of uniformity replacing diversity. It is here that we find the paradox, for these self-same plant breeders are dependent upon the availability of a pool of diverse genetic material for success in their work. They are themselves dependent upon that which they are unwittingly destroying.[14]

The paradox arises from the foundational errors of assignment of value and utility, which then make the 'modern' varieties look inherently superior, whereas they are superior only in the context of increased control over plant genetic resources and a restricted production of certain commodities for the market.

The challenge of the 1990s is based on our getting rid of false notions of obsolescence and productivity which legitimize the extinction of large parts of nature and society. The push for homogenization and uniformity comes both from the transnational corporate sector, which has to create uniformity to control markets, and from the nature of modern research systems which have grown in response to the market. Since most bio-technology research is dictated by TNCs, the sought-out solutions must have a global and homogeneous character. TNCs do not tend to work for small market niches, but aim at large market shares. In addition, researchers prefer tasks that can be simplified enough to be tackled systematically, and that produce stable and widely applicable outcomes. Diversity goes against the standardization of scientific research.

However, more production of partial outputs as measured on the market and in a monoculture is often less production when measured in the diversity of nature's economy or people's sustenance economy. In the context of diversity, increased production and improved productivity can be consonant with biodiversity conservation. In fact it is often dependent on it.

There is, however, a prevalent misconception that biotechnology development will automatically lead to biodiversity conservation. The main problem with viewing biotechnology as a miracle solution to the biodiversity crisis is related to the fact that biotechnologies are, in essence, technologies for the breeding of uniformity in plants and animals.

Biotechnology corporations do sometimes talk of contributing to genetic diversity – as when John Duesing of Ciba Geigy states: 'Patent protection will serve to stimulate the development of competing and diverse genetic solutions with access to these diverse solutions ensured by free market forces at work in biotech ecology and seed industries.'[15] However, the 'diversity' of corporate strategies and the diversity of life-forms on this planet are not the same thing, and corporate competition can hardly be treated as a substitute for nature's evolution in the creation of genetic diversity.

Corporate strategies and products can lead to diversification of commodities, but they cannot enrich nature's diversity. This confusion between commodity diversification and biodiversity conservation finds its parallel in raw material diversification. Although breeders draw genetic materials from many places as raw material input, the seed commodity that is sold back to farmers is characterized by uniformity. Uniformity and monopolistic seed supplies go hand in hand. When this monopolizing control is achieved through the molecular mind, destruction of diversity is accelerated. As Jack Kloppenburg has warned, 'Though the capacity to move genetic material *between* species is a means for introducing additional variation, it is also a means for engineering genetic uniformity across species.'[16] Production is thus driven in the direction of destruction of diversity. Production based on uniformity becomes the primary threat to biodiversity conservation, even though in the convoluted political economy of the market it is cited as the reason for conservation. The exploitation of genetic diversity for crop improvement should be the ultimate objective of the exploration and conservation of genetic resources, it is argued. The arbitrary inequality created in the status of germ plasm creates an arbitrary separation between production and conservation. Some people's germ plasm becomes a finished commodity, a 'product', other people's germ plasm becomes mere 'raw' material for that product. The manufacture of the 'product' in corporate labs is counted as production. The reproduction of the 'raw' material by nature and Third World farmers is mere conservation. The 'value added' in one domain is built on the 'value robbed' in another domain. Biotechnological development thus translates into biodiversity erosion and poverty creation.

The main challenge to biodiversity conservation is the removal of reductionist blinkers which make more look less and less look more. The social construction of growth and productivity is achieved (1) by excluding crops and parts of crops as unwanted and (2) by creating a false hierarchy of resources and knowledge, splitting diversity into dichotomy.

Not till diversity is made the logic of production can diversity be conserved. If production continues to be based on the logic of uniformity and homogenization, uniformity will continue to displace diversity.

'Improvement' from the corporate viewpoint, or from the viewpoint of Western agricultural research is often a loss for the Third World, especially the poor in the Third World. There is therefore no inevitability that production acts against diversity. Uniformity as a pattern of production becomes inevitable only in a context of control and profitability.

All systems of sustainable agriculture, whether of the past or the future, are built on the basis of the perennial principles of diversity and reciprocity. The two principles are not independent but interrelated. Diversity gives rise to the ecological space for give and take, for mutuality and reciprocity. Destruction of diversity is linked to the creation of monocultures, and with the creation of monocultures the self-regulation and decentred organization of diverse systems give way to external inputs and external and centralized control. Sustainability and diversity are ecologically linked because diversity offers the multiplicity of interactions which can heal ecological disturbance to any part of the system. Non-sustainability and uniformity mean that disturbance to one part is translated into a disturbance to all other parts. Instead of being contained, ecological destabilization tends to be amplified. Closely linked to the issue of diversity and uniformity is the issue of productivity. Higher yields and higher production have been the main push for the introduction of uniformity and the logic of the assembly line. The imperative of growth generates the imperative for monocultures. Yet this growth is, in large measure, a socially constructed, value-laden category. It exists as a 'fact' by excluding and erasing the facts of diversity and production through diversity. Sustainability, diversity and decentred self-organization are therefore linked, as are unsustainability, uniformity and centralization.

Diversity as a pattern of production, not merely of conservation, ensures pluralism and decentralization. It prevents the dichotomizing of biological systems into 'primitive' and 'advanced'. As Gandhi challenged the false concepts of obsolescence and productivity in the production of textiles by his search for the spinning wheel, groups across the Third World are challenging the false concepts of obsolescence in agricultural production by searching for seeds used by farmers over centuries and making them the basis of a future-oriented, self-reliant and sustainable agriculture.

Patents, Intellectual Property and Politics of Knowledge

As the spinning wheel was rendered backward and obsolete by an earlier technological revolution, farmers' seeds are rendered incomplete and valueless by the process that makes corporate seeds the basis of wealth creation. The indigenous varieties or land races, evolved through both natural and human selection, and produced and used by Third World farmers worldwide, are called 'primitive cultivars'. Those varieties created by modern plant breeders in international research centres or by transnational seed corporations are called 'advanced' or 'élite'. The tacit hierarchy in words like 'primitive' and 'élite' becomes an explicit one in the process of conflict. Thus the North has always used Third World germ plasm as a freely available resource and treated it as valueless. The advanced capitalist nations wish to retain free access to the developing world's storehouse of genetic diversity, while the South would like to have the proprietary varieties of the North's industry declared a similarly 'public' good. The North, however, resists this democracy based on the logic of the market. The executive secretary of the International Board for Plant Genetic Resources (IBPGR) has argued that 'it is not the original material which produces cash returns'. A 1983 forum on plant breeding, sponsored by Pioneer Hi-Bred, stated: 'Some insist that since germ plasm is a resource belonging to the public, such improved varieties would be supplied to farmers in the source country at either minimal or no cost. This overlooks the fact that 'raw' germ plasm only becomes valuable after considerable investment of time and money, both in adapting exotic germ plasm for use by applied plant breeders and in incorporating the germ plasm into varieties useful to farmers.'[17] The corporate perspective views as valuable only that which serves the market. However, all material processes serve ecological needs and social needs, and these needs are undermined by the monopolizing tendency of corporations.

The issue of patent protection for modified life forms raises a number of unresolved political questions about ownership and control of genetic resources. The problem is that in manipulating life forms you do not start from nothing, but from other life forms which belong to others – maybe through customary law. Second, genetic engineering and biotechnology do not create new genes, but merely relocate genes already existing in organisms. When genes are made the object of value through the patent system, a dangerous shift takes place in the approach to genetic resources.

Most Third World countries view genetic resources as part of the common heritage. In most countries animals and plants were excluded from the patent system until recently when the advent of biotechnologies changed concepts of ownership of life. With the new biotechnologies life can now be owned. The potential for gene manipulation reduces the organism to its genetic constituents. Centuries of innovation are totally devalued to give monopoly rights on life forms to those who manipulate genes with new technologies, placing their contribution above that of generations of Third World farmers for over 10,000 years in the areas of conservation, breeding, domestication, and development of plant and animal genetic resources. As Pat Mooney has said, 'the argument that intellectual property is only recognizable when performed in laboratories with white lab coats is fundamentally a racist view of scientific development'.[18]

Two biases are inherent in this argument. One is that the labour of Third World farmers has no value, while the labour of Western scientists adds value. The second is that value is a measure only in the market. However, it is recognized that 'the total genetic change achieved by farmers over the millennia was far greater than that achieved by the last hundred or two years of more systematic science-based efforts'.[19] Plant scientists are not the sole producers of utility in seed, a utility which has high social and ecological value, even if it has no market value. The failure of the market system to assign value can hardly be a reason for denying value to farmers' seeds and nature's seeds. It puts into question the logic of the market rather than the status of the seed or the farmers' intellects.

There is no epistemological justification for treating some germ plasm as valueless and part of the common heritage, and other germ plasm as a valuable commodity and private property. The distinction is not based on the nature of the germ plasm, but on the nature of political and economic power. Putting value on the gene through patents makes biology stand on its head. Complex organisms which have evolved over millennia in nature, and through the contributions of Third World peasants, tribal cultivators and healers, are reduced to their parts, and treated as mere inputs into genetic engineering. Patenting of genes thus leads to a devaluation of life forms by reducing them to their constituents and allowing them to be repeatedly owned as private property. This reductionism and fragmentation might be convenient for commercial concerns but it violates the integrity of life as well as the common property rights of Third World people. On these false notions of genetic resources and their ownership through intellectual property rights are based the 'biobattles' at the FAO and the trade wars at GATT. Countries like the US are using trade as a means of enforcing their patent laws and intellectual property rights on the sovereign nations of the Third World. The US has accused countries of the Third World of engaging in 'unfair trading practice' if they fail to adopt the US patent laws which allow monopoly rights in life forms. Yet it is the US which has engaged in unfair practices related to the use of Third World genetic resources. It has freely raided the biological diversity of the Third World to spin millions of dollars of profits, none of which have been shared with Third World countries, the original owners of the germ plasm. A wild tomato variety (*Lycopresicon chomrelweskii*) taken from Peru in 1962 has contributed US$8 million a year to the American tomato-processing industry by increasing the content of soluble solids. Yet none of these profits or benefits have been shared with Peru, the original source of the genetic material.

According to Prescott-Allen, wild varieties contributed US$340 million per year between 1976 and 1980 to the US farm economy. The total contribution of wild germ plasm to the American economy has been US$66 billion, which is more than the total international debt of Mexico and the Philippines combined. This wild material is 'owned' by sovereign states and by local people.[20]

Patents and intellectual property rights are at the centre of the protection of the right to profits. Human rights are at the centre of the protection of the right to life, which is threatened by the new biotechnologies as they expand the domain of capital accumulation while introducing new risks and hazards for citizens. The words 'freedom' and 'protection' have been robbed of their humane meaning and are being absorbed into the double-speak of corporate jargon. With double-speak are associated double standards, one for citizens and one for corporations, one for corporate responsibility and one for corporate profits.

The US is the most sophisticated in the practice of double standards and the destruction of people's rights to health and safety in the Third World. On the one hand it aims at restricting health and safety regulation to its own geographical boundaries, while on the other hand it aims at destroying the Indian Patents Act of 1970 and replacing it with a strong US-style system of patent protection which is heavily biased in favour of the industrially developed countries. The US government considers the transnationals' lack of patent protection as unfair trading practice. It does not consider the destruction of regulation for public safety and environmental protection as unethical and unfair for the citizens of the Third World. The US wants to limit and localize laws for the protection of people, and to universalize laws for the protection of profits. The people of India want the reverse – a universalization of the safety regulations protecting people's right to life and livelihoods, and a localization of laws relating to intellectual property and private profits.

All life is precious. It is equally precious to the rich and the poor, the white and the black, to men and women. Universalization of laws for the protection of life is an ethical imperative. On the other hand, private property and private profits are culturally and socio-economically legitimized constructs holding only for some groups. They do not hold for all societies and all cultures. Laws for the protection of private property rights, especially as related to life forms, cannot and should not be imposed globally. They need to be restrained.

Double standards also exist in the shift from private gain to social responsibility for environmental costs. When the patenting of life is at issue, arguments from the concept of 'novelty' are used. Novelty requires that the subject matter of a patent be new, that it be the result of an inventive step, and not something existing in nature. On the other hand, when it comes to legislative safeguards, the arguments shifts to the concept of 'similarity', to establishing that biotechnological products and genetically engineered organisms differ little from parent organisms.

To have one law for environmental responsibility and another for proprietary rights and profits is an expression of double standards. Double standards are ethically unjustified and illegitimate, especially when they deal with life itself. However, double standards are consistent with and necessary for the defence of private property rights. It is these double standards which allow the lives and livelihoods of the people and the planet to be sacrificed for the protection of profits.

Resistance to such anti-life technological shifts requires that we widen the circle of control and decision-making about technology, by treating technology in its social and ecological context. By keeping human rights at the centre of discourse and debate, we might be able to restrain the ultimate privatization of life itself.

Notes

This chapter was originally presented as a paper at a conference on the 'Conservation of Genetic Resources', Norway, September 1990.

1 Vandana Shiva and J. Bandyopadhyay (1982), 'Political Economy of Technological Polarisations', *Economic and Political Weekly*, Vol. XVII, No. 45, 6 November, pp. 1827–32.

2 Arasarathnam, S., 'Weavers, Merchants and Company: The Handloom Industry in South Eastern India', *The Indian Economic and Social History Review*, Vol. 17, No. 3, p. 281.

3 Borpujari, J. G., 'Indian Cotton and the Cotton Famine, 1860–65', *The Indian Economic and Social History Review*, Vol. 10, No. 1, p. 45.

4 Gadgil, D. R., *Industrial Revolution of India in Recent Times, 1860–1939*, Oxford University Press, Bombay, 1971, p. 329.

5 Quoted in Pyarelal, *Towards New Horizons*, Navjivan Press, Ahmedabad, 1959, p. 150.

6 *Ibid.*

7 Jack Kloppenburg (1988), *First the Seed: The Political Economy of Plant Biotechnology 1492–2000*, Cambridge University Press, New York.

8 Frances Moore Lappé and Joseph Collins (1982), *Food First*, Abacus, London, p. 114.

9 Claude Alvares, 'The Great Gene Robbery', *The Illustrated Weekly of India*.

10 National Research Council (1989), *Alternative Agriculture*, National Academy Press, Washington, DC.

11 Pratrap, C. Aggarwal (1990), 'Natural Farming Succeeds in Indian Village', *Return to the Good Earth*, Third World Network, Penang.

12 Vir Singh and Satya Prakash (1990), 'Indian Farmers Rediscover Advantages of Traditional Rice Varieties' in *Return to the Good Earth*, Third World Network, Penang.

13 Rolanda B. Modina and A. R. Ridao, *IRRI Rice: The Miracle That Never Was*, ACE Foundation, Quezon City, Philippines, undated.

14 Brian Ford-Lloyd and Michael Jackson (1986), *Plant Genetic Resources*, Edward Arnold, p. 1.

15 Statement of John Duesing, in meeting on patents of the European Parliament, Brussels, in February 1990.

16 Jack Kloppenburg, *op cit.*

17 Quoted in *ibid.*, p. 185.

18 Pat Mooney (1989), 'From Cabbages to Kings: Intellectual Property vs Intellectual Integrity', Proceedings of Conference on Patenting of Life Forms, ICDA Report, Brussels.

19 Norman Summonds (1979), *Principles of Crop Improvement*, Longman, New York, p. 11.

20 Hugh Iltis (1986), 'Serendipity in Exploration of Biodiversity: What Good Are Weedy Tomatoes?' in E. O. Wilson (ed.), *Biodiversity*,. National Academy Press, Washington, DC.

CHAPTER 13

Biotechnology, Patents and the Third World

CARY FOWLER

This chapter is intended to provide a very basic introduction to some of the controversies currently surrounding biological patents and an explanation as to why these debates are important to industry, to Third World development aspirations and ultimately to genetic conservation efforts.

In modern industrialized societies, the purposes and effects of patents are taken for granted. So uncritical has our thinking about them become, that indeed they are seen as a civil right, something above questioning and examination. In this atmosphere it is difficult to see patent systems as they really are – as human-created institutions designed for human purposes, as the offspring not of religion or philosophy, but of politics and economics.

Early precursors to the modern patents system date back to the seventh century BC, when the Greeks began granting short-term monopolies to cooks for new recipes. The city state of Venice instituted a patent law in 1474. England adopted its first patent law in 1623, the US in 1790, France in 1791 and Sweden in 1819. Amid great controversy, patent laws were passed, defeated or repealed by many countries during the nineteenth century. No clear consensus existed for establishing government-granted rights to inventors to exclude others from imitating, manufacturing, using or selling a product (without permission), or utilizing a patented matter or process, as patents are usually defined. Patents may be seen by some as a civil right, but it would be more appropriate to view them as a legal mechanism of control in the marketplace.

Until recently, patents were not needed for biological materials. There were more efficient mechanisms of control, which we shall consider briefly. The voyage of Columbus to the New World marked the beginning of what is called the 'Columbian Exchange'. Columbus returned from his first trip to the New World with maize, a crop of Central and South American origins. Future trips by others would bring back potatoes, squash, cassava, peanuts and common beans. But the 'exchange' was really more acquisition than exchange. Although crops moved in both directions, and new crops were introduced to the New World, they moved under colonial control.

This was particularly true of the industrial/plantation crops which were the cash crops of the day, those traded commercially.

Rubber was smuggled out of Brazil and shipped to Kew Gardens. From Kew it made its way to the botanical gardens in Singapore, where it was distributed to initiate the rubber industry of South East Asia. The South East Asia rubber boom caused a rubber bust in Brazil. The economy of north-east Brazil collapsed and hundreds of thousands of people perished as a result. In 'exchange', sugar cane travelled from South East Asia to the New World, where systems of human slavery were instituted to tend the cane on lands clear-cut of trees just for that purpose. The boom–bust–famine cycles of sugar production are well known. Coffee came from Africa and Arabia. And bananas, which were to lend their name to a particularly unbalanced form of development in the so-called 'banana republics', were brought from South East Asia.

Many native crops of the Americas were obliterated. *Amaranth*, an important grain crop of South America, was outlawed by the Spanish due to its association with 'pagan' religious ceremonies. In North America, many domesticated food crops disappeared when the cultures which valued them and the people who raised them were wiped out. In some cases we no longer know the original names of these plants (today found only in a wild state), for some 200 languages were lost when the Indians were hunted down in North America.

Colonial powers attempted to control biological materials through control of production. The Dutch limited production of cloves and nutmeg to three islands in the Moluccas. The French brandished the threat of the guillotine at anyone who dared take indigo off Antigua (Fowler and Mooney, 1990).

Explorers were not simply looking for gold and silver or shorter trading routes. They had an eye for plants. In the sixteenth century fewer than 100 new plants were introduced into England. Some 1,000 were introduced in the seventeenth century and 9,000 were brought in during the eighteenth century (Lemmon, 1968). These were the plants which were to form the basis of the European dye, chemical and pharmaceutical industries. These were the plants which made possible the plantation economies in the Third World that brought such wealth to Europe.

Europe established its first botanical gardens in the seventeenth century. By the nineteeenth century, most colonial powers had such gardens, which effectively helped to channel biodiversity to these countries for their use and even control (Brockway, 1979; Smith, 1985). For the most part the search for plants was a search for new and valuable species of plants. Intra-species diversity was not terribly important, even though the Dutch were looking for clove and nutmeg diversity in the late eighteenth century to combat problems they were having in their plantations.

The economic importance of the botanical garden as a source of material for introduction into agricultural systems began to diminish with the rise of plant breeding. The United States built a system of plant introduction stations and finally a gene bank, the modern-day equivalent of the botanical garden, for the collection and storage of diversity within species of economically important crops. The Columbian exchange continued to work. Biodiversity was still flowing from South to North under the economic and political influence of commercial interests.

From Physical to Legal Means of Control

With the rise of political independence in the Third World, the decline of plantation economies and the growing importance of plant breeding, new methods of control became necessary. Old methods of coercion and of physical control of production sites were no longer viable. Slowly, the idea of plant patents was broached after the turn of the century. Patents were still quite controversial. Most of the Third World countries that had been brought along by the major powers to sign the Paris Convention had long since repealed their patent statutes. Chemical, pharmaceutical and food patents were routinely prohibited. (Chemicals were not patentable in the Nordic countries until 1968 and in Switzerland until 1978. Many countries still reject pharmaceutical patents and Spain has no provision for chemical patents even today.) The selling of patents on 'life' was not easy. But two powerful forces were combining to make it easier.

The first was the consolidation and internationalization of the seed industry. Approximately 1,000 mergers and acquisitions have taken place in the seed industry in the past 20 years as once family-owned, locally oriented companies have been integrated into the multinational petrochemical and drug industry. As seed companies have expanded, they have become national and international in the scope of their business operations, their needs and their vision.

Old systems of control were either unavailable or increasingly inappropriate. This was particularly true of the seed industry, where new seed varieties could easily be taken and reproduced by a competitor. With much value being added to seed through plant breeding, a healthy premium could be won by anyone who could gain exclusive rights to market a new seed variety. The introduction of hybrids solved that problem for some crops, especially maize. Farmers wanting to grow maize hybrids were forced to return to the seed company yearly. Biology itself offered the companies a method of control. But for grain crops, soybeans, cotton and many vegetables, no such control was possible. In 1961 the Union for the Protection of New

Varieties of Plants (UPOV) was organized to coordinate and promote 'plant breeders' rights' (PBR), a noble term for the granting of patent-like certificates for plants. The Union was based in Europe, though by 1970 the US had passed its own Plant Variety Protection Act, which had similar aims. Typically, these laws permitted the protection of discoveries. They also provided for 'research' and 'farmer' exemptions, meaning that protected varieties could be used in research and in the breeding of new varieties, and that farmers were allowed to save the seed of protected varieties and replant that seed the following year. With these concessions, PBR laws were adopted in a number of industrialized countries. (Notably, Canada approved its law only in 1990 and Norway has yet to adopt such a system.)

PBR was a significant departure from traditional patenting systems where inventions have to be new, useful, inventive and described sufficiently to enable someone skilled in the art to reproduce the invention. In the 1960s and 1970s, it was not thought that plants could meet such strict criteria. Thus the trade which society makes with the inventor, namely the grant of monopoly rights in exchange for the contribution of the knowledge (inventive step) was compromised. To meet PBR requirements, a variety need only be distinct, uniform and stable.

The second factor encouraging the spread of life-patenting laws was the development of biotechnology. The needs of biotechnology were met neither by traditional patent systems nor by plant breeders' rights. Are the 'inventions' of biotechnology new and inventive in the legal sense? Can they be described adequately? If not, traditional patent systems offer no protection. In the US a series of court and Patent Office decisions have ameliorated some of these problems. In contrast, in Europe, the European Patent Convention expressly prohibits the patenting of plant varieties and animal breeds – a formidable obstacle.

Plant breeders' rights offered no hope of protection for genes, characteristics or processes. In any case, given the ease with which organisms multiply, PBR with its research and farmer exemptions provided too little control for the new industry. Constructing new patent laws to accommodate biotechnology might be the most logical thing to do, but political opposition to this would be far too great in most countries. Instead, there have been and continue to be a multitude of efforts to modify existing patent laws through regulatory, administrative and judicial decisions. Space does not allow us to do more than generalize. In various countries, these accommodations are taking a number of forms: new micro-organisms are being redefined so that they are no longer considered as products of nature (and thus as excludable from many patent laws), but as products of human inventiveness. Thus, invention has been interpreted as including discovery, and attempts are being made to give such an interpretation the force of law. The scope of coverage is broadening to include genes and characteristics (and plants and animals). Descriptive requirements are being loosened. It also seems that the burden of proof is in the process of being reversed. The European Commission, for example, is proposing that defendants prove their innocence by showing that they have not used a plaintiff's patented micro-organism (Newman, 1989). The result of these developments is to give more power and more control to the patent holder. The effect is to maintain the centralization of control over biodiversity which has existed since colonial times. The mode of control has simply shifted from physical to legal.

In summary, with biotechnology we have a new, lucrative technology. easily copied, coming at a time when old methods of control and even old patent systems have become inadequate. The response has been one of accommodation, the importance of which cannot easily be overestimated. The US patent office currently has a backlog of 8,000 'biotechnology' patents pending, though there are only a dozen products actually on the market now. Genentech, the premier American biotechnological company, has four times as many lawsuits to protect its patents as it has products. In the US, patent appeal cases have been consolidated into one court system with the result that the rate of patents being upheld has jumped from 30 to 80 per cent almost overnight (Dwyer, 1989). Increasingly, research is being guided by the potential for patent acquisition and enforcement rather than by the results of experiments and tests (Dwyer, 1989). Indeed, at least one company was created in the US whose 'main business' according to the *Wall Street Journal* 'is buying up broad patents and then suing other companies for alleged infringements' (Lambert and Hayes, 1990).

Moving to the International Patent Arena

Patents appear to be the only viable form of assuring control and ownership of biotechnological innovations (though trade secrets are also of importance). Yet the new techniques can be applied internationally. In order to be effective, patents must be internationally recognized. At present they are not. Patents granted in one country are not necessarily recognized by any other country. Some countries, such as India, maintain a distinctly hostile attitude towards patents.

The Third World critique of the industrial patent system is an old one. It found expression in and gained strength from work done at the UN Conference on Trade and Development in the 1960s. According to this analysis, most patents granted in the Third World simply function as a reverse system of preferences, giving legal preference, protection and monopoly rights to foreign imports. Fewer than 5 per cent of the patents granted in the Third World are used there in the production process. Fewer than 1 per cent of the patents issued in the Third World go to Third World nationals (Patel, 1989). Third World governments, then, see no evidence that patents encourage research, a benefit often cited in industrialized countries. Instead, they wonder how imported patent systems could serve their own development needs. Indeed, 'development' seems to be the question. Whereas industrialized countries are more comfortable talking about patents as 'rights', Third World governments seem to see patents in terms of development and transfer of technology policies. If a patent is to be granted, the typical Third World country will want that patent to be 'worked' inside the country. It will want the technology imported and used inside the country. If only the product is imported, its contribution to development will be slight.

The conflict of interests over patents in recent years has made international patent reform difficult to accomplish in the traditional arenas like the World Intellectual Property Organization. Given this, American industry has pressed for a change of arenas. This may explain the US initiative in the General Agreement on Tariffs and Trade (GATT) in Geneva, where the US can use its trading power to bargain for intellectual property rights.

At the beginning of the Uruguay Round of negotiations, agreement had been reached on the scope of negotiations. In the 'General Principles Governing Negotiations' (paragraph v of Section B) developed countries formally agreed that they did not expect developing countries 'to make contributions which are inconsistent with their individual development, financial and trade needs. Developed contracting parties shall therefore not seek, neither shall less-developed contracting parties be required to make, concessions that are inconsistent with the latter's development, financial and trade needs.' Nevertheless, the challenge was made. The US put forth a novel position: the absence of intellectual property rights protection (at a minimum level similar to that offered by the US) constitutes an unfair trade barrier and should be subject to trade sanctions under GATT. Strategically, the threat of trade restrictions is being offered to persuade countries into adopting foreign levels of patent protection through the only forum in which such a tactic might work across the board. As outlined by Gadbaw and Richards (1988), the strategy was fourfold:

1　attempt to persuade Third World countries of the value of intellectual property rights;

2　threaten loss of access to US markets;

3　offer increased or decreased research and development funding through the private sector; and,

4   pursue agreements on minimum patent standards through GATT.

'The primary thrust of the Uruguay Round efforts', according to Gadbaw and Gwynn (1988), 'is to draw the developing countries into a new set of rights and obligations.'

Farmers as Innovators?

Thus far we have examined the accommodation of northern, industrialized country patent systems to changes in technology and advances in the biological sciences, and looked briefly at the efforts of those systems to clone themselves in the Third World. What about the interests of the Third World amidst these changes? Does the fact that only 1 per cent of the patents go to Third World nationals mean that only 1per cent of the innovation on this planet is done in Asia, Africa and Latin America? Or, might it reflect a bias in the system, an indication of who has written patent conventions and for whom?

While it may seem impolite to say this, it can hardly be questioned that industrialized countries need protection for their inventions and desire free access to the biological resources of the South. Nowhere is this more evident than with agricultural crops. Modern plant breeding and biotechnology have made plant genetic resources extremely valuable. These are the resources which make evolution in our crops possible – yet note the curious way in which we speak of this genetic diversity, these raw materials which are the basis of our agricultural system. We hear these resources described as 'primitive' or 'Stone Age' varieties, as heirloom or traditional varieties, or as landraces. The first two terms are blatantly unscientific, inaccurate and demeaning. The other terms imply that these resources are something from the past, something which is not implicitly the product of human creativity. It is probably true that in using the term landrace scientists mean no harm or disrespect, but language often has a way of revealing unconscious feelings and hidden social relationships. Are these genetic resources in the form of varieties being grown by Third World peoples really just raw materials, or are they improved materials? Should these priceless materials remain priceless?

Such questions provided the backdrop for a remarkable series of debates in the United Nations Food and Agriculture Organization (FAO) in Rome in the 1980s. A number of Third World nations (particularly Latin American) had begun to sense inequities in patterns of seed collection and storage. Patterns of germplasm flows and usage under modern seed bank systems were similar to those under the botanical garden system of colonial days. A modern-day Columbian exchange was taking place, once again one that was less exchange than acquisition from their vantage point.

Between 1974 and 1984 over 125,000 duplicate samples were drawn from collecting expeditions under the International Board for Plant Genetic Resources (IBPGR). According to their data, over 90 per cent of these came from the Third World. Only 15 per cent of the duplicates of this material were stored in the Third World under the control of their governments. And only 25 per cent of the regional and 16 per cent of the global repositories (so designated by the IBPGR) for individual crops were in the Third World (Fowler and Mooney, 1990). Clearly the North had acted on former US Secretary of Agriculture Richard Lyng's observation that the US (and other industrialized countries) are 'totally at the mercy' of the Third World for crop germplasm. After a number of meetings and many hours of often acrimonious debate, the FAO established:

1 a Commission on Plant Genetic Resources where governments, as governments, could meet to discuss questions about the conservation and use of these resources;

2 an International Network of Gene Banks, under the auspices of the FAO;

3 an 'International Undertaking', a low-level, voluntary agreement which called for the free exchange of all classifications of germplasm, from wild varieties, mutants and the folk varieties of the Third World farmer to the breeding lines and commercial varieties of the seed company;

4 the concept of Farmers' Rights as a means of claiming that plant genetic resources are not just a raw material divorced from human creativity, and as a way of pressing forward the demand that if plant breeders' rights are to be observed and rewarded, then farmers rights must be treated similarly;

5 an International Gene Fund to finance genetic conservation and utilization programmes, and to serve, possibly, as an instrument for the concrete manifestation and recognition of the concept of farmers' rights.

Third World delegates to the FAO claim that their part of the globe has a more informal, less visible, less recognized and totally unrewarded system of innovation. If it could be shown that Third World farmers are plant breeders, the argument for a system of compensation parallel to PBR would be strengthened politically. Let us examine, briefly, what is known about the steps of the plant breeding process at the farm level in the Third World.

In the Andes, Dr Steve Brush (1986) has described folk taxonomy systems for potatoes among that region's farmers. Similar studies have shown up to five levels of classification for rice among farmers in Asia (H. Conklin, cited in Brush, 1986). Farmers may be able to describe and classify their plants, but do they know about heredity? The Pima and Tepehuan people in Mexico have ways of describing introgression of wild and weedy genes into cultivated crops and 'a sophisticated sense of the relationship between domesticated and spontaneous species', according to Dr Gary Nabhan, an ethnobotanist (Nabhan, 1989).

Can they use such knowledge of heredity? In the 1960s Dr Garrison Wilkes observed harvests of hybrids of Indian maize with *teosinte*, a wild relative of maize. In the Nabogame Valley in Mexico, he found farmers allowing and even encouraging the introgression of maize and *teosinte*. According to them the result was 'stronger' and flintier kernels (Wilkes, 1977).

In the most far-reaching study of its kind to date, Dr Paul Richards (1986) found that farmers in Sierra Leone can distinguish between 70 different rices. These are differentiated according to length to maturity, ease of husking, proportion of husk size to grain size and weight, susceptibility to bird and insect attack, appropriateness in different soils and with different levels of moisture, colour of plant parts, cooking time and qualities, taste, and other characteristics.

When harvesting, these farmers stay clear of the boundaries between different 'varieties'. They harvest panicle by panicle, saving the interesting material for future experiments. They also rogue off-types when they desire to keep a variety 'pure'. They have trial plots. They record data. They test germination rates. They try to match their rice to the local ecological niches. (Do the traits uncovered in this process constitute discovery or invention in the legal sense? Does it matter?) They multiply promising new varieties and they conduct field tests.

In summary, Third World farmers have been found to employ taxonomic systems, encourage introgression, use selection, make efforts to see that varieties are adapted, multiply seeds, field test, record data and even name their varieties. In short, they do what many northern plant breeders do, except that they do not apply for legal protection – the one step in the process which requires skills (and money) which they do not have. Do these actions deserve any less recognition or reward than those of the 13-year-old boy who discovered the world's first thornless rose and the company which eventually got the patent for this 'innovation' (Kneen, 1948)?

The actions of Third World farmers may meet the requirements of patent or plant breeders' rights laws, but the plants themselves do not. These plants may be new, distinct and useful. They are rarely uniform. The obvious question is, why should they be uniform? Uniformity is a quality sometimes needed by industrialized agricultural systems and always needed by patent laws, but its agronomic appropriateness in the Third World is highly suspect. In any case, the Third World farmer's field is at once a seed bank, a test plot and a production site. How could it be uniform? How can we ask the Third World farmer to be innovative and to produce uniformity simultaneously? We might better ask what it is about our politics, economic needs or the nature of our own scientific establishment which makes it so difficult to acknowledge the skills, creativity and contributions of others, especially in the Third World. Could it be that our lack of understanding blinds us to the reality of a different style of innovation? Dr Melaku Worede, director of Ethiopia's renowned gene bank, tells the story of an American scientist who collected a high-lysine sorghum there some years ago. After testing in the laboratory this scientist announced his discovery – a high-lysine sorghum. The locals had a name for this variety, which the scientist had not bothered to learn. It was called 'Why Bother with Wheat?' They already knew the sorghum's qualities. Who made the discovery?

It is readily acknowledged that collected seeds in gene banks are poorly documented. Often there is little 'passport' information. There is almost no information on existing uses, names, and other local characteristics. In such a situation, attributes bred by folk science can become anonymous attributes, a gift from nature, disconnected from the labour and creativity of real people – the common heritage of mankind. In the extreme case, this material can even become patentable. In this regard, one conclusion of an exclusive meeting co-sponsored by the American Society of Agronomy, the Crop Science Society of America, the American Agricultural Economics Association and the American Society of Horticultural Science is particularly interesting: 'It is important to support better characterization of material in gene banks so that characterization is known and in the public domain, available, and therefore not subject to intellectual property rights' (Anon, 1989). This statement serves to highlight the function patents may come to play in relation to Third World genetic resources. Are these organizations not suggesting that material (potentially the 'Why Bother with Wheat?' sorghum) might be patented if efforts are not soon made to catalogue what is contained in gene banks?

Conclusion

We are now entering a period of intensified conflict over questions of ownership and control of biological materials. Patents and patent-like protection will be at the centre of controversies, which will spill over into questions of access to and use of biological diversity. Industrialized countries can no longer expect the Third World graciously to donate genetic material for the improvement of northern crops and the enrichment of foreign corporations, only to be told that this material is the 'common heritage of mankind', while corporate material is private property. One cannot expect Madagascar, for example, to donate vanilla germplasm only to watch bio-technological companies begin commercial production without vanilla plants, without Madagascar's 75,000 vanilla producers and without compensation either directly or indirectly to the farmers or the country.

Patents are a means of allocating ownership, assigning control, regulating access and apportioning benefits. In the field of biology they are the latest in a series of mechanisms which date back hundreds of years and which have included colonialism, physical control of production and markets, hybrids and trade secrets. Today, the Third World is beginning to develop and employ its own mechanisms of control, strikingly similar to ones that have been employed against them – physical control, in this case over the genes themselves.

One cannot pretend that the profound changes under way in patent law exist outside a larger milieu. Patents reflect power relationships and, as such, they change. Patent systems which recognize the contributions of some but not of others are based on injustice and will be unstable, if not unsustainable. This, perhaps, is the lesson of the patent controversies of the last decade. Means should therefore be employed to soften the negative impacts of patents and provide systems of protection and compensation for forms of innovation not now covered by traditional patent systems. Concrete recognition of 'farmers' rights' through a mandatory gene fund would be one such method. Such a fund would not only reward innovation, but reward and finance conservation as well. And as the first Keystone Dialogue report notes: 'The value of a resource to a country depends on the country's present and future ability to utilize [it]. It follows that support for genetic resources conservation should be supplemented by support for plant breeding activities' (Keystone 1988). Short of totally reconceptualizing the patent system – an interesting but unrealistic goal – a fund might serve to recognize and redress some of inequalities of biological patent systems.

Decisions made regarding patents, ownership and control will inevitably affect our ability to conserve genetic resources and have access to them. The link between environmental conservation, economic development and justice is a link which cannot and should not be severed. Finally, the decisions which are made concerning the ownership and control of the planet's biological diversity will also say much about the kind of people we want to become and the kind of relationship with the world and its people we want to bequeath to future generations. As the 500th anniversary of the voyage of Columbus recedes, many will watch to see if anything has really changed in the relationship between the centres of world economic power and the periphery.

References

Anonymous. 1989. Quandary over plant patenting brings diverse group of experts together. *Diversity* 5: 36.

Brockway, L. H. 1979. *Science and Colonial Expansion. The Role of the British Royal Botanical Gardens.* Academic Press, New York.

Brush, S. B. 1986. Genetic diversity and conservation in traditional farming systems. *Journal of Ethnobiology* 6: 151–67.

Dwyer, P. 1989. The battle raging over intellectual property. *Business Week* 22 May.

Fowler, C. and P. Mooney. 1990. *Shattering: Food Politics and the Loss of Genetic Diversity.* University of Arizona Press, Tucson.

Gadbaw, R. M. and R. E. Gwynn. 1988. 'Intellectual property rights in the new GATT round', pp. 38–88. In: R. M. Gadbaw and T. J. Richards (eds) *Intellectual Property Rights. Global Consensus, Global Conflict?* Westview Press, Boulder, CO.

Gadbaw, R. M. and T. J. Richards. 1988. Introduction, pp. 1–37. In: R. M. Gadbaw and T. J. Richards (eds) *Intellectual Property Rights. Global Consensus, Global Conflict?* Westview Press, Boulder, CO.

Keystone Center. 1988. *Final Report of the Keystone International Dialogue on Plant Genetic Resources,* Session 1: Ex situ Conservation of Plant Genetic Resources. Keystone Center. Keystone, CO.

Kneen, O. H. 1948. Plant patents enrich our lives. *National Geographic* March.

Lambert, W. and A. S. Hayes. 1990. Investing in patents to file suits is curbed. *Wall Street Journal* 30 May 1990.

Lemmon, K . 1968. *Golden Age of Plant Hunters.* Barnes, Cranbury, UK.

Nabhan, G . P. 1989. *Enduring Seeds. Native American Agriculture and Wild Plant Conservation.* North Point Press, San Francisco, CA.

Newman, P. 1989. A modest proposal for European patents. *Bio/Technology* 7: 26.

Patel, S. J. 1989. Intellectual Property Rights in the Uruguay Round: A disaster for the South? *Economic and Political Weekly* 6 May.

Richards, P. 1986. *Coping With Hunger. Hazard and Experiment in an African Rice-farming System.* Allen & Unwin. London.

Smith. N. J. H. 1985. *Botanic Gardens and Greenplasm Conservation.* Harold L. Lyon Arboretum Lecture Number Fourteen. University of Hawaii Press, Honolulu.

Wilkes, H. G. 1977. Hybridization of maize and teosinte in Mexico and Guatemala, and the improvement of maize. *Econ. Bot.* 31: 254–93.

CHAPTER 14

Biotechnology and the Future of Agriculture

HENK HOBBELINK

Few newly developed technologies have occasioned as much optimism as biotechnology. Many articles appear on this issue, virtually all of them outlining the possible positive impact that this technology will have on agriculture, health, and the world's food supply. According to many authors, yields per hectare will be doubled or tripled, super-plants that produce their own fertilizer and pesticides will be developed, and new useful products will be derived from the same crops. Often it is stressed as a particular advantage of the technology that it will improve food security for small farmers in the Third World, because of its potential to reduce the need for expensive inputs and its capability to adapt crops to the marginal soils on which small farmers often have to work. It is the ideal solution to the problem of hunger, it seems. However, not everybody agrees. In its World Food Day brochure, the FAO stresses that 'several areas exist where modern biotechnology may hinder development or create serious hardship for rural communities'.[1]

In a way, biotechnology – the industrial harnessing of life forms and processes – has been with us ever since the Abyssinians brewed beer from cereals, farmers fermented cheese from milk, and people started baking yeast-leavened breads. However, today's new biotechnologies are based on a much more deterministic manipulation of DNA and the regulatory process that guides genetic functions. The techniques that are bundled under this simplistic term are quite varied. For example, tissue culture is the multiplication of cells in artificial media to multiply plants, produce specific compounds or allow scientists to scan and test materials for genetic characteristics. Recombinant DNA is what is known more popularly as genetic engineering: transferring genes from one organism to another, from bacteria to plants or from humans to cows. Enzyme technologies are new forms of fermentation to produce new substances. All of these tools are being used to develop crops with novel characteristics, new vaccines, new sources of industrial components and many other applications. Biotechnology not only breaks down the species barrier, it also allows for specific research projects to yield an array of results for agriculture, health, industrial production and energy.

Perhaps the most salient feature of the new biotechnologies is that they are predominantly developed in the North. In a report done for the World Bank it is calculated that up to 1985 only 7.5 per cent of worldwide biotechnological research was done outside the US, the EEC and Japan.[2] With Canada and Australia responsible for most of this residual amount, the Third World emerges as a complete outsider in the bio-revolution. With the explosive growth in biotechnological research in the North since 1985, this outsider role is becoming ominously inescapable. The second and perhaps more important feature is that the bulk of the research is done and controlled by large multinational corporations, or their subsidiaries, who use the new tools to further enhance their corporate interest. According to the FAO, the five largest plant biotechnology companies are all large multinational corporations with important interests in agrochemical sales: Du-Pont, ICI, Monsanto, Sandoz and Ciba-Geigy. Thus, by far the most important actors in defining the course that biotechnology will take are the giant producers of agrochemicals and pharmaceuticals as well as the major food processors.

The fact that such a powerful technology is largely in the hands of the private sector in the North can lead to biases in the type of research that is being done. It is only logical that a large company would tend to aim at large worldwide markets for their products. Such products might not necessarily be appropriate for small farmers in developing countries, who tend to work in highly variable and vulnerable ecosystems, and need seeds that are location-specific. In that sense, biotechnology might undermine food security rather that securing it. One example of the biases in current biotechnological research is the work going on to create crops that are more tolerant of herbicides. According to Don Duvick, former executive of Pioneer Hi-bred, the largest seed company in the world, the search for genetic resistance to agro-chemicals is becoming as important as the search for resistance to the pests and insects themselves.

In a recent survey by the OECD on the field testing of genetically engineered crop plants[3] it was found that the main trait tested for was tolerance of herbicides. Of the 1257 traits tested between 1986 and 1992, 740 had to do with some kind of resistance or tolerance. Of those, a full two-thirds were dedicated to herbicide tolerance, the remaining third being tests for traits such as resistance to diseases, insects and viruses. The logic of this research for the companies seems obvious: herbicide-resistant crops would increase sales of herbicides from the same or other companies. From the standpoint of small Third World farmers and food security, the logic is less obvious: more chemicals mean higher costs, more damage to the environment, and a higher risk to food security.

Uniformity for Food Security?

The race to get new biotechnological products to the market includes the development of biological pesticides and pest-resistant crops. These appear to be promising developments that could help to promote a more sustainable agriculture, fewer chemicals and better food security at the local level. But whether this will actually happen really depends on how sustainable the biotechnological solutions are. At present the research in this area focuses on an extremely narrow genetic source of pest resistance. This uniformity could seriously undermine the objective of developing a more sustainable world – and Third World – agriculture.

For example, *Bacillus thuringiensis* (Bt) is a bacterium which normally lives in the soil. It produces toxins which kill the larvae of moths and butterflies, and almost nothing else. That, and the fact that it is a 'natural' product, make Bt an almost perfect pesticide. Now biotechnological companies are massively transferring the Bt gene into major crops to make them resistant to insect pests. One report calculates that over one third of all biotechnological research on biological control agents focuses on this single micro-organism. With research efforts so concentrated on this single cure, farmers using it might soon face the old problem again. Entomologist Fred Gould puts it this way: 'If pesticidal plants are developed and used in a way that leads to rapid pest adaptation, the efficacy of these plants will be lost and agriculture will be pushed back to reliance on conventional pesticides with their inherent problem.'[4] For the companies that is not necessarily a problem: if the Bt approach becomes useless they still have the good old chemicals on the shelves to offer.

All this is not to say that the use of biotechnology to produce pest-resistant crops or 'bio-pesticides' cannot be beneficial to the farmer and to agriculture in general. We desperately need an agriculture which uses fewer harmful chemicals and other external inputs. The question is whether the current reductionist biotechnological pest control approach, almost entirely focusing on a limited number of single genes, is one which will help to solve the problems.

If current biotechnological research programmes do not take seriously the need to broaden the genetic base of agriculture, rather than further narrowing it down, we run the risk of foregoing yet another item on the long list of biotechnological promises. It is likely to switch us from the chemical treadmill to a biological one, where each time another toxic biological substance has to be found to fight off pests. If that does not work, we will be back on the chemical treadmill again, with the consequences for food security we can all imagine.

Transforming the Output

Since colonial times, developing countries have been growing crops for the North. Most of these agricultural commodities, such as sugar, cocoa, bananas or vegetable oils, now face serious problems as prices are depressed and farmers have to sell their products below production cost. This especially hits the millions of small farmers and landless plantation workers in developing countries who are dependent on these crops. Biotechnological research on tropical crops and their products is heavily concentrated within the multinational food processing companies as they search for cheaper raw materials.

The food processing companies have already used biotechnology to replace a substantial part of former sugar exports from developing countries with sweeteners derived from corn and other crops that can be grown in the North. This resulted in the collapse of entire economies in the Caribbean and of the sugar-growing regions in the Philippines. But research does not stop there, and the multinationals are now cloning genes from Third World crops to produce substances in the laboratory that are thousands times sweeter than sugar. Indeed, biotechnology puts the very future of sugarcane as a commodity crop at risk.

In yet another research focus, cocoa trees are being bred for higher production on plantations to the detriment of small cocoa farmers in Africa. The food processing companies are also using biotechnology to develop substitutes for cocoa and so end their dependence on Third World producers altogether. Countries in Africa, such as Ghana, Cameroon and Ivory Coast, where cocoa is mainly produced by small farmers, are already feeling the impact of biotechnology as the higher-yielding cocoa varieties are best adapted to plantations in Malaysia and Brazil. Consequently Africa's share of global cocoa production dropped from 70 per cent in 1961 to 52 per cent in 1991.[5] If biotechnology will further allow the multinationals to use substitutes for cocoa beans in the production of chocolate, the African countries will lose even more of this important export market. Perhaps even more important, it will be the small-scale African farmers who will be hit hardest by this development.

No crop is safe in the bio-race. Biotechnology companies have already managed to develop 'natural' vanilla in the laboratory, thus threatening the livelihood of thousands of small farmers who now produce this crop in Madagascar. There are many other examples of similar research. In all cases, small-scale Third World producers are the losers. One source estimates that in the medium term over US$20 billion worth of Third World exports could be replaced by products of the new biotechnologies developed in the North. This would represent over a quarter of what developing countries are now exporting in the form of agricultural commodities, and would mean a dramatic setback in the development of the least-developing countries especially, who would find it difficult to find alternative ways to earn the foreign currency they so desperately need. There is no doubt that such a dramatic shift in world agricultural trade would harm food security at the local level.

Biotechnology blurs the differences between commodity crops as their substances are modified to suit different needs. With the agro-chemical companies controlling the input and food processing companies modifying the output, farmers have to stop thinking in terms of kilograms per hectare and to start worrying about the amount of suitable fats, proteins and carbohydrates they provide. In that context, food production increasingly becomes an assembly line in which interchangeable components are produced. This industrialization of agriculture allows the food processing and chemical companies to choose whatever component is cheapest, thus further undermining the power of the producing Third World countries to set the conditions for the trade. As history has shown us, the losers in this process normally are not only the poorest countries but especially the small farmers and landless wage workers.

Patenting Life

Of all the policy issues surrounding the development and diffusion of modern biotechnology, one question comes across as the most profound, fundamental and far-reaching: who owns it. Intellectual property rights, and especially patents, have often been presented by their proponents as an incentive to invest in risky research and a mechanism to stimulate innovation, bringing benefits to society through the availability of scientific knowledge and assurance of technical progress. A patent is basically a compromise between society (the public interest) and an inventor (a private interest) whereby the inventor discloses his/her invention in return for an exclusive monopoly on it.

There is considerable discussion on whether and how the patent system should be applied to life forms. Biotechnologists push for this option as it would grant them more control over the marketing of their products. While the international discussion is still going on, genes, cells, plants and animals are already being patented. This is not the place for a detailed discussion on the pros and cons of the patenting of life forms. But in the North–South context, it is important to point to the fact that most of the biological and genetic diversity which provides the so-called raw material of plant breeding and biotechnology is to be found in the developing countries. And most of that material does not just lie around there; it has been created, modified, maintained and conserved by numerous generations of indigenous communities. Now biotechnologists come in, insert a gene here and there, and then call the whole thing theirs.

An example of this practice is a recent patent application on the use of a traditional African plant called *Endod* to kill Zebra mussels. These mussels are becoming a major problem in North America as they disrupt water flows by attaching themselves to pipes and other hard surfaces. *Endod,* also known as the African soapberry plant, has been selected and cultivated for centuries by indigenous people in several parts of Africa, where its berries are used as a traditional soap. Its fish-killing properties are also well known to the indigenous people. In 1990, after just a few months' testing, scientists in the USA found that the berry effectively killed Zebra mussels and applied for a patent on its use. The African communities who selected the plant in the first place, and in many ways are the real inventors of this product, are not expected to see any of the benefits.

The same story applies to two other African plants: *Katemfe* and the Serendipity berry. Both produce extremely sweet proteins, and are locally used as sweeteners. As with *Endod,* they have been selected and maintained for centuries by local communities in Western and Central Africa, but now the University of California, together with Lucky Biotech Corporation, have applied for a patent on all genetically engineered plants that contain the sweetener genes of *Katemfe* and Serendipity. The commercial value of these genes is likely to be very high as the industry is actively searching for powerful non-sugar sweeteners. Again, the African communities who have long used the plants, and who first identified their properties, are not expected to see any of these benefits.[6]

The patent system is often defended by its proponents as essentially a human right that rewards the creativity of an inventor. However, as the examples above show, it increasingly looks like a rip-off system that does not take into account the creativity and many years of work that indigenous communities put into developing products which are now the basis of a multi-million dollar industry in the North.

Biotechnology for or with Farmers?

Farmers have been actively managing genetic resources for as long as they have been tending, hunting, gathering and cultivating crops and animals. Over the past few decades, however, management of genetic resources has been progressively shifted from their control over to state programmes, international agricultural research centres and the private sector. Today, alongside calls for sustainable agriculture, more and more people are recognizing the role of local communities and especially of small-scale farmers in development. For many farming communities, diversity – be it social, cultural, economic or genetic – means security. Genetic diversity provides security for the farmer against pests, disease, and unexpected climatic conditions. It also helps small-scale farmers to maximize production in the highly variable, and often marginal or stressed environments in which they tend to cultivate their crops, herd or raise livestock, and fish.

Based on thousands of years of hands-on experience and a deep knowledge of their needs and their agricultural production systems, farming communities have developed multiple strategies for their farming systems, almost all of which hinge upon sophisticated management of genetic diversity. Traditionally, small-scale farmers not only use a wide range of crop species in their complex farming systems of intercropping, polyculture and agroforestry, but also use several varieties within each crop. It is this biological diversity that forms the basis of their production systems, and their food security.

If biotechnology needs biodiversity it does not necessarily maintain it. On the one hand, biotechnology does offer new techniques for conserving species that are hard to dry and freeze in convenient refrigerators. It allows scientists to maintain these so-called recalcitrant crops in the slow growth of a test tube. But biotechnology's main impact on biodiversity is in redesigning plants and animals, and extracting new compounds from microbes. In agriculture, the main potential market for biotechnology applications, the focus is not so much on widening the genetic base of our increasingly uniform crops and livestock, but on inserting single genes into otherwise thousandfold genomes, modifying the role of one protein over the countless others, and speeding up and rendering more precise the whole breeding process. The aim and the consequence is not to create more diversity but to gain better control over the food production system.

In trying to answer the question of how the new biotechnologies could benefit the rural poor, perhaps a useful start is to point to all the work that is not being done. Simple mass selection to improve local varieties is one example of under-supported research. Others include work on enhancing multiple cropping and rotation techniques, rationalization of the use of wild plants in local diets, and the upgrading of traditional crop protection practices. With highly promising technical solutions being heralded at every turn, the focus is often blurred. Yes, the new biotechnologies might have something to offer, but so have small farmers themselves. Research oriented towards reinforcing the solid foundations of agricultural systems which have been developed for millennia is highly sporadic and seriously underfunded. At the same time, research on the quicker, short-term and high-tech panaceas, which often result in the undermining of those foundations in the long term, attract the imagination – and most of the money. After all, money tends to go to places where it multiplies fast, which is often not in the fields of indigenous farmers.

Notes

1   *Harvesting Nature's Diversity,* FAO, Rome, October 1993, p. 19.
2   Gabrielle J. Persley, *Beyond Mendel's Garden: Biotechnology in the Service of World Agriculture,* CAB International for the World Bank, Oxon, UK, 1990, p. 48.
3   *Field Releases of Transgenetic Plants 1986–1992,* OECD, Paris, 1993, p. 12.
4   Quoted in *Seedling,* Vol 9, No.1, March 1992, GRAIN, Barcelona. p. 16
5   FAO, Agrostat computer disks.
6   Examples from: *Biodiversity, What's at Stake?,* CIIR, London, September 1993, pp. 29–30.

CHAPTER 15

The Seven Dimensions of Sustainable Agriculture

NICANOR PERLAS

The 'green revolution' paradigm has collapsed. There is global recognition that intensification of agricultural production with the use of pesticides, chemical fertilizers and related technologies is a dead-end approach. This recognition is widespread in academic, scientific and policy circles. Many are calling for a more sustainable agriculture. At the recent UN Conference on Environment and Development (UNCED), Chapter 14 of Agenda 21 called for a more sustainable approach to agriculture and rural development. Over 140 countries around the world signed their approval of Agenda 21, the global agenda for the twenty-first century.

The Consultative Group on International Agricultural Research (CGIAR), a network of international agricultural research centres launched the green revolution. CGIAR, too, is calling for more sustainable forms of agriculture. CGIAR includes Asian centres like the International Rice Research Institute (IRRI), the International Crops Research Institute for the Semi-Arid Tropics (ICRISAT) and the International Irrigation Management Institute (IIMI).

The problem, however, is that different proponents understand and use the term differently. Green revolution proponents continue their advocacy of high-tech, chemical agriculture, yet they now feel comfortable in joining the sustainable agriculture bandwagon. Even within the NGO community, the term 'sustainable agriculture' evokes different operational concepts. There is a need to articulate a far broader and comprehensive understanding of sustainability. Otherwise, wolves will appear in sheeps' clothing and the destruction of nature and communities will continue unabated under the banner of sustainable agriculture.

To be sustainable, agricultural systems must have seven attributes.

1 'Based on Integrative and Holistic Science'

Despite relatively advanced thinking by NGOs and government representatives, two thresholds were not crossed at UNCED: holistic science and total human development. These thresholds presented difficult frontiers for the participants at UNCED and the parallel international forum of NGOs and social movements. They also present almost unattainable new beginnings for many NGOs in Asia, not to mention government officials, academics and other key sectors of society.

The Achilles heel of NGOs: fixation on social factors

The first threshold concerns the very nature of science itself and how it 'understands' nature. This limitation is exemplified clearly by the glaring lack of understanding of the blindness of conventional science among both technocrats and, perhaps surprisingly, among NGOs. Technocrats, especially those from capitalist economies, predictably propose technological solutions to complex social problems. If the problem is feeding an increasing population, the answer is more science and technology along the lines of the green revolution. We can call this attitude 'technological fixation'.

Surprisingly, many NGOs display a similar naïveté regarding scientific and technological issues. The perfect example is the attitude of NGOs towards biotechnology. A significant number of NGOs are mesmerized by its promises. Like their technocratic opposites, NGOs are anxious about potential environmental and other side effects; they sincerely believe, however, that these will be minimized or done away with if NGOs and people's organizations (POs) control the technology. So they talk about community-based, or village-level, environmentally sound use of biotechnology. Redirecting the goals of biotechnological research to fit the people's agenda, NGOs mistakenly believe that 'science and technology are neutral' and that everything depends on who controls and directs the technology.

Thus NGOs demonstrate the opposite case, the 'sociological fixation'. If they can get rid of unjust social structures, and place biotechnology under social control, NGOs believe they can turn it to good use. They are not aware that this 'neutrality' conception lands them in exactly the same ideological camp as the technocrats and scientists whom they criticize for all the problems of the green revolution. While technocrats believe in the 'technological fix', many NGOs believe in the 'sociological fix'. Both are unaware of the hidden agenda of science

Reductionist science

Most conventional scientific approaches today rely heavily on reductionism. The complexity of causative factors in the real world is reduced to one or at most a few factors considered to be the cause or the dominant causes. For example, if a crop suffers an insect attack, conventional scientists, without much reflection, would immediately try to find an offending insect. No questions are asked about the farming methods or other predisposing factors that make the crop attractive and susceptible to insect attack. This type of reductionism we may call methodological or overt. Complex reality is fragmented, broken apart conceptually. A fragment of that reality is then hoisted up as *the* explanation of that reality.

There are many variants of overt reductionism: socio-cultural, techno-logical, economic and so on. The type of reductionism depends on what facet of reality is blown up out of proportion and idolized as *the* cause. But these reductionisms are merely expressions of a far more virulent and destructive reductionism, one that assumes that all natural, psychological and social reality can be fully explained by material and physical causes and processes. For short, we can call this type of reductionism materialism.

The heavy, almost addictive use of pesticides in modern agriculture provides a classic example of how a one-sided, reductionist science and its techno-projection can create large-scale environmental destruction. Today, from many quarters, we hear the cry to 'modernize' agriculture. The pro-ponents of high-tech agriculture say we need to provide more food, on less land, for an ever-increasing population on the way to becoming a Newly Industrialized Country.

To modernize agriculture inevitably means, in the high-tech approach, to use insecticides. Since insects attack plants, they say, farmers need insecticides. During the scientific research process which creates insecti-cides, however, only very narrow questions are asked, those that deal directly with the insecticide. Scientists, do not ask, for example, what the impact of chemical fertilizers may be on the emergence of insect pests. Nor do they inquire as to how monoculture, the practice of growing genetically similar crops over large areas, may induce insect pests to proliferate. Nor is there any interest in exploring how irrigation, distancing, and plant archi-tecture may actually encourage the multiplication of insect pests.

Instead, scientists prefer to slice up reality and 'reduce' their 'scientific' questions to simply asking how to kill insects. No one asks how insect pests arise in the first place, or how insecticides impact on other forms of life in addition to the insects. Such a procedure unerringly produces side effects, which apologists for insecticides say are 'unintended', even though scientific reductionism and the 'technological fix' orientation virtually guarantee that side effects will occur.

The brown planthopper in rice is a prominent example of a devastating insect pest created in this way. Until recently, the International Rice Research Institute (IRRI), and scientists at the University of the Philippines at Los Banos (UPLB) recommended saturation spraying with insecticides to control the stemborer. The insecticides partially killed off the stemborer, which today nevertheless remains a serious pest in rice. But the insecticide also wiped out most of the beneficial organisms in this farming area which had helped to control the population of the brown planthopper. The planthopper has since rapidly increased its population and become one of of the most serious pests associated with rice production. In the years since insecticides enabled it to become a major pest, the brown planthopper has eaten its way through hundreds of thousands of hectares of rice fields. Its attacks have resulted in the loss of millions of metric tons of rice, worth hundreds of millions of dollars.

Alternatives to reductionist and materialist science

It is abundantly clear that science is a major dimension of sustainability. But what type of science? The easiest alternative to reductionist science is to integrate the fragments that have fallen apart during the period of analysis or reduction. In the case of plant resistance, for example, instead of relying solely on gene transfers to confer resistance on pests, scientists could look at how the genetic endowment of crops *together with* cultural practices, environmental conditions, level of soil fertility and other factors all contribute to the final pest resistance capacity in plants.

Similarly, integration can also occur across disciplines. In the regulation of biotechnology, the government can require applicants to pass through several screens: a science screen, an ecological screen, an alternatives screen, a social screen, an ethical screen, an economic screen and an effectivity screen. The science screen will look at the validity of the scientific assumptions of the proposed biotechnological application. The ecological screen will require an assessment of the environmental and ecological impact of the product. The alternatives screen will ensure that society will not be exposed unnecessarily to products if much safer and proven alternatives already exist. For example, bovine growth hormone (BgH) will fail this test because rotational grazing outperforms BgH as a way of increasing milk production economically. The social screen will require proponents to project the social impact of their product. Similarly the ethical, economic and effectivity screens will make their contributions.

At this stage the integration can be termed 'horizontal'. All reality, biophysical or social, is still presumed to be physical and material. Science is not able to rise above its materialist episteme. Thus horizontal integration or 'holism' in science can only reach a certain point. Integrative or holistic science on the horizontal level still cannot fully grasp reality even if a systems perspective is employed. If from the beginning non-physical realities are excluded by definition, how can one integrate the banished element when it is dogmatically assumed not to be there?

A simple 'thought-experiment', as Einstein would put it, shows this inability quite directly. Take a man-made object, say a chair, and try to think about its function or concept. Without difficulty one arrives at the concept of the chair: to give support for sitting. For the next part of the experiment, take an object from nature: a stone, a leaf or a fruit will do. Then try to think about the concept or function of the stone. One notices that without adequate training one's thinking cannot penetrate into the concept or idea (a larger integration of concepts) of the natural object.

If one cannot know the ideas of nature, how can one know that after fragmenting nature, as is normally done with present-day scientific approaches, one has put nature together again in the proper way? How does one know that an authentic whole has been cognized? How does one avoid constructing an artificial whole?

Who truly knows the idea of nature? The beginning of an answer has emerged in our age. But to appreciate it, we need to take a look at a second level of integration, the 'vertical'. The materialist world view, which limits the success of horizontal integrative or holistic science, can be termed the First Scientific Revolution. This is a scientific heritage which goes back 400 years to the birth of modern science. Today the scientific community itself is recognizing that the inorganic fragmented approach to nature is one-sided and inadequate for the study of living phenomena.[1] Scientists are also abandoning the illusion that the human spirit can be captured quantitatively in a chemical retort.[2]

A Second Scientific Revolution has emerged:

• Quantum physicists have now produced experimental evidence that reality is non-local. Substances and processes of the universe are intimately connected with each other even though they are physically tens of millions of miles apart from each other.[3]

• Biologists have evidence that non-physical, 'morphogenetic fields', not DNA, govern the emergence of form in living organisms. The past forms of organisms transmit their influences to other organisms in the present and the future by means which transcend normal space–time conditions.[4]

This Second Scientific Revolution rescues qualities that have been methodologically stigmatized as subjective and unreal by the First Scientific Revolution. It is now scientifically respectable to consider life, conscious-ness, and spirit as causative agents in their own right and different from material processes, although these qualities interact with matter. The Second Scientific Revolution sees nature as alive and ensouled. It also recognizes mind and spirit as operative in the universe.[5] The Second Scientific Revolution thus provides the vertical dimension necessary for a deeper, more comprehensive and truer integration of science, previously fragmented and reduced by a dogmatic materialist frame of mind. As more research is undertaken on the new science, farmers can truly move in the direction of working in partnership with nature.

However, vertical holism is not enough. The vertical holistic scientist still remains on the same level of consciousness that created materialistic science. The difference is that the new scientists are truer to the ideals of science. The true scientist does not predefine his reality. He is continually open to new possibilities even if this would shatter old assumptions, including possibly long years of indoctrination in the practice of materialistic science. Because of this open attitude, the 'vertical' scientists obtain new intuitions and insights about nature, human beings and societies.

The new science merely points to the existence of supersensible forces, processes and realities. It does not yet experience these supersensible, non-material realities directly. Hence, while the new science points the way to the answer, it is still unable to solve the problem: who can truly know the ideas of nature?

A very important element is not observed in the normal practice of science, whether of the materialist, horizontal, or vertical variety. Scientists in all three traditions do not observe or notice their own cognitive activity while doing science. What happens if scientists take notice and strengthen the cognitive faculties of the human being? They will discover that their thinking activity becomes an organ for 'seeing' the ideas of nature.

Rudolf Steiner, founder of a new science of the spirit, posits that human consciousness can be strengthened to achieve a true spiritual knowledge of nature with the same clarity of understanding that one achieves with mathematics. He briefly describes what the experience would be like.

> In that case, we would not just see a re-created version of the outer world or an abstract mathematical picture, but we would have something formed in an entirely different manner. We would have gained something with the full character of reality, but obtained similarly to the way we obtain mathematical pictures. We would then have before us spiritually a reality that shines out toward us in the same way that the outer sense-perceptible world streams towards us. . . . [T]hrough strengthening our mathematical capacity, we would attain an inner experience, like the mathematical experience but with the character of spiritual reality.[6]

Anthroposophy constitutes a Third Scientific Revolution.[7] The Second Scientific Revolution points to the existence of spirit and spiritual processes, even if in a sometimes vague or inadequate manner. Anthroposophy actually investigates the laws and processes of non-material and spiritual forces through the disciplined schooling of the superconscious cognitive faculties slumbering in every human being. Anthroposophy can thus be called 'radical holism' because no facet of reality remains outside its reach. The mighty ideas of nature are transparent before it. In addition, its radical holism can embrace materialism as well as horizontal and vertical holism in their true meaning and elevate them to the fullness of reality.

Anthroposophy is not a theoretical fantasy land. Its practicality lies in the fact that it is able to penetrate fully the idea of nature, human beings and society. This practicality is clearly visible in the tremendous help anthroposophy has provided worldwide, as expressed in the renewal of agriculture, education, organizational development, medicine, architecture, art, mathematics, banking, the rehabilitation of drug victims and a range of other disciplines including science itself.

2 'Supportive of the Development of Human Potentials'

The discussion on holistic science already points to the next dimension of sustainability: human development, that other threshold that was not crossed at UNCED. For who does the science? Human beings, of course. But what if our leading scientists are only able to come up to a certain level of understanding? Worse, what if our leading scientists fall prey to the allure of profit? Then our scientists help trigger a chain of events, with many sectors of society participating, that we ultimately label as environmental and social problems.

Thus, to be sustainable, especially socially, agriculture must conform to the realities of human nature. Science must not debase human nature. Human beings must not be reduced to mere quantities that can figure in the statistical calculations of scientists and policy makers. Otherwise social chaos will ensue.

The three-fold nature of the human being

It is obvious and self-evident that the human being has a physical body. This is so dominant a reality that modern science has become fixated with it. The presence of the physical body is so overwhelming in the West that scientists have all but forgotten about an element of human nature that is able to interiorize what is external to it. Behavioural psychology, for example, is actually a science that systematically excludes its subject matter, the psyche. Everything is reduced to external stimulus and response. Yet our inner experience tells us we have a psyche or, in older language, a soul. Our psyche or soul is the arena of subjective feelings and thoughts. It is the location of often impulsive associational thoughts and feelings.

We also recognize the existence of the spirit, without which we would be continually caught up in the unpredictable inner dynamics of the soul, losing our ability to cognize and know the world intentionally and consciously. We could not even formulate a theory or hypothesis. We would not be able to learn anything new. Our reality would always be finished, littered with past thoughts and feelings which have their own inner logic.

Active thinking is the bridge between spirit and soul, without which we would never be able to practise mathematics. We easily recall from our school experience that to solve a mathematical problem one cannot be distracted by associational thoughts and feelings. Even when we have experienced a death in the family and our souls are heavily burdened, we have a force in us that temporarily suspends the mourning so that we may solve the mathematical problem. At that instant when this force is active, the presence of our witness or spirit and its active thinking is making itself tangible.

But active thinking can be imprisoned by the energies of associational feeling and thought. This can be experienced directly when we have a feeling or thought fixation and cannot free ourselves from it. The different types of fixations – technological, social, economic and the rest – all have their roots in the fettered area of the soul, in the arena of past, finished thoughts and feelings. And these fixations, we have seen, impose a one-sided picture of the world and create a distorted reality.

Scientists: to break free from compelling paradigms

To engage in the various types of holistic science, scientists need to reassess their qualifications. Most universities and research institutions do not bother to examine that most important scientific tool: human consciousness. They invest in very sophisticated instrumentation and equipment which merely extends, albeit erratically, the perceptual reach of the human mind. But these machines can never replace the cognitive activity which finds meaning in the thousands of isolated facts and data, and which directs the direction and process of experimentation itself.

To develop their full scientific potential, scientists initially need to recognize and take hold of the biases and blinkers that make up their paradigms. For a start, they should recognize that they have access to at least two types of thinking: one that fragments and the other which integrates. They should recognize that their scientific training imparted to them certain biases and predispositions in the way they view and work with the world: that is, that they have been educated to fragment and reduce the world. And should these fixed ideas be compelling, they should find the strength within to rise up to the real ideals of the scientific method: to find truth no matter what the personal cost may be. When they are able to do this, they may start the process of scientific empowerment by, as a first step, integrating horizontally the different facts and discoveries in their own and related fields.

NGO activists: to transcend ideologies

If there is something vaguely familiar for NGOs in the discussion concerning human development in the scientific community, there is a reason. What paradigm is for the scientist, ideology is for the NGO worker. Both need to transcend fixed ideas which are incapable of addressing and working with new realities. This constitutes the immediate human development task for the NGO activist.

Most people who work with NGOs have a socialist temperament. That is, they reach out and care for others. They want to help out. They want to improve the well-being of the impoverished and get rid of oppressing conditions. This compassion is what lives in their inner world. Now it so happens that they encountered world views and ideologies which, given their temperament, were a handle on the social world, serving to clarify certain patterns in society which reproduced the inequality and destruction they so much wanted to stop.

Now many of these social paradigms or ideologies were conceived at the height of the materialism of the nineteenth century. Like all thought structures that are frozen and contracted when they come into contact with materialism, these ideologies imported the concept of natural law into their systems of thought. And this is where the problem began. With the collapse of theoretical materialism in our time, ideologies are now vulnerable to many radical revisions.

Another important thing to note is that the variant theories of human consciousness coming from many schools of thought converge in their assumption that once somebody belongs to a specific class or culture (corporate or bureaucratic, for example) that person will articulate the values of that class or culture. Now if all the contents of human consciousness were of an associational nature they would be right on target. In fact, in situations where human consciousness is *de facto* associational people do not transcend their class or cultural consciousness. In this situation these ideologies would hold true. However not all of human consciousness is determined by associational thoughts and feelings There is a presence in the depths of human consciousness that enables individuals to break free, at any time and at any place, from all past thoughts, and from all determined contents of consciousness, including class consciousness, that have been instilled into them since birth.

This reality gives advocacy work in sustainable agriculture a certain complexity. Many ideologies contain a 'them versus us' analysis How do we now respond if some of 'them' start thinking in a way that brings 'them' closer to 'us'? NGO activists can recall vivid instances in the past when they were able to break free from the expectations of their friends, the wishes of their parents, and other external sources of intention to pursue their own goals and objectives. The very phenomenon of the emergence of the NGOs attests to the reality that many of us have transcended our own social conditioning.

Now, if this can happen to NGO activists, why should it not happen again to them now that new realities are telling them that they most probably need to outgrow the constraints of their ideologies? If NGOs can do this, why cannot this liberation happen to other individuals who are embedded in government bureaucracies, corporations, scientific centres and other institutions viewed by NGOs as inimical to their interests? Is freedom from the strictures of past consciousness, ideologies and paradigms a special province reserved only for NGOs?

There is an interesting global phenomenon which lends support to what we have been discussing and which is occurring among the ranks of those who are often perceived by NGOs as their enemies. This phenomenon is feared most by tyrants in institutions because there is no permanent response to it and not even violence will stop it. It will keep on surfacing in one form or another. The phenomenon is a symptom of what we have been discussing: it is aptly called 'whistleblowing', and the individual who does it is a 'whistleblower'. Individuals expose the shortcomings and sometimes the machinations of institutions they have worked with for a long time. They behave in a manner analogous to the referee who blows his whistle if a player is violating the rules. Whistleblowers make their protest in many forms. Some are dramatic and effective, as in some known examples where senior officials, after working with a business or government institution for a long time, resign in front of national TV, attacking the hypocrisy of the dominant power within the institution. Others are very quiet, releasing damaging information to the press.

If one takes seriously the freedom of human consciousness, this will influence more than the way in which we deal with our ideologies. The reality and unpredictability of human freedom also raises profound questions regarding the strategies or methods that NGOs use to obtain social change. NGOs know that many changes need to happen with regard to government policies, business practices, and scientific research to make all these supportive of sustainable agriculture. But is this to be achieved through confrontation or through critical dialogue? The answer to this question constitutes another area of human development particularly relevant for NGO activists.

What do we do with the whistleblowers? Do we ignore them, even though they have goals and aspirations very close to ours? Or do we empower them so that they receive reinforcement in what they are doing and are given a stronger hand against their superiors inside the institution? By entering into a dialogue, we can actually increase the propensity for whistleblowing within the target social structure or institution. Paradoxically, by apparently decreasing the outward contradiction between us and them through dialogue, we actually increase the internal contradiction within the social structure. This internal contradiction will be more difficult for the social structure to deal with, just as its more difficult for us to deal with our own contradictions.

Critical dialogue is not just a nice idea. It works in practice and its impact has proved to be powerful. In the Philippines, the Sustainable Agricultural Coalition (SAC) and the Center for Alternative Development Initiatives (CADI) have managed to turn around the pesticide establishment. SAC and CADI systematically identified the whistleblowers working inside various institutions that had a role to play in the fate of pesticides in Philippine agriculture. These institutions included the Fertilizer and Pesticide Authority (FPA), the pesticide regulatory agency, the Department of Agriculture, the national and international agricultural science communities, the media and even the United Nations agencies connected with food and agriculture. In the past, and even today, all these institutions have been responsible for the promotion of pesticides in agriculture. SAC and CADI worked with the various whistleblowers with the aim of ending the use of the more hazardous pesticides in Philippine agriculture. The strategy of critical dialogue worked. SAC and CADI convinced the FPA that it should ban four widely used pesticides, a ban which affected 60 per cent of the pesticide market in the Philippines.

NGO activists can thus hasten the emergence of new policies and infrastructures supportive of sustainable agriculture in two ways. First they engage in an inner struggle to free themselves from limiting ideologies. Part of this liberation from ideological clutter consists of recognizing that other people, in hostile camps, can also free themselves from ideological blinkers. This opens the possibility of a critical dialogue that can result in important support for sustainable agriculture.

People's empowerment, a new meaning

To truly empower farmers and, hence, advance their human development means to empower them from within. We do not mean by this statement to belittle the important efforts that are being made to empower farmers by giving them access to resources (land, credit, and so on) and technologies, and by allowing them to participate in the political processes which determine their fate. Empowering from within means complementing the more external forms of empowerment by awakening the spiritual faculties that slumber within the farmer. This can be achieved in part by evocative forms of training. Trainers often transfer knowledge and information as if one were putting water into an empty cup. Instead, the trainer can draw out the wisdom that is within the vast range of agricultural experience that the farmer has by asking questions and truly being open to what the farmer has to say. By asking questions the trainer encourages active thinking to awaken within the inner life of farmers.

Active thinking is especially essential in ecological agriculture. No two agricultural sites are the same. One can never totally transfer proven eco-farming techniques from one site to another site. Ecological agriculture is site-specific. The more vulnerable a crop, such as vegetables, the more one has to arrive at an understanding of the underlying principles so that one can create new approaches. This is impossible if active thinking is not the characteristic mode of consciousness in the farmer.

Consumers and proper nutrition

Human development is, of course, not just concerned with the non-physical dimension of the human being. It is also important that our bodies receive proper nutrition, and it is in this context that the efforts of influential institutions like the Asian Development Bank (ADB) and the Food and Agricultural Organization (FAO) of the United Nations need to be critiqued.

Food policy specialists and agricultural scientists generally give priority to calory sufficiency, which they consider to be a more basic food require-ment than protein sufficiency.[8] However, the model does not consider 'regulating' foods, including vitamins and minerals. Regulating foods do not, like calories, need to be present in large quantities. Nevertheless they play a very important role in the physiology and health of human beings. The neglect of regulating foods in so-called 'sustainable carrying capacity' policy studies can lead to serious national health problems. Illusory sustainable population figures will be generated but may not actually be supported. Meanwhile, national productivity will be impaired because of increasing health problems among a large segment of the country's population.

3 'Culturally Sensitive'

When the green revolution, conceived in the North, was implemented in the South, it displaced existing indigenous systems of agriculture and food consumption and nutrition patterns. Technological displacement ulti-mately resulted in cultural displacement. Indigenous cultural communities and peasants felt out of place and were actually displaced by the advancing mechanization and chemicalization of agriculture. They lost their spiritual centre, because reductionist science belittled their knowledge as 'primitive', a creation of 'illiterates' and therefore valueless.

This spiritual displacement ultimately resulted in massive dehumaniza-tion and alienation as peasants and indigenous peoples passively awaited the next wave of reductionist technological innovations that further marginalized their knowledge and their culture. Agriculture is clearly unsustainable under such a set of circumstances. For agriculture to be sustainable, it must be more sensitive to the culture and knowledge of the people it is supposed to serve. Cultural sensitivity primarily concerns itself with the incorporation of the set of values and knowledge specific to a culture.

Indigenous knowledge systems

Tribal communities are the cultural bearers of what increasingly have come to be known and respected in the academic and development communities as Indigenous Knowledge Systems (IKS).[9] The tremendous scope of their tacit science and knowledge can be seen from the following examples.

The IRRI is hard pressed to create a cropping system where five economic species are growing at the same time. The Hanunoos of Mindoro, however, are acquainted with 430 crops and think nothing of multiple cropping as many as 40 species at the same time throughout the year.[10] Their multi-storeyed cropping system is so finely attuned to ecological factors that some consider these complex farming systems one of the modern wonders of the world. They can achieve, at minimal cost, yields that are far ahead of intensive rice farming. The geographer Clawson did a study of multi-storeyed cropping systems in Quezon City, Philippines. He discovered that the peasant farmer harvested an equivalent of more than 49 tons of edible biomass per hectare.[11] This is far superior to the 18–20 tons of irrigated rice yields per hectare, assuming three crops of rice per year at top yields. Equally significant, the polyculture yield was achieved under rain-fed conditions!

Oral consciousness

The consciousness which produced indigenous knowledge and culture is quite different from the consciousness that produced the green revolution. During the latter part of this century, cultural and descriptive linguistics, allied with new directions in literary studies, presented very strong research results pointing to the existence of an 'oral' mentality. Orality, or verbal expression, is used to distinguish it from literacy, a consciousness expressing itself in the written word. The green revolution is the product of a literate consciousness.

This epoch-making discovery is currently altering the way scientists and development agencies are dealing with oral cultures. Oral consciousness has the following properties, among many others:

Concrete thinking. Oral consciousness does not think in abstractions. The concept 'tree' is an abstraction of concrete mangoes, avocados, citrus and so on. Oral language often does not have abstract categories, so common in literate language. Thus geometric figures are understood only in terms of the concrete. A 'circle' can be a plate or a pail. A striking example from ancient Greek literature is the word 'blameless'. In the oral consciousness of ancient Greeks, the word blameless meant 'beautiful-in-the-way-a-warrior-ready-to-fight-is-beautiful'.[12]

Tacit, holistic logic. Oral cultures have a tacit logic which does not operate according to the rules of formal logic inaugurated by Aristotle. This tacit logic also operates practically. It is always associated with the concrete. In one study, an 'illiterate' was asked: 'In the Far North, where there is snow, all bears are white. Novaya Zembia is in the Far North and there is always snow there. What colour are the bears?' The typical response was: 'I don't know. I've seen a black bear. I've never seen any others. Each locality has its own animals.'[13] Although this logic does not operate formally, it is nevertheless rational. In addition, it is able to integrate large amounts of experience into a living whole, giving oral cultures a very interesting form of indigenous science.

Minimal self-concept. Oral cultures have difficulty understanding or articulating the concept of self, so common in literate cultures as to be obsessive. Ong cites the studies of a Russian scientist, Luria, to give a graphic example of the nature of oral consciousness.

> A 38-year-old man, illiterate, from a mountain pasture camp was asked: 'What sort of person are you, what's your character like, what are your good qualities and shortcomings? How would you describe yourself?' 'I came here from Uch-Kurgan, I was very poor, and now I'm married and have children.' 'Are you satisfied with yourself or would you like to be different?' 'It would be good if I had a little more land and could sow some wheat.' *Externals command attention.* 'And what are your shortcomings?' 'This year I sowed one pound of wheat, and we're gradually fixing the shortcomings.' *More external situations.* 'Well, people are different – calm, hot-tempered or sometimes their memory is poor. What do you think of yourself?' 'We behave well – if we were bad people, no one would respect us.' *Self-evaluation modulated into group evaluation ('we') and then handled in terms of expected reactions from others.*[14] (Emphasis added. References in quoted text omitted.)

Intelligence as concrete ability. Given the propensity of oral consciousness for the concrete, it's hardly surprising that oral cultures have a very different understanding of intelligence. For them, intelligence is not what is revealed by written examinations. Intelligence has to be seen in operation. Intelligence has to be actual. For example, Puluwat Islanders in the South Pacific have very high regard for their navigators. The skills required to navigate the treacherous, high and sometimes violent seas are complex and demanding. These navigators are not called intelligent. But they are regarded as such because they are good navigators. 'Oral folk assess intelligence not as extrapolated from contrived textbook quizzes but as situated in operational contexts.'[15]

Homeostatic. Because oral consciousness always has reference to concrete situations in the present, the culture it creates is conservative of the present, of what works here and now. In other words, it is homeostatic, tending to preserve the status quo. This can be seen clearly in the usage of words. The meaning of words is connected directly to what exists out there at the present moment.

> The oral mind is uninterested in definitions. Words acquire their meanings only from their always insistent actual habitat, which is not, as in a dictionary, simply other words, but includes also gestures, vocal inflections, facial expression and the entire human existential setting in which the real, spoken word always occurs. Word meanings come continuously out of the present, though past meanings of course have shaped the present meaning in many and varied ways, no longer recognized.[16]

Pitfalls to avoid in training peasants and indigenous farmers. The most fundamental problem with conventional training approaches is the failure of trainers to understand and appreciate the oral consciousness of peasants and indigenous farmers. Hence training designs are often not appropriate to the training needs of the recipients. Abstract concepts are often not concretized through a continued linkage of the concepts with actual sense experience. The meaning of vitamin C, for example, can be discussed in terms of actual demonstrable manifestations of vitamin C deficiency.

Failure to understand the workings of oral consciousness inevitably leads to failure to understand or appreciate indigenous knowledge. As a consequence, many training programmes are hardly linked, if at all, to the indigenous science of the trainees.

Training programmes also often suffer many of the deficiencies that accompany a mass training approach without due consideration for the quality and effectiveness of the training process. The duration of the training session is often too short for an effective understanding of the intricacies of ecological cropping systems and their management throughout the varied seasons of the year. As a result, the emphasis falls on those aspects of the technology which could be physically seen and copied. The hidden relationships that express themselves through time, sequences that require an abstract, cognitive act to be perceived inwardly[17] – changing, season-attuned cropping patterns, for example – are rarely implemented, if at all. Trainers often fail to monitor adequately the progress of their trainees after the course. Thus, trainers are not certain whether those they have trained are properly applying what they have learned.

Conventional training approaches are often not evocative, even during the practical sessions in the field. Often the pedagogy is not designed for innovation, nor for a critical understanding of the principles underlying sustainable agriculture. The result is that trainees have a difficult time implementing and adapting sustainable agriculture methods to the unique ecology and socio-economic constraints of their site. Trainers who do not have their own ecological farms find it particularly difficult to impart all the nuances of sustainable agriculture practices to their trainees. A non-evocative training methodology can also, without the knowledge of the trainers, foster a culture of dependence among the trainees. As soon as contact is lost, the trainees lose interest and can even become sceptical of sustainable agriculture practices.

Training appropriate to oral consciousness. The training process should be attuned to the oral consciousness of peasants and indigenous farmers. In practical terms, this means that the most suitable and effective training approach will be apprenticeships which are culturally appropriate. An apprenticeship approach can competently address the following requirements for an effective training:

- site-specificity;
- adequate duration;
- appropriateness to oral culture;
- linkage with indigenous practices;
- avoidance of the 'blind leading the blind' dilemma;
- quality;
- less travel time for technicians;
- ultimately independent use of technology; and
- cost-effectiveness.

An apprenticeship approach implies the existence of model sustainable farms strategically located throughout the target area. If none exist, these model farms should first be established to iron out the site-specific nuances of ecological methods. At least mistakes will not be at the expense of the peasant or indigenous farmer. The model sustainable farms could then serve as field classrooms for continuous instruction. Ultimately, cooperating farmers will become the 'masters' of their craft with their own sustainable 'field classroom' farms, and they will instruct their apprentices, mostly though example and practical intelligence.[18] In effect, a farmer-to-farmer training and extension service will be set up in the project area.[19]

The apprenticeship sessions can occupy one or a few hours a day, or several hours a week. The rest of the time the apprentice works on his own farm, immediately applying what he has learned. The apprenticeship should last a minimum of six months, preferably three months during the dry season and three months during the wet season. This will allow the seasonal variations to be factored in.

The above ideas need to be refined further by a process of consultation with residents in the project area. Specifically this means asking them how they actually transfer knowledge and skills from one generation to another.

Most likely it will be through learning by doing and, possibly, the incorporation of agricultural knowledge and practice through some form of social ritual.[20] In any event, the recommendations have to be attuned to the informal education protocols that are surely operative in their culture.

4 'Founded on the Use of Appropriate Technologies'

As we have seen, technology is not neutral, but embodies a world view and a set of values. The world view of reductionist science animates green revolution technologies, endorsing the belief that nature must be cut up in order to arrive at a true knowledge of natural phenomena. As we have seen, this is not the case, and such a misreading of nature results in detrimental side effects.

Among other values that green revolution technology promotes is *de facto* centralism, with the disempowerment and dismantling of rural communities. The way the technology was conceived assumed that peasants and indigenous farmers are illiterate, needing to learn from the dazzling wisdom packaged by PhDs based in some central experimental station. In this manner knowledge became centralized and homogenized, and this centralized power has since become a form of domination over farmers.

For what, in reality, does the pesticide industry's technology tell farmers in the countryside? It tells farmers that their existing indigenous knowledge is not enough to manage pests. The promoters of pesticides do not point out that green revolution technologies have induced, to a large extent, the problem pests in contemporary agriculture. Pesticide apologists also debunk the fact that local arthropod communities are most often adequate to take care of pest problems. Instead, farmers are made to rely on external inputs.

What does this do to the farmer? First, the farmers start believing that they, because illiterate, have nothing of value to contribute to agriculture. This is the start of disempowerment. When farmers stop believing in themselves, in their own capacities, this also marks the beginning of cultural collapse. Farmers start unconsciously boycotting indigenous modes of knowledge and technological adaptation. They start listening to the radio, to what the pesticide advertisers and their suppliant scientist supporters have to say. In time, key decisions about pest management are no longer made by farmers themselves. These decisions are now externally driven. This form of disempowerment stunts human development.

The founding motives of IRRI

The IRRI was established in 1980 with funding from the Rockefeller and Ford Foundations. The objective was to breed new rice varieties along the lines of successful work with wheat in Mexico. The whole justification for IRRI's existence was to increase the yields of rice so as to counteract the spectre of an ever-increasing number of hungry people. The technology that IRRI used to realize its objectives was basically a confluence of US, European, and Japanese experiences in the intensification of wet rice agriculture.

The agricultural revolution in the United States was machine-driven until 1930. The US had large tracts of land, and initially agricultural production was increased in an extensive manner. The agricultural revolution in Europe was driven by chemicals. Chemical fertilizers were used to increase agricultural production in an intensive manner. Japan had its own agricultural revolution that, in rice, was mainly concerned with the control of water. The Japanese developed intricate methods of irrigation and drainage that boosted crop yields.

In the 1930s, the US pioneered a new era in agriculture. It introduced hybrid corn. This new agricultural revolution combined the use of machinery, chemical fertilizers, irrigation and genetics to achieve astounding increases in corn yields. In the 1940s, chemical pesticides were introduced into this package of technologies. Thus the seed became the converging point and the integrater of all the important driving forces that had created earlier agricultural revolutions.

IRRI scientists knew this. The so-called high-yielding varieties (HYVs) were going to be their beachhead into the agricultural cultures of Asia. From the birth of IRRI, however, other than purely altruistic motives were at work. The people behind IRRI also conceived of rice cultivation as a means to alter the cooperative nature of agrarian societies towards market values. The green revolution was designed to modernize Asian societies so that they would become a market for goods from industrial countries, especially US farm tools, fertilizers, pesticides, irrigation systems and other agricultural equipment.[21] 'Arthur Moses, President of the Agricultural Development Council founded by John D. Rockefeller III, argued early in the green revolution that the cooperative social structure evident in many agrarian communities needed to be dismantled in order to encourage "aggressive interest in the marketplace".'[22]

Participatory technology development

There is an effective way to prevent alien values from entering surreptitiously into a culture or society: by engaging the farmer, from the very beginning, in the evolution of new technologies.

The following steps are meant to be illustrative rather than definitive, and apply to the local setting.

1 Involve peasants and farmers in a process of participatory technology development, drawing on their oral consciousness. Among the fundamental issues to explore in this cooperative process are the following:

- How do farmers understand what literate consciousness refers to as 'problems of chemical farming'? Is there common ground between the two sets of experiences? If so, how are 'problems of chemical farming' or their present farming understood in terms of oral consciousness? This is a real issue. In our experience different farmers have different understandings of the cluster of concepts surrounding the idea of chemical farming.
- For farmers, what technology results in 'problems of chemical farming'? Care should be exercised in assuming that words used by literate NGOs or other promoters convey the same meaning in the culture. In Ifugao, for example, when asked to give an example of a 'vegetable', one mother replied: 'Rice'!

  In this interchange, NGO and other workers should be open if the farmers refer to other factors, unknown to their interviewers, as constituting part of the 'problems of chemical agriculture'. This information will be vital in designing the determinants of sustainable agriculture appropriate in the specific cultural context.
- For farmers, what are some methods of farming which can 'cure' chemical farming? How do farmers view their current practices in terms of their potential to provide alternatives to chemical farming?

2 With the aid of the farmers themselves, proponents can start redesigning the farming system to be more appropriate to the socio-economic conditions of the villagers. Proponents, together with the villagers , could also inventory existing domesticated and wild plant species with potential for green manuring practices. This would be obligatory if the participatory technology development process identified a form of green manuring as one of the traditional practices being applied.

3 Proponents may wish to supplement the above participatory technology development process by exploring, together with farmers, the best existing cropping patterns and practices in their site, and other ecologically similar food-growing areas, as indicators of what can be done.

4 If uncertainties and questions remain, and most likely they will, then proponents can co-design and conduct studies comparing preferred practices with proposed innovations. Farmer-conducted experiments are ideal because these will enhance research 'capacity building' within farmers. Proponents must also be open to existing indigenous research protocols, if any.

5 Proponents may establish a research station if it is clear that farmers can only do so much experimentation on their fields, but are wanting to learn about other technological possibilities than can improve their livelihoods. Its design should conform to what ultimately come out as the preferred technological options of the farmers themselves.

It is expected that these procedures will result in a technology truly appropriate to the farmers. Participatory technology development will also mean faster adaptation by farmers, who would have been involved in all the key decisions from the very beginning. Participatory technology development approaches will also have a favourable impact on training, since trainer and trainee will be speaking the same language, and drawing examples from the same cultural and ecological context.

Hence, one speaks of participatory technology development. Farmers have their own set of experiences, many of which have been found to be valid. Modern developments in ecological agriculture and peasant practices can be combined fruitfully for greater yields and sustainability. Participatory technology development also results in empowerment and is thus intimately concerned with the development of human potential. Project initiators who engage farmers in a process of constructive dialogue and participatory analysis support the gradual unfolding of self-reliant individuals, an important step in human development.

Balancing indigenous knowledge and holistic science

During the process of participatory technology development, it is possible that the proponents' concept of appropriateness may clash with the farmers' concept. This is a very delicate situation and requires great presence of mind. In general, if the difference lies in the cultural dimension of the technology, hardly anything can be done. For example, supporters of non-cruelty to animals (or humane agriculture), a part of the sustainable agriculture movement, will be horrified to see the way some indigenous farmers beat up chickens during rituals connected with farming. This is a cultural difference which can be reconciled with difficulty, if at all. Personal decisions will have to be made.

However, if the difference lies in the ecological basis of certain farming practices, there is the possibility of dialogue. The case of botanical pesticides is a good example. Some farmers use botanical pesticides to kill off pests. As we shall see below, there are scientific findings and experiences which indicate that these practices may not be sustainable. So how should the differing judgements be processed?

In the world of the 'concrete' (oral consciousness), often the best way is to agree to try out together the two different approaches to pest management. One will be based on the use of botanical pesticides. The other will be based on community ecology, where reliance is placed on internal biological processes, through beneficial organisms, and increasing plant vitality, through appropriate soil fertility measures. After the results are obtained, concrete comparisons can be made. Sometimes, the results are so obviously in favour of community ecology that the farmer concedes, even before the experiment is over. However, proponents of holistic science should be open to the reality that there can be botanical pesticides that are pest-specific *and* interfere only slightly with the food chain, allowing beneficial organisms to continue their existence.

Central research stations and appropriate technology

Given all the nuances and intricacies involved in participatory technology development, the temptation is great for central research stations to develop technology without meaningful input from farmers. At most, they ask a few token farmers to share their knowledge. But if they do not believe what they hear, they will simply ignore it. At worst, they pretend that they have incorporated farmers' perspectives into research, while generating technologies that are meaningful only to the input industries and already affluent farmers.

There are several barriers that have to be overcome if these central experiment stations are to be sources of appropriate technology for sustainable agriculture.

1 They should genuinely believe in the concept of people's empowerment and participation as discussed in this chapter.

2 This means that they have to respect indigenous knowledge and people's viewpoints in their research activities. They should be willing to learn from farmers, incorporating what they learn in their research protocols.

3 They should restructure their research procedure and the decision-making protocols so that farmers will truly be able to participate at every stage of the research process.

4 They should support the establishment of truly autonomous decentralized research efforts starting with farmers themselves. A significant proportion of funds should be redirected to support this people-based, decentralized research network.

5 Research should be geared towards solving scientific problems that cannot be addressed at the level of the farmers' fields.

5 'Ecologically Sound'

Although 'ecological soundness' is one of the more universally accepted dimensions of sustainable agriculture, actual implementation of the idea is fraught with wrong turns and pitfalls. Even those sympathetic to holistic science end up, in practice, with reductionist technologies.

Botanical pesticides versus community ecology

In this area of sustainable agriculture, NGOs are as guilty of the technological fix mentality as the pesticide industry people. In their sustainable agriculture projects, NGOs often rely heavily on the use of botanical pesticides as substitutes for chemical pesticides. However, botanical pesticides can suffer a number of ecological drawbacks very similar to the impact of toxic pesticides. First, insects can develop resistance to botanical insecticides in a manner similar to their response to chemical pesticides. Second, botanical pesticides can harm beneficial insects and spiders which abound in farmers' fields, leading to pest resurgence and the creation of new pests.

The real alternative to chemical pesticides is ecological pest management, specifically community ecology. This new approach examines all the components of the agro-ecosystem and assesses their impact on pest populations. An integral part of this new approach is to make sure that plants are properly fed and so do not easily succumb to disease or insect attack. This approach relies heavily on encouraging the proliferation on the farm of beneficial organisms, which almost always keep pest populations under control.

Whose Integrated Pest Management (IPM)?

With the increasing call for sustainable agriculture and the increased prohibition of pesticides all over the world, the pesticide industry is suddenly interested in IPM and hence, they claim, sustainable agriculture. A good example was the attempt by Hoechst to convince the public that their product can be used in IPM. This is a story worth telling because purveyors of pesticides will be forced to resort to similar tactics now that the world has awakened to the danger.

In January 1992, Hoechst tried to convince government regulatory officials in the Philippines that their product was safe enough to be used in IPM. They showed slides, figures and tables indicating that certain beneficial insects in coffee and cotton were not being harmed by endosulfan. Unfortunately, during the question and answer session, Hoechst's concept of IPM proved highly impractical and questionable in its fundamental design and actual operation in farmers' fields.

For a start, Hoechst was not even aware that pesticides can alter plant physiology in such a manner as to make plants more attractive to pests.[23] They had not studied whether endosulfan has this negative physiological impact or not. Unfortunately, there is a good possibility that endosulfan may actually increase the pest burden of plants. After the hearing, Dr Kern explained to CADI that endosulfan interferes with the protein metabolism of insects, especially their capacity to combine amino acids into protein. Interference with protein synthesis is exactly how pesticides can make plants more attractive to pests, according to a prominent theory.[24]

CADI also noted several inconsistencies in the Hoechst presentation. Why were mass releases of beneficial insects still necessary? If endosulfan does not harm a certain species of beneficial insect used to control coffee borer, why then does Hoechst need to engage in mass rearing of the insects and continue to release them in the field? There is an additional problem. Let us grant that endosulfan does not harm that beneficial species which they are releasing into the field. Why then are the beneficial insects not able to survive in the field? Are they starving because endosulfan has killed the pests which serve as food for the beneficial insect? (This concern is especially critical in this case, because the beneficial insect is a wasp. Wasps, being parasites, are more specialized in their feeding habits than predators, including spiders.[25] They are more vulnerable to loss of their regular insect diet.) Or are the beneficial insects being counter-controlled by hyper-parasites? In either case, the Hoechst IPM approach would be a failure. As it turned out, upon probing by CADI, Hoechst admitted that it was not sure whether the beneficial insects were controlling the harmful pests or not! At most, their combined biological and chemical control approach was achieving only a 30 per cent success rate in small-scale trials: not enough, by their own standards, to commercialize the technology.

There was an even deeper problem with Hoechst's IPM approach. Hoechst had designed its IPM strategy so that endosulfan had to be there to take on the role of the predators that endosulfan had eradicated from the agroecosystem! Of course, Hoechst did not state it so bluntly, but this was how the strategy added up.

CADI questioned the relevance of Hoechst's IPM approach to rice farming, pointing to the complex web of predator/parasite/fungus–prey relationships that are known to exist in the rice agroecosystems of the Philippines and other Asian countries. No less than 1,000 beneficial species are known to exist in rice paddies throughout Asia. In the Philippines, more than 700 animal species per hectare are found in intensified rice production areas.[26] Granted that endosulfan does not harm a few beneficial insects in coffee and cotton, what about the hundreds of other beneficial insects found in rice ecosystems? Natural biological control of pests requires the simultaneous activity of the predator-parasite complex. Why should one beneficial insect be preferred over another?

CADI's concerns about the importance of maintaining a complex of beneficial insects, not just favouring one or two, were shared by Dr Jose Medina and the late Dr Edwin Medina of the University of the Philippines at Los Banos. Dr Medina requested Hoechst to do more studies on the impact of endosulfan on other beneficial insects. Hoechst should conduct detailed studies on other crops, especially rice, and not just focus on a few biological control agents of coffee, cotton, and beans.

If Hoechst conducts such a study, they will probably encounter some important information contained in IRRI's 1980 Annual Report. IRRI scientists conducted relative studies of the toxic effect of some insecticides on brown planthopper, green leafhopper, and whitebacked planthopper. Endosulfan was one of the insecticides investigated. IRRI's data showed that endosulfan is more toxic to wolf spiders (*Lycosa pseudoannulata*) than to brown planthoppers and green leafhoppers. The study also showed that endosulfan was of similar toxicity to the wolf spider as chlorpyrifos, an insecticide banned on rice plantations in Indonesia.

This study supports the concern of CADI and Dr Magallona to determine the toxicity of endosulfan to beneficial insects. They urge that Hoechst should not use limited results obtained in a totally different ecosystem and cross-apply these to rice. Dr Magallona offered an observation which captures the central weakness of Hoechst's IPM approach:

> This [referring to CADI's concern] is the problem with pesticide use. There are numerous indigenous beneficial insects in rice ecosystems. If the farmer has a window of opportunity to spray to avoid damage to some predators, the farmer may be killing other beneficial insects. Therefore, if Hoechst has already decided that its endosulfan must be part of its IPM programme, then Hoechst has to decide which population of beneficial insects to put at risk.

Hoechst said they would be open to supporting a better approach if it were available. But further questioning by CADI showed that they were not really sincere. CADI asked Hoechst: 'If you were given a pest management strategy that did not require the use of any pesticides, would you support it? We know of cases in Mindanao where hundreds of hectares of healthy coffee are being grown without using a single drop of pesticides. We also know of instances of commercial pesticide-free rice farming'. Hoechst did not answer CADI directly. Instead it showed through the overhead projector a 1934 article which stated that chemical control must accompany biological control! In effect, Hoechst said 'no' on the basis of studies done more than 50 years ago.

In effect, what Hoechst wants is to design an IPM system which will continuously require the intervention of endosulfan so that they can continue earning money from their product. Hoechst's concern for profits creates a paradigm which ignores widespread university and farmer-level data showing ample evidence that productive, pesticide-free agro-ecosystems are practical and economically viable. Ultimately, Hoechst is not really interested in a full-blown IPM programme, one that will really reduce the use of pesticides to the barest levels, if at all. By its own calculations, Hoechst spends only 2 per cent of its R & D (research and development) budget to explore a version of IPM that is scientifically dubious to start with. So it is very clear that the pesticide industry will attempt to use IPM as a trojan horse to make their questionable products more acceptable to farmers and the general public.

Green manuring versus soil fertility management

The use of legumes as green manures is another area where even supporters of sustainable agriculture easily slip back into a reductionist perspective. Green manures have their limits. It would be difficult to control the quality of humic substances through green manuring. However, in a compost pile, one can direct the process of decomposition and ensure the production of effective humic and other organic substances. This is one reason why green manuring needs to be complemented by composting.

Green manure does not necessarily improve the long-term structure of the soil, either. In aerated soil it may even hasten the decomposition of organic matter, resulting in poorer soil structure. In this way it can have the same detrimental impact as synthetic nitrogen fertilizers. Microbes break down organic matter in the soil if there is a flush of easily available nitrogen. Microbes need the extra nitrogen to break down the carbon tied up in the organic matter of the soil. Green manures, like synthetic nitrogen fertilizers, can release nitrates which hasten the breakdown of soil organic matter.

From a broader, more holistic perspective, the true objective of sustainable agriculture, as far as the soil is concerned, is to manage its fertility. Green manuring is not a substitute for, but only one facet of soil fertility management. The following are the minimum requirements of a fertile soil:

- adequate capacity to supply plant nutrients;
- sufficient air;
- enough water;
- proper acidity;
- enough warmth;
- quality organic matter;
- diverse and vital microbial population and activity.

Integrated nutrient management: what gets integrated?

Proponents of Integrated Nutrient Management (INM) propose an integrated mix of inorganic and organic fertilizers to 'sustain' crop yields. This strategy is just about as suspicious as the earlier example of the pesticide industry. One may recall that the pesticide people are proposing environmentally sound pesticides, or integrating the use of pesticides together with beneficial insects in an integrated pest management package.

Similar remarks can be made about INM to those already made with regard to green manuring. For ecological agriculture, the objective is to manage soil fertility, not just components of it. If humic acids are not understood or included, then it is not integrated enough. If the production of colloidal nitrogen, produced in high quality compost production, is not appreciated, then it is not integrated enough – and so on. The problem with the word integrated is that really important facets of soil fertility may be integrated in the mind of the listeners but may not actually be contained in the version of those who are promoting the package.

One also needs to look seriously at what the inorganic portion of INM does to the organic portion of INM. Ammonium sulphate nitrogen, for example, increases the acidity of the soil. The resulting dominance of hydrogen ions displaces micronutrients in the active cation exchange portions of the soil. Is this being taken into consideration?

Environmentally sound biotechnology?

To illustrate the scientific shortcomings and potential ecological hazards of biotechnology, let us briefly examine whether the use of tissue culture has a place in sustainable agriculture. Take the case of tissue culture of potatoes. Let us say an NGO wanted to set-up a village-level tissue culture capability among farmers. The NGO considers this to be an environmentally sound application of biotechnology. For, after all, what harm could result in mass-producing high yielding potato varieties?

Unfortunately, the use of tissue culture for the large-scale propagation of one or a few potato varieties will be tantamount to repeating the mistakes of the green revolution. But there is a difference. Tissue culture will repeat the mistakes of the green revolution at a much faster pace. Instead of cytoplasmically narrow HYV seeds, tissue culture will be producing cytoplasmically *narrower* crops. The planting materials will almost be uniform genetically. Tissue culture will not foster intra-species biodiversity. Monocultures are also more vulnerable to pest outbreaks.

There is also an inherent defect in the method of tissue culture. Evidence is showing that it increases the propensity of plants to be attacked by insects and diseases. The experience of Malaysia with oil palm shows that tissue-cultured crops are up to six times more prone to be attacked by insects and diseases. Tissue culture can thus induce farmers to spray toxic chemicals more often to protect their crop. The reliance on mass production almost by definition precludes an intercropping approach to crop production, without which the use of pesticides would be inevitable. And if the tissue-cultured potatoes are going to be raised using chemical fertilizers, then, as we have seen, insects and diseases may flourish. Again, this is an added pressure to spray toxic chemicals. Maybe there are cropping systems and ecological practices that can minimize the problems of tissue culture. But let it not be naïvely claimed that, by giving tissue culture to the people, one is practising sustainable agriculture.

6 'Socially Just and Equitable'

The connection of social equity to the other dimensions of sustainable agriculture

From a certain perspective, what we have discussed in the other dimensions of sustainable agriculture is all related to the question of social justice, of social equity, the sixth dimension of sustainable agriculture.

Ecological soundness avoids the need to poison 25 million farmers annually with pesticides, not to think of the widespread, devastating impacts on the environment and the health of consumers. It is terribly unjust for a few people to make profits out of the poverty and oppression of many. Participatory appropriate technology development ensures the justice that people are able to incorporate their values and knowledge in the technology that they use. Empowering a dispossessed sector of society also restores the equity required to sustain agriculture. Cultural sensitivity develops the case for respecting farmers' knowledge and values. It dismantles the inequitable domination of Western forms of knowledge over the lives of millions of people in the South. Holistic science unmasks the hidden, thus manipulative, agenda of reductionist science and technology. It destroys the political use of natural science so that scientists begin to take greater responsibility for their actions. This brings justice closer to the victims of science. Finally, there is human development: establishing the sacred nature of the human being provides solid ground for the cry of 'social justice and equity'. If human beings were merely higher animals, there would be no philosophical or scientific basis on which to be concerned about justice and equity.

Structuration and policy changes

What remains to be done in this section is to indicate the general directions of policy changes needed at the macro-level in order to provide a supportive context for sustainable agriculture.

The following changes need to occur to bring about greater social equity. The list is not all-encompassing. Rather, if these changes are brought about, they will make other subsequent changes much easier and faster.

1 A culture-specific agrarian reform programme.

2 Non-token participation of all affected parties in the policy areas affecting agriculture.

3 Reform of the national research network so as to make it more responsive, in ways articulated in this chapter, to the needs of sustainable agriculture. In this respect, better support for scientists so that they will not be prey to the designs of the pesticide industry.

4 Stricter implementation of environmental and pesticide regulatory laws.

5 A redirection of government support away from the production of export crops towards meeting basic food security needs.

6 Strengthening of people's initiatives in all areas of agriculture.

7 NGO and farmer participation in the regulation of pesticides.

8 Greater incentives for the production of organic fertilizers, on-farm or off-farm, the latter being a transitional stage.

9 Redirection of credit policies so that pesticides are decoupled from credit packages and credit support for sustainable agriculture is increased.

7 'Economically Viable'

Ecological soundness leads to economic viability

Acres USA, one of the leading proponents of eco-agriculture, said it best: 'To be economical, agriculture has to be ecological.' They said this a long time ago. Now the world of conventional economics, epitomized by the World Bank, is starting to understand what they are saying. Basically, economists are beginning to realize that the global agricultural system is only a subsystem of the larger global ecological system. Agricultural intensification is rapidly filling up the ecological and social space.

Take the following into consideration. The increase in human population is forcing nations to intensify agricultural production through the use of capital-intensive inputs, including pesticides and chemical fertilizers. Meanwhile, according to the World Health Organization, pesticides poison some 25 million people, mostly poor peasants in the Third World.[27] The goodwill, the social space, for pesticides is rapidly dwindling. Many want them banned. Farmers relying on pesticides are going to find themselves increasingly marginalized in the economic market. Their costs are going to increase because of regulation and other actions that will make it expensive to put pesticides on the market. Already in Europe there are a number of countries that are taxing pesticide use by a considerable percentage. Sweden has a tax of 50 per cent on pesticides used in agriculture.

Economic activity always depends on this silent, often mute support (often forced) from both the social space and the ecological space of the planet. Agricultural economists realize too late that nature is in reality natural capital or, in accounting terms, an asset. In their rush to intensify agriculture, farmers and scientists have been depleting their natural capital instead of living off the interest obtained from wise management of the land. Thus one of the major tasks for any group supportive of sustainable agriculture is to change the accounting method, at micro and macro levels, to reflect the harmful or helpful returns on agricultural technology. These returns should be measured in terms of the ecology of the farm and its region, as well as on a national basis. It is almost certain that, if all the costs of green revolution agriculture were internalized by the conventional farmer, he would soon be out of business.

From production to total productivity

Connected with this new perspective is the necessity of changing from a mere production orientation to one of total productivity. It is not enough to say that yields have been increased. It is also useful to ask: at what cost? Agricultural economists are gradually coming round to this conception. They are starting to talk in terms of productivity. By this they mean, for example, the amount of biomass produced per unit of water, or the amount of desired yield obtained per unit of scarce resource. Or it can be an economic measure of productivity. Thus agricultural economists speak of the amount of net income earned per unit man-hour. All these are partial productivity indices, however. What is important is to move towards more holistic productivity considerations and try to see if economic quantification can be attached to these new measures of productivity. For example, economic productivity may be good, but environmental productivity is being diminished. This is the case with green revolution technology.

Reconceptualizing the market

A perennial problem for both conventional and alternative agriculturalists is the market. Our experience in the field shows that there can be two responses to this. The first possibility is to respond in the conventional manner. And this, for a long time, may be the only way to respond. Try to change your cropping pattern to suit the economics of your market. This is too location-specific an issue to offer detail on here. The important idea is that, to achieve a better livelihood, we try to enter a speciality market including vegetables. But for those who are stuck with commodity products like rice, corn and so on, the only better economic possibility is to get a reasonable premium on the product.

Customers understand. Let us say a food product cost X units of currency. Now this product is laden with pesticides, as is bound to be the case in Asian countries where pesticide regulation is weak or functionally non-existent. And because they have no choice, consumers pay the price X. Now, if a better quality product – more nutritious and no pesticides – comes along, customers are easily convinced that they have to pay more for it. With consumer consciousness moving in this direction, a second, more radical possibility exists. Growers can establish direct relationships with consumers and bypass all the marketing channels in between. In the South this is especially ideal because middlemen really exploit farmers and consumers. In the Philippines, farmers often only get 10–15 per cent, or even less, of the final retail price of their vegetables.

Conclusion

The seven dimensional principles of sustainability outlined in this chapter have found wide support. When the Sustainable Agriculture Coalition (SAC) of the Philippines was formed in June 1990, it adopted explicitly the first five dimensions of sustainable agriculture. The first four dimensions were already articulated, even if with different emphasis, by the International Alliance for Sustainable Agriculture (IASA), of which the present writer was one of four co-founders.

The first five dimensions have received wide currency in the Philippines. They have also been adopted on various occasions in the Asian region by various sustainable agriculture groups and networks. At the international level, members of the SAC managed to gather support for the first five dimensions of sustainable agriculture from 4,000 NGOs attending the International NGO Forum. This forum sponsored a conference parallel to UNCED in June 1992 in Brazil. The first five dimensions of sustainable agri-culture now constitute part of the NGO Treaty on Sustainable Agriculture. The last two dimensions are included implicitly in the first five dimensions. In this chapter, however, I have drawn them out separately for reasons already explained.

The concept of sustainability is vast, with many nuances beyond the scope of this chapter. Here, I have focused on aspects of sustainability which are not clearly understood and not even recognized to be important, and on some which have received imbalanced treatment in the past. There is also a related rationale. Past discussions have discussed the different dimensions of sustainability within the same conceptual framework that caused the problem in the first place. One cannot create the proper policy framework if these contradictions are not recognized and highlighted.

Specifically, much attention has been focused on ecological soundness, economic viability and appropriate technology. Recently, the questions of social justice and agricultural sustainability have surfaced, even if they have been treated inadequately. But equally important and less visible aspects of sustainability are not even recognized and discussed. These new dimensions of sustainability include the concern for holistic science, the role of indigenous cultural formations, and human development.

In putting greater emphasis on the little understood dimensions of sustainability, I do not judge as unimportant the other, better-known dimensions, including ecological soundness, economic viability, appropriate technology and social justice. Rather, my intention has been to broaden and build upon these valid, critical and more widely articulated dimensions of sustainability in agriculture. This is the case even when I attack agricultural solutions which focus solely or dominantly on one dimension – be it ecological only, social only, economic only, and so on – to the neglect of other dimensions of sustainability.

In discussing the well-known sustainability dimensions, I have highlighted the more subtle issues involved. Take for example the case of IPM, included in the discussion of ecological soundness. Many NGOs are not aware that the very business concerns that have wreaked havoc on people's lives and the natural environment – the pesticide industry – are advocating 'environmentally friendly' pesticides and their own version of the IPM. Unless the contradictions of the pesticide industry's IPM concept are exposed, many NGOs, government agencies and concerned consumers will be confused. A final word: one cannot separate the interactive effects of one aspect of sustainability from the others. Thus, when I have spoken of seven dimensions of sustainability, I have been distinguishing, not dividing and fragmenting, a complex reality.

Notes

1 See for example, MacRae, R. J., S. B. Hill, J. Henning and G. R. Mehuys (1989), 'Agricultural Science and Sustainable Agriculture: A Review of Existing Scientific Barriers to Sustainable Food Production and Potential Solutions', *Biological Agriculture and Horticulture*, and Norgaard, R. B. (1987), 'The Epistemiological Basis of Agroecology', *Agroecology: The Scientific Basis of Alternative Agriculture*, Boulder, Co.: Westview Press, pp. 21–7.

2 Herbert, N. (1987), *Quantum Reality: Beyond the New Physics*, Garden City, New York: Anchor Books.

3 *Ibid.*

4 Sheldrake, R. (1988), *The Presence of the Past: Morphic Resonance and the Habits of Nature*, New York: Times Books.

5 There are numerous evidences of this. Neurophysiologists, for instance, have verified experimentally the existence of the soul in laboratory experiments. Even the simplest perceptual act, the sensation of colour, already indicates a soul activity, not merely the result of brain processes. Brain scientists have even pinpointed the specific location of the soul's volitional function in an important part of the brain. See Augros, R. M. and Stanciu, G. N. (1986), *The New Story of Science*, New York: Bantam Books, pp. 11–16.

6 Steiner, R. (1991), *Anthropology and Science*, Spring Valley, New York: Mercury Press, pp. 12–21.

7 Anthroposophy preceded the Second Scientific Revolution in terms of historical time. The germs of Anthroposophy were already established by Steiner as early as 1886 in a book, *Theory of Knowledge Implicit in Goethe's World Conception*. It is a 'Third Scientific Revolution' in the following sense. The First Scientific Revolution exclusively explored the material world. It powered industrialization but the spirit in nature and humanity was banished. The Second Scientific Revolution points to the existence of a spiritual world behind matter. Anthroposophy directly experiences the realm of spirit and scientifically explores its connection with matter.

8 Berg, A. (1985), 'The Many Facets of the Nutrition Problem', *Severe Malnutrition of Filipino Pre-School Children 2, Background and Other Selected Reading Materials on Malnutrition and Development* (eds Igliseias, G. U. *et al.*), Metro Manila, Policy Studies Program, College of Public Administration, University of the Philippines, pp. 14–20.

9 Brokensha, D. *et al.* (1990), *Indigenous Knowledge Systems and Development*, Lanham, Maryland: University Press of America.

10 Conklin, H. C. (1957), 'Hanunoo Agriculture: A Report on an Integral System of Shifting Cultivation in the Philippines', FAO Forestry Development Paper No. 12, Rome: FAO.

11 Clawson, D. L. (1985), 'Small-Scale Polyculture: An Alternative Development Model', *Philippine Geographical Journal*, 29 (3–4).

12 Ong, W. J. (1982), *Orality and Literacy: The Technologizing of the Word*, New York: Methuen, p. 49.

13 *Ibid.*, 52–3.

14 *Ibid.*, 54–5.

15 *Ibid.*, 55.

16 *Ibid.*, 47.

17 This capacity belongs to the 'literal' mind.

18 'Intelligence' here is used as it is understood by oral cultures.

19 This arrangement will simultaneously encourage institutionalization, greater participation, better relevance and more appropriate technologies.

20 Interview with Dr Matthew Davisson, USA, 1983. Dr Davisson cited examples

of how rituals in the Philippines encoded vast amounts of knowledge about their natural environment. This discovery also coincides with the findings of Walter Ong regarding the role of repetition through oral literature as one form of an external memory aid in oral cultures.

21 Booth, B., 'Germ Plasm: Slave Trade of the 20th Century? Who Owns the Seeds of the Earth?', *Biodynamics*, 181 (1992), p. 6.

22 *Ibid*. Booth cites the work of Perelman, Michael, *Farming for Profit in a Hungry World*, Landmark Series, 1977.

23 Hersog, D. D., and J. E. Funderburk (1986), 'Plant Resistance and Cultural Practice Interactions with Biological Control', *Biological Control in Agriculture IPM Systems*, pp. 67–88; Lutzenberger, J. S. (1984), 'How Agrochemicals Feed the Pests that Destroy the Crops', *The Ecologist* 14 (2), pp. 79–81; Couch, H. B. (1991), 'Increases in Incidence and Severity of Target Turfgrass Diseases by Certain Fungicides', *Plant Disease* 75 (10), pp. 1064–7; Carson, M. L. (1991), 'Predisposition of Soybean Seedlings to Fusarium Root Rot with Trifluralin', *Plant Disease* 75 (4), pp. 342–6; Jones, V. P. (1900), 'Does Pesticide-Induced Activity of Two-Spotted Spider Mite (Acari: Tetranuchidae) Really Contribute to Population Increases in Orchids?' *Journal of Economic Entomology* 83 (5): pp. 1847–52; Chaboussou, F. (1976), 'Cultural Factors and the Resistance of Citrus Plants to Scale Insects and Mites', *Fertilizer Use and Plant Health*, pp. 259–80; Kogan, M. (ed.) (1986), *Ecological Theory and Integrated Pest Management Practice*, New York: John Wiley Sons.

24 Chaboussou, F. (1985), 'How Pesticides Increase Pests', *The Ecologist* 16 (1), pp. 29–35.

25 IRRI, *Beneficial Insects in Rice*.

26 Kenmore, P. (1991), 'How Rice Farmers Clean Up the Environment, Conserve Biodiversity, Raise More Food, Make Higher Profits: Indonesia's IPM – A Model for Asia', FAO, p. 13.

27 Anonymous (1990). 'Acute Pesticide Poisoning: A Major Global Health Problem', *World Health Statistics Quarterly*, 43, cited in *Global Pesticide Campaigner* (June 1991), p. 9.

Beyond Reductionism

VANDANA SHIVA

Inevitably, the future will be an age of biology. But which and whose biology will shape the future for humans and other species on this planet?

The dominant paradigm of biology characterized by genetic engineering is being pushed to new levels of reductionism, threatening to eliminate diversity and pluralism, in knowledge and action, in nature and culture. At the same time, newly emerging approaches to biology focus on the complexity and self-organization of life forms, replacing predictability with unpredictability and certainty with uncertainity in the engineering of life. Thus the potential of biological sciences is to become more pluralistic, with reductionist biology challenged by post-reductionist paradigms.[1]

While mainstream feminist theorizing, mainstream environmentalism and some indigenous communities mimic the reductionism of dominant structures, new movements are also emerging that are ecological, feminist and culturally plural, and challenge biotechnology at the epistemological, ethical, ecological and economic levels. Unpredictable convergences and partnerships are unfolding in the science–politics terrain as the age of biology is shaped by the contest between various reductionist and post-reductionist approaches to who we are, how we relate to others of our own species and to other species, and how we perceive the world we live in as being transformed by the biotechnology revolution.

Beyond Reductionist Biology:
The Machine and the Organism, Engineering versus Growing

Genetic engineering is based on a machine view of organisms; reductionism is essential to this approach to living systems. By reductionism we mean the belief that the world is made up of atomized fragments, which associate mechanistically to make larger systems; the fragments determine the system. The individual properties of the constituents are the causes, and the properties of the whole are the effects. The internal relations are ignored in determining properties and processes.

In the mechanistic, reductionist model, the building blocks are atoms or substances or matter in the Cartesian sense of *res extensa*. They are the nuts and bolts that make a machine. But nuts and bolts cannot evolve, they can only be rearranged. In biology the mechanistic model has identified genes as the atoms that constitute living systems. In this billiard ball model, the genes are assumed to be particles located on chromosomes, the genes make proteins, proteins make us, and the genes replicate themselves. In 1926, H.J. Muller, a forerunner of molecular biology, wrote that the gene can be viewed as a biological atom, solely responsible for the physiological and morphological properties of life forms.[2]

At the species level, reductionism places value on only one species – humans – and generates an instrumental value for all other species. It therefore displaces and impels towards extinction all species without, or with low instrumental value to man. Monocultures of species and bio-diversity erosion are the inevitable consequences of biological reduction-ism, especially when applied to forestry, agriculture and fisheries. We call this first order reductionism.

Reductionist biology is increasingly characterized by a second order reductionism: genetic reductionism, that is, the reduction of all behaviour of biological organisms, including humans, to genes. Second order reduction-ism amplifies the ecological risks of first order reductionism, while intro-ducing new issues such as the patenting of life forms.

Reductionist biology is also a manifestation of cultural reductionism, in that it devalues all non-reductionist forms of knowledge and ethical systems related to living organisms. This includes all non-Western agricultural and medical systems as well as all disciplines in Western biology that do not lend themselves to genetic and molecular reductionism but are necessary for dealing sustainably with the living world.

As David Ehrenfeld has stated in 'Forgetting', 'We are on the verge of losing our ability to tell one plant or animal from another, and of forgetting how the known species interact among themselves and with their environment.'[3]

Reductionism was promoted strongly by August Weismann who, nearly a century ago, postulated total separation of the reproductive cells – the germ line – from the functional body, or soma. According to Weismann, reproductive cells are already set apart in the early embryo, and continue to the next generation. This supported the non-heritability of acquired traits with no direct feedback from environment to heredity. The largely non-existent 'Weismann barrier' is still the paradigm used to discuss biodiversity conservation as 'germ plasm' conservation. The germ plasm, Weismann had earlier contended, was divorced from the outside world. Evolutionary changes toward greater fitness (meaning greater capacity to reproduce) were the result of a fortuitous error that happened to prosper in the competition of life.[4] In a classic experiment that was accepted as proof that acquired characteristics were non-inherited Weismann cut off the tails of 22 generations of mice and found that the next generation was born with normal tails. The sacrifice of mutilation in mice was not inherited.[5]

This proposition was reinforced by molecular biology and the discovery in the 1950s of the role of nucleic acid, placing Mendelian genetics on a solid material basis. Molecular biology showed a means of transferral of information from genes to proteins but, until recently, gave no indication of any transfer in the opposite direction. The inference that there could be none became what Francis Crick called the central dogma of molecular biology: 'Once "information" has passed into proteins, it cannot get out again.'[6]

Reductionism and biological determinism go hand in hand. Isolating the gene as a 'master molecule' is part of biological determinism. The 'central dogma' that genes, as DNA, make proteins is another aspect of this determinism. This dogma is preserved even though it is known that genes 'make' nothing. As Lewontin has stated:

> DNA is a dead molecule, among the most non-reactive, chemically inert molecules in the world. It has no power to reproduce itself. Rather, it is produced out of elementary materials by a complex cellular machinery of proteins. While it is often said that DNA produces proteins, in fact proteins (enzymes) produce DNA.
>
> When we refer to genes as self-replicating, we endow them with a mysterious autonomous power that seems to place them above the more ordinary materials of the body. Yet if anything in the world can be said to be self-replicating, it is not the gene, but the entire organism as a complex system.[7]

Genetic engineering is taking us into a second order reductionism: not only is the organism perceived in isolation from its environment, but genes are perceived in isolation from the organism as a whole. The doctrine of molecular biology is modelled on classical mechanics. The central dogma is the ultimate in reductionist thought.

At the very time that Max Planck, Niels Bohr, Albert Einstein, Erwin Schrödinger and their colleagues were revising the Newtonian view of the physical universe, biology was becoming more reductionist.[8] This reductionism was not an accident but a carefully planned paradigm. As Lily Kaye records in 'The Molecular Vision of Life', the Rockefeller Foundation served as a principal patron of molecular biology from the 1930s to the 1950s. The term 'molecular biology' was coined in 1938 by Warren Weaver, the director of the Rockefeller Foundation's natural science division. The term was intended to capture the essence of the Foundation's programme, its emphasis on biological entities' ultimate minuteness.

The cognitive and structural reconfigurations of biology into a reductionist paradigm were greatly facilitated by the economically powerful Rockefeller Foundation. During the period 1932–59 the Foundation poured about $25 million into the molecular biology programme in the United States, more than a quarter of its total expenditure for the biological sciences, outside of medicine (including, from the early 1940s, enormous sums for agriculture).[9]

The force of the Foundation's molecular biology programme set the trends in biology. During the 12 years following the elucidation of DNA structure in 1953, Nobel prizes were awarded to 18 scholars for research into the molecular biology of the gene: all but one were fully or partially sponsored by the Rockefeller Foundation under Weaver's guidance.[10]

The motivation underlying the vast investment in the new agenda was to develop the human sciences as a comprehensive, explanatory and applied framework of social control grounded in the natural, medical, and social sciences. Conceived during the late 1920s, the new agenda was articulated in terms of the contemporary technocratic discourse of human engineering, aiming ultimately towards restructuring human relations in congruity with the social framework of industrial capitalism. Within that agenda, the new biology (originally named 'psychobiology') was erected on the bedrock of the physical sciences in order rigorously to explain and eventually control the fundamental mechanisms governing human behaviour, placing a particularly strong emphasis on heredity. Hierarchy and inequality were thus 'naturalized'. As Lewontin states in his *Doctrine of DNA*,

> The naturalistic explanation is to say that not only do we differ in our innate capacities but that these innate capacities are themselves transmitted from generation to generation biologically. That is to say, they are in our genes. The original social and economic notion of inheritance has been turned into biological inheritance.[11]

The conjunction of cognitive and social goals in reductionist biology had a strong historical connection to eugenics. By 1930 the Rockefeller Foundation had supported a number of eugenically directed projects. By the time of the inauguration of the 'new science of man', however, the goal of social control through selective breeding was no longer socially legitimate.[12]

> Precisely because the old eugenics had lost its scientific validity, a space was created for a new program that promised to place the study of human heredity and behaviour on rigorous grounds. A concerted physicochemical attack on the gene was initiated at the moment in history when it became unacceptable to advocate social control based on crude eugenic principles and outmoded racial theories. The molecular biology program, through the study of simple biological systems and the analysis of protein structure, promised a surer, albeit much slower, way toward social planning based on sounder principles of eugenic selection.[13]

Reductionism was chosen as the preferred paradigm to economic and political control of the diversity in nature and society.

Genetic determinism and genetic reductionism go hand in hand. But to say genes are primary is more ideology than science. Genes are not independent entities but dependent parts of an entirety that gives them effect. All parts of the cell interact, and the combinations of genes are at least as important as their individual effects in the make-up of an organism. More broadly, an organism cannot be treated simply as the product of a number of proteins, each produced by the corresponding gene. Genes have multiple effects, and most traits depend on multiple genes.

Linear and reductionist causality is upheld, however, even though the very processes that make genetic engineering possible run counter to the concepts of 'master molecules' and the 'central dogma'. As Lewin has stressed,

> Restriction sites, promoters, operators, operons, and enhancers play their part. Not only does DNA make RNA, but RNA, aided by an enzyme suitably called reverse transcriptase, makes DNA.[14]

The weakness of the explanatory and theoretical power of reductionism is compensated for by its ideological power and economic and political backing.

Some biologists have gone far in exalting the gene over the organism and demoting the organism itself to the status of a mere machine. The sole purpose of this machine is its own survival and reproduction, or perhaps, more accurately put, the survival and reproduction of the DNA that is said both to programme and to dictate its operation. In Dawkins' terms, an organism is a 'survival machine': a 'lumbering robot' constructed to house its genes, those 'engines of self-preservation' whose primary property is inherent 'selfishness'. They are

> sealed off from the outside world, communicating with it by tortuous indirect routes, manipulating it by remote control. They are in you and in me; they created us, body and mind; and their preservation is the ultimate rationale for our existence.[15]

Both from within molecular biology and from other disciplines of biology, however, there is growing evidence that reductionism in biology is misplaced, and that tinkering with the genetic structure of organisms is not as predictable and certain as the machine metaphor and engineering paradigm would lead us to believe.

The genomes of all populations of organisms are fluid. They are subject to a host of destabilizing processes, so that the transferred gene may mutate, transpose or recombine within the genome and even be transferred to another organism or species. Within the biological sciences, the emergence of a post-reductionist paradigm is starting to take shape. These new insights, when added to social, ecological and feminist critiques of genetic engineering, can contribute to taking us beyond reductionism, and hence beyond the unjust and unsustainable systems of production in forestry, fisheries and agriculture.

To go beyond reductionism is also necessary, because reductionism provides the epistemological basis for intellectual property rights in life forms.

Reductionism and Intellectual Property Rights (IPR)

In 1971, General Electric and one of the company's employees, Ananda Mohan Chakravarty, applied for the US patent on a genetically engineered *Pseudomonas* bacteria. Taking plasmids from three kinds of bacteria, he transplanted them into the fourth. As he explained, 'I simply shuffled genes, changing bacteria that already existed.'

Chakravarty was granted his patent on the grounds that the micro-organism was not a product of nature, but Chakravarty's invention and therefore patentable. As Andrew Kimbrell, a leading US lawyer, recounts: 'In coming to its precedent-shattering decision, the court seemed unaware that the inventor himself had characterized his "creation" of the microbe as simply "shifting" genes, not creating life.'

On such slippery grounds the first patent on life was granted and, in spite of the exclusion of plants and animals in US Patent Law, the US has since rushed on to grant patents on all kinds of life forms. Currently, well over 190 genetically engineered animals, including fish, cows, mice and pigs, are figuratively standing in line to be patented by a variety of researchers and corporations. According to Kimbrell, 'the Supreme Court's Chakravarty decision has been extended, to be continued up the chain of life. The patenting of microbes has led inexorably to the patenting of plants, and then animals.'[16] Biodiversity has been redefined as 'biotechnological inventions' and living organisms have been redefined as 'gene constructs' to make the patenting of life forms appear less controversial. These patents are valid for 20 years and hence cover future generations of plants and animals. But even when scientists shuffle genes, they do not create the organism which they patent.

Referring to the landmark Chakravarty case in the US, in which the court found that Chakravarty 'has produced a new bacterium with markedly different characteristics than any found in nature', Key Dismukes, Study Director of the Committee on Vision of the National Academy of Sciences in the US, said:

Let us at least get one thing straight: Anand Chakravarty did not create a new form of life; he merely intervened in the normal processes by which strains of bacteria exchange genetic information, to produce a new strain with an altered metabolic pattern. 'His' bacterium lives and reproduces itself under the forces that guide all cellular life. Recent advances in recombinant DNA techniques allow more direct biochemical manipulation of bacterial genes than Chakravarty employed, but these too are only modulations of biological processes. We are incalculably far away from being able to create life *de novo*, and for that I am profoundly grateful. The argument that the bacterium is Chakravarty's handiwork and not nature's wildly exaggerates human power and displays the same hubris and ignorance of biology that have had such devastating impact on the ecology of our planet.

This display of hubris and ignorance becomes even more conspicuous when the reductionist biologists who claim patents on life declare 95 per cent of DNA as 'junk DNA'. This is not taken to imply that it is useless, but means DNA whose function is unknown. When genetic engineers claim to engineer life, they must often use this junk DNA to get their results.

Take the case of Tracy, a 'biotechnological invention' of the scientists of Pharmaceutical Proteins Ltd (PPL). Tracy is called a 'mammalian cell bioreactor' because, through the introduction of human genes, her mammary glands are engineered to produce a protein, alpha-1-antitrypsin, for the pharmaceutical industry. As Ron James, director of PPL, states, 'The mammary gland is a very good factory. Our sheep are furry little factories walking around in fields and they do a superb job.'

However, while genetic engineers claim credit for this 'biotechnological invention', the PPL scientists had to use junk DNA to obtain high yields of alpha-1-antitrypsin. As Ron James says, 'We left some of these random bits of DNA in the gene, essentially as God provided it, and that produced high yield.' In claiming the patent, it is the scientist who becomes God, the creator of the patented organism. Furthermore, the future generations of the animal are clearly not the patent holder's 'inventions', they are the product of the organism's regenerative capacity. Thus, although the metaphor for patenting is 'engineers' who 'make machines', of the 550 sheep eggs injected with hybrid DNA, 499 survived. When these were transplanted into surrogate mothers, only 112 lambs were born. Of these just five had incorporated the human gene into their DNA, and only three produced alpha-1-antitrypsin in their milk, two of which delivered only three grams of proteins per litre of milk, but Tracy, PPL's 'sheep that lays golden eggs, produces 30 grams per litre.

One characteristic of reductionist biology is to declare organisms and their functions as useless, simply on the basis of ignorance of their structure and function. Thus, crops and trees are declared 'weed',[17] forests 'scrub' and cattle breeds 'mongrel'; and DNA whose role is not understood is called junk DNA. To write off the major part of the molecule as junk because of ignorance is to fail to understand biological processes.

The fact that Tracy's protein production increased with the introduction of junk DNA illustrates the PPL scientists' ignorance, not their knowledge and creativity. Genetic engineering is modelled on determinism and predictability but it is the absence of these dualities that is characteristic of human manipulation of living organisms. In addition to the gap between the projection and practice of the engineering paradigm is that between owning benefits and rewards and owning hazards and risks.

Property rights to life forms are claimed on the basis of their being innovations, novel, not occurring in nature. When, however, environmentalists state that, as 'not natural', genetically modified organisms (GMOs) will have an ecological impact that needs to be known and assessed, and for which the 'owners' must take responsibility, the counter argument is that there is nothing new or unnatural about GMOs: they are natural, and hence safe. The issue of biosafety is therefore dismissed as unnecessary.[18] Thus, when biological organisms are required to be owned they are treated as not natural; when the responsibility for consequences of releasing GMOs is to be owned, they are treated as natural. These shifting constructions of 'natural' show how the science which claims the highest levels of objectivity is both highly subjective and also opportunistic in its approach to nature.

The inconsistency in the construction of the natural is well illustrated in the case of the manufacture of genetically engineered human proteins for infant formula. Gen Pharm, a biotechnology company, owns Herman, the world's first transgenic dairy bull. Herman was bio-engineered by company scientists to carry a human gene for producing milk with a human protein. This milk is now to be used for making infant formula. The engineered gene and the organism of which it is a part are treated as non-natural when it comes to ownership of Herman and his offspring. When, however, the issue is safety of the infant formula containing this bio-engineered ingredient the same company says, 'We're making these proteins exactly the way they're made in nature.' Gen Pharm's chief executive officer, Jonathan MacQuitty, would have us believe that infant formula made from human protein bio-engineered in the milk of transgenic dairy cattle is human milk. 'Human milk is the gold standard, and formula companies have added more and more [human elements] over the past 20 years.' In this perspective, cows, women and children are merely instruments for commodity production and profit maximization.[19] As if the inconsistency between the construction of the natural and the engineered was not enough, Gen Pharm, the 'owner' of Herman, has totally changed the objective for engineering a transgenic bull. It has now received ethical clearance to use him for breeding on the ground that the modified version of the human gene for lactoferin might benefit patients with cancer or AIDS. This changed objective has brought strong criticism of both the company and the committee.

Patents encourage two forms of violence against living organisms: (1) they are linked to the manipulation of organisms as if they were machines, thus denying their innate self-organizing capacity; and (2) to permit patenting of future generations of life forms denies the self-reproducing capacity of living organisms. Such patents also have other environmental consequences. As rewards for innovation, patents invoke the image of a solitary inventor, but in reality it is the owners of capital, not the creators of knowledge, who obtain the patent rights: patents are rewards for capital investment, not for creativity *per se*.

The 'returns on investment' logic that has guided the granting of patents to corporations also stimulates them to increase these returns by increasing the role of the patented life form in the agricultural and pharmaceutical sector. On the one hand this carries the risk of increasing uniformity and monocultures, thus accelerating genetic erosion and pushing more species to extinction. On the other hand, as in the case of Tracy, it will exacerbate the ecological costs that have already been recognized as associated with factory farming.

There are many reasons why the IPR claims on life forms based on a reductionist paradigm of biology are false. In the case of genetically engineered organisms, a patent claim is based on the false assumption that genes make organisms and therefore makers of transgenic genes make transgenic organisms. But genes do not make organisms. Proteins are made not by genes but by a complex system of chemical production involving other proteins. Genes cannot make themselves any more than they can make a protein; they are made by a complex machinery of proteins. Also, it is not genes that are self-replicating but the entire organism as a complex system.

Since the entire organism is self-replicating, and not the genes alone, relocating genes does not constitute making an entire organism; the organism 'makes' itself. To claim that an organism and its future generations are products of an 'inventor's mind' needing to be protected by IPRs as biotechnical innovations is a denial of the self-organizing, self-replicating structures of organisms. Put simply, it is a theft of nature's creativity.

Beyond Reductionist Critiques

Two kinds of reductionism characterize some of the critical perspectives on biology. The first separates technology from nature, and biotechnology from biodiversity. The second separates the different domains of living systems – micro-organisms, plants, animals and humans – as well as diverse groups of humans: women, indigenous people, farmers, healers and so on. This fragmentation militates against a coherent perspective and a coherent ethical, epistemological and ecological framework for understanding the implications of biotechnology. A fragmented politics defined on the basis of reductionist identities of social groups also erodes the ground for solidarity among them and helps build unintended partnerships between the colonizer and the colonized.

A post-reductionist perspective of biotechnology needs to evolve on the basis of the connections between technology and nature, between micro-organisms and humans, including women, indigenous people, farmers and others. It is from a web of interconnected issues and communities of resistance that the democratic conditions for accountability and responsibility will be created in the age of biology.

Biotechnology and Biodiversity: Rethinking the Relationship of Technology and Nature

Technology and nature are intimately connected. At the conceptual level, the emergence and employment of new technologies fundamentally reconstructs nature. At the material level, these technologies use natural resources as 'raw material', and also change nature through their impact on the environment. New technologies also change the status of alternatives by defining them as obsolete and primitive – as part of nature, lacking any cultural contribution. Thus farmers' seeds, which are products of centuries of innovation, are described as 'primitive cultivars' and as 'landraces', as if they embody no human creativity.

The category of biodiversity is in fact a construct of the biotechnology era. Previously, living resources were described concretely as plants, animals or humans. Biodiversity is not only categorized as a product of biotechnology, essential raw material for biotechnology, but it is also the 'environment' displaced and destabilized by the biological pollution risks posed by biotechnology. Without this systemic approach to the biodiversity-biotechnology complex, critical perspectives can become locked into a fragmented and fragmenting politics that protects and reinforces the status quo.

Feminist critiques of technology have usually focused on technology in isolation from natural resources. Feminist approaches to biotechnology rarely address the political ecology of the new technologies in the context of biodiversity; they focus exclusively on 'nature' as the 'female body'. A reductionist theory of technology thus emerges which reinforces the biological reductionism of the dominant paradigm. Feminist critique of dominant science and technology has not developed an adequate ecological concern. In the absence of an ecological framework, feminist theorizing, especially the stream characterized by reductionist constructivism (the view that nature and its diversity is *nothing but* a social construction) has an unintended convergence with the dominant reductionist philosophy of genetic engineering. Ironically, while beginning as a critique of dominant science, it ends up speaking the same language. Thus both genetic engineering and feminist theories of biotechnology contribute to the invisibility of the organism, and to the disappearance of ordered biodiversity which is the basis of ecological stability.[20] In a reductionist approach to biotechnology, issues of social justice also vanish along with concern for ecology.

The obverse of this reductionist separation of technology and nature, biotechnology and biodiversity is that issues of justice and of cultural pluralism in the context of biotechnology-biodiversity are reduced to 'bioprospecting' promoted by mainstream environmental organizations. Many environmentalists working on biodiversity conservation have barely considered biotechnology or the risks of biological pollution that will result from its deployment. More fundamental issues of how biodiversity is being reduced to genetic raw materials and people's science and technology systems marginalized are eclipsed. In addition, ethical considerations related to manipulation of life and patents on life, as well as the destruction of people's livelihoods and the disappearance of alternative technologies are deemed to be met by paying compensation to those whose lifestyles, cultures and biological and intellectual heritage are appropriated to provide raw material and markets for new technologies.

If the post-modernist tradition of feminism is to avoid supporting the uncritical acceptance of the new biotechnologies, it must open a fresh dialogue with those working on equity, ethics and ecological aspects of genetic engineering. It must become more ecological and this implies rethinking some of the categories whose origins lay in challenging the status quo, but which now support it. Two of these categories are 'essentialism' and 'crossing boundaries'.

Rethinking Essentialism

The machine metaphor for organisms is one arising from patriarchal rationality, which, when applied to organisms, denies their self-organizing, self-healing properties. Technologies based on the perception of living organisms as living systems and not machines are ecological, not engineering technologies.

Unfortunately, post-modern feminists have adopted this limited view of technology as mechanization. They therefore see an increased degree of freedom not as the freedom of an organism to adapt, to grow, to shape itself from within but as the mechanistic addition of 'metal' to 'flesh' and the 'machine' to the 'body'. The inevitable consequence is to see the one without the other as incomplete. Haraway's cyborg imaginary was supposed to suggest a way out of the maze of the dualisms in which we have explained our bodies and our tools to ourselves.

The post-modern discourse was supposed to question the privilege of the white male individual and to enable recognition of other forms of historical experience. Much Western academic feminist thinking, however, is converging closely with the perspectives of the global patriarchal élite. It is reinstituting the world view of powerful white males as a norm in an era where concern for preserving diverse forms of life, both biological and cultural, is emerging as a major challenge.

Reductionist constructivism in feminist theorizing and genetic reduction-ism underlying the genetic engineering industry converge in a move to genetic essentialism, which treats genes as more basic and essential than organisms as self-organizing systems, and species as separate and identifiable entities. However, a shift to genetic essentialism does not make essentialism disappear, but merely relocates it.

All paradigms treat something as basic and essential. Reductionism shifts the basis of life from organisms and their interactions to the gene. As Fox-Keller has pointed out, genetic reductionism leads to the

> Relocation of the essence (or basis) of life. The locus of vital activity was now to be sought neither in the physical-chemical interactions and structures of the organism-niche complex, of the organism itself, nor even of the cell, but rather, in the physical-chemical structure of one particular component of the cell; namely, in the genetic material, or more exactly, in the gene.[21]

It is not that molecular reductionism eliminates essentialism; it merely relocates it in the gene. Post-reductionist biology needs to relocate the basic unit in the internal and external relationships of organisms.

The essence of a genome is self-organizedness – elements that fit together. Complexes of effective genes form coherent wholes, which vary within usually stable patterns. As Ernst Mayer put it, 'Most genes are tied together in balanced complexes that resist change.'[22] Ecologists who focus on relationships, not on essences, also find it necessary to think of species not genes as the basic unit in biology.

It is the capacity for self-organization that makes for cultural and bio-logical diversity and pluralism. Since self-organizing systems are autonomous and self-referential, though not insulated from others, they know what they must 'import and 'export' in order to maintain and renew themselves. Self-organized systems interact with their environment, but autonomously. The environment triggers the structural changes but it neither specifies nor directs them.

Ecological stability derives from the ability of species and ecosystems to adapt, evolve and respond. In fact, the greater the freedom available to a system the greater its ability for expression, whereas external control, by curtailing a system's freedom, limits its capacity to organize and renew itself. Ecological vulnerability results when species and ecosystems have been engineered and controlled to such an extent that their capacity to adapt is lost.

Self-organizing systems are distinct and multi-dimensional, and therefore display structural and functional diversity. Mechanical systems are uniform and unidimensional and therefore are structurally uniform and functionally one-dimensional. Unlike self-organizing systems, mechanically organized systems can neither heal themselves nor adapt, but instead break down.

When organisms and systems are treated like machines and mechanically manipulated to improve a one-dimensional function, such as an increase in unidimensional productivity, either their immunity decreases, resulting in vulnerabilities to disease and/or attack by other organisms, or they dominate an ecosystem, displacing and eventually eliminating other species. Both these eventualities are aspects of biosafety.

In mechanistic and reductionist approaches, these ecological risks are always present, but never assessed or analysed. In the absence of a non-reductionist predictive ecology, each step toward one-dimensional 'improvement' of biological systems leads to increased ecological vulnerability, incidence of disease, and accelerated rates of species extinction.

The reductionist, machine view of animals overrides any ethical concern for how they are treated in order to maximize production. The mechanistic view dominates the industrial livestock production sector, as is exemplified by a meat industry manager's statement: 'The breeding sow should be thought of as, and treated as, a valuable piece of machinery, whose function is to pump out baby pigs like a sausage machine.'[23] But to treat pigs like machines seriously affects their health and behaviour; pigs are living organisms, not machines. In animal factories pigs' tails, teeth and testicles are removed or they fight and resort to what the industry calls 'cannibalism'. Eighteen per cent of piglets in factory farms are choked to death by their mother; 2–5 per cent are born with congenital defects such as splayed legs, no anus, inverted mammary glands. They are prone to sickness, such as 'banana disease' (stricken pigs arch their backs into a banana shape) or PSS (Porcine Stress Syndrome).

Such stresses and diseases will increase with genetic engineering, as is already signalled by the pig with a human growth hormone, whose body weight is greater than its legs can carry.

Animal health and welfare are intrinsically related to the impact of the new technologies on the capacity for self-regulation and healing.

> In the making of the organism, the multiplying cells seem to be instructed as to their respective destinies, and they become permanently differentiated to compose organs. But the pattern or instructions for making the whole structure remain somehow latent. When a part is injured, some cells become undifferentiated to make new specialised tissues.[24]

The challenge of biodiversity is in large measure a challenge to reinvent the relationship of humans to other species. It is the anthropocentric and instrumental approach to biodiversity that has led to animal experimentation, factory farming, and in many cases the extinction of species.

The present unique situation in which we all live is created by two unprecendented shifts: (1) genetic engineering and the patenting of life; and (2) the globalization and deregulation of commerce through GATT, including the Trade Related Intellectual Property Rights which impose patents on life, all cultures and societies. The emerging world view and legal regime makes the tradeability of life, its processes and its components sacrosant. Simultaneously the sanctity and integrity of life are perceived as mere barriers to trade and scientific progress.

This has threatening implications for everyone. Farmers' traditional right to save, use, exchange and modify seed is denied under patents and breeders' rights. Women's bodies are being redefined as 'factories' and 'mines' for pharmaceutical raw material. Indigenous communities find that their resources, knowledge and bodies are becoming raw material for the biotech industry and global trade. Consumers everywhere can expect that genetically engineered foods will make fresh, natural, locally produced food difficult to find. Finally, we are all threatened by the health and environmental impacts of genetically engineered organisms, the study of which is being stifled by assertions that they are safe and natural.

The main process of disempowerment of people under the triple colonization of biotechnology, patents and globally deregulated commerce is that what is intrinsic to people's creativity and capacity is being appropriated to generate monopoly profits. People's rights as ethical beings making value decisions are being extinguished by reducing ethics to 'irrational fears' within the GATT debates. Our rights as producers and consumers of food are being sacrificed. Our rights as knowing, innovating beings are denied as knowledge becomes imprisoned within the restrictions of patents and intellectual property rights. Empowerment of people comes from the recognition of these processes of disempowerment. It also comes from the recognition that a reductionist politics of resistance can itself become a source of disempowerment of people.

It is also necessary to go beyond reductionism in terms of addressing the ethical, ecological and economic issues of the different biodiversity domains – from micro-organisms to humans. If we need to build an earth community, the definition of community must be extended and become inclusive of all life forms in a democracy of life. Non-human species will then no longer be objects of human manipulation, but subjects in their own right, having intrinsic value. An extended and inclusive sense of community also helps overcome the fragmented politics of identity that divides communities of resistance.

In non-Western traditions, ethical problems associated with the manipulation and patenting of life are the same for micro-organisms as for humans, since all species belong to the earth family. In the Western world view, however, manipulation and patenting of micro-organisms go largely unnoticed – even though the door to patenting life forms was opened with a patent on a micro-organism. In GATT, too, the patenting of micro-organisms is a requirement in the IPR laws of all member countries. Western ethical dilemmas related to micro-organism manipulation may be minor, but the ecological risks of genetically modified micro-organisms are much higher than those related to the modification of animals.

Similarly, from the perspective of farmers in Third World societies, IPRs on seeds is an ethical, economic and political issue; in Western industrialized societies, where commodification of the seed has been the norm for most of this century, IPRs on seed is primarily an economic issue. Therefore, given the different cultural and socio-economic locations of different actors, it is important to keep all perspectives alive and to build a coherent people's perspective through solidarity and symbiosis.

Rethinking Boundaries

Boundaries have been an important construct for ecological restraint. 'Removing boundaries' has been an important metaphor for removing restraints on human actions, and allowing limitless exploitation of natural resources.

Boyle referred to the 'removal of boundaries' that native Americans had constructed to respect and conserve nature:

> that the veneration, wherewith men are imbued for what they call nature, has been a discouraging impediment to the empire of man over the inferior creatures of God: for many have not only looked upon it as an impossible thing to compass, but as something impious to attempt, the removing of those boundaries, which

nature seems to have put and settled among her productions; and whilst they look upon her as such a vererable thing, some make a kind of scruple of conscience to endeavour so to emulate any of her works, as to excel them.[25]

Two centuries later, Muller, the father of molecular biology, said:

We cannot leave forever inviolate in their recondite recesses those invisibly small yet fundamental particles, the genes, for from these genes... there radiate continually those forces, far-reaching, orderly, but elusive, that make and unmake our living worlds.[26]

In the reductionist paradigm, it is species boundaries that are crossed, and the boundaries created are those that separate the gene from the whole organism, and the patent holder from the rest of society. Crucial to the creation of transgenic organisms is the breaking down of species barriers, and the construction of the fictitious Weismann barrier that made the gene the causal determinant of the organism's evolution.

'Crossing barriers' goes hand in hand with the creation of new ones in molecular reductionism. Boundaries between species are crossed, but the Weismann barrier is erected to separate the germ plasm from the organism and its environment. Making transgenic life forms is justified on the grounds that there are no species boundaries. In genetic reductionism, there is no species identity, only DNA complexes. Shuffling genes around to cross transgenic barriers poses no problem at the ethical level. Shapiro refers to the loss of species identification as a kind of 'ontological vulnerability'.

The genetic engineer thinks less in terms of combining discrete species' ways and more in terms of gene-pools that consist of raw material and raw information. The genetic code peculiar to a given animal has no more intrinsic integrity than one filing system among many. A species is a momentary organization of a certain chunk of information. An individual animal is reduced to certain genetic information that can be readily otherwise informed.[27]

Genetic engineering requires the denial of species boundaries to move genes across species to make transgenic life forms, but the genetic engineers use species boundaries to deny ecological risks from the genetically modified organisms.For example, Dr Bishop, who used scorpion genes in a virus to control caterpillars that destroy cabbage crops, insists that the virus will not affect any non-target species because species do not cross boundaries.

Boundaries disappear when the right to manipulate and own life is claimed, but reappear when risks and responsibility have to be met. This ontological shift is part of the politics of biotechnology in which the circle of rights is expanding and the domain of responsibility is shrinking.

'Nature', 'limits and boundaries', 'organisms' and 'species' have emerged as central to the discourse and politics of ecology. Biodiversity conservation in particular includes the recognition of the intrinsic worth of species, and of ecological barriers that make diversity and distinctiveness flourish. Post-modern feminists and the genetic engineering establishment have, however, treated nature and boundaries as mere constructions, which can and should be dispensed with. Biotechnologists adopt an opportunistic approach, using or dispensing with these categories as convenient.

As I have tried to illustrate in this epilogue, there is an unintended convergence between the reductionism of constructivism and genetic reductionism. A feminist and ecological perspective requires the encouragement of other convergences that will allow a post-reductionist paradigm of biology and politics to emerge. An important challenge for a post-reductionist approach is the need to evolve an ontologically coherent discourse for the domain of rights and responsibility. The controlled and unaccountable growth of the biotechnology industry is related to the ontological split between the domain of rights and the domain of responsibility which makes for an unrestrained and unaccountable system of rights. An ethical, ecological, feminist approach to biology, biodiversity and bio-technology can contribute to the evolution of a context of accountability and social control for the new technologies.

Notes

1 This was the theme of a Third World Network conference on 'Redefining the Life Sciences' in Penang, 7–10 July 1994.

2 Evelyn Fox Keller, *A Feeling for the Organism. The Life and Work of Barbara McClintock*, Freeman & Co., New York, 1983, p. 99.

3 David Ehrenfeld, *Beginning Again*, Oxford University Press, New York, 1993, pp. 70–1.

4 Robert Wesson, *Beyond Natural Selection*, The MIT Press, Cambridge, Mass. and London, 1993, p. 19.

5 *Ibid.*, p. 11.

6 Francis Crick, 'Lessons from Biology', *Natural History*, 97 (November 1988), p. 109.

7 R. Lewontin (ed.), *The Doctrine of DNA*, Penguin Books, USA, 1993.

8 Robert Wesson, *op. cit.*, p. 29.

9 Lily E. Kay, 'The Molecular Vision of Life', in Caltech, *The Rockefeller Foundation and the Rise of the New Biology*, Oxford University Press, 1993, p.6.

10 *Ibid.*, p. 8.

11 R. Lewontin (ed.), *op. cit.*

12 Lily E. Kay, *op. cit.*

13 *Ibid.*

14 Roger Lewin, 'How Mammalian RNA Returns to its Genome', *Science*, 219 (1983), pp. 1052-4.

15 R. Dawkins, *The Selfish Gene,* Oxford University Press, Oxford, 1976.
16 Andrew Kimbrell, *The Human Body Shop,* Harper Collins Publishers, New York, 1993.
17 Vandana Shiva, *Monocultures of the Mind,* Third World Network, Penang, 1993.
18 RAFI Communique.
19 *New Scientist,* 9 January 1993.
20 Rosi Braidotti, 'Organs without Bodies', in *Differences,* 1 (1989), pp. 3–16.
21 Evelyn Fox Keller, *Secrets of Life, Secrets of Death,* Routledge, New York, 1992, p. 96.
22 Robert Wesson, *op. cit.,* p. 146.
23 L. J. Taylor, export development manager, Wall Meat Co. Ltd, in David Coat, *Old MacDonald's Factory Farm,* p. 32.
24 Robert Wesson, *op. cit.,* p. 144.
25 R. Boyle (1744, Vol. 4, p. 363), quoted in Evelyn Fox Keller, *op. cit.,* p. 65.
26 H. J. Muller (1926, pp. 200–2), quoted in *ibid.*
27 R. Shapiro, 'The Death of the Animal: Ontological Vulnerability', *Between the Species,* 5 (1989), pp. 183–4.

Glossary

Amino acid: Any one of the small molecules that constitute the building blocks of proteins.

Base: In this context it is a component of the nucleotides which make up the DNA. Four different organic bases are involved in the structure of the DNA: adenine, guanine, cytosine and thymine. Their sequence is responsible for the genetic information in the DNA.

Biotechnology: Development of products by exploiting biological processes or substances. Production may be carried out by using intact original or modified organisms, such as yeasts and bacteria, or by using active cell components, such as enzymes from organisms.

cDNA: Complementary or copy DNA is a man-made copy of the coding sequences of a gene; cDNA is produced in a test-tube – it is not a natural product. In a living cell, the protein-coding sequences of DNA are transcribed as mRNA. Molecular biologists use reverse transcriptase, an enzyme that makes DNA copies from RNA, to make copies of the mRNA. The resulting cDNA – a copy of a copy, so to speak – may then be analysed by various methods.

Chromosomes: Microscopic structures, found in the cell nucleus and in mitochondria, which are composed of DNA and proteins and are duplicated every time a cell divides. The DNA in the chromosomes carries the genes.

Cloning: The process of asexually producing a group of cells (clones), all genetically identical, from a single ancestor. In recombinant DNA technology, the use of various procedures to produce multiple copies of a single gene or segment of DNA is referred to as 'cloning DNA'.

Cosmid map: A physical map comprising a collection of bacteria contaning cosmids that carry the DNA fragments under study.

Cytogenetics: The study of genetic variation through an examination of differences in chromosomal structures.

Cytoplasm: The part of the cell that lies between the membrane and the nucleus. It contains a variety of subcellular structures that participate in the cell's functions.

Deoxyribonucleic acid (DNA): The molecule in the chromosomes that encodes genetic information and specifies the composition of proteins. It is made up of a repeating sequence of one of four possible bases, a phosphate molecule and a sugar (called deoxyribose), wound up into a helix.

Differentiation: The process of change in cells during development, resulting in structures and functions that characterize the different kinds of cells in different parts of an organism of some later phase of life history.

DNA synthesis: The chemical joining of nucleotides to create an artificial DNA molecule.

Double helix: The usual geometric configuration of DNA, consisting of two complementary strands, each made up of a long, repeating sequence of sugar and phosphate molecules, running side by side in a helical formation, and joined by the bases.

Enzyme: Any one of a large class of proteins occuring in organisms which act as catalysts, i.e. make it possible for chemical reactions to take place and occur sufficiently rapidly to meet the organism's needs.

Gene: A functional unit of DNA that specifies the composition of a protein and can be passed on from an individual to his or her descendants.

Gene expression: The process by which a gene's coded information is converted into the structures present and operating in the cell. Expressed genes include those that are transcribed into messenger RNA and then translated into protein and those that are transcribed into RNA but not translated into protein (transfer and ribosomal RNAs, for example).

Genetic engineering: A technology used to alter the genetic material of living cells through direct interference with the genome in order to make them capable of producing substances or performing functions alien to the unmanipulated cells.

Genetic mapping: Determination of the relative positions of genes on a DNA molecule (chromosome or plasmid) and of the distance, in linkage units or physical units, between them.

Genetically modified organism (GMO): An organism in which the genetic material has been altered in a way that does not occur naturally by mating and/or natural recombination, but by recombinant DNA techniques, techniques involving the direct introduction into a micro-organism of heritable material prepared outside the micro-organism, or cell fusion or hybridi-zation techniques.

Genome: All the genetic material in the chromosomes of a particular organism or species. The size of a genome is usually given in total number of base pairs. For example, the human genome is about 3 billion base pairs in length.

Genome projects: Research and technology development efforts aimed at mapping and sequencing some or all of the genome of human beings and other organisms. Collectively referred to as the 'Genome Project'.

Genotype: The total genetic, or hereditary, constitution that an individual receives from his or her parents.

Germ plasm: The total genetic variability available to a particular population of organisms.

Growth hormone: Mammalian hormone which promotes growth and stimulates the metabolism.

Hybridization, cellular: The fusion of cells from two different organisms into one cell that combines the chromosomes of both.

Library, genetic: An unordered collection of DNA clones from a particular organism.

Messenger RNA (mRNA): A class of ribonucleic acid (RNA) whose function is to carry the genetic code from the chromosome (in the nucleus) to the ribosome (in the cytoplasm) and direct protein synthesis there.

Mutation: A permanent alternation in a gene or DNA molecule.

Nucleotide: A subunit of DNA or RNA consisting of a nitrogenous base (adenine, guanine, thymine, or cytosine in DNA; adenine, guanine, uracil, or cytosine in RNA), a phosphate mole-cule, and a sugar molecule (deoxyribose in DNA and ribose in RNA). Thousands of nucleotides are linked to form DNA or RNA molecules.

Nucleus: The part of a cell that contains the chromosomes (except the mitochondrial chromo-somes) and the bulk of the cell's DNA.

Phenotype: The appearance and other physical characteristics of an organism, a result of the interaction of an individual's genetic constitution with the environment. Phenotype differs from genotype in that it includes only the outward manifestations of genes.

Physical map: An overlapping collection of DNA fragments which span a particular chromo-somal region. A common type of physical map comprises DNA fragments contained in cosmids.

Protein: A large molecule composed of one or more chains of amino acids in a specific sequence; the sequence is determined by the sequence of nucleotides in the gene coding for the protein. Proteins are required for the structure, function, and regulation of the body's cells, tissues, and organs, and each protein has unique functions.

Recombinant DNA: A DNA molecule containing strands from two or more distinct sources, formed using genetic cutting and splicing technologies.

Recombinant DNA technology: Procedures for joining together DNA segments in an environment outside of a cell or organism.

Recombination: The natural process of the breaking and rejoining of DNA strands to produce new combinations of DNA molecules and generate genetic diversity. Also called 'crossing-over'.

Reductionism: The philosophical belief that phenomena or organisms are best understood by breaking them up into smaller parts.

Replication: Duplication of a molecule by following the pattern of a template. Replication can occur *in vitro* as well as *in vivo*.

Ribosomes: The particles in the cell cytoplasm on which the base sequences brought there by messenger-RNA get translated into the amino acid sequences of proteins.

RNA (ribonucleic acid): A kind of nucleic acid that differs from DNA in that it contains the nucleotide base uracil, rather than thymine, and the sugar ribose instead of deoxyribose.

RNA splicing pattern: The combination of DNA sequences copied from a gene by messenger RNA. The mRNAs transcribed from a single gene may splice together different parts of the sequence of the gene.

Sequence: The order of nucleotides in a nucleic acid or the order of amino acids in a protein.

Transgenic animal: An animal whose cells contain genetic material originally derived from another animal. For example, transgenic mice may contain genetic material from humans.

Vector: A virus, bacteria or other piece of DNA into which a gene can be incorporated and which can then be used to introduce that gene into a cell.

A Select Guide to Further Reading

Bonss, W., R. Hohlfeld & R. Kollek (1992) 'Risiko und Kontext. Zur Unsicherheit' in der Gentechnologie', in Bechmann G. and W. Rammert (eds) *Technik und Gesellschaft*, Jahrbuch 6, Campus Verlag, Frankfurt. Forthcoming in English.

Braidotti, R., E. Charkiewicz, S. Haüsler & S. Wieringa (1994) *Women, the Environment and Sustainable Development. Towards a Theoretical Synthesis*, Zed Books and Instraw, London.

Diprose, R. (1994) *The Bodies of Women: Ethics, Embodiment and Sexual Differences* Routledge, New York.

Egziabher, T. B. G. (1993) 'Modernization, Science and Technology, and the Perturbations of Traditional Systems of Conservation of Biological Diversity' in *Proceedings of the Norway/UNEP Expert Conference on Biodiversity*, NINA/DN, Trondheim.

Emmeche, C. & J. Hofmeyer (1991) 'From Language to Nature: The Semiotic Metaphor in Biology', in *Semiotica 84 – 1/2*, 1991.

Fowler, C., E. Lachkovics, P. Mooney & H. Shand (1988) 'The Laws of Life. Another Development and the New Biotechnologies', *Development Dialogue* 1988: 1–2, Dag Hammarsköld Foundation, Uppsala.

Fowler, C. & P. Mooney (1990) *Shattering. Food, Politics, and the Loss of Genetic Diversity*, University of Arizona Press, Tucson.

Haraway, D. (1984) 'Primatology is Politics by Other Means' in Bleier R. (1986) *Feminist Approaches to Science*, Pergamon Press, New York.

Haraway, D. (1989) *Primate Visions: Gender, Race, and Nature in the World of Modern Science*, Routledge, New York.

Haraway, D. (1991) *Simians, Cyborgs and Women. The Reinvention of Nature*, Free Association Books, London.

Harding, S. (1986) *The Science Question in Feminism*, Cornell University Press, Ithaca.

Hobbelink, H. (1991) *Biotechnology and the Future of World Agriculture*, Zed Books, London.

Holtzman, N. A. (1989) *Proceed with Caution: Predicting Genetic Risks in the Recombinant DNA Era*, Johns Hopkins University Press, Baltimore.

Hubbard, R. (1990) *The Politics of Women's Biology*, Rutgers, New Brunswick.

Hubbard, R. & E. Wald (1993) *Exploding the Gene Myth*, Beacon Press, Boston.

Keller, E. F. (1985) *Reflections on Gender and Science*, Yale, New Haven.

Keller, E. F. (1993) *A Feeling for the Organism. The Life and Work of Barbara McClintock*, W. H. Freeman and Company, New York.

Keller, E .F. (1992) *Secrets of Life, Secrets of Death. Essays on Language, Gender and Science*, Routledge, New York.

Kevles, D. & L. Hood (eds) (1992) *The Code of Codes. Scientific and Social Issues in the Human Genome Project*, Harvard University Press, Cambridge, Ma.

Kollek, R. (1993) 'Controversies about Risks and their Relation to Different Paradigms in Biological Research' in Schomberg, R. von (ed.) *Science, Politics and Morality. Scientific Uncertainty and Decision Making*, Kluwer Academic Publishers, Dordrecht.

Krimsky, S. (1991) *Biotechnics and Society: The Rise of Industrial Genetics*, Praeger, New York.

Leskien, D. & J. Spangenberg (eds) (1990) *European Workshop on Law and Genetic Engineering. Proceedings*, Hamburg Dec. 1989, BBU Verlag, Bonn.

Lewontin, R. C. (1982) *Human Diversity*, Scientific American Books, New York.

Lewontin, R. C. (ed) (1993) *The Doctrine of DNA*, Penguin, London.

Lewontin, R. C., S. Rose & L. J. Kamin (1984) *Not in Our Genes. Biology, Ideology and Human Nature*, Penguin, London.

Mies, M. & V. Shiva (1993) *Ecofeminism*, Zed Books, London, Fernwood Publishing, Halifax, Kali for Women, New Delhi and Spinifex, Melbourne.

Modern Science in Crisis. A Third World Response (1988) Third World Network, Penang.

Perlas, N. (1994) *Ecological Alternatives to Agricultural Biotechnology*, Third World Network, Penang.

Perlas, N. (1994) *Overcoming Illusions about Biotechnology*, Zed Books, London and Third World Network, Penang.

Rifkin, J. (1991) *Biosphere Politics. A New Consciousness for a New Century*, Crown Publishers, Inc., New York.

Rose, H. (1992) 'Feminist/Gender Studies of Science: An Overview of the Field' in *Gender, Technology and the Sciences*, FRN, Stockholm.

Rose, H. (1994) *Love, Power and Knowledge*, Polity Press, Cambridge.

Rosendal, G. K. (1990) 'Management and Distribution of Plant Genetic Resources: A Sisyphean Victory for the Third World in FAO – Back to Square One in GATT?' in *Forum for utviklingsstudier*, Nr.2, 1990.

Sachs, W. (ed) (1993) *Global Ecology. A New Arena of Political Conflict*, Zed Books, London.

Science as Culture, Vol. 2, Part 4, No. 13, 1991, Special issue on 'Genes 'n' Greens' . Free Association Books, London.

Shiva, V. (1989) *Staying Alive: Women, Ecology and Development*, Zed Books, London and Kali for Women, New Delhi.

Shiva, V. (1991) *The Violence of the Green Revolution. Third World Agriculture, Ecology and Politics*, Zed Books, London and Third World Network, Penang.

Shiva, V. (1993) *Monocultures of the Mind. Perspectives on Biodiversity and Biotechnology*, Zed Books, London and Third World Network, Penang.

Shiva, V., P. Anderson, H. Schücking, A. Gray, L. Lohmann & D. Cooper (1991) *Biodiversity. Social and Ecological Perspectives*, World Rainforest Movement, Penang and Zed Books, London. '

Tait, J. & L. Levidow (1992) 'Proactive and Reactive Approaches to Risk Regulation. The Case of Biotechnology' in *Futures*, 24 (3).

Webster, G. & B. C. Goodwin (1982) 'The Origin of Species: a Structuralist Approach' in *Journal of Social and Biological Structures* (continues as *Journal of Social and Evolutionary Systems*), Vol. 5, No. 1, p. 15–47.

Wesson, R. (1993) *Beyound Natural Selection*, MIT Press, Cambridge, Ma.

'Women, Ecology and Health. Rebuilding Connections. Proceedings', Bangalore, India, July 1991. Published in *Development Dialogue* 1992: 1–2, Dag Hammarskjöld Foundation, Uppsala.

Index